THE CENTURY OF THE BLACK SHIPS

The Century of the Black Ships

* * *

CHRONICLES OF WAR BETWEEN JAPAN AND AMERICA

Naoki Inose

VIZ Media
San Francisco

KUROFUNE NO SEIKI by Naoki INOSE
© 1993 Naoki INOSE
All rights reserved.
Original Japanese edition published in 1993 by
Shogakukan Inc., Tokyo.

English translation by Jamie West (Diplomatt, Inc.)
Art direction by Mary Ann Levesque
Jacket design by Sean Marlowe

Published by
VIZ Media, LLC
295 Bay Street
San Francisco, CA 94133

www.viz.com

Library of Congress Cataloging-in-Publication Data

Inose, Naoki.
   [Kurofune no seiki. English]
   The century of the black ships : chronicles of war
between Japan and America / Naoki Inose.
      p. cm.
   ISBN 978-1-4215-2917-2 (alk. paper)
   1. Japan—Intellectual life—1868– 2. United States—
Relations—Japan. 3. Japan—Relations—United
States.   I. Title.   DS822.25.I56713 2009
   355.020952'09041—DC22

                              2008046681

Printed in the U.S.A.
First printing, April 2009

CONTENTS

*All Japanese and Chinese names (excluding
author's) are given in traditional sequence, with
family name preceding given name.

Prologue

BEHIND THE BAR stood the bartender. Behind the bartender stood a sooty wall. And on the wall, writ large, these words: "Be good or be gone!" It seems that blows had been exchanged in this place by tough customers for no good reason after they had downed a drink or two. These words, like old wounds, speak to us of this bygone battle.

McSorley's Old Ale House occupies the first floor of a redbrick co-op in New York's East Village. As if to compensate for the feebleness of the streetlights, the pub's green neon sign gleams brightly but unsteadily. Still, the sign at the entrance bespeaks pride as well: ESTABLISHED 1854. The place was about 80 percent full, just about right for a good time.

Order a beer here and you won't get some ordinary lager of the type Japanese are used to, but a burnt-brown stout. While I was waiting for just such a drink, I had a smoke and noticed that on the gouged and battered oak tables there were no ashtrays. The worn floor, however, was liberally sprinkled with sawdust. Easy enough to grind out a cigarette butt with the sole of your shoe.

That's right, I realized. These Irish pubs harken back to the nineteenth century, and they hate relinquishing their attachments to the past. The sawdust on the floor exactly fits James Joyce's description in *Dubliners* of how laborers in a Dublin pub "drank at intervals from their huge pint tumblers and smoked, spitting often on the floor and sometimes dragging the sawdust over their spits with their heavy boots."

One wall was nearly covered with yellowing newspaper clippings, posters, and portrait photographs. Abraham Lincoln, Theodore Roosevelt, John F. Kennedy, John's younger brother Robert. Not only American presidents, but other men idolized as American heroes. Over there was General

1

MacArthur, famous for his pride, and there, the Reverend Martin Luther King Jr. who died a violent death. All venerated as worthy "customers" of this establishment.

So this is McSorley's. "Established 1854"—it was making sense.

—Hey. You Japanese?
—Yeah.

And I nodded slightly. Oh, that was all. I had been sunk so deep in my reflections that I must have looked quite startled. But that's all it was. Be good or be gone, huh.

Ordinarily this wouldn't have interested me much, this injunction to virtue. But I was strangely intrigued by the "Established 1854." These people had been relaxing here ever since then, with not much changing, while my Japanese forebears had to struggle just a bit to fit in. They simply hadn't known Western manners, not even how to make small talk.

"Commander in Chief United States Naval Forces, East India, China and Japan Seas, and Special Ambassador to Japan"—that was the full title worn by Matthew Calbraith Perry when four Black Ships under his command (as the Japanese have always called these alien, smoke-belching, United States steamships) appeared off Uraga on July 8, 1853, at eight o'clock in the morning. Much has already been written about the shock and awe Perry's armada induced among Japanese at that time. What I should like to do here is to point out not the general Japanese reaction but rather just one item that interests me, noted in the records of the other side. And it does not require belaboring the vexed issue of Japanese formalism and feudal morality as revealed in affairs of state. It is, rather, quite an insignificant matter, one easily overlooked or forgotten.

In the words of a contemporary Japanese ditty (punning, in the original, on the name for a popular brand of tea), "It took but four, 'black,' to wake Tranquility from her Slumber; to deprive even the Night of Sleep." Having discharged his duties in this first stage of his expedition, Perry had no sooner quit Edo harbor than he made (again) for the Kingdom of the Ryukyus in present-day Okinawa, dropping anchor at Naha. Then on to Hong Kong, where he rejoined the East India Fleet. Finally he entered into formal diplomatic negotiations with Japan. To overawe the Japanese, he increased his strength to seven ships and paid another visit to Uraga.

By now it was February 13, 1854. Japanese somehow remember this pivotal encounter as a single visit by four ships, forgetting that in this second stage of his expedition, Perry augmented his expeditionary squadron to seven.

The commissioner plenipotentiary negotiating for the Bakufu (the Tokugawa Shogunate in Edo, present-day Tokyo) was Hayashi Fukusai, the Daigaku-no-Kami or head of the Confucian Academy. Under him as his aides were town magistrate Ido Tsushima, Uraga magistrate Izawa Mimasaka, superintendent Udono Nagatoshi, and government Confucian expert Matsuzaki Mitsutarō.

The fifty-three-year-old Hayashi's position and title were hereditary. Eleventh in succession after Hayashi Razan, founder of the line, he was well versed in the protocol of public affairs. Even if his opposite number were a foreigner, he would in no way lighten the gravitas of his demeanor. On the other hand, it is possible that the diminutive Japanese representative found the physical appearance of the fifty-eight-year-old Perry as imposing as the Black Ships themselves. The Japanese delegation has left us a record of their first impressions of the commodore:

> Six feet and five inches in height; stout of build and florid of complexion ["the color of cherry blossoms"—Trans.]; a prominent nose; penetrating eyes with some gold coloring; hair light blond and quite short; no beard or mustaches.[2]

Perry took the initiative and the offensive; the Bakufu representatives tried to squirm and slither out of making any concessions. The site for these negotiations was Yokohama, at the time nothing more than an isolated village. This location represented a compromise between Perry (who had originally insisted on holding the negotiations in the capital city of Edo) and the Bakufu or Shogunate (who had wanted to confine Perry to Uraga, at the gateway to Edo Bay). Subsequently, Yokohama developed rapidly as a window onto Western culture.

Perry demanded the opening of five or six ports in the southeast of Japan and two or three in the north; the Bakufu planned to offer only one port and not to include Nagasaki. After much to-ing and fro-ing, the two sides finally agreed on one port in the north, Hakodate, and one somewhat to the west of Uraga, namely Shimoda. Perry did not divulge that he had already secured the opening of Naha, in Okinawa, thus achieving his true objective of getting three ports: one in the north, one at the country's midsection, and one in the south.

And so the difficult diplomacy between the two sides was, for the time being, successfully concluded. The remaining practical work of drafting the agreements could now be entrusted safely to subordinates. At this point, Perry invited the Japanese delegation aboard one of his Black Ships for a celebratory banquet.

On board Perry's flagship, the *Powhatan*, all was festive in the extreme. The lavishly spread dining table boasted not just wine but champagne, sherry, and whisky. Moreover, it was furnished with a panoply of meat dishes, exotic luxuries to the seafood-oriented Japanese and prepared in the most elaborate fashion by a Parisian-born chef. Both the Japanese delegates and their American hosts grew red-faced as they offered each other drinks: "Here, won't you have a sip?" Add a naval band, the confusion of the bilateral mingling, sailors in blackface playing the banjo and dancing in "Negro minstrelsy," and so on, and the result was a boisterous scene indeed. For a moment it seemed as though the convivial Americans and the relaxed Japanese had become as one.

Eventually a tall, scrawny old Japanese gentleman wobbled up to Perry, who by contrast cut a proud and vigorous figure bedecked in his full dress uniform. The old man was Matsuzaki, the lowest-ranking member of the Japanese delegation. He was relatively tall for a Japanese, looked to be at or above sixty years of age, and was described in Francis L. Hawks's *Narrative of the Expedition* as having "a long, drawn-out meager body, a very yellow bilious face, an uncomfortable dyspeptic expression."[3] Perry had viewed his role in the negotiations with suspicion. The old man "took his seat constantly at rather a remote distance from the other dignitaries, on the farther end of the sedan. A scribe, who was constantly employed in taking notes of what was passing, continually crouched next to him."[4] What on earth were the duties of this old man, who was such a constant (if silent) presence? As Perry writes in the report he filed upon the conclusion of his Japan Expedition, the four delegates signed the treaty, but the fifth was obviously an advisor, or perhaps a spy.

Matsuzaki accosted Perry, and in a manner not uncommon to drunks worldwide, spoke to him with his face shoved right up to Perry's nose. Perry could only speculate that the old man must have been extremely nearsighted; but Perry was also sufficiently uninformed and inexperienced not to realize that these were merely the antics of a Japanese drunk, and that he was no spy, but a frustrated general affairs section chief unlikely to rise any higher in the world. Meanwhile, Commissioner Hayashi "always preserved his grave and dignified bearing, ate and drank sparingly." It is true that he "tasted of every dish and sipped of every kind of wine,"[5] but all in all he behaved with an air of, let us say, cautious opportunism. If we compare Matsuzaki's conduct to the restraint exercised by his younger superior, it is clear that the old gentleman was the more audacious.

For the Confucianist to draw so close to the American was already an infringement of territorial waters. Matsuzaki was skinny and tall; still, he had to throw his head back and look upward to address the giant Perry. Peering into the commodore's face with eyes that could not focus, Matsuzaki suddenly clung to him. The *Narrative of the Expedition* records the encounter thus:

The jovial Matsuzaki threw his arms about the Commodore's neck, crushing, in his tipsy embrace, a pair of new epaulets, and repeating, in Japanese, with maudlin affection, these words, as interpreted into English: "Japan and America, all the same heart."[6]

How can we ridicule Matsuzaki's feeling of relief in fulfilling a heavy responsibility, no matter how small his personal role in that mission had been? Even the naïveté of believing the business about "Japan and America, all the same heart."

Perry answered Matsuzaki's affability, rashness, and over-familiarity with a wry smile. After all, Perry had brought a small armada with him to shock and awe the Japanese and compel them to the negotiating table. Will they, nill they, they must open their ports; as a defensive strategy, the Japanese tried only to prolong the negotiations. But at the banquet, they could—as if they were different people—get tipsy and embrace the invaders. Not only did they not understand these Others, they did not know what an "Other" was.

The year was 1854. Great treaties were signed between nations, but the differences that arose between individuals were not addressed systematically. They were simply left up in the air, unresolved. On June 28, Perry quit Edo Bay and returned to Hong Kong via Naha. There he left his naval expedition and boarded an English mail steamer, the *Hindostan*, to return home.

It may be merely incidental, but what I want to draw attention to here is that to get to Japan, the Black Ships did not cross the Pacific. They came from the west, crossing the Atlantic. The image we have of Japan and America confronting each other across the Pacific is a notion that was cultivated only later.

On the way back, Perry stopped off in Great Britain. His primary purpose was to visit the writer Nathaniel Hawthorne, already famous for *The Scarlet Letter*. Perry knew that his own recent accomplishment was one of historical significance. Feeling that his expeditionary report should present a compelling account, he rather self-centeredly applied for editorial assistance to one of the leading writers of the day. Hawthorne gently declined. Still, Perry received a hero's welcome in New York. Not only was he feted in a round of receptions both public and private, but most gratifying of all, the government awarded him twenty thousand dollars, a considerable sum. On top of that, his *Narrative of the Expedition* became a best seller.

* * *

THE POPULATION OF NEW YORK at that time was seven hundred thousand, having nearly doubled during the decade of 1840 to 1850. In addition to receiving waves of immigrants from Ireland and Germany, New York was beginning to assume its position as the commercial center of the New World. John McSorley, the founder of McSorley's Old Ale House, was one of those Irishmen who could not resist the call of New York, starting out as a blacksmith and making beer on the side, as a hobby.

Perry's daughter, Caroline, married one August Belmont. This man, of Jewish descent, made a fortune acting as agent for a firm owned by the French banking family the Rothschilds and had built a splendid mansion for himself on Fifth Avenue. Not any ordinary mansion. What was truly astounding about it was that it was equipped with a ballroom large enough to accommodate several hundred pairs of dancers. The identification of Fifth Avenue with luxury and high society stemmed from this era. Perry could trace his own ancestors back to soon after the arrival of the Mayflower in 1620. Now he had forged family ties with one of the newly risen mercantile Jewish families that were supporting the rapid growth of American capitalism.

The distance from the Belmont's mansion to McSorley's Old Ale House was a matter of just six or seven hundred meters. There, it is difficult not to imagine scenes of newly arrived immigrants quaffing stout and talking up a storm. The tempestuous combination of immigration and capitalism, which so symbolizes America, was a salient characteristic of a vibrantly developing New York. And Perry's daughter's marriage occurred in 1854, too.

Attracted by this bustling Big City, a poor young printer named Samuel Clemens, later world-famous as Mark Twain, the author of *The Adventures of Tom Sawyer* and *The Adventures of Huckleberry Finn*, left St. Louis to see New York for himself. He was practically penniless when he got there. As he writes in his *Autobiography*, "I arrived in New York with two or three dollars in pocket change and a ten-dollar bank bill concealed in the lining of my coat."[7] The young man of letters, burning with ambition, strolled down Fifth Avenue, took a peek at the World's Fair, and worked part-time at a printer's. But in this year of 1854, he returned to the Mississippi River Valley. This is also the year in which the poet-philosopher Ralph Waldo Emerson gave a speech in New York on the subject of emancipating the slaves and in which Abraham Lincoln resumed his political activities at his law offices in Springfield, Illinois.

In 1861 the American Civil War broke out. And in 1869, America's first transcontinental railway service was inaugurated. Now there was a new vector to the projection of American interests and power: the Pacific.

And it was around this time that the shock caused by the Black Ships destroyed Japan's old regime, turning that country into the "Land of the Mikado."

PART I

The Pacific Ocean Vector

Why, I, in this weak piping time of peace,
Have no delight to pass away the time,
Unless to spy my shadow in the sun
And descant on mine own deformity:
And therefore, since I cannot prove a lover,
To entertain these fair well-spoken days,
I am determined to prove a villain
And hate the idle pleasures of these days.

—WILLIAM SHAKESPEARE,
Richard III (I.i.24–31)

CHAPTER ONE

External Pressures
and the Young Misfit

N ATSUME SŌSEKI'S celebrated novel *Botchan* is set in Matsuyama, in Shikoku. It was originally published in the April 1906 issue of *Hototogisu Magazine* (The Cuckoo). It so happens that Sōseki based the novel on his own experience as an English teacher at Ehime Prefectural Normal Middle School in Matsuyama, a one-year affair beginning in April 1895. That intervening period of time, a decade, is something I would like readers to keep in mind.

The author I am chiefly concerned with in this book, Mizuno Hironori, who later made his name writing about an imaginary future war between Japan and America, was born in Matsuyama. He withdrew from that same middle school in March of 1895, about a month before Sōseki took up his duties there. They just missed each other. In his youth, Mizuno's nickname was *Ikezu*, or, in the local dialect, "prankster."

After graduating from Tokyo Imperial University, Sōseki took a position as an English teacher at Tokyo Higher Normal School. By the time he took up his post in Matsuyama, he was already twenty-eight years old. The narrator and protagonist of *Botchan*, however, was a mathematics instructor on his first teaching assignment after graduating from an institute of physics. One surmises that he is about twenty years old. His youth perfectly fits a flagrantly trouble-prone protagonist whose "inherent recklessness," in the words of the novel's opening sentence, "has brought [him] nothing but trouble" ever since childhood.[1]

That there were differences between the novel and real life hardly matters— except to the locals whose Botchan dumplings are the premier souvenir of the local tourist trade, and who are apparently dissatisfied, somehow, with the novel's occasional condescension toward Matsuyama. The novel conveys how a cultured Tokyoite feels about a place located in "the back of beyond." The provinciality of the protagonist's destination is initially established by his former maid, Kiyo. When he tells her he is to leave Tokyo, heading "west," she asks, "This side of Hakone or beyond it?"[2] When he arrives at the place where he is to take up his duties, it is described thus:

> As the boat came to a stop with a deep blast of its siren, a barge pulled away from the shore and made towards us. The lighterman was completely naked, except for a red loincloth. What a barbaric place! Though, of course, nobody could have worn a kimono in that heat.[3]

To get to the town from the harbor, he has to switch to a train that is "like a matchbox."[4] And after he has introduced himself at the school where he is to teach and passed back through the school gate for a look about town, his impressions are also couched in terms of invidious comparisons with Tokyo:

> I saw the prefectural government office, an old building from the last century, and the army barracks. These were no better than those of the regiment at Azabu in Tokyo. I also saw the main street, which was about half the size of Tokyo's Kagurazaka, and whose shops were poorer. This was just a small castle town which in feudal times probably only yielded its lord a paltry million and a quarter bushels of grain. I was walking along, pitying those who brag about living in a "castle town."[5]

Strictly speaking, back then the castle town of Matsuyama had a population of thirty thousand, and its entire feudal domain was rated at 150,000 *koku* (approx. 750,000 bushels). In any event, our Botchan maintains a secret antipathy toward Matsuyama from the very beginning. One can, however, interpret this as a foreshadowing of the protagonist's future troubles, rather than as a reflection of the author's own antipathy toward the town.

From the moment Botchan first mounts the dais in his classroom, the pupils are rambunctious. Not wanting to appear weak before these country bumpkins, he uses Tokyo street language, at once sophisticated and harsh. At which point the toughest-looking student there stands up and speaks:

> You're speaking too fast. I can't understand what you say. If it's all the same to you, could you speak just a little more slower, like?

The new teacher may be a little timid, but this is not the time or place to back down. He replies, gamely,

> If I'm speaking too quickly, I'll slow down. But I'm from Tokyo and I can't speak your dialect, so if you don't understand my accent, you'll just have to wait till you get used to it.[6]

Then, as he is leaving, one of the students corners the protagonist with a request to solve some impossible-looking problems. Saying he will teach them the solutions next time, he beats a hasty retreat. This prompts a chorus of jeers, among which the protagonist can hear, "He can't do it! He can't do it!"

I suspect that Sōseki flavored such accounts with his own experiences. In any event, surrounded as Botchan is by insolent provincial students and inflexible provincial teachers, he can see that his new position will be challenging. He vents his frustrations in a letter to Kiyo in Tokyo:

> I arrived yesterday. It's a useless place. I'm sleeping in a room fifteen feet by eighteen.... I'll be home next summer. I went to school today and gave all the teachers nicknames. The headmaster is the Badger, the second master is Redshirt, the English master is the Green Pumpkin, the mathematics master is the Porcupine and the art master is the Clown. I'll write and tell you more news soon. Goodbye.[7]

As readers of this modern classic know, the only teacher the narrator gets along with is the Porcupine, "a strapping fellow, with closely cropped hair that stood up like the spines on a chestnut burr, and a face like one of those soldier-monks of the Eizan temple who were always starting revolts at the end of the Heian period."[8]

But let us return to Mizuno Hironori's story. Hironori the Prankster was also given the nickname "the Shrine." Hironori himself once asked a friend why and received the following explanation: "Because of that pointy head, dark coloring, angular features, and big mouth!"

As I write, I have before me a photograph of Mizuno Hironori during his days as an officer in the Imperial Japanese Army. Imagine, if you will, a bearded version of Atsumi Kiyoshi, the actor who played the awkward and beloved hero of the popular *Tora-san* movie series. He is narrow-eyed and square-jawed. Not a great looker. This is, rather, the face of a truculent bad-boy.

While Hironori was attending middle school in Matsuyama, a strike took place. The cause appears to have been trivial. It relates to a school excursion to Uwajima City, some fifty kilometers to the west, where a huge melee took place with some Uwajima middle school students. Both cities were in Ehime Prefecture, but the Matsuyama domain had been loyal to the Tokugawa Shogunate, to which it had belonged in hereditary vassalage, whereas Uwajima, being on the outs in the Edo era, was quicker to enter into the spirit—and to take the side—of the new Meiji regime. This opposition and tension persisted. While the great domain of Matsuyama suffered bad luck, many of the people in Uwajima, which was affiliated with the Imperial faction, rode the tides of history to great success. Feelings of resentment and opposition lingered longer and stronger in Matsuyama.

The strike agitation began immediately after the students returned from their excursion to Uwajima and expressed dissatisfaction with the fact that their own headmaster was a product of Uwajima. Students of this era were a compound of the infantile and the precocious. Influenced by the Freedom and Popular Rights Movement, they cut class to attend (and heckle) a session of their Prefectural Assembly. It was actually something of a fashion at that time to do this, hardly unique to Matsuyama. Student Alliance class moratoriums (strikes) were breaking out all over. The Ministry of Education, feeling the impact, issued this directive on May 2, 1893: "When students of schools under the purview of this Ministry seek to compel staff to retire or to transfer, they shall be punished severely."

The campaign to recall the headmaster of the Matsuyama Middle School had reached its peak in November of the previous year. The school staff all took sides, dividing into pro- and anti-headmaster camps. Finally, some students went so far as to petition the prefectural governor directly. The upshot of all this was that the headmaster was forced to transfer to another middle school in a different prefecture. The Ministry of Education's directive provided a remedy for dealing with this sort of disturbance in the future. As the headmaster forced to quit Matsuyama later reminisced, "It is shameful that such disturbances should result from my lack of virtue. I regret not having had the time to dispose properly of ruffians such as 'the Shrine.'"

It would be well to keep in mind that this was the recent history of Matsuyama when Sōseki took up his own teaching position there. The headmaster could not function unless he was a cunning old man who could speak out of both sides of his mouth; a polarized staff was now the norm. Deceit and delusion had been raised to high levels of performance, and it all directly affected personnel decisions. This sort of behavior becomes understandable in context.

The timidity some instructors exhibited toward the pupils is incisively depicted in *Botchan*. One evening, for example, the narrator, Botchan, on call for night duty, gets into his futon and finds himself in the company of fifty or sixty grasshoppers, which proceed to hop all over him as they flee the bed. He gets hold of several students and asks, "What did you put grasshoppers in my bed for?" One student feigns ignorance, "Er, what's a grasshopper?"; another suggests they were actually locusts. As Botchan recalls, "It looked as though it wasn't only the headmaster at this school who could juggle with words: the pupils were going to do it too."

The exasperated Botchan asks who put the grasshoppers in his bed.

"Nobody put them there."

"How else could they have got into my bed if nobody put them there?"

"Locusts like warm places. They probably crawled in by themselves."

"Don't talk rubbish! Grasshoppers don't just waltz their way into beds by themselves. And if you think I'm going to put up with people waltzing them in, you're mistaken. Now, come on. Speak out."

"It's all very well to say 'speak out,' but we can't explain something we didn't do."[9]

The incident precipitates a faculty meeting. The headmaster starts things off with a statement.

Whenever a misdemeanor is perpetrated by a teacher or pupil of this school, I take it as a reflection on my own lack of character. And whenever a regrettable incident occurs, I have a deep sense of shame that I, as headmaster, have failed to fulfill my duties. Sad to say, gentlemen, such an event has occurred—I refer to the recent disturbance—and for this I tender my most profound apologies to you all."[10]

The headmaster's meek, waffling response is due to his ongoing experience of the power of student rebellion. The students were here before Botchan arrived to take up his duties. They possess a history. The stranger, Botchan, has left his own history in Tokyo along with his maid, Kiyo. Alienated from the current situation, Botchan considers the local school authorities weak and vacillating. He becomes quite disgusted with everything. Only the Porcupine is a sympathetic soul: he does not pander to the students. What Botchan does not realize—and what the author, Sōseki, himself may not have known—is that the Porcupine was experienced in combating evildoers far worse than the students who instigated the grasshopper disturbance.

The Porcupine was most likely modeled on a real mathematics instructor named Watanabe Masakazu. Sōseki himself does not record this anywhere; it is merely the whispered conjecture of people in Matsuyama that this person may have been the model. But there does indeed appear to be a point of resemblance. Namely, that this mathematics master was the only teacher for whom the Shrine had a high regard.

Mizuno Hironori was incorrigibly tardy. One day, during the Autumn Festival, two groups of young people shouldering *mikoshi* (portable Shinto shrines) bumped into each other on Hironori's route to school. A fracas ensued, and the excited Hironori forgot about the time.

"Why are you late?!" the Porcupine-ish voice thundered. Now the last time Hironori was late, he had dissembled, saying, "I went to pay my respects to my ancestors' graves." And the response was an ironic "My, what an admirable example of filial piety you are." But one can visit one's ancestors' graves only so often. So this time, there was nothing to do but speak candidly.

"I went to the festival, and this fight broke out over the mikoshi, eh. People were throwing tiles from the roof. It was like a real war out there. Just so much darn fun, eh!"

"School or the festival—which is more important?! Idiot!"

"Yeah, but sensei, there's school every day, but you know, like, the festival comes only once a year, eh."

Grumbling "You're hopeless," Watanabe staged a tactical retreat.

Hironori, for his part, worn out from carrying the *mikoshi* and delivering newspapers on his morning route, was by now feeling drowsy and beginning to nod off. He was all right for a while. A student next to him poked Hironori to keep him awake, but eventually his textbook slipped off his desk, and loud snoring could be heard.

For Watanabe, this was the last straw. In high dudgeon, he leapt from the dais and slapped his pointer down on Hironori's desk.

"You're late because you were off playing hooky at the festival. You snore

in class! I will not teach someone whose conduct is so inexcusable! Get out!"
He grabbed Hironori by the ear.

"When I say get out, get out!"

Hironori's defense was a far-fetched argument. "I pay you, like, a monthly
tuition to get instructed, eh? So I figure you gotta prorate it and give me
some back, huh."

"What cheek, when you're the one falling asleep and not listening to the
lessons! You don't belong here; you're a hindrance: get out—now!"

"If I listen or if I don't listen, that's up to me, eh."

"Watch what tone you take with me! If you want your monthly tuition
prorated, go try asking at the bursar's."

Watanabe did not compromise with Hironori.

We are left with an image of the boy Mizuno Hironori's insolence and
schoolteacher Watanabe's intransigence. It would not be going too far to
say that their precedent was the *sine qua non* for the construction of the
world of *Botchan*. At the very least, there is no doubt that their existence,
and the historical environment they provide, contribute to the excitement
of the novel's milieu.

It was necessary to bring in *Botchan* in order to explain something of
the character of Mizuno, the author of Japan's first account of a future war
between Japan and America. For one thing, Mizuno was born in the town
of Matsuyama, in Shikoku, which (as we have seen above) was chosen by
Sōseki as the stage for *Botchan*.

There is another novel that has Matsuyama as its origin: Shiba Ryōtarō's
historical novel *Saka no ue no kumo* (The Cloud Above the Hill). When
one of the protagonists, based on the famous poet Masaoka Shiki, returns
to his hometown in 1895, he composes the following haiku:

> Ah, Spring!
> This once was a castle town,
> Of 150,000 koku.

This meant it was a smallish domain with a core state subsidy of 150,000
koku of rice or the equivalent thereof, one *koku* (about five bushels) being
approximately enough to feed one person for one year. By this time, the
real Shiki was in poor health. He had joined the army during the Sino-
Japanese War of 1894–95, but on his way home, his condition was already

so unsatisfactory that he was compelled to convalesce for a month or so at Suma. He returned to Matsuyama via Hiroshima just as the hot summer weather was finishing up.

In April of that year, Sōseki had already taken up his teaching position in Matsuyama. Shiki knew Sōseki from their days together in a university preparatory school in Tokyo. Shiki initially settled into his mother's house in Matsuyama, but wound up after a while in the same rooming house as Sōseki. In this establishment, run by the Ueno family, Sōseki rented the two upstairs rooms, while Shiki took the two downstairs rooms. It was after returning to his hometown, and learning that he was afflicted with tuberculosis, that Shiki composed the haiku we noted above. The illness had caused a telltale shadow on his chest X-ray. One gets a sense of the man's true character from this determination to parry and dodge all worries and instead enjoy the bright, clear sky over his hometown.

On September 17, Shiki celebrated his twenty-eighth birthday. Meanwhile, Mizuno had cut his connection with Matsuyama Middle School at the age of nineteen, just missing Sōseki as the latter arrived to take up his teaching position there. Mizuno and Sōseki were only a decade apart in age. Mizuno had actually flunked out once in 1893, but was then allowed back the following year, before withdrawing again in March of 1895. It had been a tortuous path.

It was the external pressure represented by the Black Ships that caused the collapse of the feudal system of the Tokugawa Shogunate of the Edo era. The Imperial faction, led by the domains of Satsuma and Chōshū, engaged in civil war with the Aizu domain and other supporters of the Tokugawa Shogunate. The Imperial forces emerged victorious, uniting around their symbol, the Mikado.

The Matsuyama domain was among the supporters of the Tokugawa Shogunate. And—like other such backers of the ancien régime—it paid for that stance, in one way or another, during the Meiji Restoration. The Meiji Imperial Army came from the neighboring prefecture of Kochi (formerly the domain of Tosa) and forced Matsuyama to pay a 150,000-*ryō* indemnity (about thirty million in today's U.S. dollars). Matsuyama itself sustained attacks that brought it to the brink of economic collapse. Its surviving soldiers were now destitute, reduced to an impoverished existence.

Mizuno came from a lower-ranking samurai family with a feudal pension assessed at ten *koku* per annum. In 1870, the third year of the new Meiji regime, this hereditary income was confiscated, and in its stead the family was awarded a Restoration Grant of one thousand yen. This was a lump-sum severance payment; the family was essentially left to fend for itself. It could be thought of as working capital.

Mizuno's father, Mitsuyuki, took his Restoration Grant and opened a sweets shop. It failed. Next he started up a shop selling grains and household goods. There was a household goods shop located directly across the street from his home, and it had flourished, so he tried to imitate it. But in his business practices he was the very picture of the haughty samurai. The shop did so poorly that after a while he could not retain any employees. Eventually, the former samurai and his wife were hulling the grain themselves.

In 1876, the year after Hironori's birth, his mother, Nao, died of dysentery. She was thirty-nine. He therefore had no recollection whatsoever of his mother.

In 1879, his father obtained a post with the prefectural Land Reform office, at fifteen *sen* per day. A modest wage, but at least it afforded the prospect of making ends meet. However, after working for a while, he became chronically ill, then bedridden; finally he passed away at the age of forty-nine.

As to memories the five-year-old toddler had of his father, there are only a few vignettes, such as, a "thin man with a pale face lying in front of a chest of drawers; by the pillow, bottles of medicine, and also some ginger to remedy the aftertaste of the medicine."

His father had been skinny and withdrawn, he had had few acquaintances, and the family was poor. So the funeral was a shabby one. A neighborhood child watching the funeral procession commented, "What a pathetic funeral!" in such a blunt manner that it echoed in Mizuno's ears ever after. Following the services, the family convened to determine what to do with the children. Altogether two brothers and three sisters had to be taken in by some relative or other. Hironori, the youngest, was taken in by his mother's family, the Sasais, also in Matsuyama. But Hironori did not understand what was happening.

His eldest sister put him on her back and headed toward the Sasais'. But he awoke en route, and crying, "No! I won't! I won't," threw such a tantrum that she had to turn back.

But the next morning he woke up at the Sasais'. They must have carried him there after he fell asleep. Shoving aside his grandmother, who was sleeping beside him, he dashed outdoors still in his nightclothes and made a beeline for home. When he got there, he found the front door padlocked.

No matter how he pounded on it or how loudly he called, there was no response. It was already vacated.

His father, his mother, his first home: everything that had swathed and protected the young child was now stripped from him. His final refuge was his nineteen-year-old eldest sister, who had served as his surrogate mother, but eventually she, too, left Matsuyama. She had decided to live with some distant relatives in Tokyo. The little Hironori ran after the *jinrikisha* taking her away: he ran and he ran, weeping, until he could run no more.

The current head of the Sasai family was Naho's elder brother, Masumi. Like the Mizuno family, they were lower-ranking samurai of the Matsuyama domain; their circumstances were much the same. What was different was that Hironori's forty-six-year-old uncle was square-faced, broad-shouldered, and possessed of a sturdy constitution. His way was punctilious, taciturn, straitlaced. He did not touch a drop of liquor. No one could recall seeing him smile, ever. Needless to say, he never joked. His lips were always pursed in a sour, upside-down U.

One day, this righteous martinet of an uncle launched a veritable thunderbolt. A rose bush in a corner of the garden had put forth buds. The uncle was looking forward to seeing the buds blossom. But Hironori had plucked all of the buds. He had found the sight of the tips of red petals poking out between the green calyces so intriguing, he wanted to peel them and have a peek inside. It was not out of maliciousness. Nonetheless, the uncle kicked Hironori off the porch and beat his back and behind with a broom. He treated him merely as an uncouth child in need of correction.

When Hironori entered elementary school, he graduated from such trifling matters to being suspected of having sticky fingers. For example, when some sheets of paper went missing from atop the bookcase in the parlor, Hironori was suspected. In those days, paper was a precious commodity. When the children in the Sasai household practiced their calligraphy at school, half-size sheets of paper would be used and re-used until they were almost solidly black with ink. These sheets of paper were not to be wasted, and as a rule, permission was to be asked each and every time a piece was used. Which did not prevent both Hironori and his cousin from helping each other to help themselves whenever they could. And so, one day, tidying up the parlor, Hironori's uncle sent for him.

"You stole some of the writing paper here, didn't you."

Hironori sat mute, eyes cast down, in formal *seiza* position, his legs tucked under him.

"Whenever you want paper, it's yours for the asking, but not for the taking! If you stole it, then be a man and admit you stole it!"

He didn't think of it as stealing. If one called that stealing, then his cousin was also a thief. He kept his silence, but tears began to fall onto the tatami.

"You lazy, brazen, good-for-nothing! I'll have to beat some backbone into you!"

This time, he was beaten so badly with a bamboo broomstick that it almost might have broken his backbone, if the broomstick hadn't been so weakened by insects that it broke first. All the same, it must have hurt plenty. Yet he bore it without any display of anguish.

"With the likes of you, there's no point sending you to school; can't have you around the house. Leave—get out!" His uncle spat out the words and walked away.

Hironori shut himself into a gloomy closet and refused to come out for two days. He did not eat. He did not go to school. He was so hungry he grew dizzy. Considering how things were going, for him to be unable to bring himself to leave when he was told to, you'd have to call him one stubborn child.

For Mizuno Hironori, it was his first experience of external pressure.

I should like to reflect a bit more on this incident at the Sasais'. Even when one is taken in by relatives, one can't help feeling that this is another family. The common belief that children are pure is the prejudice of adults who have, all too soon, forgotten their own pasts. In actuality, children's survival instincts are rendered so sensitive, not by rules and laws, but by exposure to natural conditions, that they naturally acquire the skill to calculate just how much strength or weakness they can display to best advantage. Soon after Hironori was taken in by the Sasai family, he encountered a distant relative, another uncle, on the street.

"So whereabouts are you going?" He was suddenly being questioned. And Hironori shot right back,

"You! So whereabouts are *you* going?"

He had only wanted to imitate the tough tone of an adult. It startled the relative so much he mentioned the encounter to Hironori's aunt at the Sasais'. And then his aunt would rehearse the entire episode to shock guests.

"'The soul at three is the soul at a hundred,'" she would intone. "I fear for the future of this brazen boy." And she would say this even when Hironori was present. She thought that such highfalutin language could not penetrate a child's heart.

"The child's not straight," his aunt was wont to say.

"The boy's an enigma," said his uncle.

One winter's day, Hironori's uncle bought him a child's shawl. At that time, children wore cotton Japanese garments and *geta* clogs. They had no overcoats, so for commuting to and from school, the fashion was to throw over the shoulders a simple shawl with a little wool mixed in. Why his uncle should buy him such a shawl all of a sudden, he had no idea. Perhaps it was because, rising early as his uncle did to sweep the garden and the street outside, he knew how cold it was. Perhaps it was because Hironori had taken honors in the year-end examinations, and the uncle meant it as a reward.

Hironori wore it with pride: "Look what my uncle gave me!"

But when he showed it off to his aunt, she gave him a quick look and a cool reply: "I see."

It would appear that his aunt then went to his uncle wearing an expression of dissatisfaction and complained. That very evening, Hironori's cousin received from his mother (Hironori's aunt) exactly the same item. For two or three days, the uncle went around with a displeased expression on his face. He was the older brother, by blood, of Hironori's mother. So there is a sign that in his own way he did recognize the wretchedness of his nephew. He was severe and dour as ever, with that downturned U of a mouth, but perhaps he was also a henpecked husband.

Hironori's aunt, Iku, was a decade younger than her husband. She was slight of build and dark-complexioned. A cheerful person, she got along well with others. And she was a good worker. As was the custom of those days, she dyed her teeth black and shaved off her eyebrows, and she did up her somewhat frizzy hair in a chignon. Every morning she rose early to complete this toilette. The dab of face powder at the tip of her nose was excuse enough for the naughty boys of the neighborhood to jeer at her, shrieking, "Yikes, a vixen!" (meaning a treacherous fox-spirit in the form of a young woman), and then run away.

Aunt Iku had also come from a lower-ranking samurai family of the Matsuyama domain. Her cousins on her father's side—the brothers Akiyama Yoshifuru and Saneyuki—served in the Russo-Japanese War: they function as the main heroes of Shiba Ryōtarō's historical novel *The Cloud Above the Hill*. Aunt Iku boasted to Hironori about such promising young relations. Now and then she would run little errands for the Akiyamas, but by this time the two brothers had already quit Matsuyama for Tokyo. Yoshifuru graduated from the Imperial Army Military Academy and rose to the rank of cavalry lieutenant. Saneyuki, nine years his junior, went up to Tokyo in the autumn of 1883. Masaoka Shiki, who had been a classmate of his at Matsuyama Middle School, had withdrawn from the school in June and gone up to Tokyo himself, one step ahead of Saneyuki. In Tokyo, the two once again sat side by side, at the classroom desks of the Tokyo University Preparatory School.

This lively aunt had quite a way with words. Evaluating Hironori, she said that he was "*kassai* and *ōdō*." By *kassai* she meant he hated to lose but loved to quarrel; by *ōdō* she meant he was bold and brash. This description may be as redundant as roofing a roof, but she was expressing a valid insight into her nephew's character.

Meanwhile the orphan was forever getting into scrapes at elementary school. The games he played, "war" and "bandits," were like real fights. He would come home with a missing sleeve and have to go back to retrieve it from where it lay in the road after having been torn off. His clothes were ripped so frequently that his aunt wove him some cloth herself, with which she made him especially sturdy clothes. Even so, he would come home with his garment's armholes ripped front to back or left to right.

"You must behave yourself," he was admonished.

In those days in Matsuyama, there was a custom they called a "recreation." By this they meant a sort of picnic excursion, with the whole family going out for a treat. The destination was the dry bed of the River Ishite, which ran through the town. Aunt Iku would pack her home-cooked meals into special stacked picnic boxes, which they would load into a crude pram made of wood. The pram was pulled by either Hironori or his cousin, who was a year younger. Every fourth of March, after the seasonal festival on the third, the dry riverbed and its banks were thronged with groups engaged in this family recreation. There were people singing, people dancing, people strumming the shamisen, people beating taiko drums. Simple and humble though this holiday was, it ushered in the spring.

Hironori's straitlaced uncle had no taste for alcohol. The fact that he was a non-drinker came out during the recreations. One tiny cup of sake and his face would light up, bright red. He would look on, glumly it seemed, as the others whooped it up, but actually he was in high enough spirits.

When Hironori was finally becoming accustomed to his uncle's household, and it looked as though the external pressure he had suffered was subsiding, he was forced to play a major role in a new incident. This occurred in the fall of 1886, when Hironori was eleven years old.

He was with a group of his pals on their way home when they surrounded another student and began poking and shoving him. A scene one might well witness even today. But by chance, a constable witnessed the bullying. Hironori's comrades instantly scattered and hid.

"Hey, stop that," the constable called out angrily as he approached. The only one for whom it was too late to flee was Hironori. What would happen in such a situation? So he wondered as he waited. Why did he wait? A manifestation of his *kassai* and *ōdō* nature, perhaps. There are many occasions throughout a man's life when one might wonder, "Why?"

Unlike the sociable neighborhood cops of today, the policemen in those days were called constables and were treated with respect.

"Why were you fighting? Come!"

Before he knew what was happening, Hironori was seized by the wrist and dragged off to the police substation at the intersection of the main road. When he tried to resist, the constable clenched one hand into a fist and punched him. The other students followed them, compelled by a morbid curiosity. And their numbers increased. The constable entered the substation and recorded Hironori's name and address in his notebook. This "bad boy" was trembling ever so slightly. The constable was scary enough, but what hurt even more was having one's name and address entered in the notebook.

"There's no way out of this."

As he strove to hold back the tears, the constable left him and went into the back rest area. His purpose was to punish the child by thus leaving him alone. However, the street outside was soon swarming with heads of black hair. At first it was merely the student onlookers; then curious adults were added.

"What's going on?"

"He was fighting or something." And the story grew from there.

"Some kids fighting? They wouldn't pull him into this place just for that. Must've pinched something at least, that's for sure."

"Hey, isn't that the kid living with the Sasais?"

News of this incident would spread far and wide.

The policeman came back. He began an interrogation. Questions Hironori should have answered straightforwardly he met with silence. This the constable took as a provocation. Hironori tended to anger adults in this way. The constable slapped him three or four times with an open palm.

It would have been only natural to cry, but Hironori did not cry. What's more, still silent, he stared at the constable as if his eyes could drill holes into him. The constable grew irritated. With his thick-soled military boots he gave the boy a swift kick. Hironori was launched heels-over-head out of the substation. He lay there without trying to get up.

"He's dead, maybe," some onlookers were saying. The constable grew somewhat flustered.

"All right, that's enough. Go on home. Try it again and you'll do time."

Some woman he did not know came up to him. "Such a little boy. He didn't have to treat you so badly. And you, what bad thing did you do?" As she spoke, she brushed the dirt off his clothing.

A lad who looked like a university student spoke words of encouragement. "You don't cry. Hey, you got grit, all right."

Thinking that the only people who got pulled into police stations were thieves and drunks, Hironori remained there not a second longer, but fled back to the Sasais'.

It was the fishmonger who told his aunt about the incident when he made a delivery. But for some reason, neither his uncle nor his aunt mentioned the matter. The next day, however, at school, he was called into the faculty room. The principal, Hironori's faculty advisor, and others were seated at the table. Spread out on the table was a copy of the local newspaper. Hironori was made to stand there as they asked him questions about yesterday's incident. When they had finished their debriefing, his faculty advisor took up the local newspaper and began to read aloud an article to him.

VIOLENCE BY A GRADE-SCHOOLER, read the headline. "Violence the likes of the Nagasaki Incident..." ran the article. Everything was put in the most exaggerated way.

"The Nagasaki Incident—like, what's that?"

What had happened was that in one fell swoop of journalistic prose, *kassai* and *ōdō* had been likened to an international incident.

The Nagasaki Incident was the event that had most excited Japanese public opinion that summer. China's North Sea Fleet had put into Nagasaki harbor on August 1, 1886. Four ships under the command of Admiral Ding Ruchang: the *Ding Yuan*, the *Zhen Yuan*, the *Cheng Yuan*, and the *Ji Yuan*, each one a world-class behemoth of a ship. Particularly powerful were the *Ding Yuan* and the *Zhen Yuan*, two German-made battleships, each with a displacement of 7,300 tons, whose hulls were reinforced with thirty-centimeter-thick steel plating. The largest steel-hulled warship Japan had at the time was in the 3,000-ton class.

This Imperial China North Sea Fleet showed up in a battle formation that appeared more than threatening to the Meiji government. Now the Black Ships were coming even from Asia.

Then some of the Chinese crew, on shore leave, got drunk and ran amok. The Japanese constabulary arrested the offenders. The next day, the town was overrun with several hundred sailors bent on revenge. It looked like a scene of urban warfare. There were almost eighty casualties altogether. This was on August 15.

The Meiji government was afraid lest China use the incident as a pretext for advancing unreasonable demands. On September 6, a joint board of inquiry established by the two countries began its investigation. However, no agreement was in sight. Japanese foreign minister Inoue Kaoru and Chinese ambassador Xu Chengzu held meetings. By February of the next year they had agreed on a balanced application of their respective laws, on reparations to be paid to injured or bereaved parties on both sides, and so on.

It was after this that Japan worked out a policy for dealing with external pressure. To counter the overwhelming superiority of the Chinese navy, shore batteries were constructed at key locations nationwide. A coast guard station had recently been established on Tsushima. And it was decided to go full speed ahead with a plan to build new warships for the navy. For the local paper to refer to all this in its article about a trivial incident involving one young boy was at least timely.

The principal handed him a sealed, formal letter addressed to his guardian.

"We'd like your uncle to read this."

It was a despondent Hironori who left school that day. He took the long way home to avoid the police substation. En route, he pondered.

"I might be forced to quit school. I might be forced to leave home too. If it comes to that, I'll kill that cursed constable, then die myself."

As soon as he got back to his uncle's, Hironori looked for the sword he had been left as a Mizuno family heirloom. But it was locked up tight in a closet, and there was nothing he could do about it. Too bad. His thoughts turned to torching the home of the constable and other schemes. But now his uncle returned from the government offices.

His aunt whispered to him, "That letter from the principal. You should hand it over to Uncle yourself. And apologize good and proper!"

Timidly, approaching no nearer than necessary, Hironori held the letter out toward his uncle. His uncle read the names of the addressee and sender, then deliberately took out a knife and broke the seal. Then he read the letter through in silence. Folding it up again and returning it to the envelope, he said, "We'll talk about this later."

Hironori waited on pins and needles. He rushed through dinner; as soon as he rested his chopsticks, he tried to go outside to play. His uncle's voice grabbed him from behind: "Hiro, you don't go out to play. You stay indoors." His cousins went out one after the other; he alone was left behind. His uncle finished dinner, then completed his prayers in front of the indoor family shrine.

"Ah, Hiro. Come over here."

His uncle was sitting down on his heels in the formal *seiza* position, his legs tucked under him.

"Looks like you've been exceptionally violent. If you were to injure another person's child, I could not face society. You must learn a little self-control. For some time you had better not go to school. And you may not go out and play."

He then proceeded to discourse earnestly on how, in order to restore the fortunes of the Mizuno family, Hironori would have to be educated into an outstanding young man. His language was so unexpectedly gentle that for the first time during this incident, Hironori was moved to tears.

The letter had read, "Punishment: three-day suspension from school."

"Come on out and play!"

When evening came and school let out, his student friends would drop by and call to him. His cousins, hearing their voices, would dash out. But Hironori the Penitent could not go out. He could hear the shouts of the children playing war and bandits. The hatred he felt toward the constable increased.

"When I grow up, I'll join the police force, that's for sure. Then when I become an inspector I'll fire that bastard!"

At the age of twenty, Mizuno Hironori entered the Naval Academy. This was after many vicissitudes, including being obliged twice to withdraw from middle school.

Before entering middle school the first time, his aunt addressed Hironori sarcastically:

"A prankster like you, there's really no point in your going into middle school. When you've finished with primary, best you get yourself a bride from Tokyo and an apprenticeship at a letterpress."

His eldest sister had in fact been taken in by distant relatives in Tokyo and then married to a man who worked at a printer's. Hironori had forgotten about her. But when he remembered how she had been like a mother to him, he felt he simply had to go join her.

"I want to go to Tokyo too!"

He did not say that out loud, but he gave it some serious thought. His uncle, however, put some pressure on him.

"You really have to make it through at least middle school. Seems like you just play all day every day, but if you're going to go to middle school, you'll have to get prepared. The restoration of the Mizuno family depends on you!"

He regretted not being able to go to Tokyo, but what his uncle said was reasonable. If he could be sent to middle school, he wanted to go. His uncle now revealed that he had been entrusted by Hironori's father with money for the boy's education.

"This money was saved up by your respected father by foregoing the sake he loved to drink. And even when he fell ill, he refused to spend money on himself on the grounds he was beyond help. Whatever little bit he could save up, he did, no matter how it inconvenienced him—and he left it for you. Misspending so much as one *ri*, one *sen*, would invite Heaven's punishment."

In those days, going to middle school was considered a luxury. So he was grateful to his uncle. But just a year later something most unfortunate occurred.

Hironori had an elder brother named Toranosuke, one of whose legs was crippled. Although he was Hironori's senior by ten years, when their father died, it was decided that succession as family head should go to Hironori instead. This was an era when such discrimination was practiced freely.

Compared to the Sasai family which took in Hironori, the family entrusted with Toranosuke's care, the Higuchis, was not stable. The head of that family, Bunzō, was a terrible drinker. Their Restoration Grant money, the family's possessions—everything was converted into drinking money. And when he got drunk, throwing around small vases was only the beginning. One day, he tossed a little two-year-old girl into the garden. The poor thing's hipbone was broken and she was handicapped ever after. He also vented his rage wildly on his wife. He would grab her by the hair and drag her to the embankment out back and leave her there, stripped naked and bound.

Toranosuke's situation was indeed a miserable one. While his father had been alive, the handicapped boy had been allowed to loll about the house. But Bunzō, wanting more money for sake, apprenticed him to a rice dealer. Pounding rice was hard labor. Toranosuke would return home utterly exhausted, only to be beaten and kicked for sport by the inebriated Bunzō.

After enduring this exploitation and abuse for two years, Toranosuke left the Higuchi household at the age of eighteen. He rented a tiny three-mat hut nearby and eked out an existence pounding rice. In addition, he would do errands for people in the vicinity, even dragging his lame leg over the mountains to the next town. And he commuted to a teacher of massage to learn that skill. Then, setting up independently as a masseur, he worked hard and lived frugally, dressing plainly and eating simply. It was a lifestyle of almost unimaginable thrift. He did not drink. He did not smoke. He woke before dawn and worked until late in the evening. In addition to being handicapped, he grew up without any opportunity for formal education. He could rely on nothing but money.

His economizing was extravagant. The year there was a cholera outbreak, rumor had it that it originated with contaminated pumpkins. Pumpkins did not sell at all; stores displayed them all out front as if they were free. Toranosuke ate nothing but pumpkin, day after day.

He would walk the streets at night to ply his services as a masseur. On his way home, he would stop by the Sasais' without fail, even if it were as late as midnight or one in the morning. He would knead the shoulders of his aunt and uncle and massage their backs. Whether a harsh rain fell at night, whether it was a cold winter's eve, he never missed a single day. The Sasais would leave the front door open till he came.

Then, all of a sudden, Aunt Iku forbade Toranosuke entrance to the house. For Hironori, it was an unforgettable scene. His brother was on his knees begging forgiveness, but his uncle would not accept his pleas and drove Toranosuke out of the house as one might chastise a dog. And Toranosuke still came by in the evenings, begging, "Uncle, forgive me! Auntie, open the door!"

The uncle suspected Toranosuke of pilfering money and other things. There were relatives with whom the Sasais were feuding; had Toranosuke become mixed up in those troubles? Hironori never really understood the causes. He could only share in his brother's misfortune. Later, even when he went to live at his brother's house, this subject was taboo. And all too soon, Hironori was to suffer the sad plight of departing the Sasais' himself.

Troubles always start small. Tiny frictions become exacerbated. The Sasais kept a bird called a bunting, a variety of sparrow. Hironori's younger cousin asked him, "Could you make it something to eat?" Spurning her request, he scoffed, "Do it yourself!" and went off to play, forgetting all about it. However, the next day, the bunting was discovered dead. It was undoubtedly a coincidence, but his cousin sobbed, "You didn't do it for me!" and so Hironori got the blame.

His uncle looked grim as he passed sentence: "You are taken in by another family, yet you are so perverse as to refuse to give their little bird so much as a morsel of food. I can't imagine what sort of behavior to expect next. You must not stay in this house."

The bunting incident may have merely provided a pretext. There was also his brother's banishment from the house. And Hironori's own back talk was becoming extremely combative. He was fourteen now and getting big. He countered his aunt's strictures with his own far-fetched logic. And he was approaching an age when any tough talk by adults, such as threatening a session of moxibustion,[11] had no effect.

Toranosuke lived in an area that had turned almost into slum. And now Hironori was descending upon this penurious, three-tatami-mat hut. The dirt-floor vestibule, about one tatami in size, was jam-packed. On the floor were crowded a bucket for uncooked rice, a bucket for pickled vegetables, and a straw bag for coal. The shelves were laden with earthenware, a portable clay stove, a tub for cooked rice, and wood tray-tables for setting on the tatami. The room itself was drab and dreary. The tatami had no trimming; its surface was reddened with age and rough with torn fibers, and here and there a hole poked through. The rice-paper panels of the inner *shōji* sliding screen were blackened with soot and torn all over. There was no ceiling—the framework of the roof was exposed. There wasn't even a single-panel *fusuma* sliding door to partition this room from the earthen-floored vestibule. A three-foot-tall cupboard was attached to the wall. In the upper portion, plastered with gold-colored paper, was the family's Buddhist altar; the lower portion held miscellaneous household junk. Off to the side, a decrepit wicker basket for storing clothes; folded on top of it, a futon that seemed as thin, and as comfortable, as a rice-cracker. About two mats' worth of floor space were left in which to move around.

Into this space were moved Hironori's possessions: chopsticks and a rice bowl, writing utensils, casual clothes and nightclothes, a faded writing desk left him by his father, one pair of wooden *geta* clogs, and so on.

It would have been bad enough sleeping side-by-side on a separate futon next to Toranosuke, who had awful underarm odor. But they had to sleep head-to-toe. This was because they had to share that one poorly stuffed, cracker-thin futon. Their dinners featured barley and rice at a proportion of sixty/forty; to go with it they had a few slivers of *takuan* (yellow pickled radish), and some other vegetable boiled in soy sauce. This wasn't enough for Hironori, still a growing boy; when Toranosuke was out, Hironori would munch on uncooked rice and filch some of the *takuan*. The tub-shaped rice container had a lock on it; he could open it only after taking great pains. "Got it!" he would say, practically jumping for joy. Once, when he removed the top, he found that his prudent elder brother had raked the top of the rice smooth and then impressed a design upon it with the rim of the wooden measuring cup. It was a last, pathetic effort on Toranosuke's part to put up a safeguard against the ravenous snacking of his younger brother.

All of Toranosuke's economizing upon economizing was done with a view toward accumulating money. He was also characterized by a fierce piety. The subject of his prayers was none other than the restoration of the Mizuno family.

Due to the kind of work he did, Toranosuke did not come back until late at night, and then had to rise early the next day. After his morning ablutions he would turn to the east and greet the rising sun with a prayer. He would then assume an odd posture and engage in deep breathing. Like a fish in an oxygen-poor tank, pressing its mouth up to the glass and gasping, he inhaled the morning air as if he would devour it all.

Next came his prayer to Shinto and Buddhist deities. The wording of the prayer never changed:

"I pray that until Hironori grows up and achieves the restoration of the Mizuno family, his uncle and aunt in the Sasai family shall remain well."

Following that, he would read aloud several dozen of the *kaimyō*, or posthumous Buddhist names, out of all those recorded for the successive generations of the Mizuno family over the course of approximately two and a half centuries. Then he would pray again: "until Hironori grows up," etc. These rituals, repeated, would take about half an hour.

Eventually, with the money he had so frugally saved up, Toranosuke was able to purchase a two-unit dwelling. He and his brother Hironori lived in an apartment with two six-mat tatami rooms. The other unit was let out. Toranosuke's short life was visited now by the only peace and security he had ever known. Alas, the Goddess of Fortune had turned to smile upon him only briefly.

Hironori's ill-starred brother began to be attacked by spasms.

When it happened, a doleful scream issued from Toranosuke. When he came out of his convulsions, he groaned with pain. What most upset Hironori, who shared a futon with his brother, was the incontinence that accompanied the start of nocturnal spasms. The spasms gradually increased in occurrence to as many as three times a day, and then even more frequently. Finally Toranosuke degenerated into seizures in which he would lose consciousness. Hironori was forced to consult their uncle. They were able to rent a tiny house from a neighbor of the Sasais. A simple renovation made one room lockable, and they locked Toranosuke in.

Hironori could not give himself to his studies. He failed the graduating examinations. He withdrew from school. After a year of care, Toranosuke's symptoms seemed to subside. He moved back in with Hironori temporarily, but Hironori no longer desired to live with him. He found separate lodgings.

Around then, something occurred which had no immediately apparent relationship to the fate of these two poor brothers in Matsuyama, Shikoku. For the first time since the Restoration, Japan was about to embark on a war with one of the great foreign powers. In the July 24, 1894 issue of the influential newspaper *Jiji shimpō* (News & Current Affairs), Fukuzawa Yukichi urged the following:

We should immediately open hostilities against China and Korea. . . . The reason our country has adopted a peace policy so far is that China had not caused us any direct harm. Now it is another story. The proof is clearly there that Li Hongzhang and Yuan Shikai and company have done their utmost to incite the Korean royal court. At this juncture, what reason does our country have to hesitate? We should declare war immediately, making their punishment clear and giving the Chinese a chance to correct themselves. This course of action would be beneficial to world civilization, at its current stage.

On July 19, 1894, the ragtag armada scraped together by this small country of Japan was grandiloquently named the "Combined Fleet." But it could boast not a single modern battleship. It even incorporated wooden ships. Its flagship was the 4,200-ton *Matsushima*. China's North Sea Fleet, on the other hand, possessed two 7,300-ton warships, the *Ding Yuan* and the *Zhen Yuan*. Japan's Combined Fleet was sent to fight a war that, on the basis of material strength, it had no chance of winning.

World affairs may have been in a tumult, but Hironori was suffering the assault of more important events. Visiting his brother's house, he found Toranosuke lying in a pool of reddish bodily wastes. Hironori straightaway notified his uncle and summoned a doctor. It was dysentery. Toranosuke was confined to a hospital in the suburbs, where, four days later, on July 26, he passed away. He was twenty-nine years old.

Hironori now had no alternative but to make his way in life all on his own. Accepting that, he thought he should get serious about entering the Naval Academy.

Six days later, on August 1, Japan sent China a declaration of war. It was generally thought that victory would depend ultimately on naval strength.

There were two institutions in Japan for the training of military officers: the Army Military Academy and the Naval Academy. The army school was in Ichigaya, Tokyo; the Naval Academy was located on Etajima, a small island in Hiroshima Prefecture. Originally, the Naval Academy was also in Tokyo, in Tsukiji. However, it had moved to a location between the naval port of Kure and the island of Itsukushima, also known as Miyajima.

Matsushima and Etajima face each other across Japan's Seto Inland Sea; they are not very far apart. When Hironori was in the fourth year of middle school, the naval warship *Fusō* (an ancient name for Japan) paid a call on Mitsuhama, on the outskirts of Matsushima. The *Fusō* was 3,700 tons and British-built. It was one class lower than the *Matsushima*, the flagship of the Combined Fleet, but for the Imperial Japanese Navy it counted as a heavyweight.

"Japan's largest warship is coming here!" trumpeted the local newspaper in Matsuyama. And thankfully, admission on board was free.

Hironori went for a look with some of his comrades-in-delinquency. But when they got to the coast, they found the beach already thick with sightseers. Just offshore was anchored a white, three-masted warship. To eyes grown used to the small craft plying the waters of the Seto Inland Sea, the *Fusō* appeared like a floating citadel, dominating the entire scene.

Mitsuhama was just a sandy beach with no wharves or jetties, but there was a lighter waiting at the beach to ferry passengers to and from ships.

Students from a girls' school were boarding and screaming at the top of their lungs that the hems of their kimonos were getting wet. Then the lighter, seemingly as seaworthy as a tree leaf, was rowed over to the *Fusō*. There, about ten of these lighters, each loaded to capacity with passengers, were already standing by, hitched to the stern. The newly arriving lighter was attached to the tail end of the immediately previous arrival. It seemed to Hironori that his turn to go on board would never come.

In the meantime, he overheard some idle chatter.

"Boy, you get shelled by those big guns, the whole castle goes poof, eh!" said a man who looked like a small-time merchant.

A young girl student with an upset expression: "I hope we board soon. I'm starting to feel sick."

Two oldsters nodded to each other. "The navy's one heck of a brave outfit, eh."

"I got a relative whose kid is in the navy, eh. It's the high life. Even ordinary sailors get Western meals every day, eh."

"If you're going to join up, it's just gotta be the navy, eh. You even get to see foreign countries, eh."

Looking up, Hironori saw a man who looked like an officer smoking as he came walking along the deck. The many brass buttons of his uniform glistened against lustrous wool. A whistle blew, and one after another, the sailors mounted rope ladders. Exclamations of admiration were heard.

"Boy, are they good, eh!"

"Just like monkeys, huh!"

When they had waited nearly an hour, and they were only two or three boats away from boarding, there came a cruel announcement: "That is all for today." In Hironori's disappointment, the image of the giant stern of the warship was burned into his consciousness.

He took the entrance examination for the Naval Academy at the end of his last year of middle school; that is, in the summer of his fifth year. It was his first time, and he failed. He also flunked his school's graduation examinations and was obliged to withdraw from school. He had only been half-serious. Then, when his brother died, he had a sudden change of heart and tried again—but failed again. In order to improve his performance, he now endured the shame of re-enrolling in the fifth year of middle school.

In March of 1895, immediately before Sōseki took up his teaching position in Matsuyama, Hironori withdrew from school again and devoted himself to preparing for the Naval Academy's summer examinations.

The Sino-Japanese War ended in a victory for Japan. The "sleeping lion's" will to fight was weak; the Peace Treaty of Shimonoseki was signed on April 17. In August, Hironori failed the entrance examination to the Naval Academy for the third time. Luckily for him, starting that year a supplementary recruitment exam was given in December. He took it, and on this fourth effort, he passed.

When Hironori passed the entrance examination to the Naval Academy, his uncle opened a document storage box and withdrew an aged-looking document.

"This is the combined will and letter of instruction written by your father before he passed away. I, for my part, have been assiduous in fulfilling his requests. Now that you will be attending the Naval Academy, I can face your father proudly when I meet him in the next world. But you must study hard, to raise your family's name to new heights, eh."

The stern, unsmiling face of his uncle was moist with tears.

The will was written in watery ink on inferior paper: a single blackish half-sheet bearing the title, "Letter of Request." It read,

"My illness is daily getting the upper hand. I am weakening to such an extreme degree, it can only be that my death is drawing nigh. I entrust all matters to you." The brushwork was weak and messy. "Please employ the children as you see fit, hiring them out or apprenticing them, whether in weaving, or in babysitting, or in silk-spinning."

Any sort of apprenticeship was all right, so long as someone was looking out for them. The letter was charged with the heartrending wishes of a father aware that it was his time to die. And thus he wrote, "This taps me out," meaning that he was dedicating absolutely his entire life savings to funding the provisions of his will: fifty yen in cash and four Restoration Bonds (from the commutation of his feudal pension) totaling six hundred yen. Invested in a savings account at 5 percent per annum, this yielded two yen and fifty sen a month. For Hironori's uncle to have tried to wring from this account the expenses for ordinary educational materials plus tuition for middle school, he must have eaten into the principal. Now a detailed accounting and the Letter of Request were turned over to the twenty-year-old Hironori. Unfriendly and socially inept as his uncle was, he gave no thought to deceiving his nephew. He was a true descendant of samurai.

Hironori had thus lost his older brother Toranosuke and broken with his uncle's family. He arrived at Etajima for matriculation into the Naval

Academy at the beginning of February 1896. Patches of snow festooned the island's "Mount Baldy." In a redbrick, Western-style building, one got a sense of the high spirits of a newly resurgent nation. But Etajima was still a tiny island only thirty-seven kilometers in circumference. Hironori's awareness of the geographical confines was intensified by the strictness of all the rules and regulations.

But the bounding main went on forever. It connected Japan to foreign countries. Hironori's present circumstances, however, were more like a jail cell. As if he had been banished into exile...

He wore a Western-style shirt for the first time. Not knowing how it worked, he put it on back-to-front and was mocked by the upperclassmen. He was pleased with his comfortable seven-button jacket and happy as well with the brass buttons of his overcoat. Even the shoes somehow felt different to the touch. And articles of daily use were all supplied.

At first, the sheer novelty was enough to keep him going, but things grew monotonous, both the classes and the scenery. To the rear, Mount Baldy; to the front, the tiny pond-like cove of Eta. That was it. There was no vigorous, dynamic atmosphere; no style, no civilization. Take one step outside the academy gates, and all you found were shabby farmhouses and acres of potato fields. It was dull. Outside of the summer and winter breaks, there was no way to savor the air of the world beyond the island.

As one self-deprecating cadet put it, "What a zoo!"

In Mizuno Hironori's class, the academy's twenty-sixth, were sixty-two other cadets. It was a four-year program, but the fourth-year students were not called seniors or upperclassmen. They were called First Classmen or, because they went on training cruises, Embarkees: the equivalent of midshipmen. There were nineteen of them. Effectively, on campus, the uppermost class were the eighteen third-year Second Classmen. The second-year Third Classmen were thirty-three in number.

The large number of Fourth Classmen had something to do with the outbreak of the Sino-Japanese War. It reflected the government's policy of naval preparedness.

A mere six days after Japan's victory in the Sino-Japanese War was confirmed by the Peace Treaty of Shimonoseki—that is to say, on April 23, 1895—the ambassadors of Germany, France, and Russia called on Japan's vice minister of foreign affairs, Hayashi Tadasu (the minister, Mutsu Munemitsu, being indisposed at the time). They "advised" Japan to return to China the Liaodong Peninsula, ceded by the terms of the treaty. This became known as the Tripartite Intervention. Germany and France represented one set of issues, but what cast a pall on the small island nation of Japan was that Russia, Japan's neighbor, was now baring its fangs.

Toward the end of that year, the state budget submitted to the ninth session of the Imperial Diet (the 1896 budget) provided for annual expenditures totaling 170 million yen, out of which 73 million yen, or some 43 percent, was devoted to the military. If one considers that before the Sino-Japanese War the annual financial resources of the Japanese government did not exceed some 80 million yen, the figures for 1896 are extraordinary. All at once, the army was augmented by six divisions, for a total of thirteen. The navy got a whopping 95 million yen in current and future expenditures dedicated to its seven-year plan to build a state-of-the-art fleet of nine capital ships.

Then, in 1897, military expenditures of 110 million yen accounted for a full 50 percent of the total state budget of 220 million yen. From then until the Russo-Japanese War of 1905, Japan was fated to continue to live beyond its means. The choices that were made were as unbalanced as that of someone living in a rented apartment who purchased a Mercedes instead of investing in a house. It seems as if people were unable to come up with a better idea for countering the external threat.

The swelling of the ranks of Fourth Classmen at the Naval Academy must be understood against this historical background of military buildup. Eighteen of them passed the entrance examinations in the summer of 1895; this should have been the size of the entering class the next year. But with the supplemental exams held in December, an additional forty-four men were admitted. Without these examinations, it is likely that Hironori, with his three strikes against him, would never have matriculated.

Once again, external pressure was a defining moment in Mizuno Hironori's life. Compared to his group of supplemental inductees, the regular inductees had a higher number of capable students, who subsequently distinguished themselves. The ambassador to the United States at the time of the outbreak of war between the U.S. and Japan, Nomura Kichisaburō, had risen to admiral, his career having begun in this program. In addition, he held such posts as minister of foreign affairs, director of the Peers' School, and privy councilor. Another graduate and admiral, Kobayashi Seizō, also fulfilled a range of assignments, serving as vice minister of the navy, commander in chief of the Combined Fleet, and governor-general of Taiwan. When, toward the end of World War II, the overthrow of the Tōjō Cabinet was plotted, he was even considered to be a potential candidate for prime minister. Kiyogawa Jun-ichi rose to the rank of vice admiral. As staff officer to Tōgō Heihachirō, he stood on the bridge of the flagship *Mikasa* during the Battle of Tsushima (known in Japan as the Battle of the Sea of Japan). And he was active in foreign relations, as a navy aide during the Washington Conference on the Limitation of Naval Armaments (1921–22) and as the navy's representative to the League of Nations.

After three years cooped up at Etajima, Mizuno Hironori finally received his formal commission as a naval cadet midshipman and boarded the 2,200-ton warship, the *Hiei*, for a three-month training cruise, ending in Yokosuka harbor.

They docked, and Mizuno went to see Tokyo for the first time. In Sōseki's *Botchan*, we recall, the scene the narrator/protagonist sees when his ship puts in near Matsuyama in Shikoku was characterized as follows: "The lighterman was completely naked, except for a red loincloth. What a barbaric place!"[12] Coming from that place, Mizuno now entered the capital of Japan, only to find the ambience as barren as a frontier town in a cowboy western. "Ginza was filthy with manure from the horse tramway," he noted in a memo book; "Around the Imperial Palace there was nothing but an expanse of rank fields." The empty area between Hibiya and Marunouchi was covered with weeds; soldiers were using it as a training ground for marching and horseback riding. Ginza and Marunouchi were spaces newly developed for the capital and made quite a contrast with the Edo spirit represented by Nihonbashi or Asakusa with their varied scenes of liveliness and calm.

After this all too brief interval of sightseeing in Tokyo, Mizuno was transported essentially in one fell swoop from the world of a tiny castle town in Shikoku into contact with the modern civilization of North America.

On March 19, 1899, the *Hiei* set sail for the west coast of North America. This oceangoing training cruise was intended to take them, over a fifty-day span, to Vancouver, then down the coast, and finally back across the Pacific via Hawaii.

The choppy seas of the Pacific Ocean made these green cadets seasick, but finally they reached the North American continent. Their first port of call was the naval port of Esquimalt in Canada's province of British Columbia. This isolated village was about six kilometers away from Victoria, the provincial capital.

In Victoria, Mizuno saw an electric train for the first time; he took a ride. Since he had previously known only horse-drawn carriages and steam locomotives, this train, which moved thanks to a single wire, was undoubtedly quite a novelty. He was awed by all the advanced technology, but what truly struck him was the urban landscape. The roads were orderly and clean. Buildings made of stone loomed, almost dismayingly gigantic in size. Tokyo was the loser by comparison.

These impressions only intensified with the ship's ensuing visit to Seattle, and when Mizuno saw San Francisco, his feelings came to a boil. He had been astonished at the standard of living in a city of a few tens of thousands of people. Now he was viewing a metropolis with a population of some 350,000. Both the Tokugawa Bakufu's (i.e., the Shogunate's) American mission, sent in 1860, and the Iwakura Mission of 1871–73, had initially arrived in San Francisco and were also overwhelmed. The polished marble floors, the high ceilings from which dangled chandeliers sparkling like cascades of gems—all this had drawn exclamations of astonishment.

In the twenty or thirty years since then, one would have expected Japan to make progress in its own "civilization and enlightenment," but the gap between the two nations had increased. The young naval cadet was duly impressed, and not merely by the marble and the chandeliers, but by the moving pictures and the huge shops, where all kinds of merchandise were gathered in one place. The moving picture had just been invented and was already tremendously popular. The department stores carried all sorts of merchandise all at once, they displayed an official price so there was no need to haggle, and they delivered.

By contrast, Mizuno noticed many of his poorly clad compatriots: pitiful immigrants in their padded kimonos and sandals, owning no other clothes. That "utter nakedness" but for the "red loincloth" may not have looked strange to the locals in Matsuyama, but here it looked pitiful and dirty.

There were also pigtailed Chinese. Mischievous white children would taunt them, crying "Monkey! Pig!" or harass them by poking them and pulling the ends of their pigtails before running away. Yet it seemed as if these Chinese had some knowledge of how to maintain a focus for their cultural identity in a foreign environment—building a Chinatown.

In his log for this voyage, Mizuno wrote that "our people" in San Francisco could be classified into four groups: "merchants, students, 'disreputables,' and vagrants." And he noted particularly that, since the proportion of the last two groups was high, the reputation of the Japanese immigrants as a whole reportedly suffered. The rows of brothels with their Japanese prostitutes he referred to as "houses of ill repute." The Japanese residents of San

Francisco were in fact concerned about the situation and inaugurated a Colonial Promotion Association in 1894. Its prospectus stated,

> Seven thousand of our compatriots have no fixed occupation. This is clear if one looks in particular at the preponderance of manual laborers. Descendants of our Yamato race can be found at every provincial railroad station: manual laborers roaming about, mantled in red blankets. Exhausted at the end of their long day, they wrap themselves in these blankets and sleep in the chilly fields, dreaming of finding a job the next day. But they don't get it that day, or the following day. They use up their travel money, and then they are up all night suffering from hunger. Or else they enter someone's home and beg for food.[13]

Compared to the Chinese immigrants, the Japanese immigrants were newcomers. The Chinese immigrants could be traced back to the famous California Gold Rush of 1848–49. In 1850, forty-four ships set sail from Hong Kong harbor; they carried twenty-five thousand people. Within a decade, they constituted a tenth of the population of California. Discord with the white population began to flare, and by the 1870s, an organized movement to expel the Chinese had begun. Their houses were burned by whites who felt robbed of employment opportunities; murders became a common occurrence. The White House could not ignore the Chinese expulsion movement. In 1880 the U.S. dispatched a delegation to China, where they signed a "Treaty Regulating Immigration from China." These legal provisions effectively stopped the flood of Chinese immigration.

Now attention shifted to a new target: the Japanese immigrants.

Under the revised Immigration Act of 1891, entry by paupers and others who might become public charges was restricted. But the fervor of Japanese to emigrate to the U.S. was undiminished. In 1898 hostilities broke out between America and Spain: it was the start of the Spanish-American War. Wages rose, and Japanese immigrants increased. Public sentiment to expel "the Japanese" was about to explode.

That was the historical context of Mizuno's arrival in San Francisco harbor. As he strolled through Chinatown, drinking in its sights with curious eyes, he may have spotted a certain white youth wandering around as well, and if he did, he could not have failed to remark upon the youth's distinctive appearance. This was Homer Lea (1876–1912), who frequented Chinatown after leaving Stanford University, where he had been a student. Due to a curvature of the spine, Homer was only about five feet tall. The arms extending from his hunched, cramped body looked longer than they otherwise might have. His hair was dark brown, his eyes were gray. Yet his face was the face of a bright young man, with a dauntless dignity that suggested that if any person were to approach him with unwanted sympathy, that person would be given very short shrift indeed. His voice, however, was low and gentle. Yet in a heated discussion, his eyes shone with excitement.

Homer Lea was essentially an American edition of Mizuno Hironori.

CHAPTER TWO

The Next Battle and
Its Consequences

I N CHILDHOOD, consciousness of one's adversary proceeds gradually outward through concentric circles of relationships, from those near oneself to the larger world. For example, attention is directed first to one's siblings, next to one's companions at play, then to students at other schools. Even pups and kittens jostle each other playfully in the struggle for food. When they get bigger, it becomes a territorial struggle.

Compared to other animals, humans introduce more complex terms into the equation. One might expect that the enemies we confront would remain within the confines of an individual's struggle for survival. However, instances arise in which the business of survival goes beyond ties of locality and blood to overlap with the interests of the nation as a whole. Circumstances producing the state of mind in which one's nation's enemy is also one's personal enemy prevail when a system allows, at least to some degree, the citizenry to participate in government on their own initiative. That is to say, after the emergence of a nation-state several hundred years ago.

If we consider the Meiji Restoration to be the birth of a nation-state, we must realize that Japanese at that time still had little experience considering other nations as enemies. In any event, people inevitably tend to conduct their lives thinking of the individual or the family as the basic unit. So, a leap of consciousness is necessary, by which the individual and the nation can be brought into overlapping focus. At times, having thus aligned one's individual consciousness with the nation, it is possible to commit follies in which one's individual existence itself is imperiled.

The objection may be raised that this has nothing necessarily to do with such matters as war. Let me rephrase: Why is it that people who are neither kith nor kin, who do not have the same alma mater, who are not so much as acquainted by sight will nonetheless cheer the same Olympic team simply because they are from the same country and find themselves excited? It is not because sports are beautiful when they test the limits of the human body. Perhaps it is because there are so few opportunities to immerse oneself in a feeling of unity.

So far, no one has been able to provide a lucid explanation. That is why I have selected the two chief personages who appear in this book. They are both runners bearing the sacred flame of crisis-consciousness. They each ignite the fuse of crisis-consciousness, one in the country that dispatched the Black Ships, the other in the country that received them.

The two are Mizuno Hironori, whose childhood we have just reviewed in some detail, and an American, Homer Lea, whose path Mizuno may well have crossed once in San Francisco's Chinatown. Their other affinities will become apparent below.

Japan and America at war. Who thought of such a thing, and when? How did it become conceivable? Or perhaps we should put it another way. When did Japanese first embrace the arrogant idea that they could attack the United States? At what point did the Western powers begin to consider Japan enough of a threat that they felt it would be prudent to spoil her debut on the world stage through the use of military force?

Examining this issue will be like watching a single spark develop into a vast conflagration. However, what I want to investigate is the epicenter of the human imagination, which is not the sort thing that can be comprehended by arranging political events along a timeline. War is summoned by acts of imagination.

At this point I feel it would be appropriate to state, briefly, a major hypothesis regarding the entire narrative that begins with the visit of the Black Ships. Japan entered the Second World War and was beaten. The major question is whether or not war between Japan and America was inevitable.

The alignments of the Second World War were quite haphazard. The opposition between the Axis powers (Japan, Germany, Italy) and the Allied powers (U.S., France, Britain) was only established at the eleventh hour. If Russia had been added permanently to the first grouping, we might well be referring to them as the Allies and to the others as the Axis. Indeed, it was with just such an alignment in mind that foreign minister Matsuoka Yōsuke negotiated a treaty of neutrality with the Soviet Union. When Hitler broke the German-Soviet Non-Aggression Pact and invaded the Soviet Union, it destroyed the possibility of the Axis bloc outnumbering the Allies.

Or one could put it like this: The real theme of the Second World War was the opposition of the full spectrum of Allies (or potential Allies) vs. the Soviet Union. At the very least, the inconsistencies of the alignments of that war gave rise to the Cold War configuration of the postwar period.

This major problem calls forth a number of lesser conundrums. Why did the Japanese military set out for Hawaii and attack America there? Was there any inevitability to it?

After the Russo-Japanese War, future-war chronicles as a genre enjoyed a boom in both Japan and the United States. From the time of the Russo-Japanese War until the Second World War, over five hundred accounts of imagined future wars between Japan and the United States were published in Japan. If one adds the works confiscated by the occupying American General Headquarters after the war, the number is even higher. By examining the traces of the fantasies common to these two countries sandwiching the Pacific—in their journalism, their imaginative literature, their commentaries on military affairs—I will reveal an "avoidable inevitability" to the U.S.-Japan conflict.

On February 7, 1904, outside of the port of Inchon (K. Chemulpo) on the Korean peninsula, the Russian cruiser *Varyag* and one other Russian warship exchanged fire with a five-ship Japanese fleet led by the cruiser *Asama*. The next day, Japanese destroyers launched a surprise attack on the Russian fleet anchored at Port Arthur.[1] In the clash off Inchon, the *Varyag* sustained major damage and withdrew to Inchon harbor. These first fruits of victory were small, but no one at that time believed in the possibility of a future Japanese victory. No one, in either Japan or Russia.

Japan could not avoid its clash with Russia. Russia intended to take possession of the Korean peninsula. If that goal were achieved, Japan would be blown away by this expanding giant of an imperialist power. It could collapse entirely. That was the consensus at the time. And that is why the heavy sacrifices made by General Nogi Maresuke in the desperate struggle over the fortifications at Port Arthur, and the tremendous naval victories by the Japanese navy under the command of Admiral Tōgō Heihachirō, have been recounted for generations as legendary accomplishments of the newly founded Japanese nation.

One may think of events such as the Russo-Japanese War as historical matters far removed from the present. But isn't this sort of prejudice infected with temporal complacency? If we measure time only in relation to our own lifespans, a concept such as a century becomes unnecessary. With the conclusion of the seemingly endless Shōwa era (1925–89), Japanese were liberated, however provisionally, from a temporal framework defined by the era's name. But it would not be a complete form of national liberation.

At the beginning of the last century, a small island empire in the Far East mounted a military challenge to Imperial Russia, one of the world's great powers. The historical circumstances, the detailed sequence of events, are vividly and passionately portrayed in Shiba Ryōtarō's historical novel, *The Cloud Above the Hill*. What I propose to relate below is what followed historically.

When Mizuno Hironori became a lieutenant in the Imperial Navy, he was made commander of a hundred-plus-ton torpedo boat. There were captains who commanded several-thousand-ton-class cruisers or battleships, but for a (roughly) thirty-year-old lieutenant like Mizuno, command of a torpedo boat was not bad at all.

Under cover of darkness, carrying multiple projectiles, the torpedo boats would approach a giant warship, swiftly fire off the torpedoes, and flee. In those days, torpedoes had to be fired from close range if they were to hit their mark. And if one did not flee quickly, it was entirely possible to be capsized by the backlash when the torpedoes hit.

After the Russo-Japanese war, Mizuno was ordered by the Japanese navy's Office of Military Command (hereinafter, Naval Command; the navy's equivalent of the army's General Staff) to participate in compiling the navy's official history of the war. This was published as *A Naval History: 1904–1905*. Mizuno also published privately his own general account of the Battle of Tsushima, titled *The Crucial Battle*. He had been ordered by Fleet Headquarters to assemble all the battle reports from the torpedo boats, but by the time his manuscript was completed, the deadline had passed—"for better or worse," as he later put it. Now, to continue with his account of the events that followed his assignment as editor, there was "nothing for it but to send it to the newspapers or magazines," where it became a hot item. "It was carried in newspapers nationwide, and such purple prose as 'the billowing smoke and the deafening boom of the thunderous naval guns' was extravagantly praised; I acquired a reputation in naval circles as a great writer."[2]

The Crucial Battle became a best seller. It was singled out for special mention in the 1912 New Year's Day issue of *Yorozu Chōhō*[3]: "Last year's Number One best-selling book, with 70 printings, was Hakubunkan's *The*

Crucial Battle (by Navy Lieutenant Commander Mizuno)." With seventy printings in the space of just nine months, *The Crucial Battle* undoubtedly set its own sales record at the time.

Tayama Katai commented critically, "The fact that it was aimed at a popular audience diminished the value of this otherwise excellent book."[4] This is the type of negative response that subsequently circulated in the established literary world. Modern Japanese literature seems to have been poor at dealing with epics ranging over the vast stage of war. Indeed, *The Crucial Battle*, which had garnered such popular support, was not taken seriously in established literary circles. This was an unfortunate turn of events, both for Mizuno and for the literary establishment, because they could not see the book for what it was—a possible starting point for a populist national literature.

The Crucial Battle was enlivened by Mizuno's accounts of his personal experiences as commander of a torpedo boat. He describes, for example, the annihilation of Russia's Baltic Fleet. The initial attack missed some enemy ships. But the orders of Japanese Fleet Command were to permit not even one Russian ship to slip back into port at Vladivostok. The torpedo boats participated in the mopping-up operation like wolves moving in on a wounded bear. As Mizuno's crew went about their urgent search for enemy vessels, they spotted lifeboats with Russian sailors bobbing in the waves.

> Around six in the evening, we came across the debris of a sunken ship. Damaged boats, blasted doors, burnt wooden material, charred hammocks; fragments of equipment from the ship all littering the surface of the water, some floating, some sinking. Most of the sailors clung to this debris as they bobbed up and down in the violent waves. When they saw our torpedo boat, they waved their hands or their caps, and cried out to us. Some were pleading to be rescued; others, robbed of their driftwood by violent waves, were fast disappearing into the deep.[5]

The plight of the Russian sailors elicited his sympathy. Some glared at Mizuno and his comrades reproachfully, but most seemed to be driven frantic with the fear of death. Clutching pieces of wood, in imminent danger of drowning, they were nonetheless so afraid of being shot that they would try to duck under the water.

A semi-submerged lifeboat, in danger of sinking, drifted close to them. On inspection it proved to contain several sailors and one officer. The officer was lying on his side, breathing unsteadily, his head swathed in bandages, his shirt so thoroughly dyed with blood it evoked the image of a Buddhist High Priest's crimson robe. Some sailors were desperately dressing the wounds of their superior officer; others were scooping water out of the boat. Already looking like it might capsize, the lifeboat was sustaining fresh assaults from oncoming waves.

"Look at yourselves now, you Russian bastards! Commander—can we shoot the lot of 'em?" That was the request of a young sailor aboard the torpedo boat.[6]

Mizuno himself had begun to feel some sympathy toward the wretched enemy sailors. But the young Japanese sailor had his reasons. He was one of three brothers, two of whom—one older than he, one younger—had both died in battle in Manchuria. The older brother had left behind a wife and child. His mother was already aged and ill when her sons were killed; following such an untimely bereavement, her condition had worsened and she had passed away, in tears.

Mizuno had a responsibility. As the commander of a small torpedo boat, he was not at leisure to take aboard wounded Russian sailors. Nor was he inclined to satisfy his subordinate's desire for revenge. Yet, in battle, there is no place either for reflection or humanistic impulses. "Thus we consigned the wretched enemy sailors to the raging billows and headed north."[7]

If Mizuno's purpose had been either to write a sentimental tearjerker or to describe the "We won, we won!" jubilation of victory in war, we could say he was pandering to popular tastes. But Mizuno's feelings were different. We know this from the objective, calm way he described his own involvement in abandoning shipwrecked sailors begging to be rescued.

Morality is not necessarily competent to judge reality. It cannot cover all of reality. There are places that cannot be reached by morality, even places that cannot be reached by the hand of God. This is what Mizuno perceived. And this is why, even as he listened attentively to the young sailor's request, he refused permission. Mizuno was being realistic. After all, he opened *The Crucial Battle* with a tone of resignation: "War is an implement fraught with danger. Howsoever the use of war is inimical to the Way of Heaven, when such use becomes unavoidable, then that use accords with the Way of Heaven." If we put this dictum into ordinary language, we will lose Mizuno's classical cadences, but let me try to restate his thinking here.

War is a tragic affair, replete with contradictions. But if one does not start the war, then one must accept the tragedy. One cannot escape that reality.

Peace is good; that is obvious. But there are cases when one does not have a free choice. Shiba Ryōtarō's *The Cloud Above the Hill* contains the following carefully chosen words.

From the nineteenth century to the present day, the nations and regions of the world have had to take one of two paths. They could become colonies of other nations; or, if they disliked that option, they could stimulate their economies and strengthen their militaries, and enter the company of the imperialist powers. Subsequent generations may fantasize that back then only a nation founded on the principles of peace toward humankind, and mutual nonaggression, constituted an ideal nation. But fixing praise and blame for a nation's behavior by introducing a fictitious phantom state into the company of actual states and international affairs manipulates history as if it were potter's clay.[8]

In other words, some wars are unavoidable. That may be an inconvenient reality, but reality it is.

Furthermore, the remarkable upsizing of armaments changed the meaning of war. This upsizing was most notably demonstrated by naval warships, in which were concentrated the most advanced technologies.

Bigger ships beat smaller ships. The range and destructive power of cannons varied in direct proportion to their size. It became clear that victory or defeat might hinge upon a ship's speed or on the thickness of its armor. Larger fleets intimidated smaller fleets. The more ships one had, the more beneficial to the development of strategy.

Outstanding admirals; sailors imbued with the fighting "Japanese spirit" (*Yamato damashii*): if these are evenly matched against one's opponent's human resources, then one can have a fight. But if, for whatever reason, there is no such balance, the fight is meaningless. Before *The Crucial Battle*, no Japanese account of war had testified so pitilessly to the physical vulnerability of even brave sailors.

When an artillery shell hits its mark, flesh is burned and bones are crushed. Sometimes all that remains are scraps of skin. In army combat, small arms were still dominant, but the navy had already seen the advent of 12-inch guns.

At any rate, the guns they carry are fierce enough to smash through armor plates ten inches thick or more. Their impact is devastating. When their targets are men, it is hardly unusual to see bodies severed in two, or heads and limbs sent flying. In extreme cases, a human being can be literally pulverized, with nothing remaining, not even a lump of flesh or a bit of bone. Furthermore, shell fragments are not rounded and smooth projectiles like bullets. Their surfaces are rough and ragged. When those shell fragments penetrate the human body, they rip it open like a ripe pomegranate, they split it like a fig. Just witnessing that brings extreme distress, so horrifically violent and painful an event it is. To express it in terms of an analogy, if a bullet wound is like a razor cut, the wound inflicted by an artillery shell is like that of a saw.[9]

The Crucial Battle describes every vessel active in the Battle of Tsushima, from the big navy ships to the smaller vessels, and every scene is covered in detail. We learn, for example, about a man whose name later resounded throughout the world in connection with the surprise attack on Pearl Harbor on December 8 (December 7 in the U.S.), 1941: Yamamoto Isoroku, then serving as a captain's orderly aboard the cruiser Nisshin.

> Around seven o'clock, a single artillery shell from a 12-inch gun hit the fore gun turret for the third time. It knocked out the left gun, wounding Paymaster Otanaka Toshikazu, Cadet Takano Isoroku, and several petty officers, while at the same time a 6-inch shell struck the top of the mainmast. Seaman Third Class Nakajima Fumiya lost his right leg, from the thigh down, to an enemy shell; blood was splattering on the deck like rain.[10]

At this point Yamamoto was still going by the surname Takano. It was later, when he was a lieutenant commander, that he was adopted by the heirless Yamamoto family of the former Nagaoka domain, who had hereditarily been the *daimyō*'s[11] chief retainers.

After receiving emergency first aid, Takano was admitted three days later to the Sasebo Naval Hospital. The bones in two fingers on his left hand were shattered; there was no choice but to amputate. He had an 18-centimeter-long gash in his lower right thigh. The flesh was torn away, and the wound was starting to rot. But this healed in time.

The public announcement was that he had been wounded by an enemy shell, but that, it seems, is not what actually happened. When naval cannon are fired continuously, the barrels must be wet down with seawater to cool them off. But as this procedure is repeated, the gun barrels become brittle. When they are fired, pressure from explosive gases builds up: there have been cases when they have in fact exploded. It is believed that Yamamoto's injuries were sustained in just such an explosion of a cannon aboard the *Nisshin*. That is modern war, in which even participants do not know for sure what is happening. The dense smoke, the deafening roar, the waves washing across the deck... Before such awesome technology, the human body is infinitely inconsequential. The still unknown Yamamoto Isoroku thus had the consequences of modern warfare engraved on his very body.

Having, in *The Crucial Battle*, described the Russo-Japanese War, the next challenge tackled by Mizuno, the military man and best-selling author, was to write *The Next Battle*. His theme: war with the United States.

The two works have similar titles, but the earlier work described a war with Russia that actually occurred. It was nonfiction, whereas the latter work described a war with America that might occur in the future and was thus a work of fiction.

Another significant difference is the direction in which the two narratives develop. *The Crucial Battle* is about a victorious war. *The Next Battle* is about a defeat in war. Still, the two share the same *basso continuo*: the crisis-consciousness of national ruin. Or one might call it the fear of the outside world.

As soon as the Russian threat had passed, a new threat, from America, awaited the Japanese. In fact, there had been two threats all along, but the first was so imminent that the other threat, a vast one, had receded in the consciousness of the Japanese. Even after defeating Russia, Japan was still poor. A poor nation had no defenses and could not survive in a Darwinian world. But then poverty was no reason for a country to neglect its military preparedness. Indeed, as one looked about, one saw the poor nations falling one after the other, becoming colonies of the great powers.

It was the psychological damage caused by the Black Ships that cleared the way for the "external pressure" narrative of insecurity, propelling *The Crucial Battle* onto the best seller lists. And that is why Mizuno sought, furthermore, to help his country sustain the strength necessary to overcome this sense of insecurity by administering the bitter medicine of the defeat described in *The Next Battle*.

Consider the scene in *The Next Battle* recounted below. No specific date is given, but the author is imagining some time in his near future, five or ten years from 1914, the time of the book's publication.

At the mansion of a former *daimyō* (that is, the former head of a domain, or fief), a splendid garden party is being given. The old lord has been made a count; he has attained the ripe old age of eighty. He strokes his goatee. His former retainers and their offspring all live in a new era, another world.

> The invited guests arrive at the mansion in automobiles and horse-drawn carriages: they range from high dignitaries such as ministers of state and generals to students strutting forth in tattered old hats and holey shoes, affecting a swagger; altogether as many as five hundred people from the old fief, now residing in Tokyo.[12]

Set up here and there throughout the well-groomed lawns and gardens of the estate are stalls offering such festive favorites as *oden* (stewed fishcakes and vegetables), *o-shiruko* (sweet adzuki-bean soup with mochi rice cakes), sushi, and beer. A stage set up for entertainment displays a sign with a double-entendre equivalent in English to "Sunshine Victory Theater and Rainfall Troupe," in which it would be understood that the "sunshine" referred to the Rising Sun, that "rain" (or "reign") referred to America, and that the "fall" of this rain/reign meant America's defeat. The Japan we see here seems, on its own terms, prosperous. It looks peaceful. Even the weather is good.

But off in a corner of the premises, like a wild gust of wind blowing in from the outside, something menaces the gay mood of the party. Two young military officers, one navy and one army, are engaged in a discussion.[13]

> What I'm saying is that we are poor. The situation is so bad that when our ships are at anchorage, to economize they don't even burn their electric lights. Whereas our adversary spares no expense in research and training.

The navy officer continues,

> "To draw an analogy, it's as if Japan were on work-study, trying to keep up with classwork on top of a milk- or newspaper-delivery route, while America is like a spoiled young heir financed by a rich family wealthy enough to afford private tutorials. It isn't that a poor work-study pupil can never outshine the scion of the wealthy classes, but if both are of equal ability, then who gets better grades is self-evident. Particularly if

you look at naval warfare, where, unlike ground combat, it isn't the spirit of the individual warrior that determines victory so much as whether the technology is sufficiently well developed and accurate. You can't get caught unprepared."

"I see. This is getting more and more discouraging. The way things are today, a conflict is unavoidable sooner or later. So we'd better grit our teeth and make it sooner rather than later, hadn't we?"

A radical statement: army's effort to keep navy in check.

By the way, if we do kick things off, what would the navy's strategy be? Just like you can't always find that tasty eel in the river even under a shady willow tree, you won't always get lucky the way you did with those nighttime torpedo attacks in the Russo-Japanese War.

But the navy officer remains unruffled, confident in his view that the course of a war against America would ultimately be decided by naval battles.

"Difficult matters like war strategy are hardly comprehensible to the likes of you and me. But after the navy takes care of a little preliminary business, well, you-all can just sit tight and watch. I'd say that by the time you get busy waving around your fixed bayonets, Japan will already be experiencing either a great victory or a tremendous defeat. By the way, what's the army's strategy?"

"Of course, to set out immediately. And I know where, too! First Army goes to the Philippines; Second Army to America."

The two officers do not display much of a sense of urgency, and the guests around them betray even less crisis-consciousness. Instead, to express his view that such complacency is fatal, Mizuno boldly chooses to portray the paradisiacal state of a world at peace. This intention becomes all too clear when things suddenly change for the worse.

An American battleship sinks; all one thousand aboard drown. The cause is not clear. And it happens in the seas near Japan. The American public is inflamed by allegations that this was Japan's doing. Dangerous words are bandied about, calling for a revenge that would take one hundred "Jap" lives for every white's life lost, urging that all the "parasite Japs" who lived in Hawaii should be burned to death, and so on. The Japanese embassy is attacked. When this is reported in Japan, the sanctity of the American embassy in Tokyo is violated, and the outraged American ambassador is recalled. The United States and Japan cut off all diplomatic relations. Soon there would be war.

Japan's Combined Fleet plans and launches a surprise attack on the Philippines, at that time a U.S.-occupied territory and military base. The attack is a success. Army divisions are landed in quick succession; they march on Manila. But just then, the invading forces are hampered by bad weather. Heavy rains fall, rivers flood, roads are cut. To make matters worse, the routed American army destroys bridges as it retreats. No sooner has the flooding subsided than the troops' strength is sapped by a heat wave, then they are further harassed by malaria.

While Japanese troops are getting bogged down in the Philippines, the U.S. military dispatch their First and Second Fleets from Pearl Harbor. The plan is for the First Fleet to confront the Japanese Combined Fleet, which has gathered off the Philippines; in a separate movement, the Second Fleet is to occupy the Ogasawara Islands in a thrust at Japan itself.

The Japanese people fear an invasion of the home islands.

Will Tokyo Bay be attacked today? Will there be an assault on Sagami Bay tomorrow? In their innermost thoughts, people are worried and afraid. They jump even at the sound of the wind. Their spirits are pained even by the beautiful cry of the crane. Our Pacific shipping has ceased. Citizens of Tokyo are even feeling a shortage of food supplies. The citizenry are by now practically half-crazed. One hears cries of despair and defeatism. All across the nation, Shinto shrines and Buddhist temples pray for the enemy's capitulation: they beat their drums and ring their bells as if to shatter them.[14]

The frantic praying of the "half-crazed" Japanese may seem comical now, but thirteen years prior to the start of the Russo-Japanese War, the same scenes had occurred. This was by no means a sudden development.

As Russian Crown Prince Nikolai (soon to be Tsar Nikolai II) made his way to Vladivostok for the ground-breaking ceremonies for the Trans-Siberian Railroad in May 1891, he visited Japan, escorted by seven warships. While he was staying in Kyoto, he and his entourage, in a procession of forty rickshaws, made an excursion to Lake Biwa, purely for pleasure. It was on their way back to Kyoto that an incident occurred. Constable Tsuda Sanzō, assigned to guard the route, drew his sword and attacked the crown prince. This became known as the Ōtsu Incident, after the place at which it occurred.

People believed that angering a great power such as Russia would mean Japan's ruin. Throughout the country people really did fall into hysteria. The crown prince, wounded in the attack, refused the assistance of Japanese doctors and was tended to by court physicians dispatched from a Russian warship anchored at Kobe, who sutured his wounds. Members of the Japanese royal family, ministers of state, famous doctors, all headed for Kyoto on a specially chartered train. Classes at the Peers' Academy and the National Academy were suspended. Keiō Academy (present-day Keiō University) sent a get-well letter in French, a language with which the Russian upper classes were said to be familiar. Rinzai Zen Buddhists offered prayers for the crown prince's recovery at services featuring the chanting of the Wisdom Sutras. At Kan-ei Temple, Tendai Buddhists held special ceremonies at triple altars; Jōdō Buddhists offered prayers for peace and security at Zōjō Temple. The Yoshiwara pleasure quarters halted all singing and dancing, and now seemed deserted.

The crown prince and his retinue cancelled the rest of their sightseeing and prepared to leave. They invited the Meiji Emperor to a farewell banquet the day of their departure, aboard one of their ships anchored off Kobe. The wharves were thronged with people worried that the emperor might be taken hostage and spirited away to Russia. Hatakeyama Yūko, a seventeen-year old girl, bearing a suicide note addressed to the crown prince, killed herself in front of the Kyoto Prefectural Building by committing *hara-kiri* and stabbing her throat with a razor.

These were the sorts of things that happened. I point to them in order to indicate the weight of external pressure of that era that the Japanese felt forced to live with. It is no laughing matter. Even today, one gets the impression that the excessive security surrounding visits to Japan by foreign dignitaries is motivated less by any direct logic of protection than by the goal of abolishing a continuing anxiety.

Let us return to Mizuno's *The Next Battle*.

The imagined battle between Japan's Combined Fleet and the American First Fleet was a fierce two-hour conflict that ended in a victory for Japan. But the winning Combined Fleet also lost half of its vessels.

The flagship's mainmast was broken in half; her forward funnel was stove in at the base; the fore bridge was blown away. The aft gun turret was damaged, it could not swivel; the barrels of the four guns in the main battery were broken in half. Her hull had been breached in about a dozen places by gashes large and small; seawater was gushing inside like a waterfall. The wooden deck was splintered like a bamboo brush; iron poles and plating were twisted like taffy; a variety of other craft— steamboats and lifeboats—had been blown to smithereens. The rigging was cut, the yardarm drooped at a slant; the white trim to the inside of the gunwales had been seared by flames and burnt black.[15]

In *The Crucial Battle*, also, unfold many such graphic descriptions of the aftermath of naval battles, scenes that truly convey the horrors of war's destruction of the human body as well.

Just counting the dead, under the rank of commander or captain, there were over one hundred lost. As to wounded, there must have been another four or five hundred. The decks were dyed crimson with blood, the gutters running along the gunwales brimmed with it. Clumps of raw flesh had been splattered against the vertical surfaces, they dangled from ceilings. Severed hands and feet and heads lay smoldering among fragments of wood and metal. The groans of the grievously injured left behind by triage, the faces of the dead, frozen in agony; everything one saw, everything one heard, everything, but everything, produced feelings of horror.[16]

In *The Next Battle*, before a Combined Fleet devastated in similar fashion, there now appears the enemy's Second Fleet, dispatched from the Ogasawara Islands. They and their allies outnumber the Japanese three to one. Furthermore, the Japanese have already exhausted their supplies of ammunition.

Ah, shall we fight? We don't have the strength. Shall we retreat? We don't have the speed. It is the hour of the annihilation of the Imperial Navy![17]

And indeed, the American Second Fleet sinks every last ship of Japan's Combined Fleet.

It was somewhat like that in the Russo-Japanese War, with the Russians deploying two fleets, the Far Eastern Fleet stationed at Port Arthur and the Baltic Fleet, which had taken half a year to steam over via the Atlantic and Indian Oceans. Despite its name, Japan's Combined Fleet was its only fleet. But by utilizing the time difference, Japan could attack Russia's fleets one at a time; whereas the Americans in *The Next Battle* deployed their two fleets simultaneously. Stripped of its sea superiority, Japan is defenseless.

Thus the rape of Japan begins without much difficulty for the aggressor, and the Japanese are hit by the very calamity they had feared, the very nightmare they had so taken to heart since the arrival of Perry's Black Ships.[18]

> They [the Americans] did not respect the human rights of the Japanese. Wherever they landed, young local women committed suicide—for reasons unknown.

Mizuno's style is euphemistic, but rather effective, though one does detect a strong whiff of cliché.

In an ending reminiscent of the conclusion of the *Tale of Heike*, Mizuno reflects on the transitory nature of all things.

> The Great Empire of Japan once ranked among the leading powers of the world. Thanks to this single defeat, it immediately sank in prestige. Now it was the Lesser Empire of Japan, cast down from the grand stage of world affairs to the smaller sphere of Asia. Ah, the rose of Sharon lasts but a single morn!

The rose of Sharon, like the morning glory and the althaea, is said to flourish only for a single morning, and then to perish. It is a classical metaphor for the evanescence of human glory.

Mizuno's narrative closes with the remarkable sententiousness of a young officer floating in the sea, about to drown after being critically wounded that night.

> Ah, we won on strength but lost on numbers! Even if in war's battles the Imperial Navy can vanquish the American navy, the Japanese people have lost to the American people in the battle to prevent war through military preparedness![19]

Someone on the point of death simply does not utter such logically composed, didactic lines. But Mizuno goes ahead and includes this direct—perhaps too direct—message to the reader.

The Crucial Battle had a literary flavor to it, an epic sweep. But one seeks that in vain in *The Next Battle*. Reading this latter work now, one finds it thick with propaganda, thick enough to choke on. Losing the war on account of "numbers" means getting beaten due to long-term neglect of precautions one might take against an enemy. If one fails to increase the defense budget and construct more warships, terrible things will ensue. Et cetera.

With his direct experience and understanding of the tragedies of modern warfare, Mizuno was in a difficult position. He had come to believe that the only way to prevent the tragedies of war was to increase military preparedness.

A small-scale model of an imaginary war story, *The Next Battle* made unexpected waves. This is because an unusual event occurred which the naval authorities were incapable of handling.

The Next Battle was actually authored pseudonymously, by "a Naval Lieutenant Commander." Mizuno had indeed been promoted from lieutenant to commander during the Russo-Japanese War. His current actual assignment was merely as navy archivist. It was an easy desk job, far from real naval combat. And yet that also made it perfect for writing *The Next Battle*. To avoid the red tape of submitting a publication request and the bother of obtaining the approval of his superiors, he published *The Next Battle* under a pseudonym without really thinking it through. He also wanted to avoid being criticized for doing extra work on the side for profit while receiving a monthly military paycheck. His debut work, *The Crucial Battle*, had ultimately gone through 140-plus printings. His finances were hardly in bad shape. Most importantly, he had, in one bound, vaulted from low-ranking officer to man of fame.

It was the Ministry of Foreign Affairs that first made an issue out of an active-duty military man publishing a work about a hypothetical war with the United States. They were worried lest the book provide a pretext for external pressure. They requested that the naval ministry launch an inquiry, and warned them of the terrible consequences of needlessly fanning the flames of anti-American sentiment. The naval ministry did indeed buy into the formal inquiry. Since Mizuno was pretty much the only one capable of writing such an account, the culprit was soon identified. In short order, Mizuno was called to appear at the naval ministry where he was grilled by the vice-chief of the naval ministry's secretariat: one Captain Taniguchi Naomi.[20]

> "The 'Naval Lieutenant Commander' listed in the newspaper ads as the author of *The Next Battle* is you, is it not?"
> "It's me."

Mizuno was choosing to be frankly insubordinate.

> "But did you get permission to publish such a work?"
> "I did not."
> "When an active-duty naval officer publishes written material, he must obtain authorization from his commanding officer. You were already aware of this."

The vice-chief is referring to the publication of *The Crucial Battle*.

> "You must have known procedure."
> "I did not. I did look into it last time, but there were no applicable regulations; I submitted a request because I was told that was customary. But this time I was publishing under a pseudonym, so I didn't think I had to bother."

At this, Captain Taniguchi held up a printed set of the *Naval Regulations*.

> There's a regulation in here. Whether you're using a pseudonym or any other alias, as an active-duty officer you are still bound by these regulations.

Mizuno gave it a look and saw that there was indeed such a regulation. It was new and he had not been aware of it. Now he must admit his error.

> I did not know about this.

But the military bureaucracy could hardly let it go at that.

> Further instructions will be forthcoming. In the mean time, I want you to ask the printer to suspend further printings.

After this, things took a turn or two and got even more complicated. The rumor reached Mizuno's ears that navy minister Yashiro Rokuro was furious and had said, "Kick this insolent punk out of the navy!" In any event, in another two or three days Mizuno was once again called before Captain Taniguchi.

The captain began, "It's really a pity, but regulations are regulations." Mizuno prepared himself for a demotion (effectively, expulsion) at last. But the results proved to be different. His punishment was unexpectedly light.

"Five days' probation, confined to quarters."

The reason for all this was that when the navy minister read *The Next Battle*, his attitude had changed. Perhaps he had expected criticism of the navy and the government; instead he found merely an argument for naval expansion. When a punishment of ten days' probation was proposed, he said, "Five is fine." And so the order stood. Publication resumed.

Around the same time, on July 28, 1914, to be precise, the First World War broke out in Europe. Japan entered the war on the side of the Allies a month later on August 23. By September 2, Japan was already landing troops at Qingdao, in China's German-held Shandong Province. Yuan Shikai, who had broken up the Chinese Revolution of 1911 (led by Sun Yatsen), feared that increased Japanese influence was threatening his own power base. He appealed to American president Woodrow Wilson not to allow the Japanese to enter the war. America was seeking to expand its initiatives in Asia. Preserving Yuan Shikai was consonant with its interests. But Yuan's schemes did not pan out, and eventually Japan entered the war. Under the circumstances, however, Japan did not want to provoke the United States. When summaries of Mizuno's *The Next Battle* started appearing in the U.S., the Foreign Ministry was once again aghast.

Once again, *The Next Battle* was obliged to cease publication. Mizuno had been putting up as best he could with his clerical sinecure as naval archivist. When he could not stand it anymore he wrote *The Next Battle*. However, he couldn't publish as he pleased, and he was still employed in the naval archives. This was equivalent to being an involuntary shut-in. He began to nurse a sense of dissatisfaction. With real anguish he mulled over the question of why he had been shunted aside to such a place.

It had begun, ironically, with his successful debut work, *The Crucial Battle*, which Mizuno undertook while he was similarly employed after the Russo-Japanese War in the navy's Office for the Compilation of War

Histories. He could not get out of his head the scenes of battle pandemonium that he had witnessed at sea. Yet Mizuno could not include them in the official record. He worked out the basic structure and composition of his book as he commuted between the redbrick buildings of the naval ministry in Kasumigaseki and his residence in Aoyama. When his official duties were done for the day, he would slave away over his book at home by lamplight, working even past midnight. His labors were rewarded with the book's reception as a best seller.

After five years in the Office for the Compilation of War Histories, Mizuno's rotation there was up. In the autumn of 1910, he was transferred to Squadron 16 of the Maizuru Torpedo Boat Division. He had been a torpedo boat commander during the Russo-Japanese War; this new assignment promoted him one rank and put him in charge of a four-boat squadron. After so long away from the sea, inhaling the moldy air of the "Redbricks," he was delighted to breathe some fresh air.

However, in the tenth month of his new assignment, he had words with his division leader, Rear Admiral Kimura Kōkichi. Mizuno had learned that one of his subordinates had been punished by the division leader for acting contrary to orders during practice maneuvers.

In the armed forces, a superior officer's command is absolute. But Mizuno's counterargument was thrust forward as aggressively as his prominent jaw and chiseled features. Nor was it mere refutation: he worked up some clever argumentation. "If you put it like that, sir," he said,

> let's fix it so that a reprimand will be issued to the commander based on my authority, as squadron leader, to punish my subordinates. I will admonish the torpedo boat commander myself.

A mere warning was what he had in mind. But in fact, the division leader had superior disciplinary authority. Rear Admiral Kimura, known for his mild temperament, replied, shaking with anger,

> Fine. I shall report this matter to my superiors. In all my long career in the navy, I have never seen such an arrogant and disrespectful person as yourself.

A few days later, Mizuno received orders to report to the assistant commandant and inspector of the Sasebo Naval Arsenal. The commandant of the arsenal was Rear Admiral Kuroi Teijirō. Mizuno had no problem with Kuroi, but one assumes Mizuno's attitude must have ruffled some feathers, judging from the fact that in just eight months, back he went to working at the naval archives.

Indeed, Mizuno had, to put it positively, a strong personality; from another point of view, he lacked the genes for cooperation. However, though he may have caused friction, he did write *The Crucial Battle* and *The Next Battle*, which went beyond the box of the conventional military mindset, so one must at least give him credit for a certain talent.

What I am particularly interested in here is how external pressure was conceptualized and made a matter of conscious reflection. The genre of imaginary or future-war chronicles provides excellent material for studying this issue. Mizuno's *The Next Battle* was the first major "record" or "chronicle" of a future U.S.-Japan conflict. Let us recall at this point the young American whom Mizuno almost met in San Francisco, back when Mizuno was a midshipman on his training cruise.

The young man was Homer Lea, whom I have called the American edition of Mizuno Hironori. The book he authored in 1909, *The Valor of Ignorance*, came to exactly the opposite conclusions from those of *The Next Battle*.

In Lea's book, Japan immediately occupies the Philippines and Hawaii. Within five weeks after hostilities start, the Japanese army lands at San Francisco and Los Angeles and with great vigor begins an invasion of the American homeland.

A Japanese translation of Lea's book came out within two years. It went through twenty-four printings in one year. To translate back into English from that translation:

> Japan has already secured a militarily superior position in Asia, from Hong Kong northwards. If Japan should desire to make herself Supreme Ruler of the Pacific, no nation on earth could prevent her—with the single exception of the United States.[21]

And the author deplores the lack of any aspiration on America's part to frustrate Japanese ambitions to rule the Pacific.

> Our people, regardless of class or race, live only for their own selfish profit. It is as if they thought to grow fat by feeding off the nation. They

care not an iota about national development and prestige. To be sure, America is wealthier than Japan. But the Japanese are as valiant as they are poor, and they are rich in their love of nation. If, together, the two nations enter the fires of war, which shall emerge triumphant? The answer should be self-evident. . . .

Should the Japanese army be successful in reaching their objectives, they would occupy the three States of Washington, Oregon, and California. Needless to say, the Union would be deprived of its rich coastal territories. From the point of view of military strategy, we would also be losing a vital base that we would never recover, for all eternity.

We shall be examining *The Valor of Ignorance* in greater detail, and we shall see that in Lea's scenario, Hawaii is subjected not to a surprise attack, but to an uprising by ethnic Japanese immigrants. This part may seem absurd, but perhaps it is best taken as an instance of the increased virulence, at the time, of America's immigrant-expulsion ideology.

CHAPTER THREE

The Adventures of
General Lea

H OMER LEA was born in Denver, Colorado in 1876, making him just
one year younger than Mizuno Hironori. It is also striking that whereas
Mizuno's *The Next Battle* (1914) ends in a Japanese defeat, Lea's *The Valor
of Ignorance* (1909) forecasts an American defeat. Thus, although the two
authors' conclusions were diametrically opposed, they were also symmetrical
in that each author imagined his own country defeated by the other.

Legend has it that Lea's birthplace was Virginia and that he was descended
from General Robert E. Lee, commander in chief of Confederate forces
during the American Civil War. How could there have been any connection
between the Colorado-born Lea and the general's family in Virginia? Despite the fact that the two were not related, Homer Lea preferred to believe
that they were. Moreover, in spite of the fact that Lea had no experience
whatsoever of the military life, he was in later years called "General Lea"
by Sun Yat-sen, leader of the Chinese Revolution of 1911. Letters are extant
in which Sun addresses Lea as "My dear General."

Homer Lea's father, Alfred A. Lea, came into this world on the outskirts
of Cleveland, Tennessee. By a circuitous route, he wound up in Denver,
Colorado. His family was led there by Lea's grandfather, a physician, who
feared becoming embroiled in the Civil War and sought to prevent that
by evacuating them to various locations. At the age of fourteen, Alfred was
placed in the care of a friend who owned a wagon train. They headed for
the Western territories, which had not yet pledged allegiance to either the
Union or the Confederacy. After an arduous journey, they reached Denver,
at the base of the Rocky Mountains.

Lea's grandfather was killed just after Alfred set out. His desperate measures
to save his family had been proven right. Hunches such as his, formulated

when face-to-face with danger, are often borne out. This intuitiveness probably ran in Lea's family.

Today Denver is the capital of Colorado. However, when Alfred arrived, the town had just been created, and the population was small. Life was hard growing up, and as an adult he found work as a peddler, making and selling digests of works that were popular back East. The business prospered, and he married Hersa Coberly from Indiana. They had two daughters and then, finally, a son.

Lea's mother died when he was still a baby, and the children were sent off to be reared by his grandmother in Indiana. Eugene Anschel, author of a study on Lea, states that

> it had been noticed as soon as Homer began to walk that he stooped to one side. Later, when he climbed stairs, he started to wheeze and had to rest frequently. His father had hoped that the return to the better air in Denver might cure what seemed to be asthma, but the little boy's condition showed no improvement. Eventually, it was discovered that he suffered from a curvature of the spine, and he was sent to the National Surgical Institute in Indianapolis, but the treatment was not successful. Gradually, he developed a hump that was to stay with him all his life.[1]

Homer Lea was raised by his grandmother, but at the age of fifteen he returned to his father in Denver. His father was now remarried, to Emma Wilson. Emma, a schoolteacher, was concerned that Lea had not attended school for quite some time; it was she who had asked that he return to Denver. As he was basically a bright child, Emma's tutelage bore results within just one year. Key Ray Chong tells us that he "developed a passion for reading, especially the exploits of great heroes and adventure stories such as *Robinson Crusoe, King Arthur's Knights of the Round Table*, and *Twenty Thousand Leagues Under the Sea*."[2]

Just before he turned sixteen, Homer entered East Denver High School. Physically handicapped as he was, he could not join the other boys in their activities. He grew quiet and depressed; he achieved emotional release by letting loose finely honed shafts of sarcasm—from a distance.

When his father moved the family to Los Angeles, Lea transferred to local schools. This proved to be the impetus for a complete reversal in his character. As Anschel describes it,

He made a number of friends, some of whom remained close to him to the end of his life. Disregarding his physical impairments, he took part in the social life of the school and made it a point to accompany his friends on strenuous excursions. He did not permit anyone to make allowances for his weaknesses, but joined in hunting and fishing trips and even took up fencing. He was active in school politics, acted as election manager for a classmate, and showed himself adept in situations that required sharp observation and rapid decision.[3]

One of Lea's school friends later recalled that "his dramatic way of speaking, his piercing eyes, the intonation of his voice, and his characteristic gesture of raising his hand with his long forefinger extended, brought home the point generated by his keen mind."[4]

It would appear that it was around this time, upon realizing that eloquence and quick judgment had no relation to any physical handicap, he began to believe that he was born to be a commander in chief. This fantasizing was only accelerated by his being occasionally shut up alone in darkened rooms.

Lea was tormented by tremendous headaches. They began in the eyes or the nose. He had several nose operations. His eyesight was deteriorating. Apparently the spinal curvature was causing the development of other physical problems. It was a doctor's recommendation that when the headaches struck, Lea be confined to a dark room. When the attacks were particularly acute, his eyes were extremely sensitive: it was thought that darkness would help spare his eyes, and that the peacefulness would also promote his speedier recovery. So whenever the attacks became frequent, Lea would draw the curtains, retire to his bed, and rest quietly, sometimes for days at a time.

At such times, his mind grew hazy and he would dream or daydream, passing in and out of sleep. In these imaginings, the dark world of his convalescence would be filled to overflowing with the world of his readings—the adventure stories, the tales of heroism. These tales became suffused with the exoticism of the denizens of a particular section of Los Angeles. Lea developed an abiding interest in the mysterious homeland of the pigtailed male residents of Los Angeles' Chinatown. His own family's cook wore the queue; from him, Lea learned of Zhu Yuanchang (1328–98), founder of the Ming Dynasty. Then Zhu appeared to Lea in a dream, a gallant figure on horseback with the noble face of a hero. On the screen of his dream, the camera zoomed in for a close-up. As Lea gazed at that face, he realized that it was, indisputably, none other than—his own! As trumpets sounded the charge, he led tens of thousands of mounted warriors into the chaos of a great battlefield of civil war: he was "General Lea." He candidly revealed to a friend what he had dreamt.

A soldier on the front lines must be physically robust. What the commander in chief needs is the ability to formulate strategy with precision. He must believe in his own correctness; he must not doubt; he must be filled with confidence. Lea's own ambition may well have derived from this dream. His friends attest to the charismatic quality they sensed whenever he chose to pitch his normally mild tone of voice in a particularly sonorous register.

After school, fooling around with his companions on the way home, Homer Lea skillfully maneuvered them into playing war games in his backyard. Transforming himself into the commander in chief, Lea would designate a bush as a fortress and press the attack with firecrackers. As one acquaintance later recalled, "He had eyes that could bury you nine feet under the ground, if you disobeyed him."[5] So they obeyed him.

With his exemplary grades, Lea first entered Occidental College near Los Angeles, then transferred to Stanford University in the suburbs of San Francisco. His attention and efforts now shifted from playing war to the specialized analysis of military affairs. Anschel points out that he also joined a debating society, "to cultivate his gift of speech."[6] In the words of a contemporary, Homer Lea was "a remarkable poker player in a small way, and an inveterate student of Napoleon's campaigns and of the military philosophy of England and Germany"; in general, "a youth of extraordinary parts—ready memory, very vivid imagination, imperturbable coolness, and an obsession for militarism and war."[7]

Finally, his day had come, as he knew it must: the start of the Spanish-American War. As Anschel puts it, "The wave of patriotism that engulfed campuses all over the United States also inundated Stanford. Military drilling became the daily routine of many students."[8] With his buddies, the twenty-one-year-old Lea volunteered for the U.S. Army. But as his friends headed off to the Philippines to serve in the military, he was left at the pier, waving goodbye with the women and children. During the Spanish-American War, his eyesight worsened. The cause: smallpox.

Meanwhile, the war ended, all too soon, with an American victory. But even as the triumphantly returning students were greeted with cheers, Lea was on his way out. He withdrew from college.

The reason was not simply illness. If he had remained on campus, he would have been labeled a war reject. It would be an unbearable humiliation. And thus it was that during the very same period when Mizuno Hironori was viewing the marvels of San Francisco on his training cruise, Lea was frequenting Chinatown. For the sick young man, this was a turning point in his life.

A year later, Lea's name was mentioned on the front page of the magazine section of the April 22, 1900 edition of the *San Francisco Call*. An article bearing the headline, YOUNG CALIFORNIAN IS PLOTTING TO BECOME COMMANDER IN CHIEF OF THE REBEL FORCES, revealed a plan conceived on a stupendous scale. The substance of the alleged plot was too fantastical, too optimistic. It was undeniably the product of sheer fantasy. Unquestionably, this was Lea publicizing his schemes.

The purported goal was "to help the Chinese emperor to the throne" of what would be transformed into a modern constitutional monarchy.[9] Not so surprising a plot, perhaps, when we consider that leading the development team for this Hollywood-style action-adventure scenario was a young man just twenty-three years of age.

The same article carried Homer Lea's photograph, a head shot. Next to it were grandly arranged photos of a number of men, including leaders of China's reform movement and of the local branch of the China Empire Reform Association. So we see that a San Francisco paper with a high circulation reported such developments with great excitement.

The Chinese reform movement had sprung up not only in San Francisco and Los Angeles, but worldwide. Sympathizers in Hong Kong, Macao, Nagasaki, and Yokohama, brimming with revolutionary zeal, had amassed several millions of dollars in donations. The article in the *Call* concluded with the information that somehow, the success or failure of this grand revolution was believed to rest on the shoulders of one American citizen: his name was Homer Lea.

Lea actually departed San Francisco for the Far East two months later on June 22. This dreamer who ventured in such high spirits across the broad Pacific to a Chinese mainland of which he had no experience had so bedazzled the *Call* with his eloquence that in a later headline it announced, TWENTY THOUSAND FOREIGN TROOPS SOON TO BE MARCHING ON CHINA SOIL.[10]

Peking, China. The summer of the year 1900. The rains are late. The crops have failed. A hundred million Chinese are hungry, and a violent wind of discontent disturbs the land. Within the foreign compound, a thousand foreigners live and work, citizens of a dozen far-off nations.

Thus declaimed the opening voiceover narration to Nicholas Ray's 1963 film, *55 Days at Peking*. The walled compound of Peking's foreign legation quarter is enveloped in yellow dust. It is morning, and it's time for the daily hoisting of the flags: the Stars and Stripes of the United States, the Union Jack of the British Empire, the Tricolor of France, the Rising Sun of Japan. The quarter is also home to the ambassadors of Germany, Russia, Italy, and Austria; and to resident military attachés and their families.

As the flags are raised, national anthems, bugle calls, and other martial music strike up. Multiple nations, simultaneously. "To the Color," "God Save the Queen," "The Marseillaise," the "Kimi ga Yo," and other tunes all mingling in cacophony. It symbolizes the discordant interests of the great powers. Yet even as they struggle for continental concessions, even as they strive to check the aspirations of their competitors, they must coexist here.

A pigtailed oldster outside the compound grumbles, "What is this terrible noise?" His companion's reply: "Different nations saying the same thing at the same time: 'We want China!'"

55 Days at Peking is a historical epic whose theme is the activities of the foreign legations—the ambassadors, the military personnel—while under siege from a secret society called the Fists of Righteous Harmony (or, by Westerners, "the Boxers") in 1900. The lead character, a major in the U.S. Marines, is played by Charlton Heston. Since Japan is one of the participants in the multinational force, a supporting role is played by Itami Jūzō as Colonel Shiba Gorō. When it is time to salute another Japanese, he bows formally—and stereotypically. This is not Itami's fault—it is Hollywood, going for the most palatable performance. It is the whites who are the good guys, while the Chinese are portrayed as both savage and sly. This too is part of the color scheme of many a Hollywood picture dealing with Asia (or Africa). Such movies follow the pattern of the cowboy Western.

And it was also in 1900, on June 22, that the twenty-three-year-old Homer Lea sailed out of San Francisco Bay, headed for China.

California journalists who wrote headlines such as TWENTY THOUSAND FOREIGN TROOPS SOON TO BE MARCHING ON CHINA SOIL were certainly under-informed. But it was not only the journalists. Ordinary Americans did not consider their personal interests directly linked to what happened in China. What they did understand was what they felt to be the trouble at home caused by waves of cheap immigrant labor stealing work from poor whites. If a San Francisco newspaper could report seriously that Homer Lea was recruiting a force of twenty thousand men, that reflected the ignorance of the actual situation in China.

In the film *55 Days at Peking*, the fighters of the Fists of Righteous Harmony are called the Boxers. They were a secret society based on folk religion; they believed that if one kept up the practice of martial arts such as boxing and stick-fighting, one would attain divine powers like the heroes of heroic novels, such as Sun Wukong (the Monkey King) and his pig-monster companion, Zhu Baijie, from the classic Chinese novel *Journey to the West*. These teachings were not really important—they merely provided an opportunity for associating in common cause.

Thanks to Westerners, China's Qing Dynasty was displaying a moth-eaten appearance; the Imperial Court was losing its dignity and prestige. The view began to gain currency that China had fallen into such a weakened, poverty-stricken state because of Westerners walking about as if they owned the place. The Manchu Court plotted to rid China of Western influence by using China's own discontented elements. And in 1899, in Shandong Province, a violent movement sprang up, instigated by the Boxers, under the slogan, "Aid the Qing; Destroy the West."

This insurrection demolished Christian churches and attacked missionaries, swelling into a mass movement that began to head toward Beijing. The court, under the empress dowager, was hoping to use this insurrection to cleanse China of Western influence. If things went well, they might actually drive the foreign powers from the land. At least, that was their overconfident plan. On June 21, 1900, China issued a declaration of war against eight foreign powers. It was just one day before Homer Lea left San Francisco.

As the film title *55 Days at Peking* suggests, the uprising was soon suppressed. The empress dowager capitulated, agreeing to pay a huge indemnity. She was even stripped of the right to station a garrison in Beijing.

Another film set during the latter days of the Qing empire is *The Last Emperor* (1987), directed by Bernardo Bertolucci. John Lone plays Pu Yi, the last emperor of the Qing Dynasty. In scenes of his early childhood, the empress dowager appears.

Deep within the recesses of the Forbidden City in Beijing, in a room made dim by the smoke of burning incense, the empress dowager holds sway, attended by her eunuchs and her ladies-in-waiting. A seventy-three-year-old matriarch, facing death, she yields the throne to the child Pu Yi by right of succession. This takes place on November 15, 1908.

Thus begins the tragedy of Pu Yi. With the empress dowager's death, the Manchu Dynasty, which had ruled China for the previous three hundred years, finally disintegrates.

At that time, China was often referred to as a sleeping lion. During the Opium War of 1842 it had been decisively defeated by England, which possessed a superior, more modern military. Yet the Sinocentrism of the Chinese was expressed literally: their country was the Middle Kingdom, the center of the world. All other peoples were beyond the pale, mere barbarians. The Chinese referred to them as *yidi*: savages; aliens. Since the Western countries were supposed to be outlying barbarian countries, their handy defeat of the Qing was shocking. Then, in the Sino-French War of 1884–85, the Qing were also beaten, and in the Sino-Japanese War of 1894–95, they lost again. The Qing had engaged the foreigners in a series of wars and lost every time.

Thus the Qing Dynasty was crumbling. Individuals began to call for the abandonment of Sinocentrism and for a more positive engagement with the West.

One such thinker was Kang Yuwei (1858–1927), a Confucian scholar who had experienced the Sino-French War at the age of twenty-seven. As a result of this war, China was stripped of its tributary state of Annan (Vietnam). The next year, Great Britain made Burma a colony. Russia also began biting off chunks of the Chinese empire in the north. Kang presented a memorial to Emperor Guangxu calling not only for the introduction of Western science and technology but also for the adoption of a parliamentary political system. China, he argued, must modernize.

But Guangxu was still in his teens, and with a weak power base, he was an emperor only in name. In reality, he was the puppet of the politically ambitious Zixi, the empress dowager.

Zixi had been the second wife of the Xianfeng Emperor, two imperial generations back. He had had no child by his first wife. After his death, the empress dowager's son, Tongzhi, had succeeded to the throne. Then, when Tongzhi died at the age of nineteen, the empress dowager swept aside all objections to engineer the succession of her four-year-old nephew, Guangxu. The consensus is that the empress dowager was a strong woman, and a Machiavellian one. In the Hollywood movie *55 Days at Peking*, she is portrayed as a stereotypical villain.

Two years before the Boxer uprising, the Reform Party of Kang Yuwei and others had been stamped out in a coup d'état. Guangxu was held incommunicado, and Kang Yuwei fled to Japan. The Reform Party was looking for an opportunity to repair its political fortunes. As part of that, secret reform support groups were organized in ethnic Chinese communities around the world. One of the many plots to oust the empress dowager from the palace was the one in which the young Homer Lea became caught up as he frequented San Francisco's Chinatown. According to the *San Francisco Call*, under its headline, TWENTY THOUSAND FOREIGN TROOPS SOON TO BE MARCHING ON CHINA SOIL, Homer would raise his fists and cry to his pigtailed friends in the secret Protect-the-Emperor Society that first, $60,000 collected by the Protect-the-Emperor Society's American comrades would be transferred to Kang Yuwei, while he was residing in Singapore. Next, in Macao, the Society would instigate a revolutionary war. Proceeding upstream as far as Fuzhou, they would construct three bases. If the Society would entrust him with sole command of the army, he would provide both American advisers and the most modern equipment and create an invincible force. They would see if they couldn't liberate the Guangxu Emperor from his heavily guarded cell and get the drop on the empress dowager. And so on and so forth. Homer Lea's bluster was perhaps typical of a youth who had not yet experienced war.

The Society's local officials supplied him with a letter of introduction, describing him as coming from an old American military family, as being possessed of outstanding military capability, and as having drawn up a plan for the establishment in China of a military school capable of training two thousand soldiers. Lea returned to the United States in the spring of 1901. If things had proceeded as envisioned by San Francisco's press upon his departure, this one-year adventure would truly have been a Hollywood spectacular. His recollections certainly read like one.

Going from Guangdong to Beijing, Lea recounts, constituted a continental incursion of hundreds of miles. Then, as planned, in the middle of the night, he met Kang Yuwei in the Forbidden City.[11] When the latter saw the hunchbacked youth, he asked him suspiciously, "Why have you come? What can you do?"

"I have come," Lea said, "to help you save China from the old Tigress [the empress dowager]. To rescue Kwang Hsu [the Guangxu Emperor].

To lead your armies to victory!" The leader of China's Reform Party, Kang was by now a handsome forty-two-year-old, reputed to have grown tired of Chinese cuisine. According to one account, "The prime minister smiled, 'You are very young to do all that.'" But having made such a long and difficult journey, Homer Lea was hardly about to give up so easily. "I am the same age," he replied, "as Napoleon was at Rivoli." Pleased with this answer, Kang "ordered Lea to proceed to Shensi, there to take over a body of volunteers." Xi'an, in Shaanxi (formerly Shensi) Province, was where the Guangxu Emperor had fled. Accordingly, the young American set out for Shaanxi with three companions. En route, a messenger arrived, bearing gifts from the emperor: a scroll and a package. Opening the scroll, Lea found a commission as lieutenant general. In the package, he found the corresponding epaulettes. He had become General Lea.

When the newly promoted general arrived at his destination, he was once again approached by a secret envoy. It was bad news. His meeting with Kang Yuwei had come to the attention of the empress dowager's spies. Apprised of this, Kang Yuwei had escaped the Forbidden City by the skin of his teeth, but with a $20,000 bounty on his head. And the "white devil" Homer Lea, whereabouts unknown, had on his own head a prize of $10,000.

To his own troops waiting in Shaanxi, Lea sent orders that until he arrived they should disperse into the hills. But before those orders arrived, the officers of his insurrectionary band had been rounded up. What General Lea found waiting for him in Xi'an were their heads, cruelly displayed on the city walls. His refusal to lose heart is a measure of his strength of will. Reconstituting his decimated legions, he marched through the countryside, recruiting additional followers. His new force of several thousand pigtailed volunteers was short on military training but long on fighting spirit.

Wearing a uniform resplendent with gold epaulettes and brandishing a sword as long as he was tall, General Lea led his troops in a furious assault on the den of corruption presided over by the empress dowager and her minions. When they reached the walls of Beijing, they witnessed the cruelty of the Boxers. The foreign powers in the legation quarter were surrounded on all sides by the insurrectionary mob; they were at the point of surrender. The empress dowager's personal army was involved, disguised as rioters. In the foreign legation quarter, women and children were also at risk. Lea was roused to action. When the revolutionary volunteers fought their way through from Tianjin, with the assistance of an eight-nation expeditionary force, they fought bravely and were ultimately victorious.

And so the Boxer Rebellion was suppressed. The empress dowager and her cronies fled for their lives; their only pursuers were Homer Lea and his volunteer army. But they were overconfident. The empress dowager set up an ambush and slipped away. The volunteers fell right into the trap. The ambush turned into a general rout. Even General Lea, the commander in chief, was left wounded on the battlefield. He was given sanctuary by Buddhist monks at a nearby temple. They dressed his wounded arm and gave him food and drink. As he reached for a cup, an old monk remarked, "Your hand is small. But it is a great hand. You will one day lead an army to victory." And at that very moment, a bird dropped dead from the branch of a large tree by the temple. According to Chinese folk tradition, this signified the fall of a regime. Qing China was about to fall.

At least that is how Homer Lea tells the story of his adventures on the Chinese mainland. In fact, the historical record cannot corroborate that when foreign troops finally suppressed the Boxers, it had anything to do with Homer Lea's phantom army. Nor are there any other indications that Kang Yuwei was even in Beijing. They mounted no insurrection, nor did Guangxu make any sort of comeback at that time. But the real feelings of the mendacious Lea were quite the opposite of the sunny story he sold to his friends. By the time Homer returned to the U.S., his story had grown into a bombastic tale of high adventure. The real story was that he had spent the time getting drunk in Shanghai.

After the foreign powers put down the Boxer Rebellion in the summer of 1900, Homer Lea accepted the hospitality of an American living in Shanghai. If all Lea had done was turn over to Kang Yuwei the money raised by the secret societies in San Francisco's Chinatown, he wouldn't have had much of a role to play in the struggle to reform China. On an unfamiliar continent, there was nothing he could do. Tex O'Reilly, later to play a secret role behind the scenes of international politics, was working in the Shanghai International Police bureau. In his biography of O'Reilly, *Born to Raise Hell*, Thomas Lowell relates how O'Reilly could not forbear from sympathizing with the indigent Lea, going out of his way to put him up for some four months.

Around the same time, the famous French naval officer Pierre Loti, author of *Madame Chrysanthème* (Madame Chrysanthemum) and *A Ball in Edo*, was also living in Shanghai. According to Tex O'Reilly, Loti's drama *La Fille du Ciel* (Daughter of Heaven), about the tragic love affair between the

Guangxu Emperor and a royal princess descended from the Ming imperial line, was based on a tale told him by Homer Lea.

O'Reilly, some three years Lea's junior, closely observed his brilliant guest.

> That marvelous mind was tied to a twisted, deformed little body, in constant pain. He suffered so horribly that he was a most unpleasant companion, irritable and cranky. And he drank all the time. He was never drunk, but he drank from morning to night, trying to get away from the pain.[12]

As one of Lea's San Francisco friends attests, alcohol was a constant feature of Lea's life after his return to the United States. I see this not simply as a means to dull the pain of his headaches. I believe his dependency on alcohol was the product of feelings of frustration.

But Homer Lea would not give up. In November 1904, he founded the Western Military Academy in Los Angeles. Not an official public institution, it was far removed from something like West Point and should be thought of more as a vocational school. The prospectus submitted to the governor of California states that the school's purpose was "instruction in . . . language and in military science and tactics."[13]

The Protect the Emperor Society, a secret society to which Lea had entrée, was recruiting volunteers for a China expeditionary force. The volunteer corps went by the impressive name of the Imperial Chinese Army, but in fact was a poorly garbed and motley crew. Any military force should have clearly defined leadership. Uniforms and ranks are meaningful because they reinforce that structural organization. From this point of view, the Imperial Chinese Army—which was not even divided into commissioned officers, noncommissioned officers, and troops—was not a real army at all.

Lea racked his brains over this particular issue. On November 1, General Order No. 8, Headquarters First Brigade, Imperial Chinese Army, was issued by command of Lieutenant General Homer Lea.[14] It governed regulations regarding uniforms for all soldiers. Clothes make the man. According to General Order No. 8, the uniforms should have the same design and color as those of the United States Army. But there was some concern that if all the men suddenly went out and ordered their own uniforms, there would be differences in quality and workmanship. So headquarters stipulated that all uniforms be ordered from Pettibone Brothers Manufacturing Company of Cincinnati, Ohio. Lea was quite involved with this issue. Nor could he have gone into such detail without being completely serious.

During the academy's first year of operation, one hundred twenty students were admitted. The teaching staff was comprised of retired U.S. military officers. They were given new ranks, from general to captain. The pigtailed recruits would complete a one-year crash-course. Then, as newly minted officers, they would be sent out all over the United States to become leaders of the Imperial Chinese Army's local detachments.

Lea made arrangements for soldiers of the Imperial Chinese Army to march in the January 1905 Tournament of Roses parade in Pasadena. The December 31st issue of the *Los Angeles Times* carried word of the impending event:

> It will be the first time in history that a company of Chinese soldiers has marched on American soil, and a great surprise is in store for those who may have looked upon the establishment of the school by Gen. Homer Lea as a burlesque. The Chinese soldiers will be one of the most striking features of the parade.[15]

And the next day, as they marched precisely and mechanically in their new uniforms and leggings, they did indeed attract attention, though they were a smallish contingent of fifty-eight soldiers. "General Lea" was on the reviewing stand, looking down with satisfaction on the splendid showing made by his men.

As if in compensation for his fruitless voyage in 1900, Lea had scored a glorious coup of a different sort, though whether it contributed to the Chinese revolution or not is something no one can say for sure. This thoroughly eccentric white man had impressed Kang Yuwei, at the time residing in London, as someone who might be useful. And one day, a letter from Kang arrived for Lea, stating, "How thankful I am to hear that you are so kind as to render assistance for our cause. I shall leave for America in a very short time, and I hope that I may soon have the pleasure of meeting you."[16] Kang promised to contact Lea after arriving in America.

Kang Yuwei was in the middle of an extensive journey throughout Europe to drum up international sympathy—and monetary contributions—for the reform cause. The trip was long but the results disappointing. And then he received heartening news of General Lea's activities.

In mid-March, Kang and his party arrived in Los Angeles. Lea dragged the mayor himself to the station to greet Kang along with Lea's uniformed troops, in formation. The only trouble was, the train was delayed by two days, so Kang's eventual arrival was not celebrated as quite as grand an event as Lea had intended it to be. Kang's welcome party, however, was a great success. The chairman of the Los Angeles Chamber of Commerce attended, along with prominent bankers, real U.S. Army generals, and celebrities from all walks of life. But some unexpected difficulties arose in the relationship between Kang Yuwei and Homer Lea.

Because Kang Yuwei's primary mission abroad was in fact fund-raising, he was inclined to go anywhere he was invited. "General Lea" was hardly in charge of all of Kang's commitments. If a man styled himself commander of an Imperial Chinese *Reform* Army, it was probably fine with Kang. At a banquet in Los Angeles, Kang met and praised just such a man, Richard A. Falkenberg: ". . . and I feel assured that China with General Falkenberg's help will be one of the foremost nations within a much shorter time than Japan succeeded in forging to the first rank."[17]

When Lea read that newspaper account, he was shocked. He had been referring to himself as commander of the Imperial Chinese Army; he had never heard of a commander of a Chinese *Reform* Army, as Falkenberg was calling himself. His vehement objections produced a public clarification. The April 8th *Los Angeles Times* quoted Kang Yuwei's proclamation, issued the previous day:

> To the American People: I desire to announce that Gen. Homer Lea of Los Angeles is the only one recognized and appointed by me as the general of all Chinese military schools in America, and furthermore, I have appointed no one such as "General Commanding," or any officer of the so-called "Imperial Chinese Reform Army," which is not in existence.[18]

Falkenberg was notorious—he had previously masqueraded as a U.S. senator. This time, it appeared he was scheming to obtain money by (ostensibly) collecting it for the Chinese Reform Party. But, while Kang Yuwei may have looked like an easy mark, he was moved by considerations that were wily enough. As long as donations were aggressively solicited on his behalf, it simply did not matter much to him whether this happened via Lea or via Falkenberg, nor did it matter with what ranks or titles the two men aggrandized their own roles in the movement.

Homer Lea was a terrific PR man for Kang Yuwei. Lea toured the various branches of the Imperial Chinese Army, accompanied by Kang, leader of the Reform Party, whose own thoughts were preoccupied with fund-raising. Not that any of General Lea's contingents were large in number, but they did all wear those uniforms and march like soldiers. Displayed before local notables, they could be counted on to be the highlight of any event, and they effectively guaranteed press coverage.

Kang's party passed through St. Louis, Chicago, and other large cities, then went on to Washington, D.C., where Kang had the opportunity to meet with President Theodore Roosevelt. The topic of the day was the anti-American boycotts then underway in China. The feelings underlying these boycotts were expressed most notably in the effort to force America to return its concessions along the Guangdong-Hankou Railway, and constituted a reaction to the U.S. expulsion movement aimed at Chinese immigrants. Kang told the newspapers that he and Roosevelt had had a worthwhile discussion of ways and means to end both the anti-American boycott and the anti-immigrant expulsion movement.

They left Washington and proceeded to Philadelphia, where they were again accorded an enthusiastic reception. Then they went on to New York. An account of their stay in New York appears in the *New York Times* for June 28, 1905. Urban newspaper that it was, the *Times* saw through the somewhat dubious character of the Kang party: the Chinese procession, led by a strange general, the pompous theatricality of the phony actors. Kang's clothing was calculated to indicate his high status. His small black cap was decorated with red and blue buttons denoting his rank in the Imperial Chinese bureaucracy. His queue was worn to a length permitted only to the illustrious. He sported gold-rimmed spectacles and a wispy mustache. His upper body was adorned with large black ornaments; the garment itself was made of silk, deep purple in color, fringed with braids of yellow cord. His bulky skirt was reddish brown, and wound around his waist was a decorative sash of a resplendent green. Black silk shoes of the highest quality completed this formal ensemble.

The journey continued to Boston, Hartford, and other cities of the northeast. In August they once again returned to New York. Kang sent a letter to the president requesting another meeting, but to no avail.

They did not even realize that their brief summer was now over. Kang and Lea's exotic show-and-tell had merely been a comical curtain-raiser to a far more serious drama. That same year, on August 10, 1905, a historic conference began in Portsmouth, New Hampshire.

It was a peace conference to end the Russo-Japanese War, and it was convened by President Theodore Roosevelt. The negotiator for Japan was Komura Jutaro; his Russian counterpart was Sergei Witte. The agreement they reached gave Japan only the southern half of Karafuto (Sakhalin) Island, and no indemnity. In Japan, there was an explosion of popular dissatisfaction. On September 5, the date the peace treaty was signed, a protest demonstration was held at Hibiya Park in Tokyo. The outraged mob attacked the residence of the minister of home affairs, the metropolitan police department, and a number of police boxes. Anarchy prevailed in Tokyo until the next day. Martial law was declared.

Later that autumn, Homer Lea received another setback. Japan's victory over Russia left the entire Chinese reform movement in a tenuous position. What preoccupied Roosevelt was the shifting spheres of influence in the Far East. When Russia withdrew from East Asia, Japanese military might seemed to him to be disproportionately large. Indeed, no sooner did the Russo-Japanese War break out than Roosevelt began to entertain secret misgivings. Chief among them was the presentiment that if Japan were to win, then at some point in the future it would wind up fighting the United States.

Roosevelt had not thought the Japanese navy capable of so thoroughly demolishing the Russian fleet. As far as the balance of power went, it was entirely desirable that the little nation of Japan had challenged the great power, Russia, and so handily won. But now there was no prospect of Russia recovering its naval power any time soon. That left a serious power vacuum that America would have to fill by building up its fleet.

Roosevelt had become president in 1901. Just prior to that, the Spanish-American War of 1898 had gained the United States the Philippines and Guam. That same year, the U.S. also annexed Hawaii. Roosevelt believed his new role was to confirm America's interests in the region. As he said in a speech delivered in San Francisco, the stage of world history had shifted from the ancient Mediterranean Sea to the Atlantic Ocean, but now it would move on to the Pacific.

In 1904, Roosevelt initiated a national defense strategy with specified hypothetical enemies. A joint board of eight army and navy chiefs, established the year before, was given the task of formulating plans. Those officers recruited included heroes of the Spanish-American War such as Admiral George Dewey and Lieutenant General Adna R. Chaffee. Taking the Russo-Japanese War as a watershed, two principal hypothetical enemies emerged: Germany in the Atlantic, and Japan in the Pacific. The appearance of Homer Lea's *The Valor of Ignorance* can only be understood against this historical background.

With Japan's victory in the Russo-Japanese War, America's attitude toward Japan underwent a profound transformation. The war plans commenced by the joint board in 1904 required the formulation of a global strategy. The portion of it that focused on Germany as a hypothetical enemy was called War Plan Black; the portion relating to England was Plan Red; the section on Japan, Plan Orange. All of South America was lumped together in Plan Purple. Canada was covered by Plan Crimson, Mexico by Plan Green.

The strategic planning that treated all surrounding regions as potentially hostile changed the following year, that is, subsequent to Japan's defeat of Russia. From that year onward, planning against hypothetical enemies was confined to Plan Black (against Germany) and Plan Orange (against Japan).

Plan Orange envisaged war between the U.S. and Japan as developing along the following lines. In the early stages, Japan invades the Philippines and Guam. America is thus obliged to dispatch reinforcements there immediately, but is initially stymied by the distribution of its navy. America's primary naval forces are concentrated in the Atlantic. Even by way of the Panama Canal (which would be completed in 1914), traversing the Pacific still takes sixty-eight days. Meanwhile, Japan marches to Manila in just eight days. The outnumbered American garrison must hold out against an assault by superior Japanese forces for at least sixty days.

Military leaders like Dewey and Chaffee, who were intimately familiar with the Philippines as a potential front in a U.S.-Japan war, recognized the need for forward bases to counter Japanese strategy effectively. For the Pacific, Hawaii's Pearl Harbor was chosen in 1908. It was the fleet heading west from Pearl Harbor that would be responsible for defending the Philippines, as described in detail in Phase III of Plan Orange.

Japanese newspaper the *Issei* published verbatim reports of first-generation immigrants (*issei*) who had come to America at the beginning of the twentieth century. For example, Mitsumori Nisuke describes thus the period when West Coast newspapers began to refer to Japan in a hostile manner:

> That a small nation like Japan could successfully wage war against a great power like Russia, and even force the surrender of Port Arthur, alarmed the American people, especially government officials and newspaper

columnists. One Los Angeles paper began to print articles filled with nothing but criticisms of Japan, warning that America must not open her doors to this dreadful group of people.[19]

The phrase, "articles filled with nothing but criticisms of Japan" refers above all to the yellow journalism of the Hearst publishing empire. Hearst's newspapers had used sensationalism to boost circulation sharply. William Randolph Hearst himself was the model for the new type of media baron depicted in Orson Welles's 1941 film *Citizen Kane*. Hearst was master of a unique concept.

In 1887, when he was twenty-four years of age, Hearst was entrusted with management of the *San Francisco Examiner* by its proprietor—his father, whose wealth derived from mines acquired during the Gold Rush. The young Hearst won a huge readership by employing original methods: a shift from hard political and economic news to crime and sex scandals, lurid photographs, and blaring headlines for top stories. His achievement was to liberate the newspaper from the intelligentsia and give it a more populist direction. One of his favorite injunctions was to spare no expense to get a story. He would report whatever his readers were likely to be interested in. But this novel sensibility was not always exercised for the larger good. Hearst would print not just the facts, but the facts as dictated by the requirements of some crusade or campaign. And even the "facts" created by such a campaign were considered by Hearst to be the truth. Sales increased; profits rose. He stood out in the unabashed zeal with which he followed the principle that sales equal profits. And Hearst rose too in the world of American publishing, building a vast media empire and earning the title "newspaper baron."

In 1938, *Readers' Digest* reprinted a *Saturday Evening Post* article that may have given the writers of *Citizen Kane* some ideas for the mise-en-scène of their film. All of his life, the piece argued, Hearst had been able to buy, buy, buy to suit his every whim and fancy. He bought several newspapers, he bought Egyptian mummies, he bought a California mountain and a herd of Tibetan yak. He acquired a monastery in Spain and had it dismantled and shipped to New York in wooden crates, where it remained, unseen by him. To that he added twenty-eight daily newspapers, fourteen magazines in the U.S. and England, eight radio stations, a telegraph company, a Hollywood production company, a newsreel company, a castle in Wales, and the world's largest private collection of art, valued at over forty million dollars.[20]

It was during the Spanish-American War that Hearst first became convinced how much more powerful a newspaper "campaign" was than mere news reporting. In *Citizen Kane*, this is portrayed in a scene occurring just before the outbreak of the war. An explosion of unknown origin sinks the *Maine*, a U.S. battleship anchored at Havana, in a Cuba that was then a colony of Spain. Spain and America dispute the cause. The newspapers in Kane's (Hearst's) chain push the idea of a Spanish plot. Kane dispatches a reporter to Havana. His reports of Spanish atrocities are designed to whip up anti-Spanish feeling among American citizens. But in Havana, all is calm. There are no signs that war is imminent. A telegram arrives from Kane's man in Havana. It reads (more or less):

THE FOOD IS MARVELOUS IN CUBA THE SENORITAS ARE BEAUTIFUL STOP I COULD SEND YOU PROSE POEMS OF PALM TREES AND SUNRISES AND TROPICAL COLORS BLENDING IN FAR OFF LANDSCAPES BUT DON'T FEEL RIGHT IN SPENDING YOUR MONEY FOR THIS STOP THERE'S NO WAR IN CUBA REGARDS WHEELER.

To which Kane is supposed to have replied along the following lines: "Dear Wheeler—You provide the prose poems—I'll provide the war." This is based on a similar exchange alleged to have occurred between Hearst and the artist Frederic Remington, who had been hired to accompany a Hearst reporter and provide illustrations for articles on the Cuban Revolution. In any event, Hearst's own newspapers did spill much ink presenting false reportage as true, inciting anti-Spanish sentiment. The White House was not inclined to go along, but it too was swept up in the war fever and obliged to declare war. This is why it is said that Hearst caused a war with the stroke of a pen.

Hearst's papers sold because they were simple to comprehend. Many Americans liked things simple. No doubt, such Americans still exist today.

When Spain had been vanquished, the next target was Japan.

Let us continue with Mitsumori's testimony of the mood of the era.

I arrived in San Francisco March or April of 1905. A man from the rooming house for Japanese came to greet me at the harbor in a one-horse wagon. There was a band of yakuza-type toughies at the harbor, and whenever they heard that Japanese were arriving they would go and beat them up. Nowadays we'd probably call them teenage radicals. Fifteen or twenty of these young gangsters would gather around, jeering, "Let's get 'em! More Japs!" We hurried off to the rooming house to avoid getting beaten up, but on the way a torrent of verbal abuse was heaped on our heads: "You Jap bastards! You shitty bastards!" One even picked up horse manure and threw it at us. I was baptized with horse manure.[21]

Mitsumori found employment as a compositor at the *Nichibei Times* (Japan–America Times), a Japanese-language newspaper. But he felt it would be dangerous to remain long in San Francisco.

At that time, American sentiment toward Japan was turning ugly. Not only could we not go out at night, we were even warned not to go out alone even in broad daylight. . . . So I made sure not to go out at night, and in the daytime not to go where the gangs of young toughs might be. Not just economically but even physically I felt I had no security. The young people who worked on the newspaper were attacked so often on their way home, it got so that a day without such an event was a day for thanksgiving. I thought living in San Francisco was no good, so I moved to Los Angeles, and then, finally, to Hawaii.[22]

The number of immigrants from the Chinese mainland had already been diminishing; those of Japanese ancestry were becoming more numerous. When Japan defeated Russia in the Russo-Japanese War, the anti-Japanese movement gained further traction. The California Legislature even sent a resolution to the White House, urging that Japanese immigration be curtailed. According to the legislation, no less than five hundred Japanese were returning from Hawaii each month. At the same time, the members of Japan's armed forces demobilized after the Russo-Japanese war were settling round the Pacific Rim in groups; their immigration to the American continent was inevitable. If that were to happen, the bill made explicit, California would be inundated in no time with groups of immoral low-wage laborers who would threaten the livelihoods of white laborers.

The next month, on April 18, 1906 to be precise, San Francisco was struck by the Great Earthquake. Over two hundred thousand people suffered directly from the calamity; among them some ten thousand of Japanese descent. When half the city's schools were lost to fire, city authorities used it as a pretext to refuse to permit Japanese to attend local public schools. President Theodore Roosevelt was able to persuade San Francisco to rescind its decision, but only at the cost of promising revisions to U.S. immigration laws.

Japanese were immigrating into California via Hawaii, Mexico, and Canada, so the key to reform was to ban this secondary immigration from those places. Immigration laws were revised in March 1907, but Japanese expulsionism increased unabated. Nothing could check its power. Pushed by popular opinion, President Roosevelt asked the Japanese government to cease issuing passports for the purpose of travel to the United States. Because the Japanese merely acceded to a request by the United States rather than concluding a new immigration treaty, this was called the "Gentleman's Agreement."

Hearst's newspapers, then in the process of being linked into a nationwide chain, mounted an anti-Japanese campaign, spreading their propaganda not just on the West Coast, but all across America. The *New York Herald Tribune*, for example, carried ominous words from Richmond Hobson, a U.S. congressman from Alabama, to the effect that he had recently seen an ultimatum sent by Japan.[23]

Hobson, now a retired navy captain, had seen action in the Spanish-American War. Indeed, his attempt to blockade the port of Santiago had made him so famous that hardly an American alive did not know his name. It was this fame that had gotten him elected to Congress. The blockade was his idea. The goal was to wrest local naval supremacy from the Spanish by blockading the entire Spanish expeditionary fleet in the Cuban port of Santiago. The Japanese blockade of the harbor of Port Arthur in the Russo-Japanese War had been the precedent: a successful effort to make such a strategy work. Hobson's plan called for sinking an aging collier in the narrow mouth of the harbor, thus sealing up the Spanish fleet inside. However, defensive fire from the enemy fleet was expected to be so intense that the crew manning the collier were unlikely to return alive. Eight men under Hobson's personal command attempted to carry out the mission. It was just the sort of Hollywood action-film scenario that Americans find so appealing.

As a naval strategist, Hobson's comments regarding Japan were highly influential. If there were war tomorrow, he said, Japan could easily destroy us in the Pacific. If they were so inclined, occupying the Philippines and Hawaii would be child's play for them. But this was not a matter of "if." Already, in the sugarcane fields of Hawaii, they await their chance.

Around that time, Nagai Kafū was living in New York. He keenly felt

the import of the campaign journalism of the day and reacted to it in his
Amerika Monogatari (Tale of America):

> Not long ago, when the issue of discrimination against Japanese school-
> children arose in California, there was much speculation in the press in
> New York and elsewhere in the country that Japan and the United States
> might go to war. Quite naturally, whenever those of us Japanese who
> were living in New York came together, the topic of conversation was
> very often developments on the Pacific Coast.[24]

Homer Lea, for his part, still cherishing his romantic dream of an expedition to China, sensitively registered the shift in public opinion. The
sleeping lion was forgotten, he lamented; now the buzz was all about the
rising sun.

Then he received a further blow, crushing one of his grandest schemes.
Something occurred that frustrated his dream of overthrowing the empress
dowager and establishing a modern constitutional monarchy. On November
14, 1908, the Guangxu Emperor, who was to rise to power on the shoulders
of Lea and Kang Yuwei, died suddenly at the young age of thirty-seven.
Since the Guangxu Emperor had not been ill, it was rumored that his death
was part of a plot by the empress dowager. And yet, the very next day, her
seventy-three-year-old life also suddenly came to an end.

The movement to modernize Qing China continued to make progress.
Japan's victory over Russia in the Russo-Japanese War strengthened those
in China who favored adopting a constitution. Japan's victory over Russia
was interpreted as the victory of constitutional politics over despotism. Even
the conservative empress dowager could not ignore this sentiment and had
announced broad plans for a constitution. And though the inauguration
of this system was put off until 1916, it was proclaimed that a constitution
would be issued and a national parliament convened.

Apart from the elimination of a key player, Lea's relationship with his
ally in the Reform Party, Kang Yuwei, grew more complicated. There are
indications that Kang was not scrupulous in some of his financial dealings,
to the point of apparently embezzling funds from the Imperial Chinese
Reform Association. "General Lea" was hard-pressed to rewrite his strategy.
Gradually, he grew estranged from Kang. In Kang's place emerged Sun Yat-
sen, who favored violent revolution rather than reform.

It was at this point that a work titled *BANZAI!* was published in New York, predicting a war between Japan and the United States. This served as a powerful stimulus to Lea's thinking. His own account of a hypothetical Japanese-American War, he thought, might attract just the right kind of attention.

CHAPTER FOUR

The Yellow Shadow
of a Stealthy Foe

As I begin this chapter, I have before me a book titled *BANZAI!* in English, which I acquired at a secondhand bookstore in Tokyo's Kanda district, famous as a center of book publishing and book selling. The middle of its front cover bears an impressed design made up of the petals of a sixteen-petaled chrysanthemum. The cover's red color was no doubt intended to evoke the Rising Sun.

Turning past the title page, one's eye is arrested by a handwritten name in faded sepia ink, written in English: "K. Tanaka," followed by (also in English) "January 1909, Washington, D.C."—evidently the date and place of purchase. One wonders who this K. Tanaka was who lived in the United States capital during this period.

More importantly, what is this book, which has taken as its title the Japanese word *banzai*? It's a strange book, indeed, especially considering the name of its putative author: "Parabellum," which can hardly be a person's real name. Its significance as a pen name, at least, is explained in the foreword. There it is stated that those who wish the Pacific Ocean to be indeed a "peaceful ocean" must not neglect armaments, and that the author thus believes, with Helmut Moltke, the father of the German military in the nineteenth century, in the old Latin proverb, *Si vis pacem, para bellum*, translated as, "If you wish for peace, prepare for war."[1] So the author's pen name itself conveys the message that peace comes through might.

Since the publication date is given as January 1909, K. Tanaka must have purchased it as soon as it hit the bookshelves. Who was he, and why did he buy this book? My search for an answer led me to examine the personnel records of the Japanese embassy in Washington for this period. An army lieutenant colonel named Tanaka Kunishige served as military attaché at the embassy; there were no other K. Tanakas. This must be the man.

Tanaka Kunishige's career trajectory followed an elite track. After graduating from the Imperial Japanese Army's Military Academy he served in the Sino-Japanese War. Then, after graduating the Army War College, he joined the Imperial Army General Staff. At the age of thirty-six he was assigned to the Japanese embassy in Washington as a military attaché. Returning to Japan, he served as a military aide at the office of the grand chamberlain. Next he was selected as a member of the Japanese delegations to the Versailles peace talks and the Washington Conference on the Limitation of Naval Armaments. The arc of his career proceeded smoothly, and he was promoted all the way to admiral.

While he served as embassy attaché in Washington, one of Tanaka's duties was to collect military intelligence. He could not fail to notice the popularity of an imaginary account of a future Japanese-American war. Neither must we. Therefore, it's time to explain the plot of *BANZAI!*

Chapter 1 begins abruptly with the exclamation of a Colonel Webster: "For God's sake, do leave me in peace with your damned yellow monkeys!"[2] This statement must have shocked Tanaka Kunishige and persuaded him that here was something he ought to pay attention to. The scene at the start of the book is set on an American military base in Manila; the conversation that takes place is held among a number of mid-ranking American military officers: colonels, commanders, and the like. The undersea cable between the Philippines and the United States has been severed; communications with headquarters have been cut off. Some suspect Japanese intrigue, but—

Before continuing with our plot outline, we must take a brief detour. I've just mentioned that an undersea cable had been cut. I was doubtful myself that one had actually been laid this early, but it turns out to be historically correct. England and America were joined by an undersea cable in 1858; the Pacific was traversed in 1902. These cables were for telegraphic communications, not telephony.

Realizing that the telegraph link has been lost, the American officers in the story now find that their Pacific Fleet, which should be in the seas nearby, has also vanished. A German steamer prepares to enter Manila harbor, and its captain confronts the American officers. It is he who is astonished. He cannot believe they do not realize their country has been at war with Japan for nearly a week. The Japanese military severed the undersea cables at the start of the war. The Americans stationed in Manila have had no information from the outside. They have been joking about the "damned yellow monkeys" without realizing that the allied fleets have been completely destroyed. Chapter 1 ends with the U.S. base in the Philippines as vulnerable as a candle in a storm.

The intention of Parabellum is cleverly worked into this opening scene. During a time of apparent peace and security, a stealthy enemy, unseen, sneaks in for a surprise attack. America had already fought England and Spain, but these wars with European nations were conducted on the basis of conventional rules of warfare. With this new enemy, such previous experience is of no help. The enemy will sidle up silently from behind—and suddenly there's a dagger at your throat. A scary foe, indeed.

The nightmare in Manila is repeated all across the American homeland itself. In New York, at the offices of a major metropolitan daily, a journalist works late on an article, ever mindful of his looming deadline.[3] On his desk, a telegram describing an attack by Japanese bandits on the Oregon train out west. The journalist's boss asks him to mention the increasing numbers of Japanese immigrants flowing across the Mexican and Canadian borders so as to encourage the authorities to take firm action to stop illegal refugees from entering the country. This news of Japanese rogues committing train robbery is well timed. The journalist sets to work, envisioning large headlines and a sensational impact: JAPANESE BANDITS—A DANGER NO LONGER CONFINED TO THE FRONTIER, BUT STALKING ABOUT IN THE HEART OF THE COUNTRY.

A staffer brings up a new batch of telegrams. The top one begins, "This morning at ten o'clock the station at Connell, Wash., was attacked by robbers, who—."

"Hm!" says the journalist. "There seems to be some connection here..." And he throws himself into his writing.

But the next telegram begins with a similar report from a different location, as does the next. Connecting the dots on a map produces a line cutting north–south through the state of Washington. An unprecedented set of simultaneous train robberies. Like the military officers in Manila, the newspaper journalist cannot grasp what is occurring. His "spirited article" closes "with a warning to the police in Washington and Oregon to put an end to this state of affairs as soon as possible." He merely chides the authorities for their lax law enforcement.

The next morning, the journalist is startled awake by the noisy ringing of his telephone. New telegrams have arrived, and his presence is urgently required at the office. His editor in chief's panic is apparent over the phone line, yet still the journalist grumbles, "There isn't any reason why [the editor] shouldn't go on with those old train-robbers."

Hastening to the office, he finds the editorial room in an uproar. The Canadian wire has reported an unidentified foreign naval squadron entering Puget Sound and heading for Seattle. Strange reports have been coming in one after another. Messages from San Francisco were held up; telegraph lines to Seattle, Tacoma, and Portland were definitely cut; word has come from Ogden, Utah, that no trains have arrived from the direction of San Francisco since Sunday noon. The journalist is suddenly struck by a realization. In a theatrical voice that surprises even himself, he turns to his editor and says, "I believe this means war!"

The editor scoffs, "We're not making war on Japan!"

To which the journalist replies, "But they're making war on us."

"Do you mean to imply that the Japanese are surprising us?" The editor stares at him. When the journalist replies affirmatively and defiantly, a reporter present interjects, "The Japanese fleet is lying off the Pacific Coast, there's no doubt about that."

The journalist then adds, "And, what's more, they're right in our country." He is now fitting the disparate pieces of information he has been receiving into his own hypothesis and is growing agitated. He realizes that the so-called bandits are in fact enemy Japanese troops.

His editor is equally appalled. "But if you really mean it . . . then it must be a gigantic plot."

And now a stenographer brings a fresh telegram from Denver that seems to confirm their worst fears:

According to uncertain dispatches, Sunday's attacks on trains were not made by gangs of robbers, but by detachments of Japanese troops, who have suddenly and in the most incomprehensible manner sprung up all over the country. Not only have single stations on the Union Pacific line been seized, but whole towns have been occupied by hostile regiments, the inhabitants having been taken so completely by surprise, that no resistance could be offered. The rumor of a battle between the Japanese ships and the coast defences at San Francisco has gained considerable currency. The concerted attacks on the various transcontinental lines have cut off the western states entirely from telegraphic communication and in addition interrupted all railway traffic.

The editor can only echo the journalist's realization of a few moments ago: "Gentlemen, I fear this means war." The journalist goes into his office and sits staring at his desk and gripping his pen, unable to write. He doodles and dawdles, gets up and locks the door, sits back down, and is consumed by a nightmarish reverie: "His thoughts flew to the far West, and everywhere he could see the eager, industrious Asiatics pouring like a yellow flood over his country."

Nowhere in *BANZAI!* is there mention of a Japanese declaration of war. The American people are suddenly enveloped in war. The Japanese are a strange, inscrutable race of invaders.

The author of this cautionary tale, Parabellum (Ferdinand Heinrich Grautoff), concentrates on describing the panic of the American populace, revealing implicitly and effectively the impact of the faceless Japanese soldiers.

When our author has brought the reader's terror to just the right pitch, he begins to pronounce upon the social ecology of this forbidding race known as the Japanese.

> In the heart of all, from the Tenno to the lowest rickshaw coolie, there exists a jealous national consciousness, as natural as the beating of the heart itself, which unites the forces of religion, of the political idea, and of intellectual culture into one indivisible element.[4]

The Westerner's view of Japan was thus delimited by the polar images of the mystical autocrat known as the Mikado and a quaint little conveyance drawn not even by a horse but by a man.

As long as they remain, quiet and inscrutable, in their island kingdom, the Japanese are nothing more than exotic playthings. But just as caged exotic animals may be thought lovable, the instant they are released they bare their true untamed ferocity.

In the same vein, Parabellum states that "when a citizen of Japan leaves his native land, he . . . can no more mix with members of another nation than a drop of oil can mix with water." This is unlike the European immigrants to America and elsewhere, who do indeed blend in. If the European immigrants think about their native country, they "sometimes retain a sentimental memory of their former home." However, "the Mongolian" is completely different. He is industrious, to be sure, but to what end is this industry is directed? His "whole energy, all his thoughts and endeavors, are directed toward the upholding of the national, intellectual, and religious unity of Japan. His country is his conscience, his faith, his deity."[5] And his attitude toward foreigners is one of stealth and secrecy. The modest bearing, the impassive countenance, conceal the dart tipped with the most frightful venom.

Let us move on to the conclusion of *BANZAI!* In Hawaii, six thousand immigrants of Japanese descent have risen in rebellion. Japan now controls that archipelago. And that's not all. The whole of the West Coast of the United States is now under Japanese control. Extending their superiority on the battlefield, the Japanese believe the time is right to secure their conquests by treaty. The terms are so humiliating that American public opinion boils over in indignation. These terms may be listed as follows:

- The states of Washington, Oregon, Nevada, and California are to become Japanese possessions, but at the same time continue as members of the Union.
- The above states are to have Japanese garrisons and to permit Japanese immigration.
- In the various state legislatures and in the municipal administration of the above states, half the members are to be Americans and half Japanese.
- Japan will relinquish all claim to further immigration of Japanese to the other states of the Union (contingent upon acceptance of the preceding terms).
- The United States is to pay Japan a war indemnity of two billion dollars, in installments, exclusive of the sums previously levied in the Pacific States.
- San Francisco is to be Japan's naval port on the Pacific Coast, and the navy yard and arsenals located there are to pass into the hands of the Japanese.
- The Philippines, Hawaii, and Guam are to be ceded to Japan.[6]

The American people are outraged. Their previously disunited, uncoordinated response now comes together under the slogan of overthrowing the detested "Japs." When their rage translates into mighty military assaults, the Japanese army is everywhere put to rout. And finally, on February 9 of the year 19–, the long-desired victory is achieved.

The novel concludes with the italicized exclamation: *"The yellow peril had been averted!"*

What is the significance of the date February 9? This tantalizing clue at the end of the novel stuck in my mind. The most significant date among American holidays is of course July 4, Independence Day. I knew George Washington's birthday was in February, so I looked it up, but it is observed on the third Monday of that month, so that does not apply either; nor does Lincoln's birthday, also in February but on the twelfth. Close, but no cigar. I broadened my parameters.

Aha! The answer eventually came from an unexpected source. Japan was considered a threat only after its defeat of Russia. And Japan's declaration of war on Russia was February 10, 1904; in America, it was still the ninth. This explains the mystery of the key phrase "yellow peril" rearing its head so surprisingly near the tail end of the narrative. The implication is that the Yellow Peril began when the yellow man first mounted a direct challenge to the white nations.

All this raises a new question: who is to fulfill the role of causing the demise of the Yellow Peril, ending the drama? This is what *BANZAI!* is all about.

This same topic is what propelled Homer Lea to the writing of *The Valor of Ignorance. BANZAI!* depicted the inscrutable Japanese with skillful brush strokes. No doubt if any Americans were to read this who were negligibly informed about Japan, they would be filled with dread of the Japanese. And in fact, even if one includes those on the West Coast brought into contact with poor people of Japanese descent, there was indeed a paucity of knowledge among Americans about Japan and the Japanese. For ignorant Americans such as these, *BANZAI!* must have had a shocking impact with its dramatic, realistic, novelistic special effects.

A novel has the potential to end in a somewhat abstract state of dread. *BANZAI!* does this, but it also partakes of genres in which aliens invade from an unfathomable outer space. What Homer Lea tried to do in *The Valor of Ignorance* was not to whip up the illusion of dread purely as an illusion, but instead to write in a more realistic style, persuasive even to hard-nosed practical types. He called himself "General." Even if this rank had been bestowed upon him merely by some exiled politician of the Qing China reform movement, he thought of himself as a military professional. He wanted to wield the authority of a war expert in order to convince readers of the possibility that Japan could invade the United States. He certainly attracted notice: a Japanese translation by Mochizuki Kotarō came out the very next year, under the title *Muchi no yūki* (a direct translation of the original title).

What does that original title, *The Valor of Ignorance*, mean? It is not immediately apparent. Fortunately, the author supplies an entry point.

> We now come to consider the American commonwealth towering as it does so mightily among nations that to those who compose it and are part of it it appears a pyramid amid the sand dunes of time. This national vanity is justifiable so long as the existence of the nation's vastness, its grandeur, and the part it has taken—as great as any other state's—as the evolution of human society continues. We only propose to examine the valor of that ignorance now endeavoring to destroy the true basis of national greatness and to replace it with a superstructure of papier-mâché, not unlike a Mardi-Gras creation, around whose gilded and painted exterior the nation is asked to dance in boastful arrogance, neither beholding nor caring at all for the sham of it nor its weakness.[7]

What then, does the phrase, "the valor of ignorance" mean? It refers to the recklessness of the American people as they charge straight into danger without knowing either their own weak points or the strengths of their enemy. Far from bravery, this is nothing more than blind conceit, the pride that goeth before a fall.

Lea's realism thus consists in trying, by closely reasoned argumentation, to warn his countrymen as to where the Japanese might invade and how they might prosecute the attack. In *BANZAI!*, the Japanese army initially disguises its invasion of America's West Coast in the form of numerous train robberies. In *The Valor of Ignorance*, Lea's flair for military analysis turns the discussion to more hard-nosed (if hypothetical) illustrations of military doctrine and tactics.

For example, in the case of a hypothetical assault on San Francisco by the Japanese army, Lea describes not a direct invasion of San Francisco harbor itself, but rather a pincer operation moving southward from Bodega Bay, and north from Monterey Bay. In the case of Los Angeles, they would not attack the port directly, but from adjacent areas. San Pedro Harbor to the south, though ineffectively fortified, would provide a narrow beachhead. But once Japan had seized Santa Monica Bay to the north, they would have acquired access to twenty miles of seaboard, placing their forces on the outskirts of Los Angeles.[8]

Lea's book even incorporated maps sketching out the likely military maneuvers. It gave readers a real feel for the way the Japanese military could encircle and besiege San Francisco and Los Angeles.

I believe that Lea had *BANZAI!* very much in mind. There was no place for him now in the Chinese Revolution, so he converted his dreams of glory to the great task of protecting the United States from invasion by Japan. *BANZAI!* was published in January 1909. By June, Lea had finished more than half the manuscript of *The Valor of Ignorance*. The argumentation of the text proper is buttressed by a dozen appended tables, the last of which is a statement of the exhaustive fieldwork Lea did for the book:

> The author spent nearly seven months exploring, from a military viewpoint, the San Jacinto, San Bernardino, San Gabriel, and Tehachapi mountains, the Mojave and its adjacent deserts, traversing between one and two thousand miles. The results are embodied in the text.[9]

One is inclined to say that Lea's work is more empirical than that of Parabellum. On the other hand, one wonders whether a person so afflicted with health problems and physical handicaps could really have traversed such distances as he claims. Whatever one's doubts, it must be acknowledged that in his hypotheses regarding enemy military actions, Lea did place a salutary emphasis on geographical conditions. In his study, "General Lea" was a one-man general staff, placing the utmost importance on situation maps as he played out mentally his imaginative simulations of war.

It was around this time that America displayed a strange increase in enthusiasm for war. William Randolph Hearst's reputed ability to start a war with the stroke of a pen was an important stimulus. And now the expression of this zeitgeist in accounts of imaginary future wars crossed back over the Atlantic to England. When H. G. Wells, already famous as the visionary author of *The Time Machine* (1895) and *The Invisible Man* (1897), contributed *The War in the Air* (1908), it confirmed and extended a boom in this genre of novel.

At the age of forty-two, Wells himself would not be satisfied with producing another futuristic novel. He began to incorporate elements of political and cultural criticism. In *The War in the Air*, he made Asia central to the story, though it had played no role in *The Time Machine* or *The Invisible Man*.

As an Englishman, Wells did not entertain the anti-Japanese sentiments so prevalent on the West Coast of the United States. And thus his focus was not restricted to a Japanese-American war: it considered a world war. The British Empire had been facing a nearly simultaneous outbreak of serious threats in addition to Japan, notably the Boxers, who caused such chaos in China, and the anti-British independence movement in India. As the curtain rose on a new century, it also announced the disintegration of the old order, the Pax Britannica.

Let us review Wells's plot. The time is the near future, the teens of the twentieth century. The hero is a young man who runs a bicycle rental and repair shop. Business is poor; the shop goes bankrupt. He becomes a street performer, but he fails at that too. Strolling dejectedly on the seashore, he sees a passenger balloon coming toward him. In it, he discovers certain design drawings. These drawings constitute detailed plans for a new type of aircraft, intended for military use. The balloon takes off with the protagonist in it. Eventually it alights unexpectedly in Germany. The protagonist hopes to garner a windfall of a different sort by selling the plans to the German government. Not only does he not manage to do that, he winds up in the middle of a war between Germany and America. His rather picaresque fate places him on board a German aerial warship, the flagship to a fleet of such vessels crossing over the Atlantic to launch an air assault upon America. The young man's own role in all of this is subsidiary yet indispensable, like one of those minor kabuki characters whose involvement is nonetheless essential to the advancement of the plot.

It is a German imperial prince who has schemed all this. A fanatical militarist, he is plotting to expand Germany's territory and to impose the German language upon all of Europe. Not even a trace now remains of the aegis of Pax Britannica, by which England had once ruled the world. England has its hands full suppressing the insurrections springing up one after another in its colonies all across the seven seas. America has occupied the Philippines, advancing into Asia, prompting Japan and Imperial China to form a defensive East Asian alliance. Japan-U.S. relations are in a perilous state over immigration issues. A world war looms.

Germany takes the initiative. Deploying an excellent attack air force, it destroys America's naval superiority in the Atlantic. The prince takes heart from this and leads an aerial bombardment of New York. Resistance by New Yorkers is futile, as is a counterattack by America's own air force. New York is reduced to rubble. Furthermore, the German air fleet openly reveals its ambition to control the entire country. They have crossed the Atlantic to attack the United States. But now their air force is threatened by a new enemy, which has crossed the Pacific. The combined military forces of the East Asian alliance devastate San Francisco and move eastward.

Finally there is a showdown between the eastward-moving East Asian armies and the German air force that annihilated New York. But whereas the German air armada draws on a worldwide fleet of some three hundred airships, the East Asians can draw on several thousand. Not only that, they have single-seater combat aircraft. If the larger airships can be thought of as giant flying nests, these one-man fighter planes are like an innumerable swarm of bats. To Westerners who despised the yellow man as incapable of original invention, this comes as quite a shock. It shakes their self-confidence. Like the German *drachenflieger* or power-glider aircraft, says Wells,

> It was built very lightly of steel and cane and chemical silk, with a transverse engine and a flapping side wing. The aeronaut carried a gun firing explosive bullets loaded with oxygen, and in addition, and true to the best tradition of Japan, a sword. The riders were Japanese, and it is characteristic that from the first it was contemplated that the aeronaut should be a swordsman. The wings of these fliers had bat-like hooks forward, by which they were to cling to their antagonist's gas-chambers while boarding him.[10]

So, civilized Westerners seem impressed by the idea that Japanese pilots would have to be swordsmen. In the face of the onslaught by this outstanding Sino-Japanese air fleet, a young German officer explains to the protagonist the dimensions of the developing world war:

> The Japanese and Chinese have joined in. That's the great fact. That's the supreme fact. They've pounced into our little quarrels. . . . The Yellow Peril was a peril after all! They've got thousands of airships. They're all over the world. We bombarded London and Paris, and the French and English have smashed up Berlin. And now Asia is at us all, and on the top of us all. . . . It's mania. China on the top. And they don't know where to stop. It's limitless. It's the last confusion.[11]

But hardly the end of the story. *The War in the Air* is rather ingeniously structured. Through the eyes of an ordinary Englishman we are shown the collapse of civilization, but the tone is not didactic. The young man proceeds by trial and error, but he also has his moments of triumph, and since the novel features an aerial war set in the near future, it has the intense technological appeal of science fiction. Moreover, it is based on a world-historical sense that envisioned a role for a new enemy, the Asians from an otherly world, with their distinctive groupist philosophies. And finally, the curtain closes on reflections, tinged with regret, regarding the course of Western civilization.

Let us continue, then, with our outline. The young protagonist escapes the battlefield where the German and East Asian forces are clashing, and by a circuitous journey searches out the American president, to whom he hopes to present the plans for the new military aircraft. The president, however, fearful of aerial bombardment, is difficult to find, concealed as he is in a subterranean bunker in an undisclosed location. But somehow the protagonist finds him and is able to turn over the plans. Through the president's good offices, the young man is able to return to England.

The England the protagonist returns to after a year's absence has been utterly destroyed by the world war. Economic activity has ceased, civilization has collapsed, the country has effectively reverted to the fifteenth century. People are reduced to livelihoods of self-sufficiency. Contagious diseases are spreading; looting is rampant. Young people attack the gangs and form vigilante groups, trying to restore public safety. Thus they become the heroes. But even with public safety restored, civilization remains destroyed and cannot be revived. *The War in the Air* may therefore be thought of as a pioneering work of pacifism. In this, it contrasts with both Parabellum's *BANZAI!* and Lea's *The Valor of Ignorance*, both of which deliberately emphasized the enemy's military capabilities, thus participating in campaigns to increase their own respective country's spending on military preparedness.

For President Theodore Roosevelt and the American military establishment, any journalism that whipped up war fever was entirely welcome. On December 16, 1907, the U.S. Atlantic Fleet set sail from its base at Hampton Roads, Virginia. Roosevelt addressed Congress. The Fleet is bound for the Pacific and for San Francisco, he said. And the Hearst newspapers crowed that the United States Navy had at last set sail for the Pacific to fight the Japanese.

A high-ranking U.S. naval official worried, rather stupidly, that the movement to the West Coast was leaving America's East Coast undefended. What if the Japanese fleet were to mount an attack from the Atlantic? It must be remembered that at this time the Panama Canal had not yet been opened. American naval defense was oriented toward Europe, and was thus concentrated on the East Coast. There was an Atlantic Fleet, but no Pacific Fleet. All America had available to protect the Philippine archipelago, which it had recently acquired in the Spanish-American War, was a small group of aging cruisers. So if the Atlantic Fleet moved into the Pacific, that did indeed leave the East Coast unguarded. And yet, not to respond to the new local preeminence of the Japanese navy, which had just defeated Russia's Baltic Fleet, would mean the collapse of the military balance of power in the Pacific. This was the insecurity that motivated the writers of works such as *BANZAI!* and *The Valor of Ignorance.*

The U.S. Atlantic Fleet had several goals. The first was to reassure the populations of San Francisco and Los Angeles. It was hoped that if it showed off the worldwide reach and power of a navy second only to England's, popular opinion would begin to support the view that the U.S. should pursue a policy of naval expansion.

Another goal was to dispatch an armada to just outside Tokyo Bay, in a show of force, a second coming of Black Ships designed to shock this new rising sun in the East. When the Atlantic Fleet left the East Coast, this plan was still secret, and unannounced by the government. But both objectives were in fact as obvious to the authors of the genre of future-war chronicles as they were to the Hearst-syndicate newspapers. In *BANZAI!*, the preface notes the author's motive for writing the book: to point out defects in the current national defense of the United States and to alert the citizenry; furthermore, to instill in them the spirit of true patriotism. In *The Valor of Ignorance*, a similar sentence warns that it is not patriotic to scorn other countries.

The U.S. Atlantic Fleet sailed south through the West Indies and down and around through the Straits of Magellan at the tip of South America, before heading north again. On March 11, 1908, the fleet put in to the port of Magdalena, Mexico. The destination was supposed to be San Francisco. But now, on the thirteenth of March, came a sudden announcement from the White House: the destination of the Atlantic Fleet was not San Francisco. This was to be a world cruise.

The Japanese government was shocked. The U.S. Atlantic Fleet comprised sixteen battleships. The flagship, the *Connecticut*, displaced 16,000 tons, as did the *Kansas*, the *Minnesota*, the *Vermont*, and the *Louisiana*. Five battleships were in the 15,000-ton class; six were in the 12,000-ton class.

It was a naval force more than double the size of Japan's Combined Fleet. The Japanese knew that yellow journalism had been inciting readers' fears that Japan planned to wage war on America, but could this dispatch of the Atlantic Fleet really be intended as a military response? Against this armada of sixteen Black Ships surging across the Pacific, Japan could deploy only seven battleships.

Japanese defense planners had to start with the fact that the U.S. Atlantic Fleet was twice the size of the Imperial Navy's Combined Fleet. If hostilities actually broke out, Japan's situation was hopeless. True, in the Russo-Japanese War, Russia's navy was also double the size of Japan's, but at the time, the Russian fleet was divided into a Far Eastern Fleet and a Baltic Fleet. First Japan pinned down Russia's Far Eastern (Pacific) Fleet at Port Arthur; then it engaged their Baltic Fleet, which had been obliged to steam all the way from Europe via the Atlantic and Indian Oceans. So, Japan battled Russia's two fleets in separate one-on-one engagements. If Japan had been forced to take on both of Russia's fleets at once, there is no doubt that Japan would have lost. Similarly, in the imaginary war described in Mizuno Hironori's *The Next Battle*, the American expeditionary force, split into two fleets, unleashes a combination one-two punch, ultimately annihilating Japan's Combined Fleet. If, in reality, America's Atlantic Fleet were to approach Japan, it would be a military threat comparable to the combined strength of Russia's Far Eastern and Baltic Fleets.

President Theodore Roosevelt had announced initially that in leaving the East Coast, the purpose of the Atlantic Fleet was to defend San Francisco Bay; Roosevelt did not hint at any other possible purpose for the redeployment. However, as the fleet approached America's West Coast, he announced abruptly that the mission was a round-the-world cruise. That was on March 13, 1908. Immediately, the Japanese government instructed its American ambassador, Takahira Kogorō, to issue an invitation to the Atlantic Fleet to visit Japan. It was now March 19, just six days after the fleet's departure. What expectations underlay this flurry of activity?

The Japanese Ministry of Foreign Affairs had already been analyzing unconfirmed reports from its embassies worldwide. The situation seemed to be developing in an unwelcome direction. Consider, for example, the telegram sent on January 5 by Kurino Shin'ichirō, ambassador to France: "French press saying Japan-America war inevitable. Japan bonds down sharply." On the same day, a dispatch came in from Inagaki Manjirō, Japan's ambassador to Spain. His report reflected conditions in a country that had recently lost a major conflict with the United States: "Local aristocrats and industrialists say if Japan goes to war with America, they will assist with war funds if requested."[12]

On February 15, Tanaka Tokichi, the Japanese consul in Seattle, sent in the following dispatch: "At Port Townsend, with its shore batteries, even when a person of Japanese ancestry merely wanted to lease land abutting the port, it became news. The suspicion was that there was a plan to seize the batteries in the event of a Japan-U.S. war."[13]

In the advanced Western nations, the fantasy of a Japan-U.S. war was clearly taking shape, acquiring its own reality. I call this the primary Japan-U.S. crisis. At the same time, Japanese public opinion displayed hardly any comparable anti-Western trends. Exhausted as the nation was by the Russo-Japanese war, it had no strength left for further conflict. The newspaper *Yorozu Chōhō* registered its surprise on January 20: "Reading the Western press, one realizes that the ordinary Westerner believes there will be a Japan-U.S. war, and that this trend is increasing remarkably."

Why did U.S.-Japan war fever grow so high in the West? The Japanese government's own attitude was relatively calm. It did not respond to the provocations of Western public opinion. The government seems to have wanted to simply ride out the storm.

So who was actually guilty of inciting war between Japan and the U.S.?

One set of culprits was comprised of writers and journalists, from press baron William Randolph Hearst to author Homer Lea. Their motivations varied. For Hearst, it was all about boosting circulation. Homer Lea was frustrated with the development of the Chinese Revolution and was also in communication with the formulators of War Plan Orange. The U.S. Navy wanted to cultivate public opinion in order to increase military budgets. All this harmonized with the president's ambition to establish a beachhead in Asia and was also part of the effort to reassure the populace on the West Coast.

What about Europe? The *Yorozu Chōhō* analysis on January 20 was that "with the Anglo-German commercial rivalry intensifying," and with "England the weaker," of the two, England had an ulterior motive in fomenting a U.S.-Japan war: namely, "to seize the opportunity to pick a fight with Germany." The English would engage in a strategic disruption of the budding friendship between Germany and the United States. It was also said at the time that Germany was the real locus of war-mongering rhetoric. Japan concluded commercial agreements with France in June 1907, with Russia in July, and with England in August. These agreements had as their background the then-current Anglo-Japanese and Franco-Russian alliances, which effectively encircled Germany. Thus isolated, Germany incited a Japanese-American war in hopes of securing America as an ally.

And what of America's intentions at the time? The evidence is scant. A biography of Theodore Roosevelt cites a revealing letter from the president to a friend. He believed, he wrote, that the likelihood that Japan was not plotting an attack was in the 90 percent range. But he could not dismiss the 10 percent chance that in fact there was a plot. If Roosevelt seriously believed in the prospect of an attack on the basis of one-in-ten odds, this is remarkable testimony. For the president to dispatch the entire Atlantic Fleet to the Pacific was quite a gamble for a leader to take.

Japan's policy of disarmament, deference, and friendliness was also something of a betting proposition. Reading Japanese news coverage one gets an impression of innocence so complete as to seem bizarre. As the American visit drew closer, the Japanese papers carried articles of welcome. They were full of language more or less along the lines of, "We Japanese welcome you Americans. We feel not the slightest bit hostile toward you. Do come and enjoy your holiday in Japan." If I were to use these articles for evidence, when asked, "What sort of people are the Japanese?" I would have to reply that they are a timid race, and a naïve one. Upon which my interlocutor would be bound to counter with the obvious follow-up, "What about World War II? Weren't they fierce and fearless then?" Perhaps both images are true, which will make this portrait of my country a bit more complex.

On October 18, 1906, the date the American fleet put in to Yokohama harbor, the *Asahi Shimbun* (Asahi Press) carried in Japanese a page two interview with Japanese statesman Ōkuma Shigenobu titled "My Views on the Coming of the American Fleet." His tone was one of admonishment toward the Japanese, as if he took the American side in the matter. He began by reviewing the initial encounters with Perry's Black Ships at the end of the Tokugawa regime, describing that event as one of great significance for Japan—a heaven-sent blessing.

The feudal system, with its rival domains, was incapable of securing a unified national policy. In the face of pressure from the outside, national unity was needed. That was when communication between the nation and the Emperor began to occur, and talk turned to the double slogan *sonnō-jōi*: Revere the Emperor, Expel the Barbarian.

Ōkuma's language may have been plain, but he was making an important point. He was saying the Black Ships had produced the Land of the Mikado. In other words, it was external pressure that gave rise to the emperor system. The slogan, "Revere the Emperor, Expel the Barbarian," referred to the centripetal principle by which the nation gathered around the emperor in order to strike back at the uncouth barbarians from foreign lands. Many fighters for the imperial cause believed in this slogan, and their discontent only deepened when the new Meiji government pursued policies not of expelling the barbarians but rather of opening the country. It was this discontent that gave rise to the Kumamoto Kamikaze League disturbances in 1876 and to the insurrection led by Saigo Takamori, resulting in the Seinan (West-South) Civil War the following year. Yet "expel the barbarian" did yield, little by little, to "open the country." And Ōkuma was saying that Japan was indebted to America for giving it the choice to open the country. As he put it,

> Perry's methods were prosecuted at a high level of skill; Consul Harris's subsequent negotiating tactics were also adroit. . . . The foreign military forces had not come to acquire other lands, nor to wage war. Rather, they were the agents of justice, peace, morality, and progress. As the logic of this gradually dawned on us, we turned our eyes, newly opened to the remarkable benefits of civilized progress, back on our own country, and we saw all the glaring defects in its unopened, primitive ways. We seemed to have become ashamed of everything Japanese. The "Expel the Barbarian" philosophy that flourished temporarily in these circumstances gradually subsided, then yielded to the sudden rise of an "Open the Country" philosophy. Finally, in 1871, this progressive "Open the Country" philosophy was adopted as national policy.

Ōkuma extended his "thanks to the Black Ships" theme even further:

> In any event, it was thus that Perry's squadron visited our ports, shattering our national stupor, and leaving his imprint on the subsequent fifty years of open-port history, a monumental achievement. This current visit by an American fleet should serve first and foremost to commemorate Perry and his squadron.

Their objectives have always been friendly. We have nothing to fear. As President Theodore Roosevelt stated in his official message, the current fleet is simply on maneuvers; they are calling on Japanese ports at the invitation of our own government. No need for alarm. Ōkuma goes on and on in this vein, and in his next passage there lurks an obsequiousness I find odd. Its very excessiveness suggests the potential for a complete reversal—a switch to contempt, hitherto latent, for the "brutish" Americans and British.

This great fleet from a friendly power, about to visit our shores, is not engaged simply in a naval exercise. Half a century ago, its predecessor came to Japan and planted a seed, a seed that was to lead to the flowering of modern civilization in our country. What, they wonder, is Japan like today? Confident though they be that the results are in fact splendid, it is to behold contemporary Japan with their own eyes, and to share with us their own joy in our achievements, that they have come. That is surely a large part of this voyage, as indeed I believe it ought to be. Half a century ago, our people were awakened by Admiral Perry from two-and-a-half centuries of slumber. Ever since, under our policy of opening the country and pursuing progress, our national prosperity has continued to break new ground, and to increase. It is up to us to show them how our current conditions now rank us among the great powers, and to accept their congratulations.

This new armada was dubbed the Great White Fleet, a nickname derived from the ceremonial white paint that coated the ships' hulls for this world cruise. Now Japan would distinguish between Perry's Black Ships and this new visitation by the White Ships.

Hidden behind Ōkuma's obsequiousness was the argument that America did in fact constitute a threat. Indeed, it was in the previous year of 1907 that the Imperial National Defense Policy first designated America Japan's number one hypothetical enemy.

The notion that the Black Ships brought civilization to Japan smacks of *a posteriori* reasoning. At the time, Japanese were simply shaken to the core. A half-century later, they again trembled at the White Ships, but the difference was that now the ones who were fearful were those in the government and the press who knew what the military matchup really was; whereas the general public, still flushed with Japan's triumph in the Russo-Japanese War, were beginning to feel confident in their strength as a nation.

In the United States, the rumors of an intended Japanese invasion spread ever wider. But in Japan, the port call by the White Ships was taken as an opportunity to launch a peace-and-friendship campaign. This, however, was a wolf-in-sheep's-clothing sort of affair.

For a fortnight prior to October 3, the anticipated date of the Atlantic Fleet's visit, the *Asahi Shimbun* ran a column headlined in Japanese, WELCOMING THE U.S. FLEET IN CONVERSATIONAL ENGLISH. It was a manual designed to help Japanese reliably guide visiting U.S. naval personnel around town: what to say, where to go, how to explain things Japanese. The first conversation takes place in Shimbashi Station in Tokyo, where an American serviceman is wandering about, unsure what to do. He is accosted by a Japanese. The conversation, as printed by the *Asahi* in English, goes as follows:

(1)
STUDENT VOLUNTEER: Good morning. You are from the American Fleet? Here is my card.
SAILOR: Yes. I am glad to see you.

(2)
STUDENT VOLUNTEER: Thank you. I have come to offer any assistance you may want of me.
SAILOR: You are very kind indeed.

(3)
STUDENT VOLUNTEER: You want to see the city, I suppose.
SAILOR: Yes. Can you come with me?

(4)
STUDENT VOLUNTEER: That is why I have come to you.
SAILOR: I shall be very glad to accept your kind service.

(5)
STUDENT VOLUNTEER: I am glad you accept my service, but please understand that I am not to be paid. You will please take me with you as a volunteer guide.
SAILOR: I feel embarrassed to take your time for nothing.

At this point, the Japanese student is obliged to declaim theatrically,

(6)

STUDENT VOLUNTEER: You know how glad we all are in welcoming you here. The whole city is of one mind in doing the best we can for you. We are determined to give you the warmest reception in our power. I am only contributing my humble effort for showing our friendly feeling to you.

SAILOR: I am really surprised to see you so earnest in helping me. I will accept your service as a very kind volunteer.

The kind Japanese student volunteer guides the American serviceman about town. When the subject of taking a *rikisha* to Shiba Park comes up, they decide to walk and talk. The student volunteer remarks, "I am a good walker and always walk when I have time. But please don't walk too fast. You see I am shorter than you are." To which the courteous sailor replies, "Very well. I will gladly adjust my steps to yours." The guidelines are constructed according to the principle, "Scratch them wherever they itch and can't reach themselves."

Prospective volunteers would read further that from Shimbashi one goes to Sakuradamon, then Ueno, then Asakusa. At Sakuradamon, tell them the story of the March 1860 assassination of the *tairō* (great elder) Ii Naosuke; add whatever background may be necessary about the political system of the Tokugawa period: say, "The shogun thus clothed with imperial authority was a perfect autocrat."

As they head back, the volunteer guide summons up the courage to make another proposal:

STUDENT VOLUNTEER: As we go back toward Shimbashi, I would recommend you to visit the Temple Sengakuji, which is between Shimbashi and Shinagawa.

SAILOR: What temple is it?

STUDENT VOLUNTEER: It is where the memories of the forty-seven rōnin are kept alive. There you will find the graves of those heroes. You know the history of those brave men?

SAILOR: Yes, I read of them some years ago with great admiration.

The student guide finally rounds off the discussion with a proud disquisition on the spirit of *bushidō*. The conduct of the forty-seven *rōnin* is still discussed today, an inspiration crossing the generations, etc.

Thus an attempt was made to popularize a rather odd strategy of welcome by means of collusion between the Japanese government and the press. But if you think about it, something strange was going on here. Check out the newspapers of the day, and you will find that all of them were plastered with images of the White Ships, regular editions and extras alike. And yet Japanese history books barely touch on the matter: Etō Jun, Hata Ikuhiko, and Ōe Shinobu are the only exceptions, and minor ones at that.[14] Any contemporary newspaper will do: pick an article, any article. All of them gave the White Ships a big welcome.

Where can one look for vestiges of Japan's previous experience with the Black Ships? Is it that instead of blustering about in a panic, Japanese now assumed an air of calmness and took the initiative in planning welcome ceremonies? Ultimately the resemblance with the Black Ships experience is that in their heart of hearts, there was unease.

Another contribution to the hoopla was the item the *Kokumin Shimbun* ran on October 18, 1908, the day the White Ships put in to the port of Yokohama: an "Ode: Welcoming the American Fleet"—in Japanese. There is no better way to convey the odd enthusiasm of this celebratory verse than to quote some of it, translated here from its pseudo-classical Japanese rhythms of five-syllable and seven-syllable lines into quatrains of more-or-less iambic pentameter:

> Pacific Ocean! Waters deep as night!
> Mount Fuji! Matchless are thy snows, so white
> In the radiance of the rising sun!
> Our friend's ships let us greet now, every one.

> Already fifty years have passed since these
> Friends first came, scolding us Japanese,
> Prodding each slumbering "I" to wake and see
> A wider world in which to act and be.

The White Ships are "our friends' ships"; it is noted that "already fifty years" have passed since the day those friends first arrived—the time of the Black Ships. And the poet gives earnest thanks that "each slumbering 'I'" was awakened. The next section of the poem continues in the same vein.

Encouraged by our friends to move and shake,
We joined the world's affairs enough to make
Our land of Rising Sun a cynosure.
Thanks, Friends, for your compassion true and pure.

Following this fulsome expression of gratitude, modest intimations of equality peek through.

In the shadow of the Sword itself lies Right.
And where Compassion? The warrior's heart, its site.
If friends be friends, yet each maintains warships,
Our Pacific will be calm, and these—Friend-Ships.

The sword of our Japan is not for show,
Nor quick to draw, as autumn waters flow.
A warrior knows a warrior's heart, indeed.
O, Friends! Know thou our hearts and minds, we plead!

The phrase "autumn waters" (*shūsui*) is now archaic. The "flow" of "autumn waters" constitutes a metaphor for clarity and purity, hence a flawlessly polished, sharp sword. This image occurred in once-common expressions such as "three feet of autumn water," meaning a long-sword. Kōtoku Shūsui (1871–1911), the socialist-anarchist executed for his peripheral involvement in the High Treason Incident of 1910, was born Kōtoku Denjirō—he changed the Denjirō to Shūsui because he liked the ring of it better. If one is alert to the nuances of the classical imagery, one can grasp his intentions. He seems to have thought of his dedicated self-sacrifice as a keen blade thrust into the government.

"The sword of our Japan is not for show." This I would interpret as a declaration of pride in Japan's Combined Fleet. And yet, one does not lightly draw and flourish the treasured heirloom sword: in the eyes of the samurai, this is a last resort. "A warrior knows a warrior's heart." Translation: "You Americans are warriors too. You must understand that discretion is the better part of valor."

Reading this carefully calibrated verse, it sounds as if it might work well set to music as a naval marching song. The lyricist was the well-known journalist Yamaji Aizan (1864–1917). But we must realize that the intended readership was not the Americans, to whom it was ostensibly addressed (though it was in Japanese). This was a message for the Japanese people.

Just as the *Asahi Shimbun* ran an editorial titled UERUKAMU (Welcome!) the *Miyako Shimbun* (Imperial Capital Press) ran banner headlines on page one proclaiming (in Japanese), AMERICAN FLEET: BANZAI! BANZAI! BAN-BANZAI! Going beyond this page-one attempt to curry favor with the Americans, we still find on page two a veritable sermon addressed to the Japanese people, urging that they take care not to give offense.

> You shopkeepers, you rickshaw pullers, you mischievous "Taros" and "Jiros": all of you, pay heed. So that the purity of our sentiments not be misunderstood, so that your own feelings not be hurt, adopt an attitude of prudence!

Corresponding to that, the *Kokumin Shimbun*, the newspaper that ran that "Ode: Welcoming the American Fleet" (October 20, 1908), added a special supplement festooned with the Stars and Stripes and with photographs of the Atlantic Fleet's commander in chief and ship captains. An editorial noted courteously, "That our Empire is all that it is today, we owe to, among other reasons, the ardent encouragement of America, her friendly admonishments, the amity of our association with her."

So the press at the time treated the White Ships with the greatest circumspection. But all these exhortations and encomiums were exercises in propaganda, and successful ones at that. They only make the underlying intent more obvious.

From the moment the White Ships docked at Yokohama on the morning of October 18, the public thronged the wharves. They first caught sight of the sixteen battleships offshore somewhat after eight o'clock in the morning. As the *Kokumin Shimbun* (Citizen's Press) described it, "Acres of waterfront were occupied by tens of thousands of people, standing even atop walls, atop houses. Men and women, jammed together without an inch between them, in rows two or three deep, were waiting, without moving, for as long as nine hours, from 5:00 AM till 2:00 PM." Those being "welcomed" in this manner must have found such a sight eerie. As the fleet dropped anchor offshore, the commander in chief, the captains, and other high-ranking officers boarded a launch and came ashore. The city of Yokohama had mobilized all of its elementary school students to greet them: the boys waving small American and Japanese flags, the girls carrying bouquets of chrysanthemums and crying, "Banzai! Banzai!" at the top of their lungs.

The next day, the delegation headed off for Tokyo aboard a railroad train. The platform at Shimbashi Station in Tokyo was practically overflowing with elementary school students: when the visitors' train arrived, they struck up a chorus of "The Stars and Stripes Forever." The leaders of the Atlantic Fleet were now swept up in a whirlwind of garden parties and banquets held by the government, financial circles, army and navy leaders, the mayor, academia, and various organizations. Day after day, the newspapers listed the details of these welcoming functions. Looking at their overcrowded schedule, one can only imagine how the visitors felt as they were dragged all over town.

Even their Japanese hosts seem to have realized that the reception was overblown. On October 25, when the Atlantic Fleet had safely left Yokohama harbor, the *Asahi Shimbun*, in an editorial titled FAREWELL TO THE WHITE SHIPS, worried "whether the guests of honor did not find their welcome somewhat oppressive." On the other hand, their faces "did not hint that they felt these favors misplaced. Cheerfully, they attended many receptions each day," and when all was done, the Japanese heaved a sigh of relief and summed up their sentiments as feelings of "profound thanks."

What I have described above is what one might call a "Great White Welcome" strategy pursued by the Japanese vis-à-vis the U.S. Atlantic Fleet. And I remarked that there was something strange about all this. What I mean by that is, why has our memory of the White Ships been so completely obliterated from the Japanese consciousness? Let me take another tack. From a different point of view as well, we shall see that the tumult over the White Ships really should not be ignored.

The commander in chief, ship captains, and other high-ranking officers did indeed receive invitations from the prime minister, the chairman of the chamber of commerce, the mayor, and so on. But how did the rest of the crew fare? What did the lower-ranking and noncommissioned officers do? What did the sailors do in Tokyo?

The *Asahi Shimbun* for October 5 estimated that "with that many sailors, if even half the fleet came ashore, it would mean at least five thousand men." If five thousand men landed, wouldn't every shop in the city sell out of all their goods? And where would they stay, the *Asahi* wondered. If the sailors slept three to a household, two thousand households could accommodate them, but wouldn't it be prudent to recruit, sooner rather than later, volunteer households throughout the Keihin (Tokyo-Yokohama) area? At least, if they were to stay at private homes, mutual understanding might thereby deepen, killing two birds with one stone.

As it turned out, there was no need to make arrangements for home stays. The sailors simply returned to their ships. Three thousand of them, though, were permitted to come ashore and go to Tokyo. Special trains were provided to take them from Yokohama to Tokyo's Shimbashi Station. There were so many of them they had to be conveyed in three trains, one thousand men to a train. From Shimbashi they marched through the center of the capital to the entrance of the Imperial Palace. After that, they were at liberty, and dispersed to see the sights at Asakusa and Ueno and other tourist spots. One sailor even asked a newspaper reporter, "Is Nikkō somewhere around here?"

Never before had as many as three thousand Westerners made an appearance all at once in downtown Tokyo. Certainly foreigners had become less unusual, but never had they piled into town en masse. We should bear in mind that this was an event without historical precedent in Japan. And thus I return to my question: why (and how) did this entire event disappear from Japan's memory?

Even as the U.S. Atlantic Fleet was being feted after its arrival in Yokohama, a small, unrelated torchlight procession was wending its way through Tokyo's Azabu and Toriizaka districts. It was part of the royal birthday ceremony celebrating the eleventh birthday of His Royal Highness Yi Un, Crown Prince of the Empire of Korea. Yi Un was studying in Japan at the time, but since he was a state hostage an imperial villa was provided for him in Toriizaka. Superficially, he was accorded the utmost courtesy. The event was attended by the crown prince of Japan (the future Taishō Emperor) and other members of the Japanese royal family, together with such dignitaries as Itō Hirobumi (1841–1909; one of the founders of Meiji Japan and at that time the resident general in Korea) and Nogi Maresuke (1849–1912; at the time, president of Gakushūin, the Peers' Academy). On the villa's broad grounds, moving pictures were shown, pigtailed Chinese magicians performed, and a naval band played. It was a scene of brilliant gaiety.

At the conclusion of these festivities, as planned, residents of Azabu and elementary schoolchildren from nearby marched in a torchlight parade to the gates of the imperial villa. The Japanese crown prince, Itō, and Nogi accompanied the young heir to Korea's Yi Dynasty to the foyer. There, standing by, were some three hundred people, who sang "Kimi ga Yo," flourished their torches, and shouted "Banzai!" (literally, "ten thousand years," the equivalent here of "Long life!") three times. At Shimbashi, Japanese school-children were made to sing "The Stars and Stripes Forever." Here, before the Korean crown prince, they sang the Japanese national anthem.

The newspapers, in the throes of White Ship fever, relegated accounts of this torchlight procession to obscure corners of their publications. Until Japan won the Russo-Japanese War, Russia had loomed large as the chief threat to Japan's security interests. The Korean peninsula functioned as a neutral zone, or buffer. Both Japan and Russia, therefore, had maneuvered to enlist Korea to their side.

When things were going Japan's way in the Russo-Japanese War, the Japa-nese military concluded the First Korean-Japanese Agreement, or convention, on August 22, 1904. This ensured that Korea would be obliged to accept Japanese or Japanese-nominated advisers in its government to administer matters of finance and foreign policy. With that, all matters relating to Korea's foreign affairs had to be determined on the basis of the consent of the Japanese government. Furthermore, on November 17, 1905, the Second Korean-Japanese Agreement was signed. This established the office of the Japanese resident general in Korea at Seoul (J. Keijō). Korean foreign affairs, finances, and domestic government fell under Japanese authority.

With the Korean peninsula effectively under Japanese control, King Kojong (J. Kōsō) tried to offer resistance. But in the face of the advancing Japanese army, he was powerless. The Japanese army penetrated even to the inner courtyard of the royal palace, lining up outside Kojong's very bedchamber and menacing him, rifles at the ready.

In 1907, Kojong was obliged to abdicate in favor of Crown Prince Sun-jong (J. Junsō). Then, in 1910, Japan formally annexed Korea. It is with these historical developments in mind that we must understand Yi Un's study-abroad sojourn in Tokyo as a hostage situation. One might say that it was Japan's fear of the Russian threat that fomented the tragedy of robbing another country of its sovereignty.

After its victory in the Russo-Japanese War, now it was Japan that fright-ened Russia. In 1907, Japan adopted an Imperial Defense Policy which, in accordance with initial proposals made by Yamagata Aritomo (1838–1922), designated Russia as Japan's chief hypothetical enemy. The navy, however, opposed this sole designation of Russia. Beginning, as they were, to be conscious of American naval power as a new threat, they succeeded in adding America as a hypothetical enemy.

One cannot identify any imperative logic connecting the annexation of Korea and the invasion of the Chinese mainland to war with America. The invasion of China did not necessitate a Japanese-American war. A Japanese-American war had already become a hypothetical possibility after the visit of the White Ships. However, while the Japanese annexation of Korea is noted as a "hard" historical fact, "soft" events that also contribute to forming the national consciousness, such as the White Ships, easily drop out of the historical record.

Two weeks after the departure from Yokohama of the White Ships that had caused such a nationwide sensation, Japan's Combined Fleet held large-scale exercises off the southeast tip of Kyushu. It split into three groups: Group one played the role of an American force occupying an island called Amami Ōshima. Groups two and three were tasked with evicting group one. Group two proceeded south from the Sasebo naval port through the Ōsumi Straits; group three started at Kure and passed through the Bungo Channel: they caught the hypothetical Americans in a pincer movement. It was a realistic simulated conflict, designed to practice maneuvers in relationship to enemy ships.

After giving the actual U.S. Atlantic Fleet such a tumultuous welcome, the Japanese saw them off and then did a 180-degree turn. The newspapers merely reported MEIJI EMPEROR TO KANSAI TO PRESIDE OVER FLEET WELCOME, and he did indeed greet Japan's Combined Fleet at Kobe harbor. The fact that they had just concluded a naval exercise that envisioned a Japanese-American war was entirely suppressed.

Gradually, secretly, preparations were made against America as a hypothetical enemy. Map maneuvers at the Naval Staff College in 1911 were predicated upon realistic assumptions, and their scenario was a revealing one.

After the start of hypothetical hostilities between Japan and the United States, Japan's Combined Fleet is concentrated at an island called Amami Ōshima, and the U.S. Atlantic Fleet sets forth from San Francisco. Before they arrive, Japan attacks the Philippines. The beachheads are at Lingayen and San Fernando—exactly what occurred in the Second World War, thirty years later. The American fleet passes through Hawaii and Guam to get to the Philippines. The battle is thus joined further north in the Pacific, off Okinawa. And the result: no victory.

In other words, according to the outcome of this exercise, Japan was defeated. Naval Command reported this to the army's General Staff office in the summer of 1911. The report, preserved among other army General

Staff office documents, is dated August 15, the date of Japan's later unconditional surrender in the real war.

There is a strong resemblance between the way this map-based simulation progressed and Mizuno Hironori's imagined war in *The Next Battle*. Since Mizuno began writing his imaginary account in the following year, it is safe to say that he was influenced by the navy's map maneuvers. One even recalls that in Mizuno's imagined war, Japan's Combined Fleet was destroyed off Okinawa in "the middle of August."[15]

One wonders, however, whence this notion came that Japan would not attack America directly, but instead take the initiative by attacking the Philippines? I would place great emphasis on the fact that toward the end of the previous year, while the map exercise was being conducted, Homer Lea's *The Valor of Ignorance* had been translated secretly and was being read in military circles in Japan.

CHAPTER FIVE

Peace: Beauty
or Beast?

HOMER LEA'S *The Valor of Ignorance* was published in the United States
toward the end of 1909. In Japan, it was translated exactly a year later,
in December of 1910, and bound into book form the following February, as
an internal military document not intended for civilian consumption.

The title page carried a notice from the army ministry's secretariat: "Un-
authorized translation: access restricted." The army minister at the time was
Terauchi Masatake (1852–1919), who came from the Chōshū area and had the
backing of the much-decorated Yamagata Aritomo, one of the inner circle of
senior Meiji leaders. Sole credit for the translation was given to Mochizuki
Kotarō (1866–1927) from Yamanashi Prefecture, a man with only a tenuous
relationship to former domain political affiliations. After graduating from
Keiō Academy (the future Keiō University), Mochizuki fell under the pa-
tronage of Yamagata Aritomo and was sent to study in England. When he
returned, he worked as Yamagata's aide, advising him on foreign affairs. At
the same time, he entered the Rikken Seiyūkai (Friends of Constitutional
Government Party), a political party created by Yamagata's fellow Chōshū
clansman Itō Hirobumi, and won election to the Diet as a Lower House
Representative from Yamanashi Prefecture. Given his expertise in foreign
affairs and his direct access to the core of the government, Mochizuki was
the perfect choice for translator of secret documents.

Since this Japanese translation was not intended as a commercial publication but rather as a historical resource for Japan's military, there was no real
need to provide a special title. Mochizuki apparently thought otherwise.
Alongside *Muchi no yūki*, a literal rendering of *The Valor of Ignorance*, he
added a second title, to which he gave priority, *Nichibei hissen ron*, or *On*

the Inevitability of a Japan-U.S. War. Mochizuki explains his choice in a foreword to the Japanese translation:

> The original title of this book is *The Valor of Ignorance*. Its purpose is to illuminate the inevitable future clash between Japan and America. To suggest the book's objective at a glance, I have therefore altered the title to *On the Inevitability of a Japan-U.S. War*.[1]

However, what really attracted my attention on examining this foreword was not so much this explanation of the title but the bizarre urgency communicated in the sentence that followed it:

> I began this draft on December 6 and finished on December 30. To my deep regret, in such a short period of time I was unable to reproduce the gracefulness of the original.

The translator pleads that we excuse the roughness of the translation he has had to produce in just three weeks' time. What exactly was the hurry?

The date on the foreword is December 31, 1910. So Mochizuki wrote the foreword in great haste on New Year's Eve, just one day after he finished the translation. There must have been some reason for rushing the job to completion before the end of the year, some serious purpose for which this Japanese translation of *The Valor of Ignorance* was necessary. Since one can very well imagine that it had something to do with a political agenda, I looked through a chronology of the period to see if that would suggest a likely candidate.

The year 1911 opens with a decision in Kōtoku Shūsui's trial in the High Treason Incident.

On January 18, Kōtoku and twenty-three other defendants in the High Treason Incident are sentenced to death by the Great Court of Cassation[2] (*Daishin'in*). On January 24, Kōtoku and ten others are executed. On the following day, Kanno Suga is executed; the others' sentences are commuted to lifetime imprisonment. This High Treason Incident, which shook the Meiji political establishment, is now thought of in Japan as having been resolved politically, redolent more of a show trial than a true judicial proceeding.

So, it seemed likely that something connected Kōtoku Shūsui, and his rejection of the Mikado, with Homer Lea and the ominous shadow of the Black Ships. But I could not see what common thread tied them together.

However, as I kept flipping through the pages of Japanese chronologies, I found recorded a rather extraordinary event:

On February 21, the new U.S.-Japan Treaty of Commerce and Navigation, together with an attached Protocol, was signed. This established Japan's autonomous control over its own customs tariffs. After half a century, the U.S.-Japan Treaty of Amity and Commerce concluded in 1858 between the Tokugawa Bakufu (or Shogunate) and the U.S. consul general, Townsend Harris, had now been thoroughly revised.

In a series of agreements with the United States and other foreign powers called the Ansei Treaties, the Tokugawa government had relinquished tariff autonomy and acknowledged extraterritoriality. These became known as the Unequal Treaties. Under the provisions for extraterritoriality, even if a foreigner broke a law in Japan, he or she could not be held accountable for it under Japanese law. Tariff autonomy refers to the independent authority of a government to set its own customs rates.

The Unequal Treaties did not provide for colonies as such, but they did create an ongoing situation that emasculated the nation's sovereignty. The Meiji government had to make the most excruciating of efforts to undo the humiliating international obligations entered into by the Tokugawa Shogunate. For example, even the nightly costume balls at the famed Rokumeikan had as their real objective the revision of the Unequal Treaties: they were public relations activities, designed to show off the extent to which Japanese were embracing Western culture. But numerous attempts to secure actual treaty negotiations failed.

In 1899, the extraterritoriality issue was resolved. Tariff autonomy was partially restored, but in many categories, lopsided duties still remained. Without the ability to set tariffs, industries that were not competitive with foreign industries would simply be crushed. What's more, there was the matter of revenue to the state. Exhausted by the Russo-Japanese War, Japan's finances were in chronic deficit. They needed those customs revenues.

It should be noted in passing that before tariff autonomy was completely recovered, customs revenues accounted for 5 percent of all state revenues. As soon as the Unequal Treaties were abolished, customs revenues jumped to 10 percent.

What I found so extraordinary about this was that the Unequal Treaties were not completely revised until the end of the Meiji period. It means that in spite of Japan's victory in the Russo-Japanese War, the great Western powers did not think of Japan as a full-fledged nation but discriminated against it. Japan, for its part, entertained no reservations about impos- ing similarly unequal treaties on the Chinese mainland or on the Korean peninsula, thinking it entirely proper to apply the same strong-arm tactics as the West.

The reason for translating *The Valor of Ignorance* in that busy period at the end of the year 1910 seems to have been related to the fact that nego- tiations for the restoration of tariff autonomy were just then coming to a head. But what exactly is the connection between *The Valor of Ignorance* and the issue of tariff autonomy?

The treaty about to be concluded was called the new U.S.-Japan Treaty of Commerce and Navigation. As I pondered the treaty's content, the mystery as to why the Japanese felt it so necessary to read *The Valor of Ignorance* was entirely dispelled.

Article 1 of the new treaty was not about tariff autonomy. Instead, it covered an issue that the Japanese and American governments thought required more immediate resolution. The issue? Japanese immigrants in the United States. The treaty stipulated that

> the citizens or subjects of each of the High Contracting Parties shall have liberty to enter, travel and reside in the territories of the other to carry on trade, wholesale and retail, to own or lease and occupy houses, manufactories, warehouses and shops, to employ agents of their choice, to lease land for residential and commercial purposes. . . .[3]

In short, Japanese and Americans had the mutual right to live and con- duct business in each other's country.

Note the language carefully. Whether for residential or commercial purposes, foreign individuals may "own or lease" buildings, but they may only "lease" land. Land ownership is not mentioned. I have stated above more than once that the anti-Japanese movement was heating up on the West Coast. This treaty language represents a subtle interweaving of that exclusionary anti-Japanese theme with the emerging sense of Japan itself as a security threat.

On January 5, just after the completion of the Japanese translation of *The Valor of Ignorance*, a bill to prohibit Japanese from owning land was introduced in the California State Senate. Japan's Ministry of Foreign Affairs was sensitive to such actions and was well aware of what was taking place in the state at the time. On November 23 of the previous year, just before

Mochizuki undertook his translation task, foreign minister Komura Jutarō had sent a secret cable to Nagai Matsuzō, Japan's deputy consul general in San Francisco. The cable noted that the pending legislation clearly targeted Japanese immigrants and that given the imminent conclusion of the new Treaty of Commerce and Navigation, Komura was not to be remiss in reporting such matters to Tokyo.

The Valor of Ignorance suggests that Japan could attack at any moment. Did this not strike fear in the hearts of Americans on the West Coast and fan the flames of the anti-Japanese exclusion movement? Lea's book repeated the inflammatory suggestion that ethnic Japanese in the United States would rise up and join such an attack from Japan.

Reports on the state of the anti-Japanese movement came in, one after another, from the Japanese consuls at San Francisco and Los Angeles. This effort in 1911 was the third year for a bill banning land ownership by Japanese to be introduced to the state legislature, following earlier attempts in 1907 and 1909. The legislation specified only those of foreign nationality. The then-current naturalization law had been drawn up in the aftermath of the Civil War, and apart from whites had concerned itself only with the descendants of other Americans, meaning blacks. Asians were not even considered.

With no legal procedures in place for ethnic Japanese to be naturalized as U.S. citizens, they were not "Japanese Americans" but Japanese wage-earners temporarily residing in America. Legal measures banning "foreigners" from owning land were thus, in reality, aimed at excluding Japanese from American society. The reasoning was devious but effective.

Not that impediments were absent on the Japanese side. Applying for naturalization in a foreign country was considered to be a renunciation of one's loyalty to the Meiji Emperor. Therefore, most Japanese hesitated to take such a step. While they hesitated, their allegiance was still directed to the Meiji Emperor, and they did not assimilate to the norms of an American society that espoused the principles of liberty and democracy. So, there were reasons for Americans to resent their Japanese compatriots.

One thesis expounded at some length in *The Valor of Ignorance* was precisely this loyalty-security threat posed by Japanese. There is no conception of Japanese as Japanese Americans. They were just Japanese, on the lookout for American soft spots into which the Imperial Japanese Army could sink its teeth. No need to hand over our land to potential invaders. This was the course into which U.S. public opinion was being directed.

The first two times Alien Land Laws went before the California State Legislature to be voted on, they failed, largely due to the opposition of President Theodore Roosevelt. Backers were hoping third try, lucky, and their time was drawing near. And the negotiations for the final revision of the Unequal Treaties were occurring at this critical juncture.

The new U.S.-Japan Treaty of Commerce and Navigation was successfully concluded. Japan's tariff autonomy was restored. But Article 1, as mentioned above, dealt only indirectly with the problem of Japanese immigration. In exchange for securing tariff autonomy, resolution of the immigration issue was effectively postponed. Or rather, Japanese had no choice but to swallow the American insistence on doing so. Critics of Article 1 pointed out that the treaty thus set a precedent for restrictions on immigration. A typical example is Ōkuma Shigenobu's comment on the subject:

> Not only is there no disposition of the issue of immigration restrictions, there is also no disposition of the matter of naturalization rights. They pay lip service to the idea of an equal treaty, but this is no equal treaty. [As Asians,] we are treated as if we rank lower, and are unworthy of naturalization. It is just as if we were slaves.[4]

The passage of the new U.S.-Japan Treaty of Commerce and Navigation did kill for a third time the Alien Land Law pending before the California State Legislature. However, the immigration issue as such was merely repressed and postponed. In 1913, the legislation came up in California for a fourth time, and this time it passed. This was the Webb-Heney Act, more generally known as the Alien Land Law of 1913, notorious for being an explictly anti-Japanese measure. The Japanese government protested, but the Americans retorted that while they sincerely regretted it, it did not conflict with the Commerce and Navigation treaty, so there was nothing the federal government could do about it. Japanese public opinion boiled over, with public calls to attack the American embassy.

It was in such heated circumstances that a book titled (in Japanese) *The Outbreak of the Japan-U.S. War: A Dream Tale* appeared in 1913. (Note that Mizuno Hironori's *The Next Battle* did not appear until the following year). The author of record was not an individual but an association: the People's Committee for Military Affairs. It is an emotional work, reminiscent of the tracts that appeared just prior to the Second World War.

> With regard to gold and machinery, Americans certainly have no worries. And truly, in those two respects Japan cannot hold a candle to America. But in Japan, there is something that can more than compensate for shortcomings in wealth and machinery. What is this "something"? There is no question about it: it is *Yamato damashi*.[5]

Yamato damashi, the Japanese soul or fighting spirit, was revived, as in days of yore. Compensating for a lack of material wealth with spiritual virtue was actively cultivated in Japan in the teens of the Shōwa Era (the late 1930s and early 1940s). However, we see that the modern roots of this disposition can be traced back to the teens of the twentieth century.

Considered as briefing material for the process of revising the Unequal Treaties, the translation of *The Valor of Ignorance* stimulated the navy's map-war gaming and also provided an opportunity for fanning the flames of U.S.-Japan war fever in the country at large. Half a year after Mochizuki's secret translation for the government, another translation, by Ike Kōkichi, was marketed commercially under the title *Nichibei sensō* (The Japan-U.S. War). This was a somewhat slipshod effort, in which the text was altered at the convenience of translator and publisher and littered with such terms as *Yamato damashi* and *bushidō*. One imagines it was this translation that mutated into *The Outbreak of the Japan-U.S. War: A Dream Tale*.

The Valor of Ignorance had fueled anti-Japanese exclusionism in the United States. But its author, Homer Lea, died in 1912, ignorant of the reaction his book was to provoke in Japan.

✳ ✳ ✳

IT WAS MISHIMA YUKIO who said, "There is a strange beauty in war," but how well do you know William Shakespeare's *Richard III*? The protagonist, Richard, Duke of Gloucester (later King Richard III), curses peace with a vengeance. Thanks to "dissembling nature," he has been "cheated of feature": born with a twisted spine and deformed limbs. His excellent talents find employment enough during national emergencies, but when the fighting is done he has too much time on his hands. Not only that. In times of peace he has no choice but to subject his deformities to scrutiny, though he is assuredly "not made to court an amorous looking-glass," nor to play the carefree lover. He therefore hates peace and seeks "to set my brother Clarence and the King / In deadly hate, the one against the other" and to seize the throne himself. The play in fact opens with Richard's famous monologue, explaining this:

> Now is the winter of our discontent
> Made glorious summer by this son of York;
> And all the clouds that lour'd upon our house
> In the deep bosom of the ocean buried.
> . . . .
> And now, instead of mounting barded steeds
> To fright the souls of fearful adversaries,
> He capers nimbly in a lady's chamber
> To the lascivious pleasing of a lute.
> But I, that am not shaped for sportive tricks,
> Nor made to court an amorous looking-glass;
> I, that am rudely stamp'd, and want love's majesty
> To strut before a wanton ambling nymph;
> I, that am curtailed of fair proportion,
> Cheated of feature by dissembling nature,
> Deformed, unfinish'd, sent before my time
> Into this breathing world, scarce half made up,
> And that so lamely and unfashionable
> That dogs bark at me as I halt by them;
> Why, I, in this weak piping time of peace,
> Have no delight to pass away the time,
> Unless to spy my shadow in the sun
> And descant on mine own deformity:
> And therefore, since I cannot prove a lover,
> To entertain these fair well-spoken days,
> I am determined to prove a villain
> And hate the idle pleasures of these days.
> (I.i.1–5, 11–32)

As I have suggested several times already, Mizuno Hironori's *The Next Battle*, which portrays a projected U.S.-Japan war from the Japanese point of view, was engendered by Homer Lea's *The Valor of Ignorance*. Both men, Mizuno and Lea, were misfits in their own societies. And each man, once in his life, had a brief personal encounter with a different culture on an unfamiliar continent. Apart from that, they had no commonalities—except, one day, a common theme with a shared dilemma. We could dismiss this as coincidence and ignore it. But permit me to indulge myself in contemplating the mystery of how these two men shared the same theme in the same time period.

In chapter 1 of this book, I selected several episodes of Mizuno's boyhood as a foster child and tried to bring out certain particulars of environment and character. If he was a bit rebellious, well, who would not be, placed like that in another family from a young age? However, in Mizuno's case, it is also true that his contrary character was not to be pacified by a mere change of environment. It was a rebelliousness of spirit that seemed to be seeking some larger object to which it could bend its fierce strength.

What of Homer Lea? He, too, was propelled by a desire that burned him up inside, to engage the extraordinary in the form of martial matters and war. Hence the quotation from Shakespeare's *Richard III*, introduced somewhat abruptly above—I wanted to focus on the psychological motif of the preternaturally gifted troublemaker or agitator. Lea developed from a leader in children's war games to an outstanding agitator for war. There was even a physical resemblance to Richard III in Lea's physical deformities. The American was a mere 150 centimeters tall, and the curvature of his spine was so pronounced that his arms seemed to project too far from his cramped body.[6] Richard III does not hate the world because of his handicaps and thus resolve to play the part of a villain. On the contrary, as Charles Lamb noted of him, the confidence he has in his own abilities lets him regard the form he sees in the mirror with equanimity.

Similarly, Homer Lea loathed the way people devour pleasure during peacetime, like maggots fattening at leisure. He hated peace more than he hated his own appearance. He had no complex about his body. His genius bloomed regardless, mediating any physical distinctions. To live a more self-fulfilled life, such a free spirit begins by arranging his environment more suitably. The ability to do so is not ambition but genius. Perhaps one may call it a genius associated with a magical power. And if this mindscape were translated into dramatic lines, it would become the long opening monologue of *Richard III*.

There is no question that the writing of Homer Lea's *The Valor of Ignorance* took place against a backdrop of mounting war fever and attendant incidents such as the visit to Japan by America's White Ships. However, discussing those circumstances alone cannot explain the birth of *The Valor of Ignorance*. That is because peace, for Lea, was merely a measure of rest in the midst of the long and violent symphony of war. Or, to put it another way, peace was not a natural and eternal condition, punctuated by warfare, but rather was itself merely a ceasefire between wars.

The Valor of Ignorance was written to justify Lea's own destiny. His hatred of peace is incorporated in the very logic of his argument:

> The beginnings of political life are not hidden absolutely from us, and though there is no exactitude in our knowledge, we are nevertheless cognizant of the fact that at one time, when primitive man lived in continuous, individual strife, there occurred, somewhere in the somber solitudes of a preglacial forest, what has proven to be to mankind a momentous combat. It was when the brawniest Paleolithic man had killed or subdued all those who fought and roamed in his immediate thickets that he established the beginning of man's domination over man, and with it the beginnings of social order and its intervals of peace. When the last blow of his crude axe had fallen and he saw about him the dead and submissive, he beheld the first nation; in himself, the first monarch; in his stone axe, the first law, and by means of it the primitive process by which, through all succeeding ages, nations were to be created or destroyed.[7]

Lea also reflects on American history, noting that the United States had gained a place among the great powers by subjugating the native peoples they called the Indians, by launching and winning a war of independence against their own mother country of Great Britain, by dominating neighboring countries, and by driving out Spanish influence from—and gaining control over—Hawaii, the Philippines, Guam, and Cuba. However, he argues,

> This country, as others that have gone before, has been built up from the spoils of combat and the conquest of defenseless tribes. . . . But its conquests have been over nations and aborigines so disproportionately weak and incapable of waging war on a basis of equality that its wars have been destructive rather than inculcative of equitable military conceptions. The very ease with which this commonwealth has expanded is responsible for the erroneous beliefs now prevalent concerning the true basis of its future greatness.[8]

And that's not all. Americans, he says, have turned to commercialism and lost their patriotism. They think only of making money, and that is not how it should be.

Industrialism is only a means to an end and not an end in itself. . . . Never can industrialism, without national destruction, be taken from this subordinate place. When a man has no aspirations, no object to attain during life, but simply lives to eat, he excites our loathing and contempt. So when a country makes industrialism the end it becomes a glutton among nations, vulgar, swinish, arrogant, whose kingdom lasts proportionately no longer than life remains to the swine among men. It is this purposeless gluttony, the outgrowth of national industry, that is commercialism.[9]

Intoning peace, Americans will become as fatted hogs.

Lea's sentiments are quite similar to the manifesto disseminated by Mishima Yukio years later, immediately prior to his self-inflicted demise:

We have seen how postwar Japan has grown besotted with economic prosperity, in the process forgetting our core values as a nation, losing our spirit as a people, focusing on details even as we neglect fundamentals, falling into expediency, hypocrisy, and spiritual emptiness.[10]

There would indeed appear to be common ground between Lea and Mishima, but for now I should like to turn to the American economic prosperity criticized by Homer Lea.

A decade after the Spanish-American War, in which Lea had hoped and failed to participate personally, America had entered a period of burgeoning capitalism, conveying the premonition that this new twentieth century was to be an American century. In the 1890s, national income per capita was $117; a decade later, it was $197, almost a 70 percent increase. Urbanization was proceeding apace; it was the birth of the mass consumer society. Henry Ford established his motorcar company in 1903. In 1902, Victor Records was still posting a mere million dollars a year in sales, but with the proliferation of its home gramophones, gross sales for 1907 reached nearly $8 million. The first movie theater, the famed Nickelodeon, debuted in 1905; by 1910 there were ten thousand of them all across America. And *The Valor of Ignorance* was published toward the end of 1909.

Through personal connections, Homer Lea asked Theodore Roosevelt, who had just retired from the presidency, to write a preface. It was a ploy typical of the celebrity-worshipping Lea, but it failed. It was perhaps in retaliation that Lea dedicated the book to the Hon. Elihu Root, the former secretary of state. The preface was finally written by Lieutenant General Chaffee, whose name came up earlier as one of the formulators of War Plan Orange. His introduction was laudatory: he proclaimed the book to be essential reading for any student of warfare or of American history.

If you flip open the gold-colored cover of *The Valor of Ignorance*, you'll find, prominently displayed before the preface, the photograph of a man in a Chinese military uniform. This man is Homer Lea. A young man with a boyish visage, he still has baby fat. The mouth is firmly closed, the eyes brim with a mysterious light. He seems to be smiling, and yet there is also a suggestion of disrespect for others, even arrogance. Bushy eyebrows; hair parted on the side (the forty/sixty split). His uniform is that of a general, with gold epaulets and a brave array of chest medals. It is the portrait of a man who blends truth and falsehood.

But now I must fast-forward to a scene some thirty years later: October 1941. A female playwright and reporter is on assignment at the U.S. military base in Manila. Her name is Clare Boothe (1903–1987). The commanding general of U.S. armed forces in the Far East, based in the Philippines, is Lieutenant General Douglas MacArthur. Boothe mingles with the hardened military men at the officers' club, sharing meals with them and asking when they expect to fight a war with Japan. And she has left us an account of the conversation.

"If it comes, where will they strike first?" I asked.

The reply came from Colonel Charles Willoughby, who after the war went to Japan on MacArthur's staff and became known as a conservative in matters of occupation policy.

Colonel Charles Willoughby drew a deft map of Luzon on the Major's tablecloth. "The main attacks will probably come here, at Lingayen Gulf," he said, making an arrow, "and then here—at Polillo Bight. Ye olde pincer movement."

It was the rainy season in Manila, and the rain beat a tattoo on the mess hall roof.

"You're not giving away military secrets?"

The officers all laughed. Colonel Willoughby pocketed his pencil. "No," he said. "Just quoting military gospel—according to Homer Lea."

"Who is Homer Lea?"

"Tell you a funny story," the Colonel said. . . ."Thirty-five years ago, a strange young man who called himself 'General' Homer Lea, wrote a book about a war to come between America and Japan. In it he described, in minutest details, the Jap campaigns against the Philippines, Hawaii, Alaska, and California."

"A sort of American Nostradamus?"

The Colonel said, "Not at all. Homer Lea was neither a mystic nor a prophet. He was a scientist. He studied the science of war—the fundamental laws of which are as immutable as those of any other science. He also sought to analyze the causes of war and diagnose the symptoms of an approaching conflict."

At this point the major, seated at the same table, said,

I read him at West Point. Damned convincing militarily—if you accepted his political premise—that our democracy wouldn't get ready in time to lick the Japs.[11]

When Boothe returned to the United States after her journalistic tour of duty, she found waiting for her the shocking news that Japan had launched a sneak attack on Pearl Harbor and was now in the process of invading the Philippines. What's more, they had gone ashore at the Gulf of Lingayen, exactly as Homer Lea had predicted. Immediately, Boothe went to the New York City Public Library. The gold cover of *The Valor of Ignorance* had lost its luster to an accumulation of dust, but when she opened the book she found it unsullied by use. Looking at the withdrawal card, she noticed that it had been borrowed only three times since its 1909 publication. And her attention was arrested, as mine had been, by Lea's photograph. She wondered who and what this man was.

Boothe embarked on research, but it was hardly smooth sailing. She visited Lea's friends and acquaintances, she sorted through stacks of old newspapers. The following year, she wrote a biographical article on Lea, titled "The Valor of Homer Lea." It was thanks to her that Homer Lea achieved a revival, albeit a short-lived one. *The Valor of Ignorance* was retitled

If America Fights with Japan and republished with Boothe's biographical article serving as introduction.

Boothe's image of Lea, however, was too simplistic. It was riddled with factual errors. This is because Lea's pronouncements to the newspapers were carefully concocted adventure tales that blurred the borderline between fact and fantasy, and Boothe swallowed them—hook, line, and sinker.

I should like to turn now to Homer Lea's career after he published *The Valor of Ignorance*. Once again, his imagination was directed to China. Even as he fell out of sympathy himself toward the leader of the Chinese reformists, Kang Yuwei—whose attitude he now found lukewarm and whose leadership he thought was flagging—Lea discovered a new comrade.

It is not generally appreciated just how close "General Lea" was to the man known as the Father of Modern China, Sun Yatsen. As Sun's biographers chronicle the career of the brilliant Chinese revolutionist, they do not seem inclined to admit that he had anything to do with this dubious American youth.

True, Lea's ultimate contribution to the success of the revolution was miniscule. However, it is a fact that at one time Sun was truly dependent on this young man, no matter how his biographers may try to distance their hero from Homer Lea. One simply cannot deny such facts.

In mid-March of 1910, Sun and Lea entered into serious discussions in Los Angeles. The chief topic: money. Whether it's politics, revolution, or war, first and foremost you need a war chest, and if you ignore this matter, then whether you're a politician, a revolutionary, or a warrior, you will achieve nothing great. The best revolutionaries generally have the best money-management skills.

Sun Yatsen's first uprising, in 1895 in Guangzhou, failed. His next effort to raise a rebellion, in 1900 in Huizhou, was suppressed. From 1907 to 1908, based in Hanoi, he attempted multiple insurrections in various places in the south, repeated and/or simultaneously launched, but was frustrated every time.

One could say that the time was not ripe, but that is an excuse that can be made at any time. Rather, some ingredient for success was lacking. Sun concluded that this missing ingredient was money: a war chest.

In search of sponsors, Sun headed to New York. It was there that he learned of the existence of a sympathizer to the revolution, a General Lea, and that if he went to Los Angeles he could meet him.

Homer Lea and his comrades reached an agreement with Sun to provide $1.5 million in aid. At a time when national income per capita in the U.S. was merely $200, this sum was considerable; if I may be permitted a rough comparison, it would be the equivalent of some $150 million today.

Once Sun was back in New York, he drew up a letter of request, stating that two million dollars in additional funds would be necessary. He had judged that if Lea and associates could raise $1.5 million, they could raise $3.5 million. This demonstrates Sun's wiliness regarding money matters.

"General Lea" himself did not have that kind of money. But he did anticipate that his silver tongue, and his personal network, could tap the world of finance. This was because, after the Russo-Japanese War, America was seeking to check the growth of Japanese interests in Manchuria; furthermore, he could take advantage of the exclusionist movement then underway on the West Coast directed at ethnic Japanese. With *The Valor of Ignorance* fanning the flames of U.S.-Japan war fever, Lea could claim a role as the perfect coordinator.

But Lea was a romantic whereas Sun was a realist, a difference that helped place them in fundamentally different relationships to the Chinese revolution. They made strange bedfellows indeed. Sun assumed the position of president; he made Lea happy by appointing him commanding general. When they had reached an understanding, Sun departed for Honolulu, and Lea immersed himself in fund-raising.

General Lea and his associates planned to approach the Morgan financial empire with their requests for aid, but negotiations proved difficult. During that time, Sun was on a fund-raising pilgrimage of his own, leaving Honolulu for Tokyo, then traveling to Penang (Malaysia). General Lea received letter after urgent letter from President Sun, dunning him for the promised funds. Even if Lea was unable to raise $500,000 for the "Canton project," for example, he was to "get as much as you can, but in any case send fifty thousand at once for preparatory work" (September 5, 1910); a few weeks later it was, "a quarter million of gold dollars will be quite enough for the whole thing."[12]

Given the overblown sums that had initially been bandied about, these figures are shockingly small. But if Sun's earlier requests had been Bunyanesque, it was simply because he wanted to be sure he could at least get sums on the order of what he finally did obtain—it is a measure of his negotiating skill.

As for Lea, he was hoping to score big off the Morgan financial interests, but at the same time he investigated sources more likely to yield revenue. He tried to chat up the military hawks who had praised *The Valor of Ignorance* so highly; he courted arms merchants. Furthermore, he sent off copies of *The Valor of Ignorance* to newspapers, legislators, and local notables, requesting assistance. He tried, with his eloquent tongue, to reap some advantage from the California state elections. But his man was defeated.

When Sun finally realized that Lea did not really have the ability to deliver the funds, he grew anxious. The time he had scheduled for his next uprising was fast approaching. At the end of that year (1910) Sun left Penang for Paris, then continued on his peregrinations to New York, San Francisco, Vancouver.

In April 1911 sad news reached Sun. His revolutionary army had risen in Guangzhou, but due to all the delays in acquiring funds and procuring weapons, the government had had sufficient time to discover that something was afoot, and the plot failed. Some of the vanguard had seen that the situation was disadvantageous and withdrawn, but over a hundred of them, led by Huang Xing, launched a suicide attack, and seventy-two of them (officially) died. They are celebrated as the Seventy-Two Martyrs of Huanghuagang (Yellow Flower Mound) after the site of their martyrdom and mausoleum. Their spirit of self-sacrifice attracted attention to the revolutionary cause not only in China but around the world.

So Homer Lea's efforts came to naught. He suffered from self-blame. The tone of Sun's letters turned icy. Lea's health was also deteriorating. He could use his eyes only for two or three hours a day, and his blood pressure was rising. The only relief was that he had proposed to his secretary, Ethel Powers, and she had consented. Ethel already had a child, and she was older than Homer. At the recommendation of a friend, Lea decided to seek treatment from an illustrious German ophthalmologist. He would take his honeymoon in Germany for that purpose.

While Lea was in Germany, he received a letter from Sun, who was in America. "Lately," wrote Sun in imperfect English, "I have received many letters urging me to return to the East soon and start the movement quick. The only thing left to be done now is the way of getting the necessary fund for the starting."[13]

Sun's letter was no lie. On October 10, Chinese revolutionary forces raised a rebellion in Wuhan. This time it looked like they might succeed. The sacrifice of the Seventy-Two Martyrs of Huanghuagang in April was being redeemed. The next day, the revolutionary army took Wuchang and

Hanko. In response, insurrections arose in province after province, each of which left the control of the Qing Dynasty: Changsha, Shaanxi, Shanxi, Yunnan, Jiangxi, Jiangsu, Xinjiang, Anhui. In November, the provinces of Shandong, Guangdong, and Sichuan each declared their independence. The Qing Dynasty was unraveling; two-thirds of the country was in revolutionary hands.

But it was still not possible to say that the outcome was guaranteed. The revolutionaries had still not stabbed at the heart of the Qing Dynasty. They therefore still needed that war chest. And there remained the daunting task of securing international recognition for the revolutionary government. General Lea cut short his honeymoon, and on November 10 rendezvoused with Sun at the Savoy Hotel in London—the same Savoy as in the theater by that name next door, which gave us the world première of the Gilbert and Sullivan operetta, *The Mikado*. "Homer is on the trail of 5 million and I hardly see him," wrote Ethel to her sister. "I hope he gets it and that Sun is grateful enough to hand me over a little lunch at least."[14]

On November 16, Lea received a new uniform made for him to wear in China as a leader of the revolution. Ethel told him it was most becoming. The next day was his thirty-fifth birthday. Sun told him he would be chief of staff—this was Sun's birthday present to him. However, the pleasant evenings at the Savoy Hotel did not last long. It had seemed like a promising beginning, but the road ahead was as long as ever.

Sun, Lea, and Ethel headed off to Paris without having achieved much of anything. In Paris, the two men divvied up the chores. Chief of staff Lea handled the bankers; President Sun petitioned French prime minister Georges Clemenceau to recognize the revolutionary government, but without success. Lea wrote Senator Elihu Root, a former U.S. secretary of state, advocating U.S. assistance at a time when England could not formally countenance aid due to repercussions involving its treaty obligations under the Anglo-Japanese Alliance of 1902: "If our country would address a secret note here . . . it would turn the scale and by a secret acquiescence I would be able to secure money."[15] But the White House did not act.

Sun, who as president was supposed to be receiving assistance, paid for his chief of staff's expenses in London and Paris. And from Paris, Sun returned to China—with Homer Lea in tow. After passing through Penang and Singapore, they arrived in Hong Kong on December 21.

In Hong Kong, Sun and Lea were greeted by Ike Kōkichi (who had published the Japanese edition of *The Valor of Ignorance*) and by such "Rōnin of the Continent" as Miyazaki Tōten, who had supported Sun. Miyazaki had been a close Sun ally ever since Sun's first uprising had failed and he had sought asylum in Japan. These supporters were apt to cast a jaundiced eye on Sun's questionable new American friend.

Miyazaki and Ike were engaged in a certain rivalry. Miyazaki scorned Ike as a "high-collar" Westernized snob trading on his ability in English and also Chinese, nor could he stomach Ike's friendliness with Lea. And he was offended by the inclusion of the Johnny-come-lately American who styled himself chief of staff. Miyazaki reminisced about this period later, after Sun lost his power struggle with Yuan Shikai:

> If Sun had been a little more practical; if he had not been so purely ideal-istic; if he had been more familiar with the ways of the workaday world, he would not so easily have been led astray by a sweet-talker like Homer Lea. He would not have imagined that simply by becoming "President" the floodgates would be opened to millions of yen. From the beginning, he would never have set his sights on goals that could not be achieved. There must have been ways to set reasonable goals, and to borrow money securely, but since Sun, the pure revolutionary, was ignorant of financial affairs, after years of effort he ended up, to his profound regret, yielding the stage to Yuan Shikai. Although Sun was still young, onlookers could only feel pity.[16]

But perhaps Sun understood the revolutionary drama and his own role better than that. Some American chief of staff was necessary to give cred-ibility to the threat (whether explicit or implicit) that if the Japanese Rōnin of the Continent did not behave themselves, scarce funds might go to Sun's American supporters instead. A flashy character like Homer Lea was perfect for the role, and Sun induced him to play the part.

Christmastime, 1911. Sun, Lea, Miyazaki, and Ike arrived in Shanghai. There was a welcome party. To the *Shanghai China Press* (as reported on December 28), Lea declared that he was chief of staff; on the same date, the *Singapore Free Press* praised Lea as the General von Moltke of China, and the man whose negotiations with the European powers were responsible for securing recognition for the Chinese revolutionary government.

On December 29, 1911, Sun was elected president of the revolutionary government by an assembly of delegates from the various provincial revo-lutionary parties. On New Year's Day, 1912, an inauguration ceremony was held at Nanjing. The Republic of China was born.

The chief of staff's period of ascendancy, however, was short-lived. Immediately after the founding of the revolutionary government in Nanjing, Yuan Shikai, chief of the Beijing-based warlords who held the real power, ordered his troops south and plundered the revolutionary strongholds of Hankou and Hanyang. Then he urged peace negotiations on Sun. Backed by overwhelming military power, Yuan demanded that in exchange for abolishing the Qing Dynasty, he be given the post of provisional president of the revolutionary government. To protect the revolutionary government, Sun had no choice but to swallow hard and accede.

America also favored Yuan over Sun as provisional president, considering that Yuan, with his military power, had the best chance of stabilizing China. And in the course of this fierce power struggle between Yuan and Sun, there was nothing Homer Lea could do. Miyazaki and his cohorts tried to get rid of this ineffectual "chief of staff."

On the morning of February 11, 1912, Homer Lea suddenly collapsed. It was influenza. His hereditary disabilities and long years of illness had left him in a debilitated state. Now his face was numbed, and he suffered from paralysis on the left side of his body. He returned, wheezing and gasping, to the United States.

Sun advocated and instigated a second revolution, but had to bow once again to Yuan's superior military and financial strength. Convalescing in Santa Monica, Sun's chief of staff received yet another request for assistance. But Lea lacked even the strength to reply. There was nothing he could do, from morning to night, but sink into his chair in his house by the sea and rest.

On November 1, 1912, Homer Lea passed away. He was thirty-six years old. Dr. David Starr Jordan, former president of Stanford University, contributed a eulogy for this strange personage who, since his student days, had been such a compound of merits and demerits, such a magnet for both praise and blame. "One [can] hardly help a kindly feeling," he said in conclusion, "for the ambitious little romancer trying to make the most of his short life, limited physique, and boundless imagination."[17]

How shall we evaluate Homer Lea, finally? In this connection I should like to cite another phrase that has made a deep impression on me. And I think this will prove that the earlier quotation from Shakespeare's *Richard III* was not inappropriate.

When Homer Lea was stricken ill in Nanjing, he was visited at his sickbed by one William Henry Donald, an Australian journalist, who has left us the following account:

> For a time he talked spiritedly, and then looking out of his window where he could see rows of ancestral grave mounds, he said morosely: "China is graves. They are all about us. Look at them. Graves, graves, graves." The "General" flung his arms in a wide arc. Then his mood changed. With a bony, crooked finger he reached out and tapped Donald on the head. "Mark me," he wheezed, "we are going to have trouble with those Russian fellows. They are [the kind of people who are] on the march to conquer the world." ... Donald rose to go, but Lea gripped him tightly by the arm. "Buy me a big horse in Shanghai," he begged. "I must have a big horse—as big as you can get. And a big sword. I'll need them. The Russians are up to no good!"[18]

One can hardly help recalling Richard III's famous line toward the end of Shakespeare's play: "A horse! a horse! my kingdom for a horse!" (V.iv.7).

PART II

The Phenomenon of Japan-U.S. Future-War Chronicles

The brown earth, the torn, blasted earth with a greasy
shine under the sun's rays; the earth is the background
of this restless, gloomy world of automatons, our
gasping is the scratching of a quill, our lips are dry,
our heads are debauched with stupor—thus we
stagger forward, and into our pierced and shattered
souls bores the torturing image of the brown earth
with the greasy sun and the convulsed and dead
soldiers, who lie there—it can't be helped—who cry
and clutch at our legs as we spring away over them.

—ERICH MARIA REMARQUE,
All Quiet on the Western Front

CHAPTER SIX

Standing in
the Wastelands
of Europe

THE EVENING SUN is just about to drop behind the horizon. The reddish-brown iron wreckage stands starkly silhouetted, like dinosaurs, towering over vegetable fields now covered with weeds. Biplanes, stuck nose down into the ground, their tail wings skyward; armored tanks, overturned, their bellies exposed; rows of abandoned shells...

Thousands upon thousands of red crosses, each marking a grave, spread out like undulating waves.

In the trenches, the blanched skeletons of German soldiers lie with their helmets still on.

Amid this wasteland, standing dumbfounded, is a solitary Japanese man. As the setting sun sets all these forms ablaze, he tries to let the entire scene be burned onto his retinas.

The man in this real-life scene was a forty-four-year-old Imperial Navy officer, freshly promoted to the rank of lieutenant: Mizuno Hironori. This was at the beginning of the summer of 1919, and Mizuno was viewing the remains of a battlefield in northeastern France, near the border with Germany.

The First World War lasted from July 1914 to November 1918. Thirty-three nations participated; 65 million soldiers were mobilized; 10 million people were killed, 20 million wounded, and 6.5 million prisoners were taken. With *All Quiet on the Western Front*, Erich Maria Remarque became instantly famous for his portrayal of that war's unprecedented horrors and of the psychology of the ordinary soldiers. If a repetition of his description is hard to take, imagine what it was to live through, over and over again:

The brown earth, the torn, blasted earth, with a greasy shine under the sun's rays; the earth is the background of this restless, gloomy world of automatons, our gasping is the scratching of a quill, our lips are dry, our heads are debauched with stupor—thus we stagger forward, and into our pierced and shattered souls bores the torturing image of the brown earth with the greasy sun and the convulsed and dead soldiers, who lie there—it can't be helped—who cry and clutch at our legs as we spring away over them.[1]

The soldiers in the trenches on the deadlocked front lines were experiencing a gradual numbing of the senses. Even though the ground around them was level, with no obstructions to their view, they could hardly see anything due to the detonation of high-grade explosives, along with smoke screens and weaponized gas. Orders were not delivered, supplies were held up. In chaotic situations in which a bullet could fly at them from any direction, soldiers could also be attacked with weapons developed expressly for this war, such as artillery, hand grenades, machine guns, and poison gas. The First World War was a modern war, in which things were handled differently from previous wars. New weapons of mass destruction were introduced, such as the airplane and the tank.

As Mizuno toured the old battlefield, he was overcome by the destructiveness of this warfare. It could not compare to his own experience of combat in the Russo-Japanese War. It was as though some unaccountable monster had trampled the Europe that had once boasted so many glories. Moving about the battlefield, Mizuno resolved to record scrupulously the horrors of this war.

* * *

THE JAPANESE NAVAL OFFICER went on to inspect the site on the western front that had seen the fiercest fighting: Verdun. Here, for a ten-month period from February 1916 to the end of the year, a desperate struggle was waged between the ferociously attacking German troops and the absolutely unyielding French defenders. This titanic clash was for possession of just a single stronghold. The German army suffered 337,000 casualties (counting both killed and wounded); the French, 377,000. These are astounding figures. By way of comparison, the casualties during the assaults on Port Arthur in 1904, a campaign after which General Nogi Maresuke, the commander, was denounced as incompetent, numbered 59,000 including both killed and wounded. Under Marshal Henri Pétain, the French army succeeded in retaining the fortress in question. However, the town of Verdun itself was annihilated.

When Mizuno visited Verdun, over two years had passed since the fierce fighting, but there were still no signs of a revival.

> The streets were completely destroyed. There were no habitable houses, merely fallen roofs and crumbled walls and broken columns and rubble strewn about here and there. One had the impression of viewing an excavation at Pompeii. The trees were all blasted up and burnt out; all I could see was lines of low, charred stumps. The whole mountain had not a single green leaf left. Broken rifles, helmets with holes, crushed gas masks, boots, canteens, and bullets were scattered all over. In the dugout shelters, shockingly, lay human bones.

And with all this sacrifice, what was achieved? To Mizuno, it was a conundrum. For those who lost, the Germans and Austrians, the answer was obvious. But what about those who won, the English and the French and the Italians? Were they really more prosperous than before the war? After all, the conventional value system provided for winners of wars to extract indemnities from their opponents, seize their lands, or deprive them of various other sources of wealth. In this conflict, however, all the combatant nations were debilitated. The "victors" did not seem to have "won." In England, returning war veterans wandered the streets, unable to find work. France alone had sustained 1.3 million dead, 4.2 million wounded, and five hundred thousand unaccounted for. Now it was suffering from a trade deficit and postwar inflation. In Italy, too, the ranks of the unemployed were swelling, and strikes were multiplying. Soldiers and civilians alike had sacrificed themselves for the nation and received nothing in return. Now a Japanese naval lieutenant, who had once believed in the concept of a righteous war, was heading for Paris in a skeptical mood.

It was around this time that the Treaty of Versailles was due to be signed between the victors and the vanquished, formally ending the Great War—the first "world war." As one of the victorious nations, Japan participated in the conference. Japan had seized German possessions in Asia. It had occupied, without much sacrifice on its part, Qingdao in Shandong Province on the Chinese mainland and the German-held islands in the South

Pacific north of the equator. Unaware of the horrendous situation along the European fronts, Japanese were excited about the economic benefits of victory. And in the city of Paris, at the very moment that the Versailles peace treaty was approved, four o'clock on the afternoon of June 28, 1919, sirens wailed. Citizens ran out of their houses; the air was full of excitement; they embraced each other indiscriminately.

At dusk, Mizuno left Paris. He put victorious France behind him and headed for vanquished Germany.

In Germany, Mizuno progressed from skepticism to an even more thorough-going change of heart. At forty-four years of age, he was beginning to gain a new point of view. He had published *The Next Battle* on being appointed to lieutenant at age thirty-nine, and his first book, *The Crucial Battle*, at age thirty-six. Thirty-six was the same age at which Homer Lea, one year Mizuno's junior, had perished on November 1, 1912.

Tasked to the naval archives, Mizuno had not seen any action in the First World War, though the war had started around the time he was promoted to lieutenant. Within the navy, Mizuno was regarded as a man full of complaints and dissatisfactions; he was also considered uncooperative. On the other hand, he was accorded respect as author of the best-selling *The Crucial Battle*. After much difficult discussion and consideration, the authorities had finally found him a safe desk job as naval archivist.

With time on his hands, archivist Mizuno had read Homer Lea's *The Valor of Ignorance*. *The Next Battle* had been written with Lea's work very much in mind. In *The Valor of Ignorance*, Lea had stated categorically that Americans had become swine, wallowing in their love of lucre. Peace merely helped develop the swine's ugliness. Lea was warning Americans not to forget the serious reality that they were surrounded by wolves. Similarly, the theme of Mizuno's *The Next Battle* was the warning that if Japan relaxed its guard, it would be destroyed by the great powers. Or rather, one great power: America. Although Homer Lea's conception of Japan was just the opposite—in that he held Japan to be one of the wolves, not one of the lambs—the logic was the same.

Mizuno's *The Next Battle* carried the notation, "This treatise on navy and army strategy in the Philippine theater conforms to the work of the American author, Homer Lea." Indeed, the debt was a deep one: Mizuno's book conformed to Homer Lea's even in concept, and Mizuno himself acknowledged as much:

In *The Valor of Ignorance*, the American author Homer Lea states incisively that "industrialism is only a means to the end of national progress; it is not the goal of national greatness. If it exceeds that role as a means and becomes an end in itself, it is no longer industrialism: it must be called commercialism. But this commercialism leads to industry's degeneration: it is a parasite, a fungoid growth, and it will bring about the final corruption of the state." All in all, there is much to what he says.[2]

Mizuno, who considered America to be a hypothetical enemy of Japan, thus thought of himself as allied in spirit with Homer Lea, for whom Japan was America's hypothetical enemy. And without knowing of the death of this worthy opponent and comrade, Mizuno had to deal with the First World War. With the war now underway, he was ordered to help compile the official war history of Japan's participation in that war. Given his previous experience chronicling the Russo-Japanese War and writing *The Crucial Battle*, it was expected that he would throw himself into his new task enthusiastically. That, at any rate, was the extent of the government's thinking on how to handle this rather troublesome figure.

However, Mizuno's innate contrariness made his reactions unpredictable. In this instance, he responded to this rather perfunctory personnel decision with a somewhat twisted logic that nonetheless hit home.

War histories should be compiled essentially as resources for later soldiers to draw on when formulating operational war plans, starting with tactics and stratagems. They are not to be composed like war tales, prizing beauty of style and variety of expression. And yet, if we look at our war histories, we find that naval authorities tend to undervalue the former conception and to overvalue the latter, so that history is subordinated to literary flair. If we seriously want to produce histories that are useful to future generations, they should be written by those who actually participated in the formulation and execution of the war's strategy. That I, who have nothing to do with strategy, but serve merely as a library guard, should be tasked with the compilation, is an insult to the very concept of a true war history.[3]

A difficult man indeed! Mizuno's contrarian subtext is clear: if they're going to have me serve as a military historian, they should put me on the elite track and take me into the military command; instead, they banish me to this trivial desk job. Thus Mizuno expressed his anger and his insubordinate spirit.

Not knowing what to do with him, the authorities sent Mizuno off to inspect battle sites, as executive officer of the armored cruiser *Izumo*. But he was in for quite a shock. When he boarded the warship, he could not help feeling like an Urashima Tarō—the Japanese equivalent to Rip Van Winkle. Over a decade had passed since the Russo-Japanese War. During that time, he had been pushing a pen at a desk, far from any battle. Now he was flabbergasted by the ship's operations that reflected the rapid advances in military science and technology over the years. And that was not all. From general training to rules and regulations, everything was different. Even the bugle calls had changed.

Mizuno realized that he could no longer serve at the front. But then, suddenly, a thought occurred to him. To study war, he should go to Europe. He still had three thousand yen left in royalties from the publication of *The Crucial Battle*. He wrote a letter of request to the naval ministry, "to go abroad at my own expense to observe and research military affairs."[4] Unexpectedly, permission was easily obtained.

With a large trunk and two pieces of hand luggage, Mizuno boarded the 11,000-ton steamer *Suwa Maru*, docked at the port of Yokohama. This was at the end of July 1916. Crossing the Indian Ocean, passing the Cape of Good Hope, they emerged into the Atlantic. Had they gone through the Suez Canal, they would have risked encounters with the German submarines infesting the Mediterranean, so they took the long way around the continent. They reached London at the end of September.

On this, his first trip to Europe, Mizuno experienced a new shock: culture shock. When he saw young couples embracing in the public parks, he wrote in his notebook, "Even cats in love avoid people's eyes. These people are shameless!"[5] But Mizuno was forgetting that these were not times of peace. He was soon to realize that these same young Londoners were also living in fear of German air raids. All over town anti-aircraft guns were set up, and at least once an evening searchlights would light up the night sky, all at once. One day, he was using the toilet when suddenly he heard a boom like a thunderclap and felt the whole building shake. Dust and plaster rained down from the ceiling. Then there was a second boom, and a third. He exited in some consternation. It was his first experience of an air raid.

There was no time to dawdle. Crowds of people were rushing like an avalanche into the basement. There was nothing for it but to go with the flow. The air outside was filled with dust. The strafing of the aircraft machine guns sounded to Mizuno like the popping of soybeans being roasted. As the sound of explosions receded, he ventured outside and saw three airplanes disappearing in the distance. The AA guns were firing after them in vain.

The target of the attack was a building that had stood a mere fifty meters away. It had collapsed, and the passageway beside it was buried in rubble. Pedestrians were lying on the ground, covered with blood. Mizuno himself had passed that building just five minutes before. He realized that if the planes had come five minutes earlier, or if he had passed by there five minutes later, he might have died. Thinking about that made him shiver. The following day it was announced in the newspaper that the air raid had killed 150 people and wounded 450 more.

In *The Crucial Battle*, Mizuno wrote of the horrors of naval warfare, which he had experienced himself. But he had never witnessed ordinary civilians fleeing and being killed. He realized that in Europe new circumstances were taking shape. His reflections on this are recorded in his notebook.

> In Japan, with our flimsy wooden buildings, one bomb would smash three to five of them to smithereens. What's more, we have no basements to escape into, no underground railroad. The loss of human life would be enormous; fires would rage everywhere; it would take only a few such attacks to reduce all of Tokyo to cinder and ash.[6]

We must realize that at the beginning of the First World War, the military use of the airplane was still a new and undeveloped technology. It was only in 1903 that Wilbur Wright and his younger brother Orville had achieved their famous first powered flight with a human passenger, at Kitty Hawk, North Carolina. That flight stayed aloft a mere twelve seconds and only covered forty meters.

After that, however, the airplane underwent fantastically rapid development. At the start of the war, technical reliability was still low; planes were usable for aerial observation at best. But when the land armies got bogged down in trench warfare, the combatants were suddenly awakened to the advantages of attacking from the air. From the second half of the First World War, airplanes began to be used more regularly for military purposes. The age of aviation had truly arrived.

At first, airplanes merely had a supporting role and were only lightly armed. Gradually, however, flight range and payload capability increased.

Before the First World War, for example, it was quite unthinkable that planes could start in Germany, conduct an air raid on London, and return to Germany. But just four years later, toward the end of the war, such exercises were part of regular operations. Altogether, more than ten thousand airplanes were sent over the front, while some fifty thousand aviators lost their lives in the European theater.

And on the Japanese side? To attack German-held Qingdao on China's Shandong Peninsula, the Japanese deployed the French-made Henri Farman biplane and Bleriot monoplane. However, there were only fourteen pilots, twelve observers, and sixteen planes all told. Given this sort of time lag between Japan and Europe, Mizuno's experience had rare value.

London was made of stone and brick; there were also shelters in basements and the underground subway railroad. Japan, on the other hand, had no such bomb shelters, and the houses were made of paper and wood, so in a modern war there was nowhere to hide. The fear Mizuno tasted derived not only from his experience but also from his imaginative powers. The personal danger he found himself in during the German air raid was a matter of chance, but he realized that if Japan were attacked from the air by an enemy, there was simply no defense. Now Mizuno could offer firsthand reports on these terrors to a Japanese public wholly ignorant of them. This alone was worth the voyage.

Mizuno spent nearly nine months in London. During that period, he also took brief trips to France and Italy. He also very much wanted to inspect conditions in Germany, as it was such a military power, but since it was an enemy country, he could not. And as he was using up his travel funds, he could not extend his stay indefinitely.

The war seemed like it would last forever. Three years, and still no end in sight. It had already lasted twice as long as the Russo-Japanese War, yet both allies and enemies were holding out. At the end of June 1917, Mizuno finally gave up the idea of visiting Germany and decided to return to Japan via the United States. The ship he sailed on was the *St. Paul*, of the type known at the time as a cruiser-in-disguise: it was registered as a passenger ship and sailed with its cannons sheeted.

Like the Mediterranean, the Atlantic was infested with German submarines called U-boats, for *Unterseeboot* (undersea-boat). As a new form of military technology, the submarine surprised Mizuno no less than the airplane had. To redress their losses, the Germans adopted an indiscriminate submarine warfare strategy, attacking even commercial ships without warning. Various goods were being sent from America to Europe via commercial ships to support the Allies' war effort. In order to sever that line of supply, Germany attacked commercial ships one by one as they sailed the Atlantic. This indiscriminate form of attack violated international treaties and angered U.S. president Woodrow Wilson. This is what finally tilted America toward its declaration of war in April 1917, which led to Germany's defeat.

Mizuno was tormented by the prospect of unexpected attacks by unseen underwater ships. There was always a lookout perched on the *St. Paul*'s mainmast. The ship traveled in a zigzag. Just in case of a torpedo attack in the middle of the night, Mizuno slept with lifesaving gear handy. He drew up a will. For three days and nights, he fretted. When the ship had passed out of the submarine danger zone, the ship's captain finally appeared in the dining hall. Seeing the expressions of relief on the faces of the crew, the passengers relaxed and opened up to each other.

Mizuno wondered what he had been so afraid of. He felt a bit ashamed. He hummed a well-known tune whose lyrics went, "Crossing the line of death, looking back, wave upon wave." Certainly the submarine threat had been terrifying. But the fear that Mizuno had fallen into was of some unknown monster. Later, the submarine would meet its own natural enemy, the destroyer, which would stalk the submarine throughout the seven seas. But in Mizuno's present state of mind, he felt as though he had been thrown bodily into an ocean full of sharks.

After an eighteen-year absence, Mizuno finally reached America, safe and sound. It was in 1899, when he was twenty-four years old, that he had first landed on the country's west coast on his long-distance training cruise. Now he was a naval lieutenant, and the city at which he was landing was America's largest, New York. On the approach to San Francisco he had been astonished. New York was beyond comparison. As he approached the city's harbor, the head of the Statue of Liberty was shrouded in rain. The skyscrapers were like giant trees of concrete, lined up in rows and crowned with clouds. This city of the future had amazing depth to it. Trains were passing to and fro incessantly on three levels: underground, ground level, and above ground on elevated tracks. The lines of automobiles were like unbroken processions of ants. Mizuno was, in his own words, "simply astounded."

He wrote that he had been overwhelmed by London and Paris, but that New York was on another scale entirely. No matter how we try to foster our hostility toward America, he said, or to whip up our patriotism, we can't compete. New York is simply stupendous.

The Mizuno who authored *The Next Battle* had believed America to be a hypothetical enemy. He had believed that the Alien Land Laws in California discriminated against Japanese. And before he left on his current trip, he had been warned by knowledgeable military colleagues in Japan that as a Japanese he would be subject to harassment when he entered the U.S. However, the immigration officer had actually been courteous. Mizuno had heard that American customs officers were corrupt and would definitely expect a bribe. But when he tried to press some small change upon the officer, he was mildly rebuffed.

In Washington, Mizuno met up again with Nomura Kichisaburō, who was serving as naval attaché at the Japanese embassy. Nomura was a classmate from the Naval Academy who had entered on the elite track. Later, he was to be the special ambassador serving in America at the start of the war between the two countries. Nomura took him to see Congress in action.

Parting from Nomura, Mizuno traveled to Chicago and Los Angeles. Then he stopped by San Francisco, which brought back memories. Chinatown was still lively, but Little Tokyo was comparatively subdued.

Back then, "picture brides" were popular. Immigrants' success stories were bandied about back in the Japanese villages that contributed the most to the influx. Hoping to secure a portion of the American dream, farmers competed to send their daughters over to the United States. From America, photos of young male immigrants were sent back to Japan. The ones taken at professional studios usually showed them dressed up nicely in clean suits, lending credence to their success stories.

These matches were usually arranged through intermediaries who managed the correspondence. Groups of brides numbering in the dozens would be sent across the Pacific by ship, traveling in third-class cabins. When they came ashore at the pier at San Francisco, each with her fiancé's photo in hand, it was a strange scene. American newspapers mocked the practice. Politicians fomenting anti-Japanese sentiment cited it to foster contempt, while feminists complained of discrimination against women.

In the city of San Francisco there was an inn called Iyada-ya, meaning the "Hate-Him Hotel." (Its real name was different, but in the Japanese community it was known as Iyada-ya.) The picture brides would go there after arrival and would change out of their traveling clothes. Then the grooms would come for their first meeting with their fiancées. It was at that point that the women discovered that what they had expected and what they were getting was often very different. "I hate him! I hate him!" they would scream through their tears.

"So that's why it's called Iyada-ya," thought Mizuno, when he found out. But larger issues were also at stake.

A Japanese American issued a cautionary observation:

> The Japanese who have come here already are by now Americans. To live here, we must become accustomed to the ways here. But back in the home country, they think of emigration as a kind of apprenticeship. Fine, but when children are sent off as apprentices, the family shouldn't interfere: they must do as the employer wishes. If they make a fuss, crying, "anti-Japanese, anti-Japanese," they have to realize that it may reach the ears of the employer, and the apprentice will suffer.[7]

When Mizuno heard this, he felt some remorse. His book, *The Next Battle*, constituted just this sort of interference from the home country. Excerpts from the English translation of *The Next Battle* were carried in the *New York Sun* as examples of Japanese anti-American sentiment. Mizuno had not seriously been thinking about America or its Japanese immigrants. He had merely invoked them to help justify his call for increased military preparedness. He had used superficially impressive but ultimately hollow arguments such as the following:

> Sixty years ago came [Perry, leading the Black Ships]. In his hand, the gun of a murderer; on his lips, sweet talk of the welfare of the human race. America forced us to open our country, taking no cognizance of the internal debate then raging. Now, without justice or reason, they endeavor to lock up their own country and exclude us. . . . When things come to such a pass, the "freedom and equality" that these Americans are forever professing, their "justice and humanity," prove to be nothing more than hypocritical window-dressing. Historically, when America has wanted to invade another country's territory, they have employed treachery or applied violence; their means have always been insidious and villainous in the extreme. So it was in the Philippines. So it was in Hawaii, so it was, too, in Panama. If anybody doubts this, let him go ask the Mexicans! Ask the Colombians![8]

After a total of two months in the United States, Mizuno returned home to Japan. The port of Yokohama looked shabby to him now.

For the number one port in Japan, the harbor facilities were pathetic; for a treaty-port town, the buildings were dingy and dirty; for the people of an advanced nation, their manners were uncouth. When I considered that this was my native land I felt regret, I felt shame, and I felt resentment.[9]

There was something else that stuck in Mizuno's craw when he reentered the country. Compared to America, Japanese customs practices were dysfunctional and hidebound, rendered inflexible by an institutional superiority complex. After more than a year abroad, it was only natural that Mizuno's luggage had increased. Yet the customs officer glared at it all and thrust some red tape at him rudely. The paperwork read, "The undersigned humbly requests permission to bring into Japan the articles of baggage specified below. . . ." Mizuno was miserable at having to abase himself thus with a petition written in honorific language, when it was just a matter of getting his personal luggage through customs. What kind of backward island nation was this?

Now that he was back, Mizuno was once again faced with boredom. The work the navy assigned him was in support of the Military Affairs Research Committee. He was told to write something in the nature of a report on what he had observed in Europe, and then he was let alone. By now, Mizuno was used to this sinecure, so he wrote some journal and newspaper articles and generally did as he pleased. At the end of this year, he was promoted to the rank of navy captain. It was a seniority system, so graduates of the Naval Academy usually got at least this far. Front-line captains would command battleships; those on the elite track would enter the Naval Staff College and then join Naval Command as core strategists.

As soon as Mizuno finished his report for the Military Affairs Research Committee, he was returned to his old and moldy post of archivist. Now the chance of becoming a flag officer was forever closed to him. At age forty-three, he had reached a career impasse. But he had an abundant sense of mission—it was as though he believed that the Imperial Navy needed him. On November 9, 1918, a revolution broke out in Germany. Emperor Wilhelm II abdicated and defected; Friedrich Ebert, leader of the Social Democratic Party, came to power. Two days later, a ceasefire treaty was signed between Germany and the Allies, and the four-year-long First World War was finally at an end.

Pacifism now emerged in Japan as well as in Europe. It even became somewhat fashionable. Professor Anezaki Masaharu, an authority on religious studies at Tokyo Imperial University, wrote an essay for the *Ōsaka Mainichi Shimbun*, titled, "The Scourge of Militarism and the Ruin It Brings" (December 3, 1918). His pacifism was based on the theory that people are inherently good; it was informed by the humanism that was characteristic of the Taishō period (1912–25). In sentiment, it resembles Mushakōji Saneatsu's famous dictum, "A good relationship is a lovely thing."

Mizuno immediately rose to the bait with an article in the 1919 New Year's issue of the journal *Chūō Kōron*.

The outcome of this last European war cannot be described (as the good professor would have us believe) in terms of the victory of Allied liberalism and the defeat of German militarism. And by no means was this (as the Yanks and Brits would have us believe) the victory of Allied righteousness and humanism over German oppression and tyranny. Why, then, did the Allies win, and why did the German side lose? The answer can be stated with brevity and clarity. I maintain that it was the superior manpower, financial power, and material power of the Allies, led by the United States, that defeated the Central European alliance led by Germany.

The outcome of a war, then, does not depend on right, but on military and national might. That was Mizuno's conclusion, after he had got a good taste of the power of modern military technology on his recent voyage: the airplanes, the submarines, and so forth.

At the time, the First World War was called the Great War. The designations "First" and "Second" (or I and II) were generally applied only after the Second World War had broken out, to make the sequence of these two world wars clear.

The Great War. This refers not simply to its scale, but to its novel form. Wars used to occur as bilateral confrontations, between England and France, for example, or between France and Germany. The new shape of warfare, however, would be determined by the choosing of sides in a conflict between competing leagues of nations, as almost all the countries of Europe found their interests affected and themselves getting caught up in entangling alliances. Japan had sailed through the Sino-Japanese and Russo-Japanese Wars, and thus its experience of war was purely bilateral. It could not adjust imaginatively to the circumstances of the Great War.

A writer should be sensitive to events that stimulate the imagination. Yet the main concern of the novelists of Taishō Japan was the inner development of their own psyches. The concerns of an active-duty military man like Mizuno were different from those of an ordinary writer. What is happening in Europe now, he wondered; what kind of war will be next?

In March 1919 he took a second trip to Europe. For his first trip, he had applied to conduct research abroad at his own expense for two years; he had received permission, but returned after only one year. So he reasoned he should be able to go again, for another one-year stay. But to the naval authorities, this seemed like a purely self-interested request. It was to be expected that they would be hesitant, but since Mizuno's position was, after all, a sinecure, and since they were well aware that Mizuno would hardly take a simple no for an answer, they gave in. He was determined to go again, mainly because he could not go to Germany during the first trip.

Mizuno had wanted to visit such a military powerhouse as Germany during the Great War, and that the reason he could not was that it was an enemy country. Now the Germany he was heading off to was a Germany in defeat.

Mizuno entered Germany via France and Switzerland.[10] As it was just after the war, border crossings took time. There were customs offices near both ends of a bridge connecting Switzerland and Germany. One might have thought that the baggage inspection on the Swiss side would have settled things, but on the German side there was another meticulous check. Not only did Germany levy a duty of 30 marks on every 200 cigarettes, but foodstuffs, clothes—anything new, at least—were taxed without mercy. When Mizuno switched to a German train, it suddenly dawned on him why this was the case. The first class carriage was so in name only: it was poorly appointed and had not been cleaned. The ceramic basin in the washroom was cracked; the wallpaper was peeling; there was neither cup nor soap nor paper nor towel. And the carriage shook alarmingly. It was a passenger car, all right, but on the verge of being scrapped. Germany's postwar plight was telegraphed by every oscillation of the car. Every time it pulled into a station, people would rush the train, crowding in eight people to a four-person compartment. The very corridors and bathrooms were bursting with riders. There were even people who tried to force their way in through the windows. Every single pane of glass was broken; nothing covered the open space. Mizuno commented in his notebook,

> This was a German railway? Number one in the world for organization, control, orderliness, and punctuality? Germany has collapsed not only physically and materially but also mentally and spiritually.

A German passenger who boarded en route spoke to Mizuno: "You Japanese?" He was a middle-aged man with a shaved head, no doubt military. Navy, he said. He called out a few Japanese place names, repeating them: "Nagasaki. Yokohama." And then, in broken English, the sailor asked, "Why didn't Japan side with Germany?" And then he grumbled about how unfair things were. He pointed out the window. There was a row of factories.

> Look at those chimneys. Lots and lots of chimneys. Not one of them putting out any smoke. No raw materials; no coal. The French have seized our coal-mining area.

Thinking Mizuno still had not got the point, the man continued with his explanation.

> We've no money to buy either the coal that fuels the machinery or the raw materials to make things with. And when we do work and make any profit, it's taken by the French.

Mizuno asked, "How do you feel about this last war?" The man replied,

> Right, the war. Strange thing, that. It's tough. It hurts. After three years I was already sick to death of it. Paris will fall any day, they said. England is surrendering, they said. We were dragged along by the government's propaganda, the war just grinding on and on. And what we get, in the end, is this state of affairs!

What state of affairs? As soon as the train arrived in Berlin, Mizuno understood. The plaza in front of the station was covered with horse manure, and the stench assaulted his nose. Unclean and unsanitary. Automobiles had been seized by default to pay off war indemnities. Hansom cabs and horse-drawn carts clattered up and down the broad asphalt boulevards of the capital. The horses were so underfed their ribs were showing. Their iron trappings were rusted. The sight of these horses straining, frothing, as they hauled their heavy loads—it was a doleful thing to behold, and it overlapped in his mind with images of Germans. "So this is what defeat looks like," thought Mizuno.

The Berlin streets were awash with khaki. The street-side newspaper vendors, the men who cleaned the horse manure off the street, the drivers of broken-down carts, the porters at the station—all were in khaki. They were wearing their old military uniforms and caps, stripped of insignia. During the war, Germany had mobilized over ten million men. Mizuno estimated that an average of one out of every 2.5 men was dyed in khaki. They were almost all discharged soldiers. Commodities were in short supply; people had no clothes. So towns and villages alike were inundated with a flood of khaki. Germany was impoverished and unemployment high. There was no way to accommodate these legions of demobilized soldiers.

A whole khaki, without defect, was fortunate enough. Wounded soldiers were discarded on the street like so much trash. Whether it was under the scorching summer sun or in the cold of a driving winter blizzard, khaki-clothed veterans without hands, without legs, without eyes, squatted on street corners and lay about under the trees. Silent, pitiful, reproachful, they stretched their arms out toward passersby, begging.

There was one beggar in particular that Mizuno could not get out of his mind. A biting winter wind was blowing in Berlin. The cobblestones were cold as ice. Yet there this beggar sat, his shirtsleeves and trousers rolled up deliberately to expose his painful wounds to the winter wind to elicit sympathy. No one could bear to look at those wounds. One arm had been severed at the shoulder. One leg was gone from the knee down. At the points of dismemberment the flesh was purple and swollen and festering.

The war numbered among its victims not only adults, but children as well. Beside the beggars lay crying infants, emaciated from malnutrition. Women were desperate to survive.[11]

Among the prostitutes loitering on the street corners were the daughters of former barons, the younger sisters of former major generals and rear admirals, the widows of former captains and lieutenants; even lady schoolteachers. In department store lounges or on park benches at dusk, these women . . .

Though Mizuno's conclusions are questionable by today's standards,

Mizuno reasoned that German women stood better chances of survival than their male counterparts:

> Even if the jobless men went down on their knees, even if they screamed, or wept, or raged, no one would treat them to so much as a slice of bread. The women are fortunate to have a stable source of income.

Then there were the ravages of inflation. In the one month Mizuno was in Germany, the mark's value dropped by two-thirds. Half a year later, it had dropped by 90 percent. And two years later (by which time Mizuno had left the country), they were only printing mark notes in denominations of 100 million and 1 trillion. This was hyperinflation.

Mizuno also took note of the opinions of the intelligentsia. A once plump and ruddy-cheeked university professor lamented that he himself had grown thin, wan, and wrinkled. When they had a meal together at a restaurant, the man grew emotional: "I haven't had such a feast as this in three years!" During dessert, he did not put sugar in his coffee, and when Mizuno asked, "Don't you like sugar?" he replied, "No, it's not that. In my household we haven't tasted sugar for years now. I'm going to save this and let my children enjoy it." And then, as they were leaving, he said, half in jest and half in earnest, "Look, Germany lost this war. People say that Japan is a second Germany, so take care."[12]

The young female elementary school teacher who was teaching Mizuno German also confessed, with tears in her eyes,

> The first half a year after the end of the war, it was a real struggle to keep from starving. In class or on the athletic field, students one after another were fainting for lack of nourishment. More and more children were stealing food. I looked into it, and found kids who simply wanted to give an egg to their ailing grandfather, or some milk to their baby brother since their mother was too ill to breastfeed. I had no strength to scold them.[13]

Mizuno's observations gradually began to take on the air of prophecy. In time, the people of this defeated country embraced a leader with an insane hatred of Jews. Mizuno noticed the status of the Jews and expressed his misgivings about them, as the only ones in this defeated country who had avoided the worst of the current calamity.[14]

Almost all the people are impoverished now, but the war also produced some nouveaux riches. They reaped huge profits from smuggling, or from cornering some market, or from speculating in marks. By forging links with diplomatic delegations and capitalists sent by the Allies, they obtained privileges amounting to a kind of extraterritoriality and managed to keep their profits safe and secure. They were beyond the reach of the authorities. Most Germans regarded them as "a base group of people who took advantage of the nation's distress."

Indeed, the popular atmosphere in Germany was rife with the sentiment that it was on account of the Jews that the war was lost. It was natural for people to look for an excuse, a defense. They found the notion of a Jewish conspiracy handy to explain not only their own defeat, but also the Communist revolution in Russia. But Mizuno was looking at the Jews objectively. He was not a fanatic. He realized that the Jews were without a homeland and thus had no state to rely upon. Historically, they were taught they had no one and nothing to protect them but their own strength. Since ancient times they had wandered the earth, experiencing oppression but enduring, overcoming. It is only natural that they should excel in willpower and spiritual strength. Among this wandering tribe a wealthy man appears. A great scholar appears. Soon, the Germans feel that their financial institutions, their public forums, their political institutions, are all being led around by the nose. It is this that galled the Germans, but not Mizuno.

For better or worse, the Jews are not the people of some small nation, but of the wider world. And it is precisely because they are so cosmopolitan that they are hated by other peoples and expelled from individual countries. When you consider that it is the most one-sided chauvinists who get the best reception in such countries, the logic of the situation becomes self-evident.

Mizuno had been an advocate of a Japanese arms buildup, but his look at the consequences of Germany's defeat in the First World War changed his view of life. Or rather, it changed his view of the entire world.

August 31 was the birthday of the reigning Taishō Emperor. It was called the Festival of the Lord of Heaven. To mark this event, Japanese living in Berlin gathered at the Kaiserkeller, a posh hotel, for a ceremony and celebration. Diplomats, military, businessmen, and journalists attended, only about two dozen altogether. I should like to emphasize here that while the Japanese back home were still flush with the profits of a wartime economic boom, only this handful of their compatriots were in a position to observe closely the effects of war on a defeated nation. A few of them stood up and gave speeches. As a celebrity, Mizuno was among those designated to speak.[15]

Mizuno began his address to the assembled dignitaries in the following fashion:

> As I look around at all of us gathered here this evening, I would imagine that very few have not borne witness to the aftermath of the war in northern France. Gazing upon the terrible destruction at the battle sites, those scenes of hideous devastation, was there any among us who did not find a great shadow falling across his heart, confronted thus with the cataclysmic nature of modern war? Observing the gruesome realities of daily life for the people here in Germany, is there anyone who has not been shocked by the sad consequences of defeat?

As he spoke, scenes of the battle sites of northern France passed before his mind's eye: the crashed biplanes with their noses thrust into the ground and their tails sticking up into the sky; the tanks, belly up and exposed; the rows of abandoned shells; the undulating lines of thousands of grave markers; the bleached white bones of the corpses of German soldiers lying in the trenches. Mizuno launched into a full-blown speech, waxing passionately. In such a war, he argued, there are no winners. Those who survive are just so many more victims. And that is not all. The malice of each nation—of each people—toward their former enemies will not vanish from the earth.

> Can there be any human being, possessed of reason and a conscience, who does not detest and curse this atrocious yet meaningless war? How can we avoid any more such detestable and accursed wars? Not only has this great responsibility been thrust upon us moderns who have tasted this bitter experience; I believe it is our glorious mission to find a way.

He concluded his speech in the following manner; his great concern, the fate of Japan.

> Considered "the second Germany," Japan is now the object of world suspicion. I believe we must devote the greatest thinking and the utmost effort to finding ways to avoid war. Therefore I believe we should lead

the other powers in advocating to the entire world the abolishment of armaments. I believe that this is the safest way for Japan to ensure its continued existence.

The Japanese army attaché opposed Mizuno's view on the grounds that peace with arms is also possible. But the other guests greeted Mizuno's speech with applause. Here it was the pacifists who were the mainstream.

Yet these men, who understood the hell of modern war, numbered only about two dozen. And there was only one among them who was determined to take back to his homeland what he had seen and heard of this hell on earth: Mizuno Hironori.

CHAPTER SEVEN

War as the Greatest Adventure

With *THE NEXT BATTLE*, Mizuno Hironori had fanned the flames of war fever in Japan in addition to pushing for a naval buildup. But he was shocked to see the havoc and waste wrought in Europe by World War I. It changed his perspective 180 degrees. As he stated his new position, "I believe [our country] should lead the other powers in advocating to the entire world the abolishment of armaments."

Mizuno thus returned home with new convictions. The former hawk had come back a dove. Ironically, the Japan he was returning to was one in which there would soon be a boom in the genre known as Japan-U.S. future-war chronicles.

The magazine *Shin Seinen* (New Youth) published its inaugural issue on January 1, 1920. Later, this magazine would help launch the careers of famous authors such as Yokomizo Seishi and Edogawa Rampo. But the lead item in its founding issue was the first installment of a piece by an author whose name is no longer known today, Higuchi Reiyō. The title: *A Future Chronicle of the Japan-U.S. War: A Novel.*

The publisher of *New Youth* was Hakubunkan, one of the largest publishing houses of its day, though today it is known primarily for its diaries. Whatever biographical footprints Higuchi Reiyō left in the sands of time seem to have vanished. This is common among the authors of these Japan-U.S. future-war chronicles. For many such authors, we do not even know their birthdates. That such popular authors have vanished from literary history is evidence of scholarly neglect. The postwar atmosphere did not help. Not only did U.S. General Headquarters scrap many such books as being tainted with militarism, but Japanese themselves ignored them completely.

Fishing around in rare bookshops, rooting around in libraries and archives, I have managed to peruse some of these future-war chronicles. I have been struck by the marginalia: *Stupid! Stupid!* or *If we really fought a war, Japan would win*, or *Of course!* or *NO! NO! NO!* From such scribblings one can get a real sense of how people felt.

And in what frame of mind were people then confronting the country of the Black Ships? Assessing their thoughts, I felt as if I were peeking into my own DNA, witnessing my own hereditary molecular structure. This produced a somewhat painful nostalgia. Let me return to Higuchi Reiyō, whose *A Future Chronicle of the Japan-U.S. War* achieved tremendous popularity.

The editorial board of *New Youth* whetted their readers' appetite for future installments of this serialized novel, and challenged their forecasting skills, by offering a yen's worth of book coupons to one hundred people who correctly guessed the answer to the compound question, "Will Japan win? Or will America win?" at the end of the novel. They received 43,081 responses, of which 8,936 were correct. *New Youth* chose the lucky hundred winners from among that group, by lot. The winners were announced in the July 1921 issue, which carried the final installment of the novel.

So what was the novel's outcome? What was it that so stirred up these readers? To answer these questions and solve the riddle ourselves, we first need to go over the basic outline of the plot.

> Japan-U.S. war! Japan-U.S. war!... This earth-shaking event burst upon the scene on a certain day of a certain month of a certain year in the late 1900s by the Western calendar, at some point very near the year 2000 and when the hands of the clock pointed to 12:35 AM.

The battle was at last joined.

> The Japanese navy attacked an awesome American armada that was steaming eastward to assault the entire coastline of Japan. Simultaneously, several large fleets left their rendezvous points with the mission of occupying the Philippines and Hawaii. Meanwhile, the army had its own war to fight. It mobilized numerous units and began to dispatch them from military ports and other ports along Japan's Pacific coast in fiercely guarded troop transports that were sent out across the vast ocean to attack the North American continent. The cheers of "Banzai!" arising

from the lips of the enthusiastic populace along the railroad tracks, at every military port and at the troop transport centers, swelled to a roar like a myriad of thunderclaps, so powerful as to shatter the pillars of Heaven and shake the Earth off its very axis.

Pretty upbeat, at the beginning.

But what of the *casus belli*? At first, we are told merely that "this Japan-U.S. clash was not some sudden phenomenon incapable of being imagined or foretold." The explanation, however, is left for later. Strangely enough, although the novel is set at the end of the twentieth century, international relations seem to be frozen as they were at the time of the Treaty of Versailles that ended World War I. Well, perhaps that's forgivable. But let us proceed.

The rumors of an impending Japan-U.S. war, which started with the American anti-Japanese movement, have temporarily quieted down, thanks to the Great War. All the peoples of the world hope that in the postwar era, with the establishment of the League of Nations, peace will return to the world. But this is not to be. And the blame—Higuchi is very clear on this—lies with America and Australia, but particularly America, for the following reasons.

Australia bears a grudge toward Japan because Australia lost out to Japan at the Versailles Conference on the matter of control over the formerly German territories in the South Pacific. An anti-Japanese movement arises. The American attitude is even worse. They incite the Chinese to rise up against Japan and actively encourage the Koreans to launch an independence movement. Furthermore, when Russia is shaken by revolution, America lets it be known that it intends to take the opportunity to seize Siberia.

Britain and France, the chief actors in the League of Nations, are sympathetic to Japan, and an International Court of Arbitration announces sanctions against America. Displeased with this verdict, America teams up with Australia to ignore the course pursued by the League. The League resolves that Japan should punish the arrogant Americans. Mexico and the countries of Central and South America remember their own oppression at the hands of the Americans and offer aid. And thus the war begins. Everything is America's fault.

Higuchi's reasoning is itself bellicose. It would appear that he was an amateur in military affairs, so this sort of run-up to war sufficed for him. His writing philosophy seems to have been that whatever plays, stays.

New weapons start appearing one after another. The Americans, for example, invent a radio-guided, air-launched torpedo. This weapon is responsible for the utter annihilation of Japan's Combined Fleet as it sails for Hawaii. But the air-launched torpedoes sink only Japan's surface ships. Its submarines, which Japan believes to be the best in the world, are left unscathed. Still, when the Japanese people learn of the destruction of the Combined Fleet, they are distraught. "Many Millions Mourn" is the phrase of the day, and popular morale sinks as precipitously as did the fleet.

More bad news is to come. China issues a declaration of war against Japan. Then American spies infiltrate Japan and succeed in blowing up munitions depots. The Empire of Dai Nippon—Great Japan—is but a candle before the wind.

It is at this low point in Japan's fortunes that the prime minister delivers a rousing speech: "My fellow Japanese!" he says, "As of today, Japan is now saved from this grave crisis, and you may all feel safe and secure again." He reveals that Japan has perfected a great invention that can counter America's air-launched torpedoes. It is a military airship, equipped with air-launched torpedoes and defenses against them, superior in quality to what America has. But the new weaponry is not used. As the American fleet enters the waters near Japan, they are attacked by the surviving Japanese subs lurking there.

Neutral countries that hate American tyranny, such as Great Britain, France, Russia, Germany, and Italy, intervene as mediators, opening a peace conference. America responds; that is, it has no choice but to respond. Without disparaging the extraordinary efforts of the European powers, it is Japan's development of new weaponry, a matter of power, that really creates the conditions for peace.

And thus concludes Higuchi Reiyō's novel, *A Future Chronicle of the Japan-U.S. War*. It was published in book form by Daimeidō Shoten and sold so well that "The Japan-U.S. War: Picture Postcards from the Future" even appeared. The publisher hoped to make a little extra money by shipping some of these postcards off to America for sale. A painstaking examination of Japan Foreign Ministry records reveals that a number of items relating to these Japan-U.S. future-war chronicles were indeed shipped off, the postcards among them.

Of course, not all the future-war chronicles were officially noted. As long as Japanese were simply reading them and discarding them, there was no need for the Foreign Ministry to be concerned. It was when there was fear that by crossing the Pacific they would inflame American public opinion that they became subject to inspection. A secret document titled "Secrets Cat. B, No. 558" and dated October 23, 1920 was sent by the superintendent general of the Tokyo Metropolitan Police to the Europe/America desk of the Foreign Ministry, reporting the halting of the export of "The Japan-U.S. War: Picture Postcards from the Future."

The postcards had gained some popularity among Japanese Americans, and the Foreign Ministry wanted to know what could be done about it. The superintendent responded to their request for intervention by reporting the results of his investigation. He said, "[With regard to this matter of the postcards,] they are selling well domestically and continue to be exported to America." His report quoted Kobe Fumisaburō, proprietor of Daimeidō, as follows.

> Circumstances now are such that a Japan-U.S. war is inevitable. When it might begin has become a matter of public interest. That is why we have published Higuchi Reiyō's *A Future Chronicle of the Japan-U.S. War*: to appeal to our patriotic fighters. Japanese intellectuals have hitherto been cool to Japan-U.S. issues; now, not only they but the public as a whole have been greatly stimulated. A fuse has been lit, and I can fairly see it sizzling as it burns toward a consciousness of national unity. We hereby commemorate this occasion and opportunity with the publication (at Dr. Higuchi's suggestion) of 31,800 copies of "The Japan-U.S. War: Picture Postcards from the Future," as propaganda that will fund public studies of our policy toward America and encourage national unity. We also plan to export them to America.

At the tail end of this report, the superintendent notes casually, "The bulk of them have been seized."

This particular "advance" upon the United States was stopped. On the other hand, the publishing industry had arrived at a consensus that these Japan-U.S. future-war chronicles represented real commercial possibilities.

Higuchi's own conclusion in his *Future Chronicle of the Japan-U.S. War* was half-baked. The answer to the publisher's challenge to readers to describe the ending was "it ends with mediation by a third party." Having teased the readers with the question, "Will Japan win? Or will America win?" and then to end, as it did, in a draw, the editorial department of *New*

Youth felt constrained to add the apology, "Our readers may find this quite unsatisfactory." Accordingly, the next month, Higuchi began to serialize *A Future Chronicle of the Japan-U.S. War, Continued: A Future Chronicle of the Second World War*.

This continuation, however, does not venture to ask, "Will Japan win? Or will America win?" Instead, the Japan-U.S. war ends with a peace treaty. In America and Australia, the anti-Japanese movements grow even shriller. The League of Nations collapses. The world splits into two camps. One alliance comprises Japan, Germany, Russia, Italy, Belgium, Mexico, and China. It is opposed by an alliance including England, France, America, and Australia. Now a world war ensues. The human race is on the brink of self-destruction. Just as the aforementioned new Japanese air-launched torpedo is about to be deployed, the continuation is discontinued. Higuchi gave his reasons in the March 1921 issue of *New Youth*.

> How will these travails of war come to an end? That is the question. But to describe that adequately would take the rest of the year. Indeed, depending on how the war developed, it might not be brought to a conclusion even if the telling of it took the whole of the following year as well. If readers were led on for so long, they would wind up simply washing their hands of it. And that is the reason why I am stopping here, with no conclusion for a conclusion.

Considering that readers had already been led on, with pounding hearts and bated breath, for some fourteen months now, this was irresponsible. The editorial department seems to have felt the need to prepare for a new solution.

Higuchi's yarn was preposterous, but his use of the phrase "the Second World War" does deserve some attention. It reflected the crisis-consciousness that the next war would be a world war. Higuchi's confidence that the readership would accept this was rooted in his experience of the novel's long and popular serialization.

At the same time that Higuchi was serializing *A Future Chronicle of the Japan-U.S. War, Continued: A Future Chronicle of the Second World War*, he was also writing another novel. The title was *As Expected: The Japan-U.S. ******. The book was published in June 1921.

Given the recent background of the authorities' suppression of the post-cards, the "*****" may be thought to suggest jittery official censorship. In reality, it was a deliberate effort at sensationalism. The apparent censorship itself creates an atmosphere of danger around the book. Since the title begins with "As Expected," the readers of that era would have had no trouble mentally replacing the asterisks (circles in Japanese) with "Final Battle" or "War," understanding the title as a whole to refer to the inevitability of a conflict between Japan and the United States.

If you consider Higuchi's three works together, you can triangulate his main area of concern. Certainly this third book is written with a lot of high-spirited dash: "The entire fleet, from the commanders on down," exhibited the highest morale, "as if to say, 'What is the American military to us? What can those arrogant Yankees do to us? We shall make them worship the acme of perfection to which the Japanese man has brought his fighting skills.'" No gloom and doom here.

As before, awesome new weapons appear. The Germans had used poison gas in World War I. When an assassination by means unknown occurs in *As Expected: The Japan-U.S. ******, the agent turns out to be a newly developed gas. America, the enemy, also makes new inventions.

> Even foodstuffs for the civilian population are now researched scientifically, and in one hour, one newly invented machine can produce enough to feed one hundred thousand people for one day. Everything is large-scale, everything is scientific, everything is designed for durability, everything is thoroughly systematized.

So now we realize: Higuchi is aiming for a science fiction–type adventure tale.

It is worth considering why such an author appeared at that time. In our current postwar period, Japanese have made war taboo as a topic. If one of us says "war," another will shout "peace" in a knee-jerk reaction. But it is too easy to talk simply of war when in fact the ramifications are many and varied. As a result, we have lost our ability to think imaginatively about war.

In the prewar period, however, many imaginative works appeared, from realistic military tales and propaganda to fantastic adventure stories. An actual battlefield where people kill people is a horrific place, but war does provide the most outstanding theatrical space, a grand backdrop for love and adventure. Prose fiction abounds with this sort of thing; one sees plenty of it in popular films too. Back in 1900, Oshikawa Shunrō had debuted with a pioneering war-based adventure tale, titled *Warship at the Bottom of the Sea*.

* * *

OSHIKAWA SHUNRŌ was born on March 21, 1876 in Matsuyama City in Ehime Prefecture. In other words, he was a fellow townsman of Mizuno Hironori, who was just a year older. When I learned that his father had been a samurai retainer of that domain during the Edo period, I thought that he and Mizuno might have been childhood friends and might have exerted some influence on each other. But it turns out that is not a possibility.

When Oshikawa was eight months old, his family moved to Niigata. The Oshikawas were a low-ranking samurai family with a stipend of only ten *koku*. However, as one of the domain's promising young elite, Shunrō's father, Masayoshi, entered Kaiseijo, the forerunner of Tokyo Imperial University. There, Masayoshi was influenced by a missionary dispatched from the United States and became a Christian. The reason he left Matsuyama for Niigata right after Shunrō's birth was in order to proselytize. He traveled around the Niigata and Hokuriku areas and founded a mission center in Sendai. This is the origin of Tohoku Gakuin University.

Shunrō completed elementary school through high school in Sendai and then matriculated at Meiji Academy. He became fanatical about baseball, which was then the latest sports fad. Shunrō flunked out twice and was called back to Tohoku Academy, where his father was president. But there he continued his wayward behavior. As Shunrō later told a magazine, he once poured kerosene on the hair of a student sitting in front of him in English class. The student's hair caught fire, and Shunrō caught hell. Presidential scion he may have been, Shunrō was nevertheless expelled.

Next, he became a privately funded auditor at the famous Sapporo Agricultural College in Hokkaido. Tiring of this as well, Shunrō returned to Tokyo. There he entered the Fisheries Institute (the forerunner of Tokyo Fisheries College) but didn't see that through either. Next he entered Tokyo Technical College, the forerunner to Waseda University. Beginning his studies at age nineteen, he spent three years as a student in the English department before transferring to Politics. He plunged himself into his readings: Victor Hugo's *Les Misérables*, Alexandre Dumas's *The Count of Monte Cristo*, Jules Verne's *Twenty Thousand Leagues Under the Sea*, etc.

A number of overlapping elements thus went into the making of adventure author Oshikawa Shunrō. For one thing, we noted above that Shunrō's father was a convert to Christianity who lived in a milieu of foreign missionaries and himself moved about constantly from mission school to mission school; his own character was unbridled. For another, when Shunrō was at Tokyo

Technical College, he attended the "Saturday Club," a student literary salon, where he made the acquaintance of author Nagai Kafū, and also of the author Iwaya Sazanami, editor in chief of a youth magazine.

Shunrō wanted Japanese people to have adventure-story heroes of their own that could compare with the protagonists of Western novels, such as Jean Valjean, the Count of Monte Cristo, and Captain Nemo. When he published his maiden effort, *Warship at the Bottom of the Sea*, at age twenty-four, he was on his way to becoming a best-selling author. This debut work was indeed an adventure story, influenced by both Verne's *Twenty Thousand Leagues Under the Sea* and Yano Ryūkei's *The Tale of the Floating Castle*. The warship in question was a submarine, something that was not yet a naval reality. The hero was a stand-in for the author; room was also made for a beautiful heroine and for a young boy with whom the readers could identify.

The heroine had the "graceful eyebrows and gracious lips" of a Celestial Maiden: "as in her outward appearance, so too in spirit, she was beautiful, the most noble lady in the world." The boy loved to play war and would say such things as, "Every single day I fly the flag of the Rising Sun as I play at war all over town. And say, isn't that Rising Sun a grand flag?" Then, added to the hero, the heroine, and the boy, are science fiction elements.

The submarine that appears in *Warship at the Bottom of the Sea* is forty meters long and seven meters wide. In shape "it bears a striking resemblance to the spear used by South Indian savages to fell an elephant with a single blow or to slaughter a tiger. At both ends the submarine is strangely shaped and sharply angled." It can fire seventy-eight torpedoes a minute and travel at a speed of 107 knots. It also has equipment that can break down seawater, producing oxygen to breathe underwater. It can travel underwater for dozens of hours at a time.

After *Warship at the Bottom of the Sea*, Oshikawa published one best seller after another. From the titles one can get an idea of his originality: *The Giant Airship, The Great World Struggle by Land and by Sea, The World a Thousand Years from Now, Desert Island Warship, Where the Demons Are, The Electric Fleet*. Having so rapidly become a popular author, Oshikawa found himself approached, hat in hand, by the giant publisher Hakubunkan. They wanted to profile him as the lead author in the inaugural issue of their *The World of Adventure* magazine. Accordingly, the first issue, published in January 1908, began with the following declaration from Oshikawa, titled "Off we go, into the World of Adventure!"

The twentieth century furnishes a great live stage for the enterprising, the aggressive, the bold. In a broad sense, he who has the spirit of adventure will prevail. Indeed, in the broadest sense, what human affair does not partake of adventure? War is a great adventure, sailing is a great adventure; in any righteous activity there is always to be found a story of adventure and courage. Most of the grand undertakings in this wide world of ours are possible only via great adventures. To extend this line of argument, riding a locomotive is also an adventure; strolling about the city is also an adventure. Indeed, to push this notion to an extreme, it is already an adventure merely for human beings to try to live on this earth. We can never know when the earth will collide with some comet and be pulverized, or when our cities will be struck by earthquakes and burn to the ground.

So everything is an adventure, even riding on a train or walking about town. But the greatest adventure of all is war and sea-travel—as in *Warship at the Bottom of the Sea*. Oshikawa's world neither promotes arms expansion nor offers paeans to peace. Just as boys in any era enjoy playing war, Oshikawa enjoyed the free play of imagination and the prospect of live theater.

Creativity knows no bounds, and Oshikawa's "stage" expanded without borders across the entire globe. Thus we have his *Crossing the Vastness of Asia, Wonders of India and the South Seas, Airship over the North Pole, World Travel by Bicycle (and on a Shoestring), Mysterious Fire under the Frost, Hot Wind and High Seas*, and *Around Africa*.

However, Oshikawa gave up writing for *The World of Adventure* and founded a publishing house and a magazine of his own. The inaugural issue of his magazine, *The World of Chivalry*, was published in January 1912. And as Oshikawa moved from the former world into the latter, his writing took on a different aroma, or rather smell. If we compare the manifesto for *The World of Adventure* with the following pronunciamento from *The World of Chivalry*, we can get an idea of the great divide between the two worlds.

The World of Chivalry has arisen to carry the spear that bears the brilliant standard of heroism, and to vanquish the demons that spew their vile venom at our nation. Selfishness and avarice, unpatriotic thought, decadence, vanity, dangerous beliefs—all these are our enemies. We have arisen to exterminate these poisonous pests once and for all, to assist our national spirit to flourish, to encourage chivalry of soul, to observe the principle of a sound mind in a sound body, to foster to the best of our ability the nurturing of the physique that accompanies the cultivation of wisdom, and by all this to discharge our responsibility to provide our country with an adamantine, rock-solid national security.

Why did a writer of tales of pure imagination start spouting off like some moralist and xenophobe? Over this change of heart I see cast the shadows of two figures: Homer Lea and Mizuno Hironori.

Lea's *The Valor of Ignorance* was first published in the United States in 1909. A year later, Mochizuki Kotarō translated it in secrecy for the army's internal use. In 1911, it was bound and distributed. In October of the same year, Ike Kōkichi's translation of Lea came out under the altered title of *The Japan-U.S. War.* The publisher was Hakubunkan. But even before the publication of this translation, Hakubunkan knew about the original. The April 1910 issue of *The World of Adventure* had carried a novel titled *Dream Tales of a Japan-U.S. War,* by the pseudonymous Torahige Tai-i (General Tigerwhisker). The author's real name was Abu Shin'ichi; he is also known by the pen name of Tenpū. His main literary activity was in *The World of Adventure.* Born in 1882, he was six years younger than Oshikawa Shunrō. He came from Yamaguchi Prefecture and was in the same entering cohort at the Naval Academy as Yamamoto Isoroku in 1901. When he was still a candidate for midshipman, he participated in the Battle of Tsushima and was wounded. In the Russo-Japanese War he was in the reserves. He seems to have aspired to become a second Oshikawa Shunrō. Nothing else is known of his career.

In *Dream Tales of a Japan-U.S. War,* as in Oshikawa's stories, the hero is a Japanese man loved by a beautiful woman. The heroine is an American actress. As to the adventure part, the hero goes gallivanting around in a newfangled aeroplane, and that's about that. It's not much of a story. But the opening statement does grab one's attention: "In America, the coming war with Japan is a fashionable topic; I thought I would give it a shot too." And the conclusion is also worth a look.

We are barely on the verge of this war. One wonders what its outcome will be. Which side will win? The answer seems obvious. You, our readers, believe, without harboring a doubt, in the victory of our Empire. Nor do our journalists doubt it. But if one is not careful, one never knows what might happen. Americans cry war, but today's Foreign Ministry and journalists simply deny that with "It can't be! It can't be!" which is not a clever way to respond. Readers! From now on, you take care—understood?

The magazine's editors added their own boxed epigraph.

In America they have what they call the "yellow papers." These are newspapers of the most dishonest variety, which try to distract from their incompetence by raising a stink; their clamor is intolerable. If Japan and America go to war, Japan will lose one battle after another—or so say that lot.

It was while Hearst's papers were thus fanning U.S.-Japan war fever in the United States, and when Homer Lea had just put out *The Valor of Ignorance*, that this *Dream Tales of a Japan-U.S. War* was written. The line of influence is clear. The next year, Mizuno Hironori's *The Next Battle* became a best seller. And at the same time, Ike Kōkichi's *The Japan-U.S. War* sold an epoch-making 84,000 copies.

After becoming independent of *The World of Adventure*, the first piece Oshikawa wrote for *The World of Chivalry* was titled "Japan-U.S. Duel." I read it anticipating something in the genre of the future-war chronicles, but it turned out to be the same old adventure-story format, with a hero and a beauty. An admiral in the Imperial Japanese Navy slays a viciously evil Yankee in Acapulco, restoring peace to the area. The citizenry are grateful to this epitome of righteousness and *Yamato damashi* (the Spartan spirit of ancient Japan) and hold a banquet in his honor. A railroad baron named Lee or Lea (the Japanese is phonetic, and it is unclear if this is meant to invoke Homer Lea) entreats the admiral to marry his daughter (the heroine). But the Japanese admiral declines, saying, "I am the loyal child of the Great Empire of Japan, with its tradition of bloodlines unbroken over myriad generations."

In *Warship at the Bottom of the Sea*, the hero engages many foreigners in sumo and dispatches them all with ease, putting him in a great mood until he is trounced by an American. When he tries his luck at a footrace, he comes in not first, but third. So he is not necessarily the strongest, the handsomest, the most right. Therein lies the story's originality and charm. But in "Japan-U.S. Duel," the hero sides with the weak and crushes the strong in the manner of a typical stuffed personage in a didactic novel. It ceases to be interesting.

There is another reason for the decline in the vitality of Oshikawa's novels. He was swimming in sake. He would go on a binge, then produce a stream of adventure stories. Gradually, however, it was the alcohol that consumed him. On November 16, 1914, his physical condition took a turn for the worse, and he suddenly died. He was thirty-eight years old.

All in all, however, Oshikawa was a genius of the adventure-story genre, churning out one idea after another. When he left *The World of Adventure* for *The World of Chivalry*, the former declined in readership. When he died, the adventure-story genre itself petered out. At *The World of Adventure*, Abu Tenpū was next in the batter's box after Oshikawa, but he was lucky to get base hits. The Hakubunkan editors decided to retire the team. They stopped publication abruptly and in 1920 started up *New Youth*. They still needed to find a new Oshikawa.

The nod went to Higuchi Reiyō, whose *The Imperial Strategy*, based on the Yellow Peril doctrine of German Emperor Wilhelm II, had become a best seller thanks to the timing of its publication, which coincided neatly with the outbreak of the Great War. The novel tells the dubious tale of a French spy who overhears the kaiser musing to himself about his delusions of grandeur and specifically his fantasy of world conquest. The spy transcribes this and translates it. Higuchi published a number of similar tales during the conflict.

The magazine *New Youth* started publishing just after the end of the First World War, at which point the Hakubunkan editors planned the next big thing for Higuchi, something they thought would produce sales. Namely, the theme of a Japan-U.S. war. Thus they made his *A Future Chronicle of the Japan-U.S. War* the centerpiece of their inaugural issue. We noted above the esteem Higuchi garnered with that serialization, and the excellent sales. But his writing was weak and the novel poorly structured. He had simply caught the trend of the times. He had originally debuted as a poet. His two collections of verse, *The Laurel Wreath* and *Remaining Blossoms* were titled somewhat after the fashion of Shimazaki Tōson's works. It was derivative verse of the following sort: "Do not say that love delights. / Hand in hand with a beautiful maiden, / I wept at the fragrance of white lilies, / And sorrow ruled my breast." Et cetera, et cetera.

The reason that *A Future Chronicle of the Japan-U.S. War* contained elements of both science fiction and the adventure story is that it appeared at the end of this spate of chronicles of imaginary wars, which had begun with the works of Oshikawa Shunrō.

172 | PART II

After Oshikawa Shunrō's piece, the biggest buzz around the inaugural issue of *New Youth* was devoted to Higuchi Reiyō's future-war chronicle, which also answered the question, "Who wins, Japan or the U.S.?" with "It's a draw." To resolve readers' dissatisfaction, the editors required Reiyō also to write a sequel. But the sequel dealt with the problem by embroiling the Japan-U.S. conflict in a larger world war, and the plot broke down.

Now it seemed as though every pot was boiling a Japan-U.S. war scenario. With readers thus attracted and stimulated, fresh topicality had to be added to the recipe to keep them hungry for more. The Hakubunkan editorial board accordingly dredged up a new chef. This new talent, who took Higuchi's place in the limelight, was Satō Kōjirō, whose *Dream Tales of a Japan-U.S. War* was published in the April 1921 issue of *New Youth*.

Until just four years prior, Satō Kōjirō had been an active-duty lieutenant general in the army. He was born in 1862 into a samurai family in the domain of Owari. After graduating from the Army Academy, he served in both the Sino-Japanese and Russo-Japanese wars. Then, after a period of study in Germany, he was given a series of postings as an elite military attaché. So he had experience of living abroad and was nearing the ripe old age of sixty. As a lieutenant general, his bona fides in military matters were irreproachable. For a personage of such standing to author such a work as *Dream Tales of a Japan-U.S. War* was, at the time, sufficiently novel and noteworthy.

Still, one wonders, why was Higuchi replaced with Satō? With readers' responses in mind, the editors made the following simple calculation. Rather than continue with the line of adventure stories that traced its genealogy from Oshikawa Shunrō to Higuchi Reiyō, they would respond to the developing market for reality-based forecasting. The editors made their expectations of the new *Dream-Tale* author clear in a preface to the next issue:

The author is one of our country's preeminent soldier-statesmen: a military strategist who is also a literary stylist; the author of the excellent *If Japan and America Fight*, a work which has already proved he can gain and keep the whole world's attention. We mean none other than His Excellency Lieutenant General Satō Kōjirō of the Imperial Japanese Army.

The editors chose to mention Satō's rank and his previous hypothetical-war publication, *If Japan and America Fight*; in fact, he was retired from the army and had also published, immediately after leaving active duty, a treatise titled *National Mobilization for a People's War* (1918). While he was on active duty, Satō had been obliged to keep his grander visions to himself. It was only when he retired that he felt he could finally trot out his pet theories, which Satō did in his book on national mobilization. This was the first time the topic had been propagandized journalistically.

In the realm of politics it took some twenty years after Satō's proposal for a national general mobilization law for it to be enacted in Japan. This happened in 1938, when the war with China was finally underway in earnest. The law put under state control not only the munitions industry but many facets of the economy, including raw materials, production, capital, labor, trade, transportation, and communications. Not only that, it also provided for the enlistment of the citizenry, and even for that trump card of the wartime system: control over freedom of expression. The state thus gathered unto itself authority to control virtually all aspects of the people's life. It was a law that provided a foundation for fascism.

For Satō to be writing in this vein so early makes him an ominous prophet indeed. His tone was certainly portentous (or at least pompous) enough:

> I say that victory or defeat in a People's War necessarily depends upon that people's spiritual strength; I say it depends upon the nation's strength in military recruitment; I say it depends upon the nation's material and financial strength, and I say it depends upon the nation's industrial strength. In other words, what is meant by national mobilization is the submission to government control of virtually all of the nation's military manpower, wealth, and industrial capacity, so that the war can be prosecuted to the last man.

Satō's big ideas were born of his admiration for Germany. Germany was overwhelmingly powerful not only under Hitler but also at the beginning of the First World War. Satō flattered himself that he knew the secret to this strength. "The Sino-Japanese War was finger-wrestling; the Russo-Japanese War was arm-wrestling; the struggle from now on is the real thing, into which we must pour the strength of our entire body politic." Germany is, "even in ordinary times, united from top to bottom, meticulously thorough, and absolutely complete in its preparations for a people's war." Therefore, like Germany, Japan should "mobilize the entire workforce, mobilize the entire manufacturing sector and all of business, and mobilize the railroad, shipping, and financial sectors: everything must come directly under the purview of the state." Satō's tone and premise is that in all things we must follow Germany.

Nor is national mobilization, in Satō's conception, reduced to purely spiritual exhortations. He does not neglect to point to detailed policy proposals for its realization. For example, "[German] park benches are built in such a fashion that they can be installed in trains that are converted into troop transports." And "chemical factories that normally produce celluloid are designed so that when occasion demands, they can readily be converted to the production of explosives."

Satō says that "in reality there is no blame accruing to German militarism." However, his partiality is so evident that one cannot help feeling he is like a man possessed. As to why, remember that at the time he was writing this, Japan was participating in the war on the side of the Allies. And that Germany was on the verge of losing.

Satō further censures England and France for their lack of military preparedness and assigns the blame to the low status of military people in those two countries.

What of America? Satō too has read Homer Lea's *The Valor of Ignorance* and been influenced by it. America has fallen into money worship and is not thinking seriously about national defense.

> To reduce armaments and instead devote all one's efforts to industry: that could be done only by the Americans. If one devotes all one's efforts to industry in this manner, then it is a matter of course that the country will grow wealthy. Many individuals have indeed attained great wealth. In truth they have become shamefully addicted to gold, and the resultant harm has been manifold. Intelligent Americans are greatly concerned and have tried to awaken their countrymen to these dangers. In just such a manner, Homer Lea, the author of *On the Inevitability of a Japan-U.S. War* [Mochizuki Kotarō's Japanese translation of *Valor of Ignorance*], endeavors as its chief goal to alert his countrymen.

To Satō, as the author of *National Mobilization for a People's War*, Germany's defeat was contrary to all expectations.

Satō's next book was *If Japan and America Fight*. To switch formats so readily may suggest that the author has lost some of his seriousness of purpose, but it is the way of political leaders to insist, at the outset of a war, that the war will solve any problem at hand. War is clearly an extension of politics. However, wars sometimes end not only without the resolution of old problems but with the engendering of new ones.

When the Versailles peace treaty ended the Great War, nothing was resolved regarding the Pacific or the Far East. Japan's demands for concessions in the Shandong peninsula and for occupation of Germany's former South Pacific islands was supported by England, France, and Italy, but shelved due to the strong opposition of the United States. One must acknowledge that behind this lay America's own ambitions in China. The theory gained currency in Japan that the anti-Japanese movement in China involved some American string-pulling.

For Satō, whose praise of Germany had turned out to be misplaced, the American threat was most satisfactory grist for his national mobilization mill. One wonders how Mizuno Hironori himself would have reacted had he not personally observed Germany's miserable state after the war. He might very well have held the same opinions as Satō.

If Japan and America Fight provided the foundation for *Dream Tales of a Japan-U.S. War*. The earlier work explicitly stated that its purpose was "to serve as a wake-up call to our own people, and at the same time a warning to the Americans." It was replete with confidence that "if the Americans read this work," they will understand "the stupidity of attacking Japan." The Japanese navy, the author noted, had played a prominent and victorious role in both the Sino-Japanese and Russo-Japanese wars. "In contrast, the American fleet, though modern, has never been deployed in any large-scale engagements." And the Japanese army was the best in the world. Japan had "learned the arts of war, first from the French, then from the Germans, finally from England," making it stronger than America. Japan, he thought, would never attack American territories "as Homer Lea fears." But if America were to attack Japan, then "rather than occupying ourselves with exclusively defensive measures," Japan should counterattack, as with the Baltic Fleet. And to that end we should prepare ourselves by laying down a ten-year plan for a system of national mobilization. Satō's conclusion was that if his advice were followed, America would "suffer the same fate as the Mongol invasions" of 1274 and 1281. (It was, of course, the *kamikaze*, or "divine wind," of a hurricane that had ended the Mongols' dreams of a conquest.)

That such a work as *If Japan and America Fight* should be written by someone who had been so high up in Japan's military command structure made the Foreign Ministry apprehensive. Amid the voluminous reports on the subject in the archives of the Ministry of Foreign Affairs is a document sent to foreign minister Uchida Kōsai from the Japanese consul general in Seattle, Saitō Hiroshi. In it, Saitō says that if indeed war arises between Japan and the United States, it will be as a result of exaggerating a small struggle in such a way that conjectures about a coming crisis begin to spread far and wide. This would involve immigration issues, which easily inflame popular opinion in both countries. It was well known that both Japan and America were brimming with war sentiment. Therefore, Saitō thinks, it is their absolute duty to eradicate anything that advocates a Japan-U.S. war, even if it is not hard-line material.

It is worth paraphrasing Saitō's criticisms of Lieutenant General Satō a little further, since he mixes in personal views that go beyond the framework of what is required by his position. Lieutenant General Satō's ethos, he says, is completely different from his own. If the views of the lieutenant general and his ilk percolate through to bilateral relations, it will encourage a bellicose spirit on both sides, producing a dangerous international situation. It is this that most stirs the writer's apprehensions. The only way to avoid incurring the mistrust of the world is to create a progressive and democratic government.

It is certainly true that the publication of Satō's book indicates the gradual acknowledgement of freedom of expression in Japan. But for a book like this to come out also presents problems for freedom of expression. Denying Lieutenant General Satō's views is also freedom of expression. Thus it makes sense to counter his views with reasonable arguments, correcting his fallacies and throttling off any pernicious influence on the U.S. Consul. Saitō was born in 1875, making him thirty-five years old at the time of this exchange, a man of sound mind and body.

* * *

SATŌ BEGAN SERIALIZING his *Dream Tales of a Japan-U.S. War* in the April 1921 issue of *New Youth* at the invitation of its editors. What sort of a tale was this? As I read, I began to get angry. "Whether or not we can cut through our present difficulties depends entirely on the discipline of the communal life of the populace." When I am exposed to something like this, I cannot help having a strong negative reaction.

But as I kept turning the pages, I thought to myself, "Wait a minute. Why does he have to dramatize this national crisis, this crisis-consciousness, to such an extent?" Is living in this island nation that dangerous? What is the efficacy of stressing "the discipline of the communal life of the populace" in countering the menace of the Black Ships—the enormous shadow cast over the imagination by the United States of America? Is that "discipline of the communal life of the populace" some sort of hole card that will enable us finally to trump that threat? Or is it merely a tranquilizer? If we have to be kept in a constant state of fear and anxiety, we are a most naïve people indeed.

The narrative begins as follows. One day, at the invitation of an association of local military personnel, a certain white-haired general heads off to give a lecture at the town of S on the Tōkaidō, or Eastern Sea Highway. He is identified as General Genkai. His topic is "The Japan-U.S. Problem and Spiritual Mobilization." The meeting hall is abuzz with the conversation of 1,400 or 1,500 townspeople, young and old. The general says he has come to "iterate and reiterate" the "urgent necessity of conducting a spiritual mobilization" to respond to "the gravest crisis since the founding of our nation": namely, the Japan-U.S. problem.

General Genkai spends the night at the home of one of the local notables. This man is an elderly gentleman, whose commercial wealth and kind character ensure a steady flow of guests; his home is the town's cultural salon. The next evening, a number of townspeople are gathered there, and they recount the dreams they had following General Genkai's lecture the previous night (hence the novel's title, *Dream Tales of a Japan-U.S. War*).

One "nervous-looking old maid," who had taught school in Nagoya and Nara after graduating teacher-training college, starts out by disclosing that "I had the most horrible dream that our Empire was on the verge of utter ruin." She continues in the following vein:

> One day, I had the feeling that there was some great social unrest that was arising. I couldn't just stay cooped up in the countryside, so I immediately went to Tokyo, where I found society changed, agitated. Extra editions of the newspapers were being hawked about town every other hour or so. According to these extras, Japanese-American diplomatic relations were at the breaking point, and either that day or the next the Americans were due to issue an ultimatum. Reportedly, a great American armada was approaching and was preparing to reduce our land to scorched earth with a single blow.

In the dream, the people collectively shudder at the threat posed by this approaching American fleet. The ex-schoolteacher further notices that the soldiers and police officers patrolling the town are all women. And that they are of robust physique. It is not that no men are about, but rather that the men are weak and frail, so they are not entrusted with this sort of work, and they do not stand out. At a gathering held in Hibiya Park by the Citizens' Council on Policy Toward America, the entire audience is female. On the dais a fat woman appears. She is Speaker of the Lower House of the National Diet. This crisis, she declaims, has come upon us because the entire lot of male politicians has followed the bad example set by Ii Naosuke back at the end of the feudal regime. Quaking in fear of America, they made no preparations for the national defense. Furthermore, the general populace have spent morning, noon, and night indulging themselves in extravagance and are contaminated by foreign ideas. They have become distanced from the ideals of loyalty and patriotism. Most of the menfolk have slipped into an effete sophistication; by contrast it is the women who have awakened and arisen and grown strong. Given this situation, such goals as universal fairness and national unity can be achieved only by transferring half of the political power to the women.

The old maid's dream ends here, abruptly. That is because General Genkai interjects,

> One does greatly desire the advancement of women, but of course one also hopes that Japanese women will not lose their commitment to being good wives and wise mothers. However, if our young men do not exert themselves a little more, they might very well lose out to women like those in this dream tale. Wouldn't that be something! Ah, hah, hah, hah, hah!

To Satō, a man of the nation-building Meiji era, the young men of the following era of Taishō democracy could hardly avoid appearing spineless. He could only wonder uneasily, if the younger generation are turning out like this, who is going to protect the country? And indeed, it was in 1920 that the feminist Hiratsuka Raichō (1886–1971), who had founded the Bluestocking Society in 1911, established the New Woman's Association to fight for women's civil rights. With these social conditions in the background, the mise-en-scène of this dream tale becomes more understandable.

Satō, advocating (through General Genkai) that women restrict themselves to their dual role as "good wives and wise mothers," could not bring himself to acknowledge Hiratsuka and other members of the movement to expand women's rights. However, in his earlier *National Mobilization for a People's War*, he did emphasize how, in the Europe of the Great War, due to the decline in the numbers and availability of men, women did not serve merely as nurses accompanying the troops but took up such professions as schoolteacher, car driver, train conductor, mail deliverer, and police officer. And he commented (intending it as propaganda for national mobilization) that "the awakening of women as women is more to be feared than the advent of mannish women."

Meanwhile, in *Dream Tales of a Japan-U.S. War*, people appear one after another to tell their own strange dream-tales, as if handing off the baton in a relay. The head of the local branch of the veterans' association, who was decorated with the Order of the Golden Kite for his service in the Russo-Japanese War, comes forward in an episode that furnishes a typical example of the psychological wound left by the Black Ships. His dream is set fifteen or sixteen years in the future. Americans are acting the bully in China. Japanese there were limited to laundrymen, hairdressers, houseboys, nannies, and prostitutes. An American lady rebukes her Japanese houseboy and nanny for having an affair. The houseboy asserts their innocence, saying nothing of the sort occurred. In his excitement, he inadvertently pushes the American lady. She cries out for help. Over a dozen American men rush up, gang up on the houseboy and the nanny, and beat them to death. As the narrator of this dream says, "It was exactly like the lynchings that Americans even nowadays give to the blacks." In response to the white man's outrageous conduct in China, Japanese anti-American movements multiply throughout China. Upon which the American government demands that every last Japanese resident in China be obliged to return to Japan. When the Japanese government firmly resists this, the American government sends an ultimatum. And so war begins.

Thus in this work, the Japanese-American war crisis is discussed in terms of American ambitions in China. Given what was also heard from Japanese Americans regarding their own circumstances in California, all this made for an increased feeling of reality and immediacy. It keenly stimulated the Japanese consciousness that Japanese were discriminated against, that they were the victims of the ideology of white supremacy. In this regard it is important to keep in mind that the American counterparts of these chronicles of future war treat the Japanese immigrants who have crossed the Pacific in a panicked tone that borders on complete fantasy.

Immigrants from Japan did not readily change their habits and customs or try to assimilate into their new country. Everything they did seemed to the majority culture like some kind of secret or mystery. It was feared that behind their inscrutable countenances, they were sharpening the fangs of an alien culture. A typical example was already mentioned in connection with chapter 4 of *BANZAI!* Like the soldiers hidden in the giant Trojan Horse of Greek mythology, the Japanese Americans mount surprise attacks in multiple locations, coordinated with the Japanese fleet that has arrived via the Pacific. The faceless Japanese raise the specter of a yellow tidal wave flooding in.

Both *Dream Tales of a Japan-U.S. War* and *BANZAI!* can be categorized as xenophobic literature. And it would be fair to say that if both works try to inflame readers concerning an enemy threat but focus more on their own people's predicament and presumed reactions than on the alien culture itself, that is proof that in both cases their understanding of that other culture is shallow.

What the editors of *New Youth* asked of *Dream Tales of a Japan-U.S. War* was that it be an adventure tale. Lieutenant General Satō therefore framed the ending of the dream as the adventure story of "an army major who lost his right arm during the Siberian Intervention" of 1918–22. This tale recounts how Japan invented a Laputian aerial troop transport called the Celestial Rock Ship and used it to send a suicide corps to America to bring the enemy to their knees.

Lieutenant General Satō then boldly added something so excessive it must be ascribed to his pride as a proponent of national mobilization. His narrative closes with the following observation by General Genkai:

In terms of material power, no matter what the angle from which one looks at it, at the present time Japan is not America's enemy. To start with, America's national wealth is some 440 billion yen, nine times that of Japan. National income per annum is 76 billion yen, or some sixteen times that of Japan. There is no comparison. In terms of scientific progress America is of course more advanced, though not by so much as the difference in national wealth. The key is spiritual mobilization. With national unity and the concentrated application of all our individual spiritual energies to the military arts, an invention like the Celestial Rock Ship is by no means impossible.

In September 1923, two years after the serialization of this *Dream Tale* had ended, Lieutenant General Satō passed away at the age of sixty. As we have seen, he was the last of a stream of authors, including Oshikawa Shunrō and Higuchi Reiyō, whose works—as one can tell from their titles or from the titles of the magazines and books in which they were originally serialized or published—were ultimately nothing more than tall tales of adventures and dreams. But the *Dream Tales* of Lieutenant General Satō, a military professional whose fiction was heavily laden with ideology, represents a turning point, and suggests the shape that future-war chronicles would take thereafter. Readers were demanding more graphic descriptions, more specialized technical information, and greater detail. Higuchi Reiyō had successfully ridden the currents of the time with *A Future Chronicle of the Japan-U.S. War: A Novel*, and *A Future Chronicle of the Japan-U.S. War, Continued: A Future Chronicle of the Second World War*, and *As Expected: The Japan-U.S. ******—but now he had no place to go.

In 1926, he published *Ah, Future Chronicles of Japan!* Subsequently, he churned out a long line of potboilers with such titles as *A History of the Shame of Great Japan*; *From Siberia to Tokyo: A Military Novel*; *A Comical History of Japan*; *New Ways to Utilize Banks*; *The Secret of Diplomacy: The Silver Tongue of Cordiality*; *A New Method of Dealing with People*; and *Marx on Capital*. He fell ill and died in September 1932.

Let us now resume chronicling the career of Mizuno Hironori prior to his quitting the navy. His inspection tour of post–World War I Europe had been outside the normal scope of his duties, and he had funded it privately on a leave of absence. Because he had been given this leeway, he felt it was only proper that upon his return to Japan he pay a courtesy call on the office of the navy minister. The navy minister at that time was Admiral Katō Tomosaburō, age fifty-nine. As chief of staff of the Combined Fleet during the Battle of Tsushima, he had stood with Admiral Tōgō Heihachirō on the bridge of the admiral's flagship, the *Mikasa*. He had a reputation for being cool and unflappable, poker-faced, someone whose real feelings were hard to gauge.

The old admiral looked at Mizuno and asked, "So, did you get anything out of your tour of inspection in Europe?" To which Mizuno replied,

Quite a bit. I was astonished at the scale of the European war, and compelled to contemplate the miserable state of a defeated Germany. I keenly felt that a poor country such as Japan—one that is, furthermore, greatly isolated in the world—should consider not how to win wars, but how to avoid them.

As Mizuno delivered his reply, Katō remained silent, without so much as batting an eyelid. Then the admiral glared at Mizuno briefly through his spectacles and said merely, "I see." That was all. Mizuno could not tell if Katō was being sympathetic or was simply giving him the brush-off.

With his strong self-consciousness, Mizuno could hardly leave it at that. The next year, 1922, Mizuno again made trouble. Katō put Mizuno on a one-month's suspension, with confinement to quarters. What had happened was that at the beginning of January Mizuno had begun serializing "The Military Psychology" in five parts in a newspaper called *The Tokyo Daily* (*Tōkyō Nichinichi Shimbun*). Postwar inflation in Europe, he pointed out, had doubled prices, and then tripled them. Daily life was a struggle. Strikes by workers were common. The military was no different: its stagnant wages produced pent-up dissatisfaction. "So far," wrote Mizuno, "I have not heard of a protest demonstration by the military," but "since even the military is part of society, they cannot help but be stimulated and influenced by social currents." That being the general drift of Mizuno's article, the military authorities were quite capable of interpreting it as radical, extremist thought.

On February 19, the day before his punishment was due to end, Mizuno received a visit from Nomura Kichisaburō, a former classmate now working as a high-level aide to the navy minister. "The minister's intentions..." he began, "are to discover whether you wish to return to the navy or not. If you do, I will convey that to him."

Mizuno was taken aback. He was already resigned to being shunted into the naval reserve. "No. I've had it. I'll retire," was his immediate response. If he returned to the navy, he would just be stuck in some meaningless desk job again. And besides, he was a man who had seen the hell of modern war. He had no regrets.

CHAPTER EIGHT

Recollections of a Spy

WOULD WAR break out soon in the Pacific? Certainly Homer Lea
stressed this possibility. But he did so in a way that left him open
to criticism by the Englishman Hector C. Bywater in his *Sea Power in the
Pacific*, first published in March 1921 in London. What exactly did Bywater
find so objectionable? Although Lea had turned a creative and informed
mind to American vulnerabilities in the Far East, he had overstated the case
for an invasion of the American homeland.

> More harm than good has been done by the well-meant efforts of writers
> such as Homer Lea, whose sensational forecast of Japanese operations
> against the United States was so demonstrably absurd that it encouraged
> American public opinion. Every intelligent American knows that his
> home coasts are, humanly speaking, secure against invasion from the Far
> East. It is some ten years since Homer Lea wrote his book, in which he
> described at great length the transport of a huge Japanese army across
> the Pacific, its landings in Washington, Oregon, and California, and
> its eventual conquest of the whole Pacific slope. Even at that date the
> American Navy was quite strong enough to have made such an operation
> absolutely impossible; and since, in the interval, its position of relative
> strength *vis à vis* the Japanese Navy has substantially improved, there is
> less reason than ever to include an invasion of the American mainland
> among the possible events of a future war.[1]

The genre of Japan-U.S. future-war chronicles at that time was also
endeavoring to enter a new era of realism. It was passé now to whip up a
sense of crisis irresponsibly, or to fantasize about new weaponry, or to have
the hero gallivanting about on romantic adventures.

Sea Power in the Pacific went through three printings that year. It was also well received in America. The president of the United States Naval War College, William Sims, who had served as commander of naval forces in Europe during World War I, went out of his way to write a rave review of it for the *Atlantic Monthly*. Sims praised it as a study "which the lay reader should find easily understandable, and most interesting, and which the student of war will recognize as authoritative in its assemblage of facts"; adding, "The reading public is fortunate in having presented to it at this time a treatise so thoroughly excellent, by a writer both authoritative and impartial."[2]

Japanese military people, too, could not fail to hear of this work. Lieutenant General Satō himself must have obtained a copy of the English edition, for he promptly wove a reference to *Sea Power in the Pacific* into the middle of his serialization of *Dream Tales of a Japan-U.S. War* in the June 1921 issue of *New Youth*. He has one of the characters who relate their dreams say, "But you know, it's just like that Englishman, Hector C. Bywater, says. The whole notion of launching a strike against America from Japan—in reality, that'd be a suicidal strategy." Judging from the timing of its serialization, one would imagine that Satō must have devoured a first edition of Bywater's work in great haste after having had it shipped from London.

Sea Power in the Pacific was quickly translated into Japanese. Translated excerpts were carried as early as the September 5, 1921 edition of *Foreign Newspapers and Magazines*. In the same month, Naval Command translated the full work and distributed mimeographed copies as internal documents. By July of the following year, the publisher Suikō Sha had put out a limited "not for sale" edition.

Who was this Hector C. Bywater, whose *Sea Power in the Pacific* had garnered such international attention? The Japanese publication, *Foreign Newspapers and Magazines*, introduced him as "a noted British naval authority." His translated excerpts were also prefaced with a concise summary of the work.

The author first explains how the core of the naval question has moved from Europe in the West to the Pacific in the East. He gives an overview of the U.S.-Japan dispute. Then he breaks to a new chapter for a detailed account of the development, organization, and current status of both Japan's and America's naval forces. Next he attempts a discussion, in concrete terms, of naval strategy and warfare in the Pacific. Lastly he takes up various political and economic issues and sketches his reasons why war between the two countries would not be right. Both "tigers" would sustain injuries, but in particular the economic injuries to Japan might prove fatal. It would be better to refrain from war.

Japanese readers may well have been disappointed to hear this. Whenever the subject of hypothetical Japan-U.S. wars had come up, they had been fed a diet of future-war chronicles in which the battle was joined straight off, and the question was which side would emerge victorious. But Bywater's conclusion was that both countries should avoid war. What stood out in particular was his stated concern for Japan: do not be provoked into war, for your loss will be greater.

Thus, unlike the genre of future-war chronicles, *Sea Power in the Pacific* did not irresponsibly incite war fever. Neither, however, did it neglect to warn that a war crisis was ever-present. But the question I want to address at the moment is why was this Englishman, Hector C. Bywater, so sympathetic toward Japan?

Just when Bywater was publishing the first edition of his *Sea Power in the Pacific*, that is to say in March of 1921, Crown Prince Hirohito (the future Shōwa Emperor) was leaving for Europe aboard the imperial vessel, the *Katori*. He visited England, France, Belgium, the Netherlands, and Italy before returning to Japan in September.

Why was America not included in the crown prince's foreign itinerary? My conjecture is that there is some connection with Bywater's line of argument, and that by lobbing yet another "why" here we may solve the whole matter.

Ever since the Iwakura Mission of 1871–73, Japan's leaders had been traveling to both Europe and America. Actually, more Japanese had studied in America than in Europe. So no matter how you look at it, for America to drop out of the equation on this rare royal tour abroad is unnatural. And yet, none of our history books deals with this question. What's more, when I started looking into it myself, I found that people at that time also considered it strange. On March 3, 1921, for example, it was reported by the *Ōsaka Mainichi* in a front-page article with the subtly doubtful headline, CURRENT ROYAL TOUR WITHOUT HISTORICAL PRECEDENT. The article then offered an explanation couched in rather euphemistic phraseology.

Word has it that His Highness the Crown Prince will not be visiting

America. We, his loyal subjects, cannot imagine the many duties discharged and hardships borne by His Highness on such a voyage. . . . To add an American sojourn would clearly mean increasing those burdens unacceptably.

Perhaps the newspaper was resisting swallowing the government's announcement whole, for it added in a more accusatory vein, "One imagines that His Highness himself finds this regrettable."

America shared this uneasiness over the crown prince's non-visit. Around the time that Crown Prince Hirohito was in London and Paris, the June 1921 issue of the journal *Current Opinion* began to raise doubts as to Japan's fundamental intentions. The initial plan, it noted, was to cross over to America after the European tour, passing through New York and then returning to Japan via San Francisco. This, it said, was the crown prince's own wishes; the plan had been changed hastily at the last minute.

Later, the Shōwa Emperor had occasion to reflect pleasantly upon memories of his European tour: "For myself, who had been as a bird in a cage, that tour was my first experience of a free life." Furthermore, when asked at a news conference on September 17, 1970, to name the most important events of his life, he replied, "It goes without saying that right off the top I would mention the hardships suffered during great wars. But after that, I would mention the trip to Europe."

But if the Shōwa Emperor had in fact visited America on that trip . . . One wouldn't be able to claim that the Japan-U.S. war would never have happened. However, such a trip might have shed some subtle yet significant light onto the political process in the otherwise murky early Shōwa period.

Since the subject of World War II has been raised, I'd like to review some obvious matters that I perhaps carelessly neglected to cover earlier. During the Second World War, in Japan the Americans and British were lumped together in the slogan, "Those fiendish brutes, the Yanks and Brits." The two countries were thought of in the same breath. However, even when Crown Prince Hirohito went on his observation tour of Europe, relations between Great Britain and America were certainly not the best. They were in fact rather tense. So delicate was the situation that the crown prince's visits had to be scheduled in circumstances in which giving priority to one destination meant slighting another.

The Anglo-Japanese Alliance goes back to 1902. It provided for a cooperative relationship between the two countries, with Russia as the hypothetical enemy of both. At that time, Great Britain had the most powerful navy in the world. The Japanese navy was modeled on Britain's with respect to not only the purchase of warships but all other matters, hard and soft. After Japan beat Russia in the Russo-Japanese War, the confrontation between Great Britain and Germany became the main theme of the Alliance. With the collapse of Imperial Russia and then Germany due to the impact of World War I, the Alliance's *raison d'être* could not help but fade.

Meanwhile, after the Russo-Japanese War, Japanese-American relations steadily deteriorated. As far as Japan was concerned, if it came to war with America, Japan would like to be able to count on Great Britain's assistance. Anglo-Japanese cooperative relations were in fact the greatest fear the United States had. This was understandable. If the U.S. were attacked on both its Atlantic and Pacific coasts, its military power would be divided.

American suspicions were thus directed even toward the crown prince's foreign tour. Here we must establish things by checking the records of the Foreign Ministry. And the information is indeed there. The following is from the transcript of a telegram received on March 15, 1921, addressed to the ambassador to the United Kingdom, Hayashi Gonsuke, from foreign minister Uchida Kōsai.

> With regard to the European visit by His Highness the Crown Prince, some of the Chinese-language newspapers, particularly the Chinese-American ones, argue that the plan is to use the Crown Prince's relations with the British royal house to effect the continuation of the Anglo-Japanese Alliance.

However, in 1911 the Anglo-Japanese Alliance had been revised, so that even in the event of a Japan-U.S. war, Great Britain would not have to go to Japan's aid. Legally speaking, there was no obligation to enter such a war. Still, America feared an Anglo-Japanese alignment. To drive a wedge between them, the United States began to maneuver within the emerging Commonwealth of Nations. It had some success with neighboring Canada, but Australia and New Zealand cared more about maintaining their national security in the Pacific and chose to extend their participation in the Anglo-Japanese Alliance.

For example, the *Sydney Morning Herald* for February 4, 1921, ran an editorial noting that Japan was an ally of Great Britain, and that the crown prince's visit must have had something to do with a renewal of the

Anglo-Japanese Alliance. England had repeatedly declared its intention to renew the Alliance, and the crown prince's trip bore that out. The editorial urged that England serve as an honest broker between competing military interests in the Pacific.

An Imperial Conference was opened in London that June, just when the crown prince had left Britain for his observation tour of the Continent. At the Imperial Conference, representatives gathered from Canada, Australia, New Zealand, South Africa, and elsewhere. But the Conference did not come to any conclusion regarding revisions to the Anglo-Japanese Alliance. However, Great Britain did propose trilateral talks between Great Britain, the United States, and Japan. The United States countered by holding an international conference of nine nations with interests in East Asia and the Pacific. The group comprised Japan, Great Britain, the United States, France, Italy, Belgium, Holland, Portugal, and China. This was the Washington Conference.

At the 1921 Washington Conference, the Anglo-Japanese Alliance was scrapped. At the same time, the world's first arms limitation treaty was concluded, with the United States, Great Britain, and Japan fixing the ratio of their capital ships at 5:5:3 with respect to tonnage. Japan's 60 percent position relative to the United States or Great Britain gave rise to some dissatisfaction within the Japanese navy among those hardliners eventually referred to as the Fleet Faction. Opposed to them were the more conciliatory Treaty Faction, who thought such limitations inevitable. The military-expansionists in the Fleet Faction argued that the 5:5:3 ratio would be ruinous to Japan. But in point of fact, the "8-8" fleet plan that had got underway immediately prior to the conclusion of the Washington Treaty, assuming America as a hypothetical enemy, was already taking up one-third of Japan's national budget for 1921, reaching the limit of what the economy could bear. Therefore, even the militarists were demanding merely 70 percent vis-à-vis the United States or Great Britain, rather than 60 percent.

Thus, behind the boom in future-war chronicles by the likes of Higuchi Reiyō and Satō Kōjirō there was this triangular shipbuilding competition between Japan, the United States, and Great Britain.

But even if the militarists had managed to achieve 70 percent, they would lose a war with America. There is no practical difference between 60 percent and 70 percent in this context. So what was left was a sense of surrender. A 5:5:5 ratio would have been a more clear-cut outcome, but the Japanese economy was incapable of keeping up with that. Deep down, the militarist faction knew that too, but they needed some grand pretext to lower the fist they had raised so menacingly. The militarists demanded abrogation of the Washington Treaty, but if there had really been a free and unlimited naval arms race, there was the possibility that America's economic power might increase. However, with the U.S. stock market crash of 1929 and the ensuing Great Depression, the view gained currency in militarist circles that the United States had been weakened, and that worries to the contrary were groundless.

* * *

BEHIND THE EVAPORATION of the American leg of Crown Prince Hirohito's grand tour lay some delicate issues involving the trilateral relationship of Japan, Great Britain, and the United States. Japan wanted to extend the Anglo-Japanese Alliance. The crown prince's tour was indeed planned in order to deepen Japan's friendship with the British royal family. But America was a different story. Not including America in the itinerary was not really satisfactory, but then, America was at that time in the throes of an anti-Japanese movement. What if some untoward event should occur during the crown prince's visit? Great Britain also had its own schemes. It could take the initiative to ameliorate Japan-U.S. tensions, flaunting its cooperative relations with Japan. This would be an opportunity to display to magnificent effect Britain's skill at complex diplomatic maneuvering.

And that is why, in his *Sea Power in the Pacific*, Hector C. Bywater demonstrated a sympathetic attitude toward Japan while hinting at a Japan-U.S. war crisis. Bywater's stance may be summed up as follows: The argument that with Germany crushed, Great Britain no longer need maintain a huge fleet is erroneous. The British Empire's concessions and rights in the Far East are at least as great as America's. From an Englishman's perspective, it is desirable that no one power gain absolute supremacy in the Pacific. If war were to arise between Japan and the United States, that would also have a negative impact on Great Britain. Something must be done to improve Japan-U.S. relations. Britain should take the initiative. And in order to do so, it must be thoroughly familiar with issues relating to the Pacific...

So, Englishman that he was, Bywater had clear and present patriotic reasons for writing a U.S.-Japan hypothetical war scenario. Given that, he could hardly dash something off based on insufficient information. Information is essential to military analysis, and in his case, Hector C. Bywater was certainly confident of the quality of his information. As he wrote in his preface, "No trouble has been spared to ensure completeness and accuracy of information concerning the ships, dockyards, and personnel of the two navies, not to mention the administration and organization of their naval forces." And Bywater made the fullest possible use not only of published studies by specialists, but also of connections who could supply him with public documents and publications, drawing on the resources of the United States Navy in Washington and the Japanese consulate in London.[3]

A Captain Kobayashi served on the general staff aboard the battleship *Fusō* during the Battle of Tsushima. He had been a classmate of Mizuno Hironori's at the Naval Academy. Unlike Mizuno, however, he had gone on to the Naval Staff College on the elite track, later assuming such important posts as governor-general of Taiwan. During World War II, when the Senior Statesmen were plotting the overthrow of the Tōjō Hideki Cabinet, he had been selected as a possible candidate to head a subsequent administration. Cautious to a fault, however, Kobayashi took care to distance himself from the planned coup d'état.

Kobayashi was considered to be in the pro-British wing of the military, and as such he probably helped Bywater gather information for his book. Bywater himself got his journalistic start thanks to the surprise attack Japan's Combined Fleet launched on the Russians in the Russo-Japanese War.

In *Sea Power in the Pacific*, after citing his sources for data on Japanese and American military power, as well as material concerning their relative political and economic power, Hector Bywater was confident enough to take "full and undivided responsibility" for the conclusions "in the chapters on Pacific strategy and the possible features of a naval campaign."[4]

To understand why the celebrated British naval correspondent laid such stress on information, we must understand the first half of his life, which is filled with mystery. Furthermore, at the conclusion of *Sea Power in the Pacific*, Bywater foresees the likely outcome of a Japan-U.S. war and urges that Japan absolutely refrain from going to war with America. I want to examine an event that took place in the summer of 1912 in order to see what led Bywater to that conclusion.[5]

On one of my trips to Berlin I kept an appointment with a correspondent who had previously given me a considerable amount of useful information. Although German by nationality, he had a Polish mother. He was highly intelligent, but most excitable, and I had always foreseen trouble with him.

On this occasion he came to the meeting-place in a state of extreme nervous tension. The police were on his track, he assured me, and he had been shadowed for several days. He also believed that his correspondence was being opened. He lived in fear of arrest at any moment. He could not sleep, and he was drinking too much. So he had made up his mind to go to the police and confess.

By implicating me he expected to get off lightly, as he knew the authorities would consider me a valuable catch. It was something in his favour that he had come to warn me of what he proposed to do. Had he gone to the police first I should have been caught red-handed, for they would naturally have instructed him to pass incriminating documents to me before they came to make the arrest.

Even as things were, it was an awkward situation. Schneider, as I will call him, was in that condition of extreme fear which makes the veriest poltroon take desperate risks if he sees the faintest chance of saving his skin. I argued with him for a long time, assuring him that his fears were baseless, and pointing out that even confession would not save him from a stiff term of imprisonment. But it was all in vain. He was going straight to the police, and no one should stop him.

That did not suit me at all. If he persisted in his intention, I must at least have time to get clear of Berlin, and once the police were on the alert this would be difficult, if not impossible.

It was clearly a case for drastic methods. Schneider made for the door, but I reached it first, locked it, and put the key in my pocket. He struggled with me, and I had to hit him—hard. I did this reluctantly, for until then he had been exceedingly useful to me, and in any case I did not want to make him a personal enemy.

He collapsed in a chair. I gave him a drink and then produced a revolver, just for moral effect. Then I talked to him.

It's easy to fall prey to the illusion that one is reading a spy thriller. The account is from a memoir I acquired at a secondhand bookshop in London. Its clothbound cover was orange, with faded black lettering announcing the title, *Strange Intelligence*. One other thing that struck my eye was the name of one of the two co-authors: Bywater. The book was badly soiled and damaged, the cloth binding worn and fraying; it looked like it was about to fall apart. Published in 1931, it must have passed through the hands of a number of readers. The endpaper on the front cover carries the signatures of more than one purchaser, with different handwriting and a series of dates, from 1934 to 1965, that must have been the years of purchase. The incident we have been recounting here is said to be narrated by a former member of the British Secret Service; there are reasons to assume it is Bywater's personal reminiscence, partly fictionalized but based on truth.

Let us return, then, to Bywater's narrative.

It's amazing how fertile one's imagination becomes in a crisis like this. I painted a lurid picture of our Secret Service, of its ramifications all over the world, and of the ruthless treatment it meted out to betrayers. Its agents worked in couples, I said, though only one actually operated at a time; the other remained in the background, ready to execute swift vengeance if his colleague came to harm.

"You tell me you've been shadowed these last few days, Schneider," I said. "Well, that happens to be true. But it wasn't by the police. You have been kept under close observation by my colleague. We always shadow people like you as a matter of routine. It is extremely fortunate for you that you did not attempt to go to the police before seeing me again. Had you attempted to do so you would have been a dead man by now. On leaving this house you will again be followed, and I advise you to go straight home. Otherwise something will happen to you."

He was inclined to be skeptical at first, but although I was bluffing, the knowledge of my own danger made me feel, and probably look, rather grim. Gradually I could see conviction dawning in his eyes. And this much was true enough: that I was not going to let him out of my sight until I was reasonably sure that his lips were sealed.

Finally he said that he would not make his confession till the following morning, so that I would have the whole night in which to escape. But I saw through this stratagem, for it was obvious that, unless he could produce me, his story would merely convict himself without securing lenient treatment from the authorities. It was necessary to use more powerful arguments.

I warned him that betrayal of me at any time would infallibly be punished.

"If the police allow you to go free, it will only be a question of days, perhaps hours, before something very unpleasant happens to you. If you get a prison sentence, no matter how long it may be, my friends will be waiting for you when you are released. Go where you will, you cannot escape them!"

Then I tried a further bluff.

"And here's another thing, my friend. Hasn't it occurred to you that you are more at my mercy than I am at yours? Now that you have shown yourself to be untrustworthy, I am half inclined to give you a dose of your own medicine. I am going to summon one of my colleagues" (turning to the telephone as I spoke) "who will see that you are kept quiet for the next day or two, by which time I shall be out of Germany. You will then be anonymously denounced to the police as a spy, and conclusive evidence of your guilt will be placed in their hands. If you try to implicate me you probably won't be believed, and in any case it won't help you. You will be safe for ten years, and, as you know, the prison people have orders to make things especially severe for men convicted of *Landesverrat*. Yes, that is by far the best plan—" And I made as if to lift the telephone receiver.

The bluff had undoubtedly worked. Schneider was now in a more pitiable state of terror than before. He saw that my threat could really be put into execution, and he capitulated without further ado. He swore that he would not go to the police, promised to do anything I told him, and, as evidence of good faith, there and then produced some information which was really valuable.

But still I was not satisfied. In his present state of agitation he was not to be trusted. So I determined to keep him with me all night, hoping that by morning he would have recovered his nerve. It was a long and trying night, and more than once I had to make play with the revolver to keep him quiet.

After certain forms of moral suasion had been employed, he drew up, in his own handwriting, a full confession of the work he had done for me—giving dates and all details—and signed it. This I put into an envelope and addressed it to the Chief of Police, Berlin.

"Now, Schneider," I said; "if in the future I have any reason to doubt you, this envelope goes into the post at once. You must see that there's no escape if you ever attempt to give me away."

He obviously did see it, and I began to feel more confident. In the morning I called a taxi and drove him to his rooms in Charlottenburg. He was pretty much of a wreck by then, but the nervous crisis was over, and he was quite subdued. I had paid him off, and privately decided not to employ him again. . . . As weeks passed and nothing happened, it became evident that he was holding his tongue. I never saw or heard of him again.

From *Strange Intelligence*, one can certainly appreciate both Bywater's icy cool and his love of country. "It was always a risky business," he noted, "dealing with such people, for a man who will sell his own country will, as a rule, make nothing of selling those for whom he works."[6]

Hector Bywater was not a typical member of the elite. His educational background was nothing to speak of, but his lively mind absorbed knowledge from reality like a sponge. He was born on October 21, 1884, the youngest of four siblings. In a strange, karmic way, his birthdate has a motif-like significance for his career. For any Englishman, October 21 is famous as the date on which Admiral Horatio Nelson's fleet defeated the united fleets of Spain and France under Vice Admiral Pierre-Charles de Villeneuve, off Cape Trafalgar, crushing Napoleon's greatest ambition. In Bywater's England, whenever the anniversary date came round, all of England was given over to celebration. The navy shipyards were opened to civilians so that they could see close-up the grandeur of the warships of the world's mightiest navy. The young Hector went every year and pored over such tomes as *Brassey's Naval Annual* and *Jane's Fighting Ships*. He had committed to memory the plans of every ship and the details of its equipment. Sometimes when the public guide was describing one of these warships, he would, diffidently but confidently, contradict him. And the young Hector was always right. By the time he was ten years old, he was already such an expert in naval affairs that an article he wrote, discussing the Japanese victory over Qing China's North Sea Fleet in the Yellow Sea, was printed in a magazine.

His father, Peter D. Bywater, was a large, heavyset Welshman with a thick beard, who rather resembled a storybook pirate captain. And not just in appearance, but in character as well, he seems to have been an eccentric person. For most of his life he never settled down, but wandered from one place to another. He worked as a traveling salesman, a printer-engraver, a Pony Express rider, a secret agent for the Union army in the Civil War, an instructor of Greek. He went from job to job. It was Bywater Sr.'s knowledge of Greek that led him to name his boys Ulysses and Hector, after the heroes of the Trojan War. While Hector was between the ages of thirteen and seventeen, the Bywaters lived in America, Canada, West Africa, and Germany. After that, the family scattered.

Hector Bywater moved to Brooklyn, New York by himself. He worked as a tram conductor and as an employee of the Union Railroad Company. Brooklyn was the site of the New York Naval Shipyard (or Brooklyn Navy Yard), so when he had time he snooped around. Old submarines were mothballed there, and new warships were under construction, so he was never bored. Scrupulously noting down his observations, he made them the basis for some reportage about the Brooklyn Navy Yard. He sent his observations to the *New York Herald*. This led to his being hired as a reporter. He was nineteen years old. It was shortly after that, on February 7, 1904, that the Japanese navy launched their surprise attack on the Russian fleet at Port Arthur, and the Russo-Japanese War began. The New York office received an incessant stream of messages in Morse code, and the office was abuzz with the news. Which warships played decisive roles; what were the names of the ships that sank? Soon Bywater could recite the information by heart. It was a rousing experience for a young journalist, and it served to fix his gaze on the Far East.

In 1907, when he was twenty-three, Bywater was invited by his brother Ulysses to join him in Germany. Ulysses, two years his senior, worked at the American consulate in Dresden. Known as "the Florence of Germany," Dresden was a cultured city, with its historic opera house and museums. Hector loved music, so to Germany he went, but he had other reasons as well to accept his brother's invitation.

Just at that time in Germany Kaiser Wilhelm II was going forward with a military buildup. One after another, battleships were being built, and the German navy was attracting the attention of the entire world. The balance of power was ever so slightly beginning to tilt. It appeared as though the British navy's supremacy was crumbling.

Hector Bywater became the editor of the *Daily Record*, an English-language newspaper published in Dresden. At the same time, he worked as special correspondent on naval affairs for the *New York Herald*. He even began to send articles to the British navy's own *Navy League Journal*. His articles were somehow unusual. His expertise was thorough-going, and his writing was far more than a listing-up of facts; it had a dynamic brilliance to it. His Dresden bylines were noted in London. William Honan has pieced together the origin and outline of Bywater's career as an undercover agent, and it, too, reads like a thriller.[7]

Shortly after he began to write regular columns from Dresden about the German navy, Bywater received a visit from an Englishman who told him that if he ever took a holiday in England it would be to his advantage to telephone a certain friend of his. Intrigued, Bywater pursued the suggestion on his next visit to London. Telephoning the number he had been given, he was directed to 2, Whitehall Court, a palatial structure that looked like a French chateau in the heart of the government section of London. The building housed the Authors' Club, Golfers' Club, and the Junior Army and Navy Club. Bywater was told to take the lift to the top floor, just above the Authors' Club. He followed the instructions apprehensively because he still had no idea of what he was getting into. At the top landing, his identification was checked by two men who appeared as though they were carrying concealed revolvers. When satisfied, they instructed him to climb a flight of stairs and enter a suite of rooms in what was evidently the attic.

In one of his books, Bywater described the scene:

"The apartment, large and airy, is furnished as an office. Its most conspicuous feature is a huge steel safe, painted green. The walls are adorned with large maps and charts and one picture, the latter depicting the execution of a group of French villagers by a Prussian firing squad in the war of 1870. There are three tables, at the largest of which sits an elderly man, grey-haired, clean shaven, wearing a monocle. His figure inclines to stoutness, but the weather-tanned face, with its keen grey eyes, stamps him as an out-of-door man. He is, in fact, a post-captain on the retired list of the Royal Navy."

The year was 1909, and Bywater was discovering his destiny. Let us continue with Honan's account.

The gentleman was to play a large role in Bywater's life over the next six years, although throughout most of that time he would be known to him only as C. He was Sir Mansfield Cumming, the head of the newly formed Foreign Section of British Secret Service—officially known as M.I.i(c)— a power in the world at that time. Unlike today's Secret Service chiefs who inspire novels and movies, C was completely unknown during his lifetime. Many high-ranking government officials, including some who communicated with him regularly, did not know his identity.

Bywater recalled that C began the interview by explaining in an avuncular manner that he was the head of an agency within the Foreign Office whose speciality was gathering information from around the world that might have a bearing on the security of the British Empire. Quite obviously, he said, the growth of the German navy was a matter of serious concern, but dependable information about it was exceedingly hard to come by.

C went on to say,

We are almost entirely dependent on the naval attaché's reports and such news as Tirpitz chooses to give the German press, which is precious little. Then we get reports from an agent in Brussels, and occasionally from two very dubious agencies in the same city. . . . The stuff I get from this source struck me as being highly suspicious and probably worthless.

At this point, I should point out that when Bywater first moved to Dresden two years earlier at his brother's invitation, he had entertained friendly feelings toward Germans. Honan notes that "he had made a number of German friends in New York and on previous visits to Germany, and his reading of Carlyle's *Frederick the Great* had given him a sincere appreciation of the qualities which raised Prussia to major-power status."[8] But then he became aware that Germany considered England an enemy and had begun preparations for war. Let's resume our peek into Bywater's meeting with C.

C said he knew all about Bywater's background and was confident that he would able to perform an invaluable job for his country. So as not to arouse suspicion, he should continue to work for the *Daily Record* in Dresden, and to contribute articles to the service publications for which he was currently writing, but he should start sending reports back to C immediately.

Bywater was to initiate a second, parallel, secret career: that of spy.

The first [of his reports] should cover the fortifications on Borkum, a small island off the Friesland coast, which was one of the strategically key positions in the North Sea. Where were the bombproof shelters located and how many were there? How many 28-centimeter howitzers in fixed positions, and how many mobile 4.1 centimeter high-velocity guns in among the sand dunes? Where were the secret telegraph and telephone cables leading from the garrison headquarters to the mainland? A map would be extremely useful.

C's next words were ominous.

You must exercise extreme caution, and understand that if you should be caught violating the German law against espionage you would be disavowed by the British Foreign Office and would have to fend for yourself. His Majesty's Government cannot be implicated under any circumstances.

Bywater responded with equanimity: he and his brother Ulysses were already representing themselves, he said, as Americans. C endorsed this, and urged Bywater to have Uly take advantage of his position at the American consulate to certify this officially. But Bywater did have one reservation.

Bywater was aware that his wife back in Dresden was now pregnant. Getting up his courage, he explained to C that he was honoured by the invitation but, also mindful of approaching fatherhood, he would be glad to know how much he would be paid.

C said he was surprised to hear any mention of monetary compensation since it was a patriotic honour to serve one's country in time of need. Bywater persisted, firmly yet politely, and as he spoke C recalled the reports by Bywater he had been reading in the *Navy League Journal* and the *Naval & Military Record* which packed more fresh and vital information into a column of newsprint than he could get from all the naval attachés and agents in Europe. Consequently, C relented. In short order, the two men shook hands and the newest recruit to the British Secret Service was strolling confidently along the Victoria Embankment having been promised the pay and allowances of a lieutenant commander in the Royal Navy.

Toward the end of 1911, over two years since Bywater had become a full-fledged spy, John Fisher, an aide to Winston Churchill, then First Lord of the Admiralty, sent Churchill a letter in which he praised Bywater as our "splendid spy in Germany."[9]

Bywater himself listed the following attributes of the effective spy: (1) a legitimate career, (2) fluency in the language of the country to which one is assigned, and (3) the ability to mix freely and frankly with people of all social classes and personalities.

If one thinks about it, these qualities are the very ones that would serve as the qualifications for a good journalist. For the secret agent, it is precisely the information that his quarry does not wish to let slip that has the highest value. In journalism, that is called a scoop. But that is not all. The assembling of facts alone is meaningless. One must be decisive in discarding the dross. The nugget of truth one seeks may be miniscule. One then takes that tiny bit of truth and subjects it to bold logical analysis and hypothesis as a first step toward capturing the larger prize.

Hector Bywater served as a secret agent for nine years, from 1909 until the end the Great War in 1918.

Naturally Bywater's vast knowledge of naval affairs was augmented by his practical experience. This was not borrowed from others but was a product of the journalist's own initiative. Under such conditions, he had an unequaled opportunity to nurture his creativity as well. *Sea Power in the Pacific* was written from this unprecedented perspective. It is an achievement that is inconceivable if one subtracts Bywater's personal experience as a spy. But it was also natural that information did not sprout wings and fly to Bywater at his convenience. Rather, he had to exert all his wiles to coax it out. Bywater describes part of the process as follows.

A walking cane discreetly marked off, said Bywater, was useful for measuring the thickness of armor plating. To the practiced eye, it was easy to estimate the capacity of coal depots or crude-oil storage tanks. For details regarding new ships—their features, their facilities, their artillery equipment and sighting mechanisms and so on—a tiny camera that would fit in the palm of one's hand did nicely. That was fieldwork.

The business about mixing freely and frankly with all sorts of people did not mean merely being amiable. The following incident shows how behavior always entered into the picture, along with familiarity with the local language and culture:

An English spy was once invited by a German officer to a private party where the guests were mostly German military men. The beer flowed and the banquet was in full swing when the singing began. It began with old German folk songs, then some charming Schubert lieder, eventually some of the patriotic ballads that are such a feature of the German repertoire. The men loosened their belt buckles and undid their stiff collars. The next table over was a veritable mountain range of cloaks with red-stripe insignia, tall military hats, gleaming short swords. Jokes were bandied about, punctuated by bursts of laughter.

At a sudden lull in the conversation, a rather high-pitched voice struck up a patriotic song. An old patriotic song, "The Song of the Sword." It was said to have been composed by the Saxon poet Karl Körner just hours before he fell in action at the Battle of Leipzig. When it became apparent that the singer was none other than the English guest, an enthusiastic wave of applause swept the room. Amid cheers and further applause, a toast was drunk to the health of the worthy Englishman.

When things finally quieted down, the conversation turned to the war situation. The war was already a year old, so talk of it was no longer theoretical. With the beer and the merriment everyone's tongue was sufficiently loosened. An infantry second lieutenant spoke up. Obviously, he said, Germany could not fight France and Russia simultaneously. The question was which to mobilize against so as to improve the success of an attack. The speaker advocated attacking France first and occupying Paris. It should take about a month, after which the army could turn its attention back to the east. It was well known that Russia could not mobilize its entire army in less than six weeks.

But one of his comrades had a different opinion. France won't fall in a month, he said. The fortifications at Verdun, he said, were formidable. The second lieutenant pounded the table and called the man a coward. What kind of fortifications were these, he demanded. What of them? Why, he demanded, were the huge railroad depots at Eupen and Malmedy constructed? So that once they got the "go" sign, the army could cross the borders of Luxembourg and Belgium in a flash. This was no secret, he said.

But others offered counterarguments. Such an action would violate terms of neutrality. (The objectors had a point. Later, Germany did in fact trample upon the neutrality of Luxembourg and Belgium in order to invade France, bringing worldwide condemnation.)

Besides, the Belgians would resist. Their army was small, but the cities of Liège (near the border with Germany) and Namur (a strategic point sixty-two kilometers southeast of Brussels) would not be taken so easily. Their fortifications were strong, as in France.

At this point a technical second lieutenant diffidently entered the fray. He agreed that Liège was strong. Last summer, he said, he had spent a month in Belgium, subjecting Liège and Namur to the most detailed scrutiny. The revolving gun turrets at Liège were protected with 9-inch steel armor. According to manuals, the bomb-proof shelters were made of four-foot-thick, steel-reinforced concrete. Their 12-inch howitzers could not take them down. But there was no need to worry. His elder brother in the army ministry had told him of a new weapon that had just been developed. Far more impressive than a 12-inch gun. Truly unbelievable. The weapons were being prepared at Essen, the center of the industrial Ruhr valley in west-central Germany. The shells were astonishingly large, weighing approximately...

At this point his narrative was cut short by an artillery colonel who had been in another conversational group and had just noticed what the second lieutenant was talking about. He told him to watch out. There was an uncomfortable silence. The colonel stood up and beckoned to the second lieutenant. The second lieutenant snapped to attention for his regimental commander and went off with him to a far corner of the room.

There was some grumbling among the other officers, who didn't see the harm in such discussion among comrades. For the moment, the Englishman had so completely blended into the group that his presence had been quite overlooked. He had been engaged in a debate with the man seated next to him regarding the relative merits of lager and stout.

It was only much later that the spectacular life of spies became known the world over. Before the espionage game became systematized during World War I, spies could hardly be compared to the CIA and KGB operatives of later years. Their very existence was not publicly acknowledged. Bywater himself may be said to be the harbinger of the new era.

Bywater has summed up the rewards these unsung heroes enjoyed after risking so much to get the inside story:

> Their names will never be known. Today the few survivors of that service find their only excitement in a debate in committee at the golf club, or in the purchase of a sweepstake ticket under the eyes of a local J.P. That is about the wildest extravagance they can afford on their "savings."[10]

That is, perhaps, a matter of course. Looking ahead a bit, we find that both the beguiling Mata Hari and the beautiful cross-dressing Kawashima Yoshiko were famous spies, but that their fame was for the violent ends they met, not for any great intelligence coups. The more dramatic the heroine, and the more she is the victim of something beyond her control, the less it reflects any systematized activity.

W. Somerset Maugham, later famous for *The Moon and Sixpence* and *Of Human Bondage*, was recruited into Britain's secret service like Bywater during World War I. His status as a playwright and fiction writer appealed to the authorities, as it could serve as a cover for his peregrinations. Maugham collected a number of stories about his own experiences and published them in 1928 under the title *Ashenden: Or the British Agent*. He reflects on what it is to be a spy, in language sometimes reminiscent of Bywater's. The life of a spy, he writes, is on the whole rather monotonous, and much of it probably useless. The only parts that are suitable material for fiction are scattered fragments of experience. It is the role of the author to coerce these fragments into some sort of coherent whole and to provide sufficient dramatic interest.

So the realism of this new era was engraved in the very souls of spy-story writers such as Bywater and Maugham. An instructive contrast can be found in the works of Arthur Conan Doyle, creator of Sherlock Holmes. These stories treat spying in a world that still partakes of a lyrical nineteenth-century romanticism. There was a generation gap here. Older than Bywater by a quarter-century, Conan Doyle could not comprehend the harsh realities and inhuman cruelties of twentieth-century espionage.

Arthur Conan Doyle was born in 1859. His father, Charles Doyle, was a civil servant of the city of Edinburgh, and Arthur was brought up in a middle-class household. He entered a Catholic parochial school, received a rigorous education, and was admitted to study in the Faculty of Medicine at the prestigious University of Edinburgh.

After graduating, Conan Doyle worked for some time as ship's doctor aboard cargo ships involved in the African trade. He competed against native swimmers in the sea off Nigeria; he explored mangrove swamps; he hunted crocodiles. Upon his return, with the help of a friend, he opened a private ophthalmological clinic.

In 1887, at the age of twenty-seven, Conan Doyle published "A Study in Scarlet" in the *Strand Magazine*, and the activities of the famed consulting detective Sherlock Holmes achieved great popularity. He then entered his own literary golden age, with *The Sign of Four* (1890) and such series as *The Adventures of Sherlock Holmes* (1892; serialized 1891–92; including "A Scandal in Bohemia" and "The Red-Headed League") and *The Memoirs of Sherlock Holmes* (1894; serialized 1892–93; including "Silver Blaze," "The Stock-broker's Clerk," and "The Final Problem"). Having reached a peak as a writer in a very short period, he then put an abrupt full-stop to the Holmes series. To readers, it could only seem capricious.

In "The Final Problem," Arthur Conan Doyle killed off Holmes at the Reichenbach Falls. It provoked a veritable flood of protest letters from readers. But Holmes was not revived until the twentieth century. Reader demand was still overwhelming. Conan Doyle also succumbed to the temptation of the wealth he knew more Holmes stories would generate. When a number of other projects and ventures failed, circumstances finally compelled him to write books that would sell.

Holmes was thus resurrected nearly a decade after his prime. *The Hound of the Baskervilles* (1902), a novel, was followed by *The Return of Sherlock Holmes* (1905; serialized 1903–1904; including "The Empty House," "The Dancing Men," and "The Second Stain"). Doyle's explanation for the resurrection was ingenious. Holmes had indeed been locked in mortal combat with his archenemy, the sinister Professor Moriarty, but he had survived thanks to his expertise in what he termed "baritsu," meaning *bujitsu*, or martial arts. Besides, the fans were wonderful. They were so greedy that they forgave a little implausibility in exchange for the return of their beloved Holmes. And Arthur Conan Doyle tried to reward that loyalty by catering to the readers' wishes, setting the new series of Holmes stories ten years prior so as to reduce the sense of discontinuity.

But historical reality had, in the interim, entered a new era. Conan Doyle and his Holmes-hungry readers were wallowing in nostalgia for a nineteenth century that had passed as a new era of warfare dawned. The British crime novelist had already achieved wealth and fame. Then, during the decade in which his great detective apparently lay dead under the Reichenbach Falls, the detective's creator and destroyer had indulged a number of whims, chief among them being his participation in the Boer War.

The Boers were people of Dutch extraction living in South Africa. By the end of the nineteenth century they had founded the Transvaal Republic and the Orange Free State. When diamond and gold were discovered in this region, Great Britain endeavored to wrest control, openly interfering in the two states' internal affairs. Resistance by the Boers, however, was unexpectedly strong, and Great Britain finally mounted an invasion. Beginning in 1899, the war lasted three years—which speaks to how tough a fight Great Britain had picked.

The Boers had a population of only five hundred thousand, out of which they could muster an army of but fifty thousand. They were attacked by a British force of 250,000. The British pursued their campaign to the point of genocide, indiscriminately rounding up noncombatants and forcing them into concentration camps where conditions were so poor as to drive the Boers to the brink of ethnic extinction. In this crisis, the Boers were forced to surrender. International opinion favored them, Great Britain's high-handedness coming in for much criticism.

After parting with Holmes, Arthur Conan Doyle participated in this southern African conflict. He had missed the opportunity to go to war when he was younger. Now that he was on the downhill side of forty, he felt that this would be his last chance to see wartime action. When he told his mother,

Mary, she was shocked and tried to dissuade him. Surely the world was full of men who, learning that the creator of Sherlock Holmes was heading off to war, would volunteer to serve in his place. She had opposed the Boer War from the beginning and remonstrated with Arthur, then in London, in a letter she sent from Edinburgh. To drive that small nation into such a horrid strip of land, and then administer to them such a beating, showed a lack of magnanimity, entirely unbecoming to a great people.

Doyle's mother was a rather perspicacious woman. She pleaded with him forcefully:

> For God's sake listen to me. Even at your age I am God's representative in you. Do not go, Arthur! That is my first and last word. If these politicians and journalists who so lightly drift into war had to go to the front themselves they would be a great deal more careful. They pushed the country into this, and you shall not be their victim if I can help it.[11]

But Arthur remained unmoved. Indeed, immediately after the war broke out, he had written a letter to the *Times*, saying, for example, that the Empire should send sportsmen skilled in riding and shooting into battle as mounted infantry. At this late date he could hardly back out. As he told his mother, "I was honor-bound, as I had suggested it, to be the first to volunteer." He went on, "What I feel is that I have perhaps the strongest influence over young men, especially young sporting men, of anyone in England bar Kipling. That being so, it is really important that I should give them a lead." And, he added, in response to his mother's objection to this particular war, "As to the merits of the quarrel: from the day they invaded Natal that becomes merely academic."[12]

So Conan Doyle was gung ho, but the authorities politely declined to accept him as a volunteer on the grounds that he was past the usual age. Finally, he was allowed to participate in the war as a member of a medical corps led by a friend of his. At the field hospital, Conan Doyle worked in a tropical pith helmet and khaki fatigues with gaiters.

Mortimer Mempes, an artist dispatched by the *Illustrated London News*, visited the field hospital in order to sketch Conan Doyle. Conan Doyle's first words of welcome were, "Just look at this inferno!" but immediately the famous man pointed out two black-robed Sisters of Mercy: "They are angels," he said. "They are angels." Many of the wounded suffered from infectious diseases, and Conan Doyle's devotion to them was heroic. As Mempes observed,

Dr. Conan Doyle worked like a horse, until he had to drag himself up on a kopje to get fresh air, saturated as he was with enteric. He is one of the men who make England great.[13]

In between his volunteer duty shifts, Conan Doyle toured the battle sites. One day, as he was following an artillery unit on horseback through a grassy field, he suddenly heard the whine of artillery shells. The enemy was firing on them. Shells and shrapnel hitting the earth were scattering dirt all about. Britain was at that time the world's preeminent naval power, but the army was not yet modernized. The South African farmers that the British so looked down on were armed with excellent weapons, whereas the British themselves, still equipped with sabers and lances, did not even know that they should dig trenches to protect themselves from enemy fire. And the Boer army's artillery had longer range. No matter how the British squinted into the distance, they could not see the enemy firing upon them. The shells rained down. The British soldiers, panicking, fired their own weapons randomly and uselessly at an enemy equipped with superior German armaments.

It was a strange scene indeed. Amid the carnage, the officers, scions of the upper class, wore their monocles even on the battlefield and did not deign to modify their aristocratic drawl. Conan Doyle presented practical recommendations for army reform in an article titled, "Some Military Lessons of the War," concluding as follows:

> Above all, let us have done with the fuss and feathers, the gold lace, and the frippery! Let us have done also with the tailoring, the too-luxurious habits of the mess, the unnecessary extravagance which makes it so hard for a poor man to accept a commission! If only this good came from all our trials and our efforts, they would be well worth all that they have cost us.[14]

In other words, the days of the purely aristocratic officer corps were numbered. As applied to defense of the home islands, one of Arthur Conan Doyle's biographers, John Dickson Carr, has summed up Doyle's arguments as follows:

> Defense of Empire was not the business of a special warrior-caste; it was the business of everybody. If every able-bodied youth and man in Great Britain were taught to use a rifle, those riflemen when combined with

artillery could beat back an invasion of England with comparatively few regular troops to assist them. It was the new long-bow, the men of Agincourt sprung to life.[15]

One could say that Arthur Conan Doyle's proposals resembled universal conscription, opening the discursive door to something like the advanced national mobilization ideology of Japanese captain Satō Kōjirō.

Thus Conan Doyle returned home from the Boer War in a state of some indignation. He was also conscious of the absence of Queen Victoria. She had succeeded to the throne in 1837 and reigned until her death in 1901. For sixty-three years she had been the figurehead of England's brilliant rise to ascendancy in the world. In Japanese history, the length of her reign compares to that of the Shōwa Emperor (1925–1989), and her death caused a national shock akin to the passing of the Meiji Emperor in 1912.

Sherlock Holmes had resolved case after case as the hero of the palmiest days of Victoria Regina. The unshakable confidence of this hero reflected a stable world in which yesterday did not differ very much from today, nor today from tomorrow. Thus Holmes's resurrection, as a symbol and guardian of order, was a consolation devoutly to be wished by Conan Doyle as well as his readers. This is what lay behind the public's joyful reception of *The Return of Sherlock Holmes*.

Arthur Conan Doyle now entered upon two projects simultaneously. One was the resurrection of Sherlock Holmes. The other was a rebuttal of the international condemnation of Great Britain for the Boer War.

The news that reached all parts of Europe, accompanied by illustrations, was of British soldiers bayoneting babies and raping women one after another. Conan Doyle believed that behind this "news" was the German propaganda machine. Indeed, we have already noted that the Boers were equipped with German arms, and there we do see German machinations at work. Conan Doyle wrote a defense of the Boer War, titled *The War in South Africa: Its Cause and Conduct* (1902), which sold out of an initial run of three hundred thousand copies in less than three months. A further five hundred thousand copies were sold in the United States and Canada. Those were just the English editions. The book was also translated into French, German, Russian, Italian, etc., and distributed all over Europe. If disease was prevalent among the subjugated Boers, he wrote, it was not from British neglect or worse, but from their own ignorance and contrariness. As one witness he quotes put it,

Many of the women would not open their tents to admit fresh air, and, instead of giving the proper medicines supplied by the military, preferred to give them home remedies. The mothers would not sponge the children.... The cause of the high death-rate is that the women let their children out as soon as the measles-rash has subsided. They persist in giving their children meat and other indigestible foods, even when we forbid it.[16]

Arthur Conan Doyle's concerns were on-target. This disquieting era continued. Eventually came the era of the battle with Germany: the Great War, otherwise referred to as World War I.

In 1917, at the author's whim, Holmes was revived again, not just once, but three times. In "His Last Bow," the great detective served as a spy against Germany.

When an author grows chauvinist, his works grow tedious. They lose subtlety. Conan Doyle's stories of the great detective Sherlock Holmes furnish a prime example: none is more tedious than "His Last Bow." I say this with all due apologies to Holmes fans enamored of the entire canon, but even Homer nods, and this work is a case in point.

All the action of "His Last Bow" takes place on the night of August 2, 1914, just two days before the outbreak of World War I. (The story itself was written in 1917.)

Since according to Conan Doyle, Holmes was born on January 6, 1854, this meant pressing him into duty as a spy when the great detective was an older man, sixty years of age. In fact, he is described as follows: "He was a tall, gaunt man of sixty, with clear-cut features and a small goatee beard which gave him a general resemblance to the caricatures of Uncle Sam."[17] At this point in the story, Holmes has not revealed his identity. He is disguised as one Altamont, an Irish American.

Since this book is easily obtainable (unlike the other hypothetical war stories we have considered), I will limit my plot outline to the barest of details. In 1904, Conan Doyle had written "The Second Stain," later collected in *The Return of Sherlock Holmes*. In that work, Holmes is portrayed as having retired from the detective business, living a comfortable, self-satisfied existence now in a second home in the country where he keeps bees and devotes himself to his writing. But in "His Last Bow," the recluse is visited by the prime minister himself and asked to help expose a German spy ring active in England. The spymaster is one Von Bork, described as follows:

> A remarkable man this Von Bork—a man who could hardly be matched among all the devoted agents of the Kaiser. It was his talents which had first recommended him for the English mission, the most important mission of all, but since he had taken it over those talents had become more and more manifest to the half-dozen people in the world who were really in touch with the truth.[18]

At the beginning of the story, Von Bork is in conversation with Baron Von Herling, chief secretary to the German legation in London. Von Bork expands upon the stupidity of Englishmen:

> It is an inconceivable thing, but even our special war tax of fifty million, which one would think made our purpose as clear as if we had advertised it on the front page of the *Times*, has not roused these people from their slumbers. Here and there one hears a question. It is my business to find an answer. Here and there also there is an irritation. It is my business to soothe it. But I can assure you that so far as the essentials go—the storage of munitions, the preparation for submarine attack, the arrangements for making high explosives—nothing is prepared.[19]

The tenor of this argument should be rather reminiscent to the reader. Remember Homer Lea's *The Valor of Ignorance*? The burden of that tract was that the American people were lost in profit-taking and idle reverie, and that while they slept, a formidable foe—Japan—was advancing upon them. This sour note ill-suited the dry dialogue and British wit that constituted part of the appeal of the Holmes stories. Yet Conan Doyle was doing his level best to agitate the public in order to awaken the patriotism and vigilance of the British people. But the more moralizing the tone, the less entertaining the tale.

Von Bork has employed the Irish American tough, Altamont, to obtain the new British Naval Signals—their communications codebook. Altamont has sent the following telegram:

> Will come without fail tonight and bring new sparking plugs.
> Altamont[20]

Altamont arrives, with a chauffeur, and the two are admitted into Von Bork's residence. Some interesting conversation takes place regarding the codes and Von Bork's spy ring, and when the German turns his back to peruse the new purloined information, he is caught from behind by an iron grip, and finds placed over his face a chloroform-soaked sponge, and he becomes putty in the hands of—none other than Sherlock Holmes, who had merely been disguised as Altamont. The chauffeur was Watson.

The story ends with a discussion between Holmes and Watson, as they look out over a moonlit sea. Holmes shakes his head thoughtfully.

"There's an east wind coming, Watson."

"I think not, Holmes. It is very warm."

"Good old Watson! You are the one fixed point in a changing age. There's an east wind coming all the same, such a wind as never blew on England yet. It will be cold and bitter, Watson, and a good many of us may wither before its blast. But it's God's own wind none the less, and a cleaner, better, stronger land will lie in the sunshine when the storm has cleared."[21]

When I suggested above that this was a boring story, I had in mind that the story gives us neither excitement nor denouement. So the question is, why did Arthur Conan Doyle write "His Last Bow"?

The answer is that his mood inclined him less toward Holmes and more toward war. In 1913, he published an article, "Great Britain and the Next War," in the *Fortnightly Review*. The following year it was published as a single volume. The subtitle was *A Reply to Bernhardi's "Germany and the Next War."* Before I discuss Conan Doyle's tract, I should like to review Bernhardi's book, which was published in 1911.

The Japanese translation of General Friedrich von Bernhardi's work came out in 1914. Its Japanese title, rendered into English, reads, *The Culture of War in Germany: A Country that Wrongs Itself and Wreaks Havoc on Others*, which suggests that in Japan, Germany was seen as an enemy nation. The preface was written by Takada Sanae, president of Waseda University in Tokyo. Takada noted that on a trip he'd recently taken to Europe and the United States, Bernhardi's book was being read avidly by virtually every traveler he came across. In the United States, it was even a best seller. Takada returned to Japan impressed with this publishing phenomenon.

Bernhardi was a retired lieutenant general who had served on the German General Staff. His book was written not only to direct the German people in their psychological preparations for the war that was coming, but also to claim the legitimacy of Germany's position before the court of world opinion. Let us return to Takada's preface to the Japanese edition.

Takada stated in his preface that he found it intolerable that, although war had begun, Japanese had no knowledge of a book so widely read abroad. Japanese, he said, "have an urgent need to know Germany's true intentions in opening hostilities," and thus he made haste to publish a Japanese edition.

That such a work should be read all over the world could not but offend Arthur Conan Doyle. Though he was not a military professional like Bernhardi, at least Conan Doyle had been so bold as to write *Great Britain and the Next War*, despite his lack of experience.

Books that try to stimulate a sense of crisis tend to fall into a pattern. Mizuno Hironori's *The Next Battle* and Homer Lea's *The Valor of Ignorance* both speak of their countrymen slumbering as a powerful enemy prepares to attack. While the enemy is sharpening its fangs, our own people are oblivious, blinded by their pursuit of wealth. My self-indulgent countrymen—awake! Bernhardi is true to type. History verifies, he says, the contention that his nation is the most warlike in Europe, words of praise as far as he is concerned. And yet Germany has now become one of the most peaceful of peoples. What is particularly shameful is the way in which the facilitation of trade has become our sole preoccupation. We have completely forgotten that the land in which we live was won through armed struggle. We have become an utterly agreeable people.

What did Arthur Conan Doyle have to say about this? He too wanted to waken his slumbering countrymen. One could not simply dismiss Bernhardi's pan-Germanist sentiments as the ravings of a lunatic. But no matter how angry Conan Doyle might get, German efforts to make the submarine more practical and effective—that is to say the threat of the U-boats—loomed ever larger in his mind.

In fact, as soon as the war began, London sustained strikes from the air. Conan Doyle had not envisioned fighter planes or aerial battleships. He thought that even if aerial weaponry were more developed, the threat would not be great. His concern was exclusively with the U-boats. Here is how he put it:

What effect a swarm of submarines, lying off the mouth of the Channel and the Irish Sea, would produce upon the victualing of these islands is a problem that is beyond my conjecture.[22]

If the ships supplying Great Britain's commodities and raw materials fell prey one after another to the submarine, its people could not survive. Arthur Conan Doyle therefore backed three policies to address this situation. First, he advocated sharp increases in duties on imported foodstuffs so as to encourage production at home. Second, he advocated building transport ships that would be as invisible as the submarines that were hunting them. The third policy he backed was to dig a tunnel under the English Channel. He thought this could be a way to transport food and troops safely between France and England.

However, none of his plans had much chance of being realized. No realists gave them serious thought. But Arthur Conan Doyle did, and his motive for doing so was spelled out in the conclusion to his tract denouncing Bernhardi:

> Every one of his propositions I dispute. But that is all beside the question. We have not to do with his argument, but with its results. Those results are that he, a man whose opinion is of weight and a member of the ruling class in Germany, tells us frankly that Germany will attack us the moment she sees a favorable opportunity. I repeat that we should be mad if we did not take very serious notice of the warning.[23]

Following this statement, Conan Doyle penned a story titled "Danger! Being the Log of Captain John Sirius," which appeared in the July 1914 edition of the *Strand Magazine*. This was immediately before the outbreak of the Great War. In the story, England was already at war with a small, imaginary country called Norland. The plot revolved around the ability of Norland's submarine fleet of eight ships to inflict heavy losses on Britain's merchant fleets, precipitating a food crisis. It was a novelistic development of the propositions first stated in *Great Britain and the Next War*.

In the course of these propagandistic activities, Conan Doyle once again mobilized the great detective Sherlock Holmes in the service of his country. Hence 1917's "His Last Bow," in which the novelist has Holmes utter the famous line quoted above, "There's an east wind coming, Watson." This was an attempt by Conan Doyle to prove how early he had recognized the danger England faced. And this must be why his stories became so dull. He was not writing for his readers' sake so much as for his own self-satisfaction. "His Last Bow," a work derided by a number of critics for its inexpert balancing of politics and detective story form, concludes with the claim that "a cleaner, better, stronger land will lie in the sunshine when the storm has cleared."

Germany in fact did lose the Great War, but the victors paid a terrible price as well. British casualties (both killed and wounded) numbered some three million. The conflict's tragedy touched Arthur Conan Doyle's life personally. The younger brother of his second wife Jean lost his life in the conflict. The husband of Lottie Oldham, his younger sister, was also killed. The son of Connie Hornung, another younger sister, was killed in battle. Jean's close friend, who was staying with the Conan Doyles, lost three siblings. The bitterest blow of all was the mortal wounds sustained by Kingsley, Arthur Conan Doyle's eldest son by his first wife, Louise, at the Battle of the Somme in July 1917. He died from those wounds in October 1918, right around the end of the war.

Surrounded, as it were, by dead people, Conan Doyle turned to spiritualism. The British upper and middle classes were sending their sons to war as frontline officers who personally led their troops as they charged the enemy. On the western front, it was not at all uncommon for such an officer to lose his life within a fortnight of his arrival. When, all at once, so many Britons were grieving the loss of so many of their close friends and relations, spiritualism gained quite a following. The mediums, who offered to manage communications with the dead, subsequently prospered. The detective novelist was merely another grief-stricken survivor of the Great War. In *The New Revelation* he speaks of being drawn into the world of spiritualism.

> The War came, and when the War came it brought earnestness into all our souls and made us look more closely at our own beliefs and reassess their values. In the presence of an agonized world, hearing every day of the deaths of the flower of our race in the first promise of their unfulfilled youth, seeing around one the wives and mothers who had no clear conception whither their loved ones had gone to, I seemed suddenly to see that this subject with which I had so long dallied was not merely a study of a force outside the rules of science, but that it was really something

tremendous, a breaking down of the walls between two worlds, a direct undeniable message from beyond, a call of hope and of guidance to the human race at the time of its deepest affliction.[24]

As an evangelist of spiritualism, Conan Doyle gave lectures all over Europe. In his final years he published one last collection featuring his beloved detective: *The Casebook of Sherlock Holmes*. On July 7, 1930, he died of heart failure. He was seventy-one years old.

The confidence of the great detective in the late nineteenth century. The horrors of the first great modern war. In the great gap between— confronted by the vast numbers of those who had just perished—Conan Doyle's patriotism foundered. Similarly aghast at the catastrophe of modern war, Mizuno Hironori struggled to convey to his fellow Japanese all that he had seen in Europe. He felt that he and his countrymen "should lead the other powers in advocating to the entire world the abolishment of armaments." As for Hector C. Bywater, the rare experience of the life of the spy was enriching for him. War is made up of quantities and technologies and information. He thought that extraneous emotions clouded one's vision. Of all those whose views we have considered, he may have had the coolest temperament.

CHAPTER NINE

An Englishman's "Great Pacific War"

JAPANESE are used to dating events by the reign name of each of its emperors. This way of marking national history has some advantages, but not when situating Japan in the context of world history. Then, it becomes a truly troublesome obstacle. The reign-name sequences chop up historical timelines too finely. When the unit of comparison is the century, they pose serious limitations to the study of historical events.

Sir Arthur Conan Doyle is a case in point. In the traditional Japanese system, one would have to say that he was born in the sixth year of Ansei but died in Shōwa 5; furthermore, that he lived through no less than eight reign-eras: Ansei, Man'en, Bunkyū, Genji, Keiō, Meiji, Taishō, and Shōwa. From a Western perspective, this is truly hard to grasp.

Properly speaking, the twentieth century is one era. Yet the Taishō era corresponds only to the segment from 1912 to 1926 on the Western calendar. Within it, one finds neatly bracketed the entire four years of World War I, from 1914 to 1918. The very period that Japanese designate so favorably with the epithet "Taishō democracy," as an era that extolled peace, was in Europe a time of unprecedented calamity. At times like these, the convenience of a reign-name can thus be deceptive.

Mizuno Hironori, who was active earlier in our discussion as something of a militarist, now embraced a new mission: to convey to his homeland the tragedy of the Great War in Europe. But he returned to a Japan at peace.

Hector C. Bywater, nine years his junior, was born in the seventeenth year of Meiji (1884). Bywater had a son and a daughter. The son was born in Meiji 43, or 1910, so he must have had childhood memories of World War I. The daughter, however, would have been less than four years old at that time.

Some 200 kilometers northwest of London by car one finds the town of Derby, with a population of 230,000. When one says "Derby," one thinks of horse racing, but there is in fact no racetrack in Derby. The association derives rather from that famous aristocrat Edward Smith Stanley, the Twelfth Earl of Derby, who raced four-year-old thoroughbreds.

The trip there by auto takes about two hours, first zooming along the M-1 motorway, then switching to the slower A-6. Derby is a provincial town in a green and pleasant locale. I visited in September 1991, just after an IRA terrorist incident in which the British army's local recruiting station had been attacked, killing a sergeant. If one hadn't known about it, one wouldn't have believed such a bloody event could have taken place there.

Twenty minutes from downtown Derby, in a section of broad flatlands, lies a community of retirees living in cottages. Cottages, but made of brick. And in one of those cottages, where I visited him, lived Hector C. Bywater Jr., known as "Junior." My voyage back in time had led me all the way to the outskirts of Derby to investigate the human riddle that was his father.

Bywater Sr. had experiences more real than the spying activities attributed to the Great Detective, Sherlock Holmes, in Sir Arthur Conan Doyle's "His Last Bow." He actually was a spy during World War I. But why was this Englishman concerned for the future of Japan?

Bywater Jr., eighty-one years of age, greeted his visitor from afar and led me into the cottage on unsteady legs. He explained that he was suffering from rheumatism, and also, with a regretful smile, that the deterioration of vision in his right eye made it impossible to read much.

"I've been the minister here for some time."[1] Bywater Sr. had been a tall man with piercing eyes. Junior was of middling weight and height, and mild-mannered. A small table next to a sofa was decorated with framed photographs, fading and sepia-toned. They were photos of Bywater Sr. and his wife in their younger days. I was told the photos were taken in Dresden. Bywater Sr. stood, dressed in a three-piece suit, his right hand in his pocket. He smiled slightly for the camera. The eyes were as penetrating as ever, but one sensed a brooding melancholy there. His wife, Emma, was also tall, even a little taller than Bywater Sr. himself. In the background were a number of overlapping human figures. This photo would appear to have been taken during a party. Emma was a beauty, though her facial features were largish. Her expression was unaffected and casual as if to say, "Oh, you're taking a photo?" Perhaps I am trying too hard to spot dissonance in a single photo. I was told that it was soon after this picture was taken that they were divorced.

Junior's earliest recollection was from when he was four years old—the very moment World War I began. As the train they were riding pulled into the station, his father abruptly stood up and cried, "It's war!" He had seen the huge headlines on the newspapers lined up on racks on the platform: WAR DECLARED!

From 1909, Bywater Sr. was based in Dresden and concentrating on his information-gathering activities. So as not to involve his family in this dangerous business, he moved them to London the following year. After that, he lived and worked abroad alone, mainly in Germany, though he was also sent to America. When he returned to London it was to make his reports and to rest.

As soon as the war ended, Bywater was liberated from his work as a spy. Prior to that he had requested several times to be relieved of his duties, and every time the naval ministry had made sure he was retained. Even at war's end, the authorities promised honors commensurate with his achievements in an effort to persuade him to stay on. But Bywater refused. Otherwise, there would never be any end to it.

After giving up the life of a spy, Bywater moved to a suburb ten miles south of London. There, he concentrated on his writings. I went looking for the place: No. 23, Whitmore Road, Beckenham. It was the kind of partitioned house one often sees in London, called a semi-detached house. This house, however, was a little larger than usual and had a garret. Given Bywater's relatively carefree lifestyle after he gave up spying, he and his wife and children should now, finally, have been able to spend time together here as a cozy family. On weekends, they went on picnics together. Junior was given a model train set. He has numerous recollections.

"My dad liked to go out. When he had the time, he'd take me on walks with him. He even took me to the seashore by car. Seemed like a sociable person, right?" But, added Junior, "Dad really had two sides. . . . Toward people who knew him, his behavior was unembarrassed. At small parties, he was the liveliest. He was great with his friends, completely reliable. But in respect of his work—how shall I put it?—there was a facet of his life that had to remain hidden. The other side was public. You understand."

Bywater Jr. spoke of his father's career as a spy with some reticence. He did mention the following incident. Once, during the Great War, his father suddenly took to wearing sunglasses, explaining that he had injured an eye. He told all his friends and neighbors that he had to go to America for some special ophthalmological surgery. He came back in a few weeks.

Of course it was only much later that Junior understood what had really been going on. "Not only did he not confide about his life as a spy to me, his son, he didn't even confide it to my mother. In that sense he betrayed even his wife."

Life at No. 23, Whitmore Road should have been peaceful. Certainly Bywater was able to mark some time and present a smiling countenance to his family. But to the extent that his thoughts were still occupied by the sea and war, it cannot be said that it was a happy family life in the true sense of the phrase. A chill wind blew between Bywater and Emma.

One day, in the back garden, Junior was playing with his father, who had brought out some model warships he had made himself. Suddenly, a cork shell, fired from one of the warship's miniature cannons, flew in an unfortunate direction. Emma was also outside, drying the wash. The cork barely missed hitting her in the aft. Junior still remembers being upset by his mother's unwonted fury. And the widening rift in his parents' marital relations proved too great to repair. "I think my father had too many secrets. When the war was over, then it was the writing. He spent too long sequestered up in his garret, working."

From Junior's snatches of memories of his father emerge a picture of a man consumed by war. Even when he was passing time with his family, his thoughts were elsewhere. He was focusing solely on the next war: "My father was somehow always living under intense pressure." What Bywater Sr. was so engrossed in writing was *Sea Power in the Pacific*. He looked past the destruction of the German navy to the postwar world and saw the kindling for a new Great War beginning to smolder at the next flashpoint: the Pacific. Something must be done.

In accordance with the policy that had been in effect for some time, namely one that designated the United States as the hypothetical adversary, the Japanese navy was in the process of its "8-8" fleet expansion plan: that is, the construction of eight new battleships and eight new battle cruisers. The military budget for 1920 was 650 million yen, accounting for 48 percent of the total annual budget. The next year, 1921, those expenditures stood at 730 million yen, or 49 percent. This level of nearly 50 percent of the national budget was inordinate. Two-thirds of that was devoted to the construction of new warships. Naturally, it was the people who bore the burden of arms expenditures.

The United States also adopted a gigantic naval construction program in 1916. In just one three-year period, starting the next year, the plan was to expand the fleet by ten new battleships and six new battle cruisers. The naval shipbuilding race between Japan and the United States was overheating. *Sea Power in the Pacific* was published just when the results of this competition were becoming clear in March of 1921. Bywater began his opening chapter as follows:

> When the German High Sea Fleet surrendered for internment on the twenty-first of November 1918, a brief but pregnant chapter in the history of sea power was brought to a close. The next chapter may be said to have opened in August 1919, with the passage of the newly created United States Pacific Fleet through the Panama Canal en route to its base in San Francisco Bay.[2]

Bywater was trying to inculcate something different from the notions of Homer Lea and others—different from their belief that the Japanese military would come charging across the Pacific like the surging billows of the ocean itself, invading and occupying the West Coast of North America.

> It is some ten years since Homer Lea wrote his book, in which he described at great length the transport of a huge Japanese army across the Pacific, its landings in Washington, Oregon, and California, and its eventual conquest of the whole Pacific slope. Even at that date the American navy was quite strong enough to have made such an operation absolutely impossible, and since, in the interval, its position of relative strength vis à vis the Japanese Navy has substantially improved, there is less reason than ever to include an invasion of the American mainland among the possible events of a future war."[3]

Indeed, in Bywater's judgment, the battleground of an American-Japanese conflict would be not the American mainland, but America's Pacific possessions.

America was occupying the Philippines and Guam. Then there was Hawaii. If America tried to attack Japan, the Japanese military would mount a stiff defense from their chain of naval bases ranging from the Chishima Islands through the Japanese archipelago to Okinawa and Taiwan. They would be able to parry any American thrust at the home islands.

Furthermore, during World War I, Japan had gained control over the

German mandates in the South Pacific, such as the Marshall and Caroline island groups. The Japanese military proceeded to fortify them one by one. What's more, if Japan attacked the Philippines, it would be possible to occupy that archipelago without much difficulty. The distances from the home country of each side were entirely different. Any American relief would arrive too late. The naval bases at Luzon, Mindanao, and elsewhere in the Philippines were all inadequate for the repair of battleships, and the American fleet based there was meager. The key to the defense of the Philippines was held by Guam, which should have been fortified by now, but at present, "no steps have been taken to carry out such work, and the island remains to the present date a mere coaling station, without any adequate defences and with no facilities for the upkeep of a naval squadron."[4]

What about Hawaii? Facilities there too were unsatisfactory. They were quite incapable of hosting a large fleet. If a powerful fleet were based at Pearl Harbor, it would enable a broad sphere of defense, from Alaska to Samoa. Yet an American Pacific strategy was as good as nonexistent. They were not making full use of the islands scattered across the Pacific. Bywater requires the reader to share this assessment as a precondition for imagining a future Japan-U.S. war.

The war would begin with—of all things!—a surprise attack by the Japanese. First on the hit list: the Philippines and Guam. Guam would be seized by Japan in a matter of weeks. Once Guam had fallen, it would be easy for the Japanese military to occupy the Philippines. The initial rounds of the war would thus belong to Japan. And once Guam and the Philippines had been seized, it would be difficult to recover them. Quite difficult. It would take a great deal of time indeed.

What was America to do? First, it would have to concentrate its entire fleet in Hawaii. Then it would have to use Wake Island (between Hawaii and Guam) as a forward base with which to threaten the Japanese coastline and recover Guam. But the Japanese navy would act to contain any such movements. It was impossible for Japan to mount an invasion so far away as the American mainland, but America's possessions in the Pacific would certainly come under attack.

The war scenario outlined above shows an America deprived of any offensive military power. Thus we see that Bywater's *Sea Power in the Pacific* diverges in obvious ways from Homer Lea's *The Valor of Ignorance*. Indeed, with regard to objective reality, their views are 180 degrees apart. The military critics and authors who were Bywater's contemporaries also differed from him. This is because Bywater's criteria were not limited to fleet size, and his analysis was not overwhelmed by patriotic gush.

After discussing the theoretical possibilities in *Sea Power in the Pacific*, Bywater next wrote a novelistic treatment of his ideas: *The Great Pacific War*. As a novel, *The Great Pacific War* naturally conveyed more of a sense of immediacy.

It must be said that, in and of itself, it was uncommon for a foreigner to be engaged in forecasting the future of Japan. As a rule, one can easily dismiss such a forecast when it's misguided or a matter of out-and-out meddling. But what about when it's absolutely the opposite case? If a foreigner were to forecast Japan's future more accurately than a Japanese, the ignorance of the Japanese would be a poor excuse.

The Great Pacific War, written in 1924, describes a Japan-U.S. war that purportedly takes place in 1931. On March 2 of that year, to be precise, a Rear Admiral Ribley, commanding the United States' Pacific Fleet that is stationed in the Philippines, feels uneasy at the sharply worsening relations and indeed state of crisis between Japan and the U.S. and requests that naval reinforcements be sent from the U.S. mainland. Subsequently, the undersea cable from Manila is cut. Wireless transmissions from Guam and Eastern Samoa are also compromised, possibly by electronic interference of some kind, rendering them nonoperational.

The next day, March 3, a merchant ship from Osaka, the *Akashi-maru*, traversing the Panama Canal, explodes with a loud bang and sinks. The *Akashi-maru* is a huge 12,000-ton cargo ship, and the explosion literally shakes heaven and earth as the giant ship is blown to smithereens, smothering both banks of the canal with an avalanche of debris. The wreckage renders the Panama Canal impassable.

The rupturing of communications lines at Manila and the explosion at the Panama Canal have been both meticulously planned by the Japanese, but at this point there is no declaration of war. In fact, the two events are camouflaged as accidents precisely in order to serve as the preliminaries to a surprise attack. Thanks to the break in lines of communication, America's Pacific Fleet is isolated; and with the Panama Canal out of service, America's Atlantic Fleet, currently stationed on the East Coast, cannot cross to the Pacific. It could attempt the difficult passage around the South American Cape Horn, but the Panama Canal is the best route and will have to be repaired—and that will take half a year.

Meanwhile, the Japanese commander, Vice Admiral Hiraga, heads for the Philippines aboard his flagship the *Kongo* together with a flotilla of six light cruisers including the *Hiei* and the *Kirishima*, accompanied by the aircraft carrier *Hōshō* and trailed by two dozen destroyers.

Before daybreak on March 6, an American reconnaissance plane spots the huge Japanese armada. But it is too late. The Japanese are already attacking the western shore of Lingayen Bay. Already, on the afternoon of March 5, Count Sakatani, the Japanese ambassador in Washington, has informed the American government that Japanese diplomatic personnel are being withdrawn. This is effectively a declaration of war.

The American fleet at Manila tries to counterattack the Japanese fleet as it closes in, but the battle lasts only three hours. The paltry American naval forces are no match for the Japanese armada.

With the telegraph lines cut, Washington does not get the news immediately. When it does, it is through unconfirmed reports that reach Washington via Hong Kong and London. Everybody hopes it is just a bad dream. But a follow-up report includes irrefutable confirmation. There is no way now to avoid the truth. The report is from a Dutch trading vessel, which has rescued seven survivors of the destroyer *Crosby*. To the American public, it is a bolt from the blue. Their only military capability in the Far East has disappeared. The Japanese government issues the following formal announcement:

> In the forenoon of March 6 our South Sea naval forces, under the command of Vice Admiral Hiraga, encountered the American Asiatic Squadron outside Manila Bay. By skillful maneuvers it was brought to action under favorable conditions, the battle lasting three hours. The enemy force was totally destroyed, in spite of a brave defence. We sank five cruisers, one large auxiliary, nine destroyers, and several submarines. Two store ships were sunk and one was captured. A number of prisoners have been taken. Our losses are small. . . .[5]

Generally, Japanese government announcements are distinctive for their lack of embellishment. They capture the gist of things in terse sentences. If we contrast the testimony of an American staff officer (and battle survivor) with the announcement of the Japanese government, the situation becomes all the clearer. Let me quote from the officer's notes, published after the war (remember, of course, that this is all Bywater's fiction). The memoirist is one Admiral Elkins, second-in-command to Rear Admiral Ribley aboard the flagship *Missouri*.

> Thinking he had given us enough rope, the Japanese admiral must have decided to end the game without further ado. What followed is beyond description; all around us the sea spouted and boiled; there were half a dozen terrific explosions in as many seconds; I heard one appalling crash as if a giant redwood tree had toppled athwart our deck; then there was a blaze of light, another ear-splitting crash, and everything came to an end for me. When I recovered my senses I was being dragged into a boat from the destroyer *Hulbert*. They told me the flagship had foundered at 11.30, having been practically blown to pieces. There were only six survivors besides myself. The Admiral had gone down with the ship; probably he had been killed by the shell that knocked me senseless.[6]

The matter of casualties is also recorded in the memoir in detail.

> Our squadron had been wiped out, and upwards of 2,500 gallant comrades had fallen, but at least we could say that we had upheld the honor of the flag. The only Japanese ships sunk were the *Tatsuta* and two destroyers. Their casualties throughout the fleet were returned as 600. But considering the enormous disparity between their force and ours it was remarkable that they suffered any loss at all.[7]

Bywater imagined this early, stunning blow by Japan to have occurred on the exact same day of the year, December 7 (December 8, Japan time), as the actual 1941 Pearl Harbor attack in which 2,402 lives were lost. And Bywater's tragedy in Manila seems to the American people, if not to their leaders, to come like a bolt from the blue.

> The bad news from the Far East sent a wave of grief over the United States. For the time being little heed was paid to the peril which menaced the Philippines. The country was thinking of those thousands of gallant seamen who had gone to their doom, fighting to the last against tremendous odds, with the old flag still flying as the waters closed above the torn and battered hulls of their ships.[8]

Considering that upwards of a thousand men lost their lives on the battleship *Arizona* alone when it sank and they were buried alive inside, it is as if Bywater's fictional memoirist were an eyewitness to real history.

The Great Pacific War thus has hostilities commencing with a surprise attack by Japan, as in the actual Japan-U.S. war, the sole difference being the omission of Hawaii. At the time Hector C. Bywater wrote his hypothetical scenario, Pearl Harbor was little better than a supply station, and the strategy Japan adopted (fictively) was to pin down the U.S. Atlantic Fleet by shutting down the Panama Canal. In the 1931 of Bywater's novel, the effect of shutting down the Panama Canal was the same as the actual 1941 annihilation of the fleet concentrated in Pearl Harbor.

The significance of this preliminary action is plainly stated: "The destruction of Admiral Ribley's squadron left the way open for the invasion of the Philippines" by an expeditionary force of five divisions, or about one hundred thousand men.[9]

> Ere yet the last battered American ship had vanished from sight a radio message from the Japanese Commander in Chief set in motion the fleet of transports which had been lying at Kure and other ports for some days past, with a hundred thousand fighting men on board. The whole convoy, with its naval and air escort, was under way at dusk on March 6. Steaming south at a speed of 12 knots, it was timed to reach the shores of Luzon in four and a half days.

Troop strength differentials alone do not determine the success or failure of a strategy. Japanese troop transports were still vulnerable to aerial bombing by the islands' defenders.

> According to the last report from Japanese agents, not more than fifty serviceable planes were in the islands at the end of February. But on the 25th of that month a transport had arrived at Manila bringing thirty machines of a new and powerful type. These . . . played a very important part in the defence of Luzon.

In the real Pacific War, the surprise attack on Pearl Harbor was followed within a matter of hours by an attack on the Clark airbase in the Philippines. The American military there had by then received word, over the wireless, that Hawaii had been attacked, and the base was on high alert. Fighter planes were dispatched. However, due to a thick fog, the Japanese attack was delayed until the noon hour, when almost all the American pilots were back on base having lunch. One hundred and twelve fighter planes were being prepped. They were sitting ducks.

Let us take an abbreviated look at the Japanese strategy for invading the Philippines principally via the west shore of Lingayen Bay on the island of Luzon, as described in *The Great Pacific War*.

At 3:00 PM on March 11, 1931, several Japanese warships appear in the waters a thousand meters off Lingayen Bay. They commence a concerted naval bombardment of the American military base there. The Americans return fire with their own artillery. At 5:00 PM, under cover provided by the warships, two dozen troop transports approach shore. The Americans scramble forty bombers. The aircraft, making long aerial arcs, climb to a height of three thousand meters to escape anti-aircraft fire from the warships, before attacking the troop transports following the warships. This aerial bombing is successful. The Japanese lose eleven of their troop transports, with six thousand men killed or injured.

The success enjoyed by the American warplanes, however, is fleeting. It cannot ultimately prevent the landing of so large an invasion force. The Japanese naval gunners are accurate. That is because Japanese reconnaissance planes are spotting for them. And the Americans have been compromised by poor defensive planning. They have huge artillery on rails up on the hills commanding Lingayen Bay, but the rails are sabotaged by Japanese spies, and the Americans cannot move these guns to other locations in time to bombard the disembarking Japanese troops.

At 8:00 PM, under cover of darkness, the landing craft carrying the invasion force draws near the shore. Carrying their rifles over their heads and shouting war cries, smallish figures in khaki uniforms leap into the water and charge ashore. They are undaunted even by crossfire. Many are mown down. The beachhead is soon piled high with mountains of casualties. But the veritable tide of Japanese soldiers eventually overwhelms the American trenches. The U.S. garrison retreats to Manila.

Simultaneously with the Japanese landing at Lingayen Bay on the western side of Luzon, there is another landing, at Lamon Bay on the eastern side of the island. The strategy is to catch Manila in a pincer movement.

On March 12, at 5:00 PM, the Japanese fleet, screened by fighter planes and bombers, advances on Lamon Bay. Here there is no interception by American warplanes. The Japanese fleet approaches the shore, and for half an hour it shells the woods where American troops may be supposed to be concealed. But there is no return fire. Indeed, there is no garrison stationed there after all. However, since the Japanese troop transports have been spotted by an American reconnaissance plane, it is not long before twenty American fighter planes show up and attack. In the skies above Lamon Bay, a Japanese-American dogfight ensues. The Americans lose half their fighters, but the remaining ten bear down on the Japanese troop transports. Of the twenty-one transports, one is sunk and three are damaged.

But that is the extent of the resistance. The next morning, before dawn on March 13, thirty thousand Japanese troops land, and they march on Manila.

It would be appropriate at this point to make some remarks on the course the Pacific War actually took.

Whether or not it was due to the influence of *The Great Pacific War*, the American military did not in fact leave Lamon Bay undefended. As the 16th Division under Lieutenant General Morioka Susumu forced its way onto the beach during the real war, they came under withering fire and suffered many casualties. One who died of severe wounds sustained during the battle was Second Lieutenant Ōe Sueo, a medalist in the pole vault at the 1936 Berlin Olympics. At the Olympics, it had been a tough, five-hour struggle, at the end of which an American had taken the gold, while Ōe and fellow record-holder Nishida Shūhei literally split the silver and bronze medals, recombining the halves to make two half-bronze, half-silver medals. This story was once included in school textbooks as a moral of heroic competition and shared triumph. In any event, the 16th Division numbered seven thousand men. The main force was landing at Lingayen Bay.

The force that landed at Lingayen Bay came at Manila from the north; the force that landed at Lamon Bay came at it from the south. Still, it was an essentially east-west pincer strategy—and the very one described in Homer Lea's *The Valor of Ignorance*. Lea had one of the two pincer arms start at Polilio Island rather than Lamon Bay, but since Polilio is just to the east of Lamon, it amounts to the same thing.

Mizuno Hironori's *The Next Battle* followed Homer Lea blindly in this regard. But Hector C. Bywater did not. His interest in a Lamon Bay landing was spurred by his independent judgment regarding the difficulty of getting past the mighty fortress of Corregidor guarding Manila harbor. A direct attempt on the harbor, he felt, would cost too many casualties.

The commander in chief of Japan's actual attack force in the Philippines was Lieutenant General Honma Masaharu. His opposite number, in charge of the defense of the islands, was General Douglas MacArthur. Prior to implementing the main landing at Lingayen Bay, Lieutenant General Honma carried out another maneuver on a smaller scale. Landing operations were conducted at Lagaspi at the southwest of Luzon Island, at Aparri in the north, and at Vigan in the west. However, MacArthur rightly saw through these diversionary tactics as attempts to split his forces. He was confident the main landing would be at Lingayen Bay, and he situated his forces accordingly. It is fair to say that what gave him confidence in this decision was the psychological influence of Homer Lea's *The Valor of Ignorance*. Nevertheless, the Japanese onslaught was so fierce that MacArthur was unable to counter it. He withdrew from the Philippines, and, at a news conference at Darwin, Australia, uttered his famous grim pledge, "I shall return."

Let us return to *The Great Pacific War*. The American garrison in the Philippines undertakes to make a hopeless stand against the advancing Japanese soldiers. But there is nothing they can do against an enemy force that outnumbers them ten to one. On March 19, 1931, the commandant of U.S. Army forces stationed in the Philippines, General O'Neill, learns that he has less than two thousand men left under his command. Rather than expose Manila to bombardment, he retreats on March 20, and the Japanese triumphantly enter the city. The day before that, a separate Japanese expeditionary force of five thousand men invaded Mindanao Island at Sindangan Bay. All the Philippine Islands are thus brought under Japanese control. The Americans are obliged to organize a resistance.

These early victories by surprise attack also occurred in the actual Pacific War. The problem is what came next. In Bywater's novel, even with the western Pacific falling under Japanese control, the eastern Pacific is still controlled by the U.S. The Philippines and Guam may have fallen, but the main American naval force has come to Hawaii. The Aleutian island chain and Samoa both have U.S. bases. These bases give the U.S. strategic points from which to dominate the sea-lanes west from Hawaii. And the U.S. Navy is almost unscathed. Its Pacific Fleet at the Philippines does not constitute part of its core strength. The Pacific Fleet that assembles at Pearl Harbor draws on the military ports of San Francisco, San Pedro, and San Diego. In addition to twelve battleships (the *West Virginia*, the *Maryland*, the *Colorado*, the *California*, the *Tennessee*, the *New Mexico*, the *Idaho*, the *Mississippi*, the *Pennsylvania*, the *Arizona*, the *Oklahoma*, and the *Nevada*),

Bywater's Pacific Fleet includes twenty cruisers, two aircraft carriers, forty-one submarines, and other craft. (In the actual attack on Pearl Harbor, the *Arizona* and the *Oklahoma* were both sunk, and the *West Virginia*, the *California*, and the *Nevada* were seriously damaged. The *Maryland*, the *Tennessee*, and the *Pennsylvania* also sustained damage.)

The Pacific Fleet is larger than the Atlantic Fleet, which has six battleships, ten cruisers, two aircraft carriers, and seventy submarines. However, as we noted above, the Japanese have sunk a giant steamer in the Panama Canal, blocking passage and thus pinning down the U.S. Atlantic Fleet—preventing it from joining up with the Pacific Fleet. The Atlantic Fleet makes shift to transport their personnel to the West Coast by rail.

The standoff across the Pacific continues. Neither side can press an attack against the other. The risk is too great. The situation is, in fact, deadlocked. Even the fleet at Pearl Harbor cannot move out. To break the stalemate, the Japanese launch a guerilla strategy. On May 20 in the seas near Hawaii, and on May 25 at the entrance to San Diego harbor, mines laid by the Japanese are discovered. They must have been laid by submarines, or possibly by fishing boats. The entrance to San Diego harbor is cleared at the relatively light cost of damage to three American destroyers.

On June 17, the Japanese navy's submarine No. 54 bombards the mainland from a position south of Santa Ana. Its target is a freight train packed with military supplies and materiel. Cars are knocked off the tracks and catch fire; many casualties are sustained. The submarine turns and proceeds north, and outside San Francisco's Golden Gate Bridge it attacks and sinks four merchant ships. That evening, it sinks a tanker off Los Angeles. Finally, on June 22, twenty Japanese bombers are seen above San Francisco, Oakland, and Los Angeles. San Francisco is well equipped to fight fires, and fire damage is sustained in only one contained area. But in Los Angeles, oil storage facilities are set ablaze, and when Hollywood burns, many priceless films go up in smoke.

On August 9, as the Atlantic Fleet passes through the Straits of Magellan on its way to link up with the Pacific Fleet at Pearl Harbor, it comes under attack by Japanese submarines.

With these multiple guerilla attacks, American public opinion is at the boiling point. The White House is under pressure to take decisive action. The president assembles his cabinet secretaries and his army and navy chiefs to confer on strategy. Fleet Admiral Morrison proposes a radical strategy. If the Ogasawara island group were occupied, it would place the U.S.

Navy just five hundred nautical miles from Tokyo Bay. At full speed, that distance could be traversed in a single day and night. The Japanese will not be expecting an attack to be launched from so close. Says Morrison: "The plan was an exceptionally bold one, but its very audacity held out the best promise of success."[10]

If the U.S. are successful in occupying the Ogasawaras, the Japanese will have to send their fleet's main strength against it. At the point that fleet leaves the military port of Yokosuka would be the time to strike it. There is much dissent, but as no alternative proposals are forthcoming, this is the plan that is agreed upon. To take and hold a base camp at the Ogasawara Islands, 22,000 troops are dispatched aboard troop transport ships, guarded by four cruisers, thirty destroyers, and four aircraft carriers. The convoy leaves Pearl Harbor on December 20.

Six days later they reach the Midway Islands. The next day they head for Wake Island, but suddenly the weather takes a turn for the worse. The convoy is beset by a fierce squall coming up from the southwest. Two of the troop transports sink; a thousand men drown. And then the aircraft carriers they are supposed to hook up with are nowhere in sight. The hundred American warplanes on board were to have dropped poison gas on the Japanese garrison on the Ogasawaras. While plans continue to unravel in this fashion, the convoy is discovered by Japanese submarines.

At this point the troop transports are attacked from the rear by four Japanese cruisers. They scurry, limping, back to Wake. The Ogasawara strategy collapses, and Fleet Admiral Morrison is reassigned. His successor as chief of naval operations is the more cautious Admiral Lincoln Muller. Joseph Harper, who as governor and commandant of Guam has only recently risen from captain to rear admiral, is named assistant chief. His knowledge of the Pacific theater is valued; so too is his fighting spirit.

Rear Admiral Harper has had the experience of being held prisoner by the Japanese. As he is being transported on a Japanese destroyer, it comes under attack by an Allied submarine. The destroyer is sunk, and Harper narrowly escapes with his life. The incident is reminiscent of MacArthur's experience on a boat while fleeing the Philippines.

The plan Harper draws up is to use the mid-Pacific islands as stepping-stones over which to advance westward toward Manila. The U.S. begins to implement this strategy by sending wooden mockups of warships to Dutch Harbor in the Aleutians. These are decoys. The real ships are sent south. Troops are also sent to Tutuila Island in American-occupied Samoa.

America has naval supremacy east of Hawaii, so there is no way Japan can discover the deception early on. And by using Tutuila as a supply base, the Americans will be able to undertake an assault on the Truk Islands in the Carolines.

The U.S. captures Ponape (Pohnpei, in the Caroline Islands) and Yalut (Jaluit, in the Marshall Islands) simultaneously. Now the supply routes to the Hawaiian Islands are secured. The next part of the plan is to build an advance base at Angaur (Ngeaur) Island in the Palau group and to attack the Philippines. Meanwhile, the U.S. steps up development of a feint toward Japanese-held Guam and Yap. The goal is to lure Japan's Combined Fleet out of its safe haven at Yokosuka.

Harper's strategy is dead-on. The Japanese launch an aerial assault on Dutch Harbor in the Aleutians. In fact, they go so far as to dispatch a task force, the aircraft carrier *Hōshū* serving as flagship. They are completely taken in by the decoys.

The Truk Islands are a small archipelago of about a dozen coral reef islands lined up like the serrated edge of a blade. After the First World War they are transferred as trust territories from Germany to Japan, but no garrison is stationed there. Both Ponape and Yalut are occupied easily, with almost no casualties. And the strategy of luring out Japan's Combined Fleet also works. The Japanese play right into the hands of the Americans.

Already a year and a half has passed since the beginning of the war.

On September 17, the Japanese Combined Fleet leaves Yokosuka harbor. On October 15, it enters Manila. The Fleet comprises seven battleships, five battle cruisers, four aircraft carriers, twenty-three cruisers, one hundred destroyers, and ninety-four submarines. The Americans' main force consists of sixteen battleships, five aircraft carriers, twenty-three cruisers, 115 destroyers, and eighty submarines. The Americans have the edge in numbers of battleships, but the Japanese have the advantage in terms of speed. It is seen as a match of quantity versus quality. The battle between these two great fleets, rivaling the Battle of Tsushima during the Russo-Japanese War, commences on November 21, 1932.

Before relating the outcome of the battle, it is imperative to reproduce the circumstances that obtained immediately prior, based on the (fictional) historical record. This is because one aspect of naval warfare is the psychological battle.

In the postwar period in Bywater's novel a book titled *The Japanese Fleet in the American War* by Japanese author Nakabashi Rokuro is published in

Japan, in Japanese, by Seikyo-sha in 1933. This is, of course, all Bywater's fiction, but Seikyo-sha appears to denote the same company, Seikyō Sha, that in the real prewar Japan put out the nationalistic journal *Japan and the Japanese*. Bywater had done his homework.

This postwar account carries a fictional battle log, which provides a rather convincing portrayal of how anguished the commander in chief of the Combined Fleet was at being unable to fathom the American strategy.[11]

> During the morning of November 17, a report from Submarine *Ro. 60*, patrolling north of the Pelews, came to hand, announcing it had sighted a large fleet of enemy warships and transports steering N.N.E. . . . From this intelligence we assumed that the threatened invasion of Yap was about to take place.

It is not immediately clear that this fleet heading toward Yap is in fact a decoy maneuver.

> At 10 AM on the 18th we had a message from Yap, reporting hostile battle-ships within sight of the island, bearing S.W. At 10.45 came a second report: "Ten battleships bombarding us; fleet of transports lying out of range. Our batteries are in action."

Commander in chief Hiraga forces the pace of the response. If the Yap Islands are occupied by the enemy before the defenders can be relieved, the fleet that has just been sighted will slip through his grasp. He has no choice but to head there at full speed. But strangely, it seems that "the attack was being conducted with a singular want of vigor":

> At 10 PM came a message: "Enemy no longer in sight."

This is a problem. Had they slipped away after all? Fleet Admiral Hiraga is disheartened.

> Conceive, then, the relief we felt on learning at 8 AM that hostile battle-ships were again off the island and had reopened their bombardment.

Hiraga is indeed relieved. They have still not fled. But suddenly he is beset by misgivings. He can't say that the American campaign is being prosecuted half-heartedly, but there is something strange about it nonetheless. If a truly all-out assault had been mounted, the enemy would have taken Yap, lickety-split. If the idea were to inflict damage and then flee in hit-and-run fashion, that was also doable. But these attacks qualify for neither tactic. The enemy must know that such feckless conduct invites an attack from the rear by the Combined Fleet. It is strange.

At 9 PM came the usual report: "Enemy withdrawing to sea. We are endeavoring to repair our batteries, but have only two guns left in action."

Hiraga is expecting to arrive at Yap by evening of the very next day, and yet at the eleventh hour, as it were, the enemy is fleeing. This is not good.

At dawn we received from Yap a message reporting that the enemy was no longer in sight.

They have already slipped through his grasp. Now there is nothing for it but to put in at Yap, resupply, and settle on a new strategy. But while Admiral Hiraga is being tantalized by the reports from Yap, the Americans are outflanking him and pulling up behind his Combined Fleet.

Again there came news that the enemy fleet had been sighted—not, however, where we supposed it to be, some hundreds of miles to the east, but almost due west of us, and only 100 miles away!

It is a report from a patrol submarine. From the opposite direction! What is going on here? Do the Americans have a fleet to the west as well as to the east? The fleet that retreated from Yap was merely a decoy. The main fleet has circled around to the west and is ready for battle. Japan's Combined Fleet hastens to draw itself up into battle formation. Admiral Hiraga now tries to repeat Tōgō Heihachirō's T-formation from the Battle of Tsushima, in which he turned his fleet in a line perpendicular to the line of advancing enemy ships and subjected each of the enemy ships successively to concentrated firepower. But the Americans will have none of his T. Before Hiraga can fully bring his ships around, the Americans engage.

Let us omit a full description of the battle here and instead add a few words of analysis. The battle lasts five hours. The Combined Fleet loses, giving the Americans mastery of the Pacific. Hector C. Bywater permits the U.S. victory here because he wanted to point up the glaring preponderance of American military power.

The Japanese knew that if the American Atlantic and Pacific Fleets were to combine, Japan could not hope to win. Hence, in Bywater's novel, the blockage of the Panama Canal. And hence Mizuno Hironori's version in *The Next Battle*, in which Japan's pyrrhic victory over the U.S. First Fleet sets it up for defeat by the U.S. Second Fleet.

But Bywater unquestionably had an additional message in mind. Namely, that even if the Panama Canal were dynamited, the two U.S. fleets would still unite, and Japan would still lose. In the Russo-Japanese War, the strategy of blocking up Russia's Far Eastern Fleet in Port Arthur succeeded. Japan was then able to turn its attention to attacking the incoming Baltic Fleet, and defeated it. The Baltic Fleet had to leave its base in the Baltic Sea, and travel through the Atlantic and around Africa via the Cape of Good Hope, and then cross the Indian Ocean. The seven-month voyage left ships and crews depleted and exhausted, giving Japan a good shot at winning. But it could not work this way in the Pacific. Japan would have to fight both American fleets united in one grand armada.

Back to Bywater's hypothetical history. With Japan's Combined Fleet defeated, the U.S. seizes Guam and the Philippines. It is merely a matter of time before Japan itself will be brought under aerial attack. U.S. aircraft carriers approach Japan's coasts, and one would think that Japan's capitulation is nigh.

On the evening of January 30, 1933, fifty American warplanes appeared over Tokyo. Tokyo immediately fell into a panic. However, what the American planes dropped was not bombs, but countless leaflets. They were written in Japanese, and they said, "Further loss of life is pointless. The American people appeal to the conscience of the Japanese to put an end to this unjustified, pointless war. We call for a cease-fire."

On May 15, 1933, a peace treaty is signed in Shanghai. Its terms are not onerous to the Japanese. Japan is to cede the protectorates of the Marshall and Caroline islands to the United States. Otherwise, the status quo will remain, with America demanding no indemnity.

* * *

ANYONE can take it upon himself or herself to predict the outcome of a conflict. It is an author's prerogative. What we must ask ourselves is, what of value does Bywater's *The Great Pacific War* contribute that distinguishes it from other hypothetical accounts of Japan-U.S. wars?

One aspect we have already touched on: the detailed verisimilitude Bywater's novel exhibits as a simulation or hypothetical scenario. It closely resembles real, later wartime conditions, and in that, it is corroborated by history. As a journalist of the first rank, Bywater gathered the most accurate information he could, and he based his predictions on hard data.

Secondly, Bywater's method was hardly armchair theorizing. In response to a question from me, Bywater Jr. (eighty-one years old at the time I interviewed him) contributed the following recollection about his father.

> My father was quite expert at building model battleships. And he recruited me and Sylvia, my younger sister, to help him. Then he'd float them in the pond, and play war. I say, "play war," but it was hardly an idle pursuit.

Even when constructing a miniature of a battleship, Bywater made it accurate to the tiniest detail. He would carve the main body of the ship out of pine, then cover it with tin plate. The brass deck-cannon fired "shells" made of cork. Finally, he would outfit the craft with a motor, rigged so as to maintain a constant speed.

Near the Bywaters' residence at 23 Whitmore Road in London's Beckenham district was a small pond. It was about the size of an elementary school swimming pool, and it was handy for sailing model battleships. But it wasn't just Hector Bywater Sr. who engaged in this: his journalist friends helped him out, playing war. Battle cries would come from one side of the pond. Then the opposing side would respond in kind as the ships were drawn up into battle formations and commenced hostile action.

Suddenly, the little pond was transformed into the Pacific Ocean. For the decisive battle, the opposing fleets would mobilize battleships, cruisers, destroyers, submarines, and aircraft carriers. In considering actual fighting strength, the sheer number of battleships is really the name of the game. It far outweighs other factors, such as the power and range of the cannon, the thickness of the armor plating, the class of the ships. In reality, supply ships also have their role to play, but they can be ignored in simulations.

Seven Japanese battleships appear in *The Great Pacific War*: the *Nagato*, the *Kaga*, the *Mutsu*, the *Ise*, the *Hyūga*, the *Fusō*, the *Yamashiro*. These were names of real ships. The American Atlantic and Pacific Fleets combined have eighteen battleships, of which sixteen confront Japan's Combined Fleet in the decisive battle.

The difference in numbers of ships made the imbalance in fighting strength quite apparent. Simply put, the American fleet outnumbered the Japanese fleet. It was all very well to say that anyone with any experience would draw the obvious conclusion. It still had to be verified by deploying the model ships in various hypothetical battle formations.

At the pond, Bywater himself was transformed into a Gulliver. Up to his waist in the pond-water of this little Pacific, he would set the two mighty miniature fleets against each other. Propeller-screws buzzed and corks popped as the battleships exchanged "fire."

The Great Pacific War also incorporates elements of the psychological battle. Without an understanding of the military basics, however, that would not amount to much. And with his many and varied simulations, Bywater was led to one inescapable and frightening conclusion.

If opposing battleships approached each other and exchanged fire, both would sustain grievous damage. Not only had there been substantial improvements in the efficacy of the naval guns themselves, aerial spotting had also improved accuracy. It would be difficult for either side to win unscathed. Not only the vanquished but the victor would suffer great harm.

It might seem obvious, but the best solution was to avoid war. Particularly because henceforth, winning would always be unsatisfactory. This was the main point Bywater wanted to drive home with *The Great Pacific War*. That is why he has America, though victorious in its war with Japan, abandon the demand for indemnities when the treaty is finally concluded. Let us have it in his own words.

Now that peace has been re-established on a sound and apparently permanent basis, the historian may be permitted to marvel at the folly of Japan in wantonly attacking a country with whom she had no real cause for enmity, and whose friendship was, indeed, essential to her own welfare. As a result of this unprovoked conflict, Japan was brought to the verge of ruin, nor is it conceivable that she will regain her former status as a first-rank Power during the present generation.

If the United States emerged victorious from the fray, it cannot be said that she derived any substantial benefit beyond the elimination of that menace of war which had been for many years a perpetual source of anxiety to her statesmen. Her shipping trade was virtually destroyed, and as yet it shows no sign of recovery. The enormous expenditure in which she had been involved left its inevitable aftermath of high taxation and consequent social unrest. War is never a paying proposition from any national point of view, and the great conflict of which the salient phases are described in the foregoing pages has proved, in its material aspects at least, scarcely less disastrous to victors than to vanquished.[12]

This was a point of view not seen hitherto in "future chronicles" of a Japan-U.S. war. In *The Valor of Ignorance*, Homer Lea insisted that in Japan, the martial spirit rules all aspects of national life. In *BANZAI!*, Parabellum described fear of a Japanese army that would inundate the country like a yellow flood.

There was a line of thought that held that Japanese culture was so different as to be inscrutable, unknowable. One only knew that it had acquired advanced Western arms, improved upon them, and was now forcing itself upon the world. Yet even back then, Bywater had no use for such prejudiced thinking. Significantly, even Mizuno Hironori ended *The Next Battle* with a defeated Japan losing all at once the international position it had labored so intensely to construct for itself ever since the advent of the Black Ships—and yet he said nothing about America as the victor.

Before the First World War, it is true that only the defeated side fell into an economic abyss. The victors did not suffer deep economic wounds. But in carrying out his spying activities during the Great War, Bywater was obliged to experience in some way the terrible realities of that war. Like Mizuno Hironori, he understood the new reality that in modern war there could be no true victor.

War does not arise simply out of fear of a different culture. For Homer Lea or Parabellum, even for Satō Kōjirō (author of *Dream Tales of a Japan-U.S. War*), such cultural divergences were indeed the seeds of war, but in Bywater's conception of war they had no place. His interest was piqued, rather, by such practical questions as who had what hardware—that is, ships—and how it could be deployed to secure victory.

Hector Bywater's attitude is redolent of game-playing. But not in the sense of idle amusement. Strategy is always a game. And to the extent that it is a game, the participants must adhere to certain rules. The military men who appear in *The Great Pacific War*, from generals to privates, are all described as people who follow certain rules of behavior.

The Japanese military men who appear in Bywater's novel are gentlemanly to a fault, engaging in conduct informed with the spirit of *bushidō* in the best sense of the word. Consider what happens when the Japanese army invades the Philippines and the American army capitulates. Praising the brave defense mounted by his enemy, General Kimura permits the American commander in chief and his staff to retain their personal swords. Prisoners of war are treated according to international law. Noncombatants, whether locals or foreigners, are treated the same in their daily lives. They are permitted to resume their prewar occupations.

The same is true (in Bywater's novel) on the high seas. The German U-boats attack shipping indiscriminately, regardless whether a given craft is a battleship or a commercial vessel. But Japanese submarines do not operate that way. In one incident, when a Japanese submarine spots an American supply ship traversing the South Pacific, instead of instantly attacking, it first issues an order to heave-to. However, the American supply ship tries desperately to flee, so the Japanese fire upon its engines to force it to a halt. This results in casualties: five dead and many wounded. Enemy casualties are carried aboard the submarine and their injuries medically treated. They and their surviving crew members are then turned over to a British commercial vessel that happens to be passing through that area. The supply ship is deemed unrecoverable, and it is sent to the bottom of the sea.

Let us look at some other examples. A passenger ship on its way from Honolulu to San Francisco unexpectedly encounters a Japanese submarine. Given America's local mastery of the sea, no armed escort is felt needed. Although it is a passenger ship, this voyage is also intended to train new naval recruits and to carry military personnel back to the mainland for rest and recreation. Yet there are also families with children aboard. The ship is immediately captured. A Japanese officer accompanied by four sailors board the passenger ship and deliver the following warning: "My captain may let the ship proceed if the men give their parole not to serve in the war."[3] Even at war, the Japanese military conduct themselves like gentlemen.

In another instance, a squadron comprised of four cruisers and ten destroyers spot an American cruiser that has run aground. After only a single fusillade from the Japanese ship, the cruiser begins to sink, upon which the Japanese admiral orders a cease-fire. A destroyer approaches the stricken American vessel, and thanks to its rendering of life-saving assistance, almost the entire American crew survives.

Of course, similarly laudable behavior occurs on the American side. I believe that Bywater considered scenes of naval battles as settings for the portrayal of the correct deportment of military men. When the First World War became a tale of immense carnage and destruction, even noncombatants, including women, were sacrificed. Then, such concepts as chivalry and *bushidō* seemed obsolete.

It is interesting at this juncture to refer to *The Grand Illusion*, the 1937 Jean Renoir film starring Jean Gabin. The setting is the First World War; the theme is the conflict between French officers who are prisoners of war and a German P.O.W. camp commandant. It is a work in which enmity is interwoven with a strange sort of amity. The aristocratic commandant and the equally wellborn French officers exchange words along the following general lines:

> "I know not which side will emerge victorious in this war, but whichever wins in the end, it will certainly be the end for you and for me."
> "I fear the world no longer needs our class."

The aristocracy is comprised of those whose full measure of wealth and honor is redeemed by leading the defense of a country that does not regret even the sacrifice of one's life in that cause. Living in a world defined by pledges of bravery and devotion, it is possible to develop a sort of aesthetic sense that transcends reality. Their era had, in fact, already passed. And while on the one hand, one could say that the logic formerly used by individuals in passing judgments was now universalized as norms of international law, one would also be hard put to deny that Bywater exhibited the same sort of nostalgia as that evidenced by the characters in *The Grand Illusion*.

The greatest event that took place during Hector C. Bywater's career as a journalist was the Russo-Japanese War. In that war, General Maresuke Nogi permitted his defeated counterpart, the Russian general Anatolii Mikhailovich Stessel to continue to wear his personal sword. Bywater must have remembered the interview that took place between the famous commanders. Or perhaps he had a lingering impression of the courteous deportment of Admiral Tōgō Heihachirō toward Rear Admiral Zinovy Rozhestvensky, commander of the captured Baltic Fleet. And he must have read Nitobe Inazō's *Bushido: The Soul of Japan*, published in English in 1899.

Since we, a generation or more removed from Bywater, know the outcome of World War II, we are apt to hear only the pathetic antithesis of these sorts of heroic tales and dispositions. Why should this be so? For Bywater, chivalry and *bushidō* were not different in substance. And he chose to focus on the commonalities rather than on cultural differences.

Thus, for Bywater, the Japanese navy was an object of admiration and respect, not some scary invading force. Hence his treatment of Japanese immigrants to Hawaii was different from the yellow journalism reflected in such works as *The Valor of Ignorance* and *BANZAI!* In previous Japan-U.S. future-war tales, an insurrection by Japanese immigrants in Hawaii had always occupied a prominent place. Infiltrating the local population of Japanese immigrants, Japan's soldiers found it easy to occupy the islands. But Bywater wrote of no such thing.

True, *The Great Pacific War* tells of an attack by several thousand Japanese immigrants on the barracks of the American garrison in Hawaii. But this disturbance is predicted before the war, since Japanese immigrants numbered 140,000 out of a total local population of 330,000. The ethnic Japanese who participate in the insurrection show behavior indicative of organization and direction. They destroy means of communication, such as telephone and telegraph, in downtown Honolulu; they take over the railroad station. The very next afternoon, however, the twelve warships anchored at Pearl Harbor shell the headquarters of the insurrection, succeeding in quashing it.

Even Bywater could not ignore the Japanese immigrants in Hawaii. But he did not make their action into anything more than a single episode in the war. And it has no effect whatsoever upon the progress of the war.

During this period, many future-war chronicles were published in Japan and the U.S., and both countries were buffeted by the sympathies such accounts elicited and the errors they perpetuated. But the Englishman Bywater had reason to be concerned about truly ominous storm clouds gathering on the horizon of the far Pacific.

He wrote of some more practical concerns to Ferris Greenslet, editor in chief of Houghton Mifflin, the American publisher of *Sea Power in the Pacific*:

Herewith please find the first chapters of the War Story I spoke to you about. They are subject to drastic revision, as they were written before the earthquake, and many changes will need to be made.[14]

The letter was dated June 12, 1924.

By "the earthquake," Hector Bywater no doubt meant the Great Kanto Earthquake of September 1923. But he might as well have meant the anti-Japanese, exclusionary National Origins Law (otherwise known as the Reed-Johnson Immigration Act) that had just been passed by Congress on April 16. When news of this legislation crossed the Pacific, the shock was substantial and did considerable damage to bilateral relations. The Japanese were stimulated to think along lines that led to a boom in Japan-U.S. future-war chronicles. We shall come back to this later.

Houghton Mifflin was a venerable old Boston publishing house. At Harvard University's Houghton Library, one can peruse the correspondence between editors and authors active in the early twentieth century. A careful examination of the dealings between Bywater and Greenslet sheds light on how this second "earthquake" affected the publication of *The Great Pacific War*.

As I have indicated above, Bywater took great pride in the accuracy of his data. In the same letter referred to above, he appealed to Greenslet as follows:

> The point about this narrative is that it will be written with a scrupulous regard for the technical points of naval warfare, and with a close knowledge of the geography and topography of the localities mentioned. In other words, "local color" will be super-added to dramatic interest, and no naval expert will be able to put his finger on any statement or incident and say, "That is wrong or technically impossible."

Why this emphasis on a carefully thought-out structure and accurate data? It was because Bywater expected his writing to have definite influence.

> With regard to the book on Pacific naval-political problems I mentioned to you, your remarks as to the reluctance of the reading public to repeat . . . sank into my mind, and I have come to the conclusion that perhaps the time is not quite ripe for another effort along the lines indicated. In view, however, of recent developments in the American-Japanese situation, it seems to me that a revised edition of my original book would be worthwhile preparing, since if the crisis between Washington and Tokyo became, or even threatened to become, at all acute, there would, I think, be a large demand for a volume that presented the current political and naval situation in clear and understandable terms.

At the root of the distrust Americans generally harbored toward Japan was the Japanese victory in the Russo-Japanese War. This had lain dormant during the First World War. Then, with the signing of the Washington Naval Limitation Treaty in 1922, the U.S., Great Britain, and Japan fixed the tonnage of their capital ships at a 5:5:3 ratio. Japan had been effectively put in its place.

The Japanese dissatisfaction with this treaty had no outlet. But at least a stable world order had been formed for the post–Great War period. So the Washington Treaty also provided a framework for Japan-U.S. amity. One flashpoint remained smoldering. The immigration problem.

In a sense, Homer Lea with *The Valor of Ignorance* and Parabellum with *BANZAI!* correctly reflected the sentiments of Americans who lived on the West Coast of the U.S. For them, Japan's military threat and the immigration issue could not be considered separately. Indeed, they were two sides of the same coin.

With California's anti-Japanese Alien Land Law of 1913, Japanese were prohibited from owning land. However, this legislation had little actual effect, so in 1924 federal anti-Japanese immigration legislation surfaced, with a provision prohibiting Japanese from entering the country. From early that year, the bill was hotly debated in both the Senate and the House, finally passing Congress. Academic and religious spokesmen objected to such discrimination, but on May 26 President Calvin Coolidge, despite his own reservations, finally signed it into law.

Japan-U.S. relations were rendered untenable for the Japanese, and understandably so. It is against this background that we must understand how boldly Hector Bywater moved forward with his plan to write a book addressing the theme of Japan-U.S. war. And also why Greenslet's reply of August 19 contains reservations.[15]

I think you have begun most brilliantly. After the first few pages, the thing laid hold of my imagination, and I read it with an almost breathless excitement. More than any other "future war" book that I have ever read, it has the authentic accent of past history.

The only doubt in my mind is whether it [is] sound public service to publish the thing here. From one point of view I am inclined to think that it might possibly foment trouble. Then again I see a different set of considerations leading me to believe that it would be more likely to forestall and prevent it. We wouldn't want to come to a definite decision without seeing the complete manuscript, and perhaps taking council with authority.

Greenslet then recommends, in a roundabout way, that Bywater publish it in England instead.

> It has occurred to us that possibly it would be more likely to operate as oil on the waters rather than as gasoline on the flame, if it were manufactured in England and then imported into this market as an article of strictly British—that is to say, neutral—manufacture.
>
> I think the chance of the book's being published and making a success are sufficiently bright to warrant you going ahead with its completion at your leisure. Is this sufficiently definite for you now?

In the ambivalence Greenslet demonstrated even as he praised Bywater's manuscript to the skies, we see reflected the caution of the American intellectuals of that era. The anti-Japanese immigration legislation was enacted in such an inflammatory atmosphere that even the president hesitated to affix his signature.

At a time when Japanese sentiment toward America was worsening precipitously, one would hesitate to publish a Japan-U.S. future-war chronicle in America of all places. In Japan, journalistic rhetoric was flaring up with the bright flames of simple anti-Americanism. Immediately after the anti-Japanese immigration legislation was passed by Congress, fifteen Tokyo newspapers issued a joint proclamation:

> The injustice and immorality of the Japanese exclusion bill that has just passed both chambers of the U.S. Congress are strikingly evident. We are hard put to believe that this represents the will of the majority of Americans, who have taken upon themselves the mantle of champions of peace and defenders of justice.

Summer was at its height when a Citizens' Council on Policy Toward the U.S. was held in Ueno, as advocated by the leader of the right-wing Black Dragon Society (*Kokuryū-kai*), Uchida Ryōhei. One celebrity after another ascended the dais to speak. Take, for example, Tokyo Imperial University professor and constitutional scholar Uesugi Shinkichi. It was he who attacked Dr. Minobe Tatsukichi for his "organ theory" of imperial authority (that the emperor was not absolute but an organ of the state), in a controversy that ended with Minobe's public disgrace a decade later. "I must confess to a sort of racial bias here. No matter what, I dislike Americans. Come what may, I dislike them." The meeting hall erupted in fierce applause.

Military affairs commentator Kawashima Seijirō followed. This was someone intimately acquainted with statist/nationalist figures such as Kita Ikki and Ōkawa Shūmei.

A person named Homer Lea has written a famous work called *The Valor of Ignorance*. He argues that Japan could swoop down on America, occupying her Pacific Coast, sending 200,000 troops in the first four weeks, 500,000 within four months, and over one million by the tenth month. If Japan's army is victorious, we may very well be able to fill this order.

Sustained applause.

When Uchida Ryōhei stepped up to the podium and began to talk, the strange mood in the hall deepened. "Japan and the U.S. will go to war in or around 1928," he said. "Since the founding of our nation, no country has prospered long that has fought Japan."

An elderly man named Matsumura Kaiseki, born in 1859, proceeded to deliver an impassioned speech. He had originally been a follower of Christianity, but was now concocting a blend of Confucianism and Christianity called the Church of Japan (*Nippon Kyōkai*).

It will not do to abase ourselves continually before the Americans. We must say at least one "NO." Else they will never understand Japan, and always mock us. I have long been concerned with this problem, and for the past thirty years I have been explaining it to the Ministry of Foreign Affairs. They do not understand. Whatever is said to them [by the Americans], their response is "YES, YES."

This sort of gathering was not confined to Tokyo, but also took place in provincial cities and country villages. More than one protester was upset to the point of suicide. One forty-something man committed *hara-kiri* in the estate gardens of Viscount Inoue Katsuzumi, next to the grounds of the American embassy. By the body was found a letter, a last will, titled "An Appeal to the American People." Reportedly, the man had intended to commit suicide at the American embassy and had entered the wrong garden.

One might also cite a report by the Ministry of Foreign Affairs concerning what happened at a meeting room at the Imperial Hotel, where about a hundred guests, including foreigners, had been invited to a ball. Upwards of a dozen young-bloods in crested kimono and formal *hakama* (culottes) forced their way in. Declaiming in an oratorical fashion, they demanded to know how, at a time when the fate of the nation hung in the balance, the guests could allow themselves to be distracted by such trivial amusements as social dancing. The group brandished Japanese swords and performed a sword dance, demonstrating the *i-ai* technique of swordsmanship: drawing, slicing, and sheathing, all in one swift motion. Hotel management were quick-witted enough to have the band strike up the "Kimi ga Yo" (the Japanese national anthem), which the appeased intruders took as their cue to leave.

It was in such a superheated atmosphere that Japan-U.S. future-war chronicles and other works related to that genre came out one after another. Let us examine the line-up.

The year 1924 saw the publication of Higuchi Reiyō's *Japan's Crisis: The American Calamity* (March 1924); Sakai Katsutoki's *Let Us Willingly Make Our Enemy* (May 1924); Fujiwara Tomo-o's *A Japan-U.S. War?* (July 1924); Sudō Shigeo's *A Present Danger, A New Defense* (August 1924); Ishii Tsunezō's *The Empire's Crisis and the People's Readiness* (September 1924); Kuki Moritaka's *The Unification of the Universe: A Divinely Inspired Novel* (December 1924); Citizens' Council on Policy Toward the U.S. (eds.), *Collected Essays on Policy toward the U.S.*; Ishimaru Tōda's *Victory at Sea* (December 1924; the translation of a work by W. S. Sims); and Ishimaru Tōda's own *Japan-U.S. War: Japan Won't Lose* (December 1924).

The next two years produced a long string of such publications. Among them were no less than three Japanese translation/adaptations of Hector C. Bywater's *The Great Pacific War*; Hori Toshikazu's *A Future Record of Japan-U.S. Relations—The Pacific War* (February 1925); Kitagami Ryōji's *Struggle for Supremacy in the Pacific* (November 1925); and Ishimaru Tōda's *The Pacific War, with Critique* (January 1926; commentary attached).

The others in the genre were Ishimaru Tōda's own *Can This Possibly Be World Peace?: Japan and the World after the Washington Conference* (February 1925); Kawashima Kiyojirō's *U.S.-Japan Showdown: The Fear That Dare Not Speak Its Name* (also February 1925); Tamura Shōichirō's *If Japan Fights the U.S.* (May 1926); Ono Torao's *The World Fifty Years Hence* (July 1926); Ishimaru Tōda's *Japan-U.S. War As the U.S. Sees It* (August 1926); Itō Masanori's *Our Hypothetical Enemy* (September 1926), and Uesugi Shingō's *The*

Inevitable Japan-U.S. Clash: Are the People Ready? (September 1926).

Simply by scanning the titles of the future-war chronicles that eventually flooded the Japanese market we can understand Greenslet's reservations about publishing Hector Bywater's novel. But Bywater was intent on publishing *The Great Pacific War* in the United States. On August 28, 1924 he replied to Greenslet as follows:

> My book on a future war in the Pacific ... represents the fruits of long years of study of naval elements—material and personal—and the strategical, geographical, and political conditions that would play a part in determining the course and outcome of a war such as that foreshadowed.
>
> As I wrote you before, my aim is to put down nothing that an expert could challenge on the score of inaccuracy or improbability. The succeeding chapters, so far as I have outlined them, should surpass in interest those which you have already seen. The average story of this type fails to carry conviction because the author almost invariably resorts to sensationalism to cover up his limited knowledge of technicalities.

Bywater was sensitive to the traps the hypothetical-war genre could easily fall into. He knew that it tended to be the most ephemeral sort of writing, and to be regarded as such. And that is why he sought verisimilitude. Instead of "bad money driving out the good" one could have the good money driving out the bad for a change.

> ... I do not think that any harm would be done by the publication of such a book in the United States. At least three books of a similar character have been published in Japan during recent years—one by a military officer of high rank—and American literature on the military aspect of the Pacific problems has already assumed imposing dimensions. There is no gainsaying the fact that possibilities of such a war are being freely canvassed in both countries.

When Bywater remarks that "at least three books of a similar character have been published in Japan during recent years," he must be referring to some among the group of titles cited above. Excerpts of Mizuno Hironori's *The Next Battle* had been published in English translation in a newspaper, and the "military officer of high rank" may well refer to the Lieutenant General Satō who wrote *If Japan Fights the U.S.*

In the same letter, Bywater makes clear his intentions and expectations for

The Great Pacific War: "I am sure that, so far as the will to war is concerned, the effect of the book would be deterrent rather than provocative."

On March 10, 1925 he wired his editor, Greenslet, that he had completed the manuscript. He followed that up with a letter dated March 13:

> The story throughout has been kept well within the bounds of possibility, and all technical details—whether relating to ships' naval organisation, topography, [or] strategy—will bear expert scrutiny. As you will see, I have been careful to avoid offending Japanese sensibilities, and neither the gruesome nor the more sensational aspects of warfare have been over-emphasized.

Bywater had rushed the writing. He was worried lest reality overtake fiction.

It was just at this time that a huge American fleet was beginning the largest naval exercise in history, starting in the Pacific. The hypothetical attack target, it was rumored, was Japan. The U.S. Atlantic Fleet had passed through the Panama Canal in February. In March it put in to the naval port of San Pedro, and in April it was scheduled to be united with the Pacific Fleet at San Francisco. The two fleets were combined under one unified command, making it the largest fleet in the world. Battleships, aircraft carriers, cruisers, destroyers, submarines: the grand fleet stood at 145 warships.

Recall that it was to prevent this very possibility that the Japanese in *The Great Pacific War* had scuttled the steamship in the Panama Canal and rendered it impassable. If the U.S. Atlantic and Pacific Fleets combined, Japan had no chance of winning a war with America. The strategy of the surprise attacks on the Philippines and Guam had already been adopted by Japan. Now, as Bywater heard reports of the exercise by the American navy, he added elements to his fictional story.

The real American ships were ostensibly heading for Australia and New Zealand. But when the fleets united at San Francisco, the combined fleet aimed for Hawaii. It was only after offensive and defensive maneuvers there that it headed for Australia.

At Hawaii, the attack team was comprised of ten battleships and two infantry divisions. They were met by a defensive force of 15,000 troops and nineteen submarines. This was war-gaming on a gigantic scale. So if an attack on U.S. interests were to come, what country was envisioned as being the attacker? What enemy was hypothesized, that it was felt so necessary to drill like this? No need for any doubts. Everyone at the time knew this presumed enemy's real identity.

From Hawaii to Australia is about five thousand miles—exactly the same distance as to the Philippines. When the Great White Fleet made a similar circuit, the government and people of Japan welcomed the Americans and rode out the crisis. But the goal of the grand exercise of 1925 was different. This time, intimidating Japan was merely a superficial purpose. The real goal of the exercise was practical: to prepare for a future Japan-U.S. war.

In addition to the combat force per se, there were thirteen oil tankers, four hospital ships, two provisions store ships, and other supply ships participating in the exercise. These ships were essential to the logistics of keeping a fleet at sea for extended maneuvers. In the event that America's military bases in the Philippines were attacked by Japan, such a fleet would have to cross the Pacific rapidly. If they were unable to make port calls at islands in the South Seas, they would exhaust their fuel. The only alternative was seaborne refueling, but that was still a new technology. During the exercise, training in seaborne refueling was attempted, but a number of the older tankers failed to keep pace with the latest-model battleships. That this would occur might seem obvious, but it took the attempt during the exercise to throw the problem into relief.

Hector Bywater solved this fuel resupply problem by employing the strategy of island-hopping.

* * *

AROUND THE SAME TIME, "not to provoke war, but to deter it," Mizuno Hironori published an article in the February 1925 issue of *Chūō Kōron* (The Central Review) titled, "A Warning to the People of Japan and of the United States, Concerning the Grand Exercise by the American Navy." Mizuno had retired from the Japanese navy in August 1921. He was forty-six years old. From that time on he devoted himself to his writing. His principal venue was *Chūō Kōron*.

Chūō Kōron was at that time publicizing the arms reduction arguments of Yoshino Sakuzō, Ishibashi Tanzan, and Abe Yoshishige. They were all members of the Lesser League for Arms Reduction promoted by Ozaki Yukio. And their membership rolls also carried the name of navy captain (ret.) Mizuno Hironori.

The phenomenon known as Taishō Democracy does characterize one trend of the times. Before the Russo-Japanese War, Japan was a weak nation that believed in victory in war as the way to guarantee national security. The Taishō era, however, was a time when this sort of nationalism seemed to drop out of the equation. It was an era of individualism, or it might be thought of as an era mad with money-making. And since everybody wanted lighter taxes, latent dissatisfaction toward Japan's excessive arms buildup had been intensifying. In the memoirs of military personnel, one repeatedly reads of their mortification when they rode the municipal streetcars in uniform, and other riders would deliberately let them hear epithets such as "Tax robbers!" Such was the era.

Mizuno could therefore write as he pleased. When the Washington Naval Limitation Treaty was signed, and the tonnage of Japan's capital ships was fixed at 60 percent that of the U.S. or Britain, one would expect a military man to vent some anger. But in *Chūō Kōron*, Mizuno wrote that "whatever their lapses and flaws," the Washington treaties were "more or less, both materially and spiritually, a success" for Japan. Since the Washington Treaty stood for naval arms limitation, that was close enough to the author's own position.

Early in the summer of 1922, Mizuno was on holiday, traveling by train to the Bōsō Peninsula, when he overheard a conversation. It took place among farming people on their way back from a Peace Memorial Exposition held in Tokyo as part of the celebration of the signing of the Washington Treaties.

"First time I ever saw one of those aero-planes or whatchamacallems. Sure is huge. That thing goes on a tear, the kites and crows won't be happy."

"Was that one of those ones that pisses burning oil all around, incinerates enemy towns?"

"Young feller back from the military, he said we take on the U.S., our village [Kujūkurihama] is the very first one gets hit. We better make a lot of them [planes]."

"Scary, world, huh. Stuff like this, even Nichiren had no idea."

At the mention of the Buddhist monk Nichiren (1222–82), founder of the sect that bears his name, they all burst out laughing. The train was headed for Katsuura, but they knew that before reaching Katsuura it would pass through Kominato, Nichiren's birthplace.

For *Chūō Kōron's* July 1922 issue, titled "The Sea," the editors solicited from Mizuno an essay-cum-travelogue. When he thought about it, he realized that he had been oriented toward the sea ever since he joined the navy. *The Crucial Battle* had described the Russo-Japanese War. He had also written *War Shadows* (*Kaneo Bun'endō*, 1914). But the theme had always been war and naval warfare. Indeed, for Mizuno the sea was never "pacific" but rather a world of bloody battles.

So to look at the sea afresh, he voyaged now to the seashore with his wife and son. Never before had they set off like this, *en famille*. They were looking forward to making their way toward a quiet ocean, with no rough waves or violent winds. However, a conversation like the one related above could not fail to catch his attention.

Mizuno had married his wife, Morie, when he was thirty-three years old and rising to the rank of lieutenant commander. His own family background was samurai, but extremely impoverished. That he could take to wife the daughter of a village headman was due to his being a military man. At the time of his marriage, he had just started to write *The Crucial Battle*. He had his daytime duties, then a second, separate work life at night. Midsummer nights were tough. In those days he had only an oil lamp to write by, and of course no electric fan. Morie would sit by his side, sending a cool breeze his way with a handheld fan and driving away the mosquitoes. It must be said, Mizuno was a stubborn character. While he was on active duty in the navy, he was forever clashing with superiors and fellow officers. He finally left and achieved his freedom.

So now he could consider what, after all, the sea meant to him. As he gazed out the train window at the peaceful, early-summer seaside landscape now passing before him, he thought long and hard.

The first time I was conscious of viewing the sea was when I was around eight, nine years old. It was during a school outing. Only a *ri* and a half [about six kilometers] separated where I lived from the sea, but there was no steam locomotive or electric railway nearby, and I didn't even know the word "sea-bathing." I thought, in my childish heart, what a faraway world the sea is![16]

He did not even imagine such at thing as the navy.

At the inn, as they were unpacking and changing, Morie was clearly in pain. Ever since their son, Mitsunori, had entered Musashi Middle School that spring, her health had been deteriorating, and she spent an increasing number of days bedridden. Mizuno had taken on this particular writing assignment partly to assist her convalescence. After the family had fallen asleep, he would go onto the verandah alone and gaze out at the deep, dark sea: "As I observe the ever-revolving flashing of the lighthouse, I can't help but be reminded of the blockade of Port Arthur."

Morie did not recover. She lay ill, bedridden until her death two years later. It was during the period when America was instituting its anti-Japanese immigration legislation. Mizuno found himself once more involved in public affairs. This period also saw the beginning of the boom in Japan-U.S. future-war chronicles.

It was Mizuno's *The Next Battle* that served as the original spark for the Japan-U.S. future-war chronicles. Now more than a decade had passed since its publication. The reader will recall that it ends with the annihilation of Japan's fleet in its battle with the two American fleets acting in concert off the Philippines.

The conclusion is the same as Bywater's *The Great Pacific War*, in the sense that they both end in Japan's defeat. However, Mizuno's motives at the time were different. His goal was to warn his readers that without expansion of armaments a catastrophic outcome awaited Japan. He had been an arms expansionist. Then, after witnessing the First World War, he became an arms reductionist.

The Japan-U.S. future-war chronicles that were written after Mizuno's second book took positions that resembled his former position. He commenced criticizing them. When he did so, the *Kokumin* newspaper published an article under the headline, NEXT BATTLE SCRIBE LIEUTENANT COMMANDER MIZUNO TO JOIN LEFTIST ORG.; SCORNS MILITARISM; NOW DEEMED THREAT BY GOV'T:

In any event, the aforesaid's speech of late has intensified antithetical feelings among those in the navy and in local military associations. Their attacks on him have been growing sharper. And within the Kempeitai [military police] and the Special Higher Police ["thought police"], he is being treated as an object of ideological suspicion.[17]

Mizuno had begun to be treated as a dangerous person.

And now, just at the time when anti-Japanese immigration legislation was being institutionalized in the United States, provoking anti-Americanism in

Japan, a great American naval exercise was about to unfold over the vast Pacific.

In "A Warning to the People of Japan and the United States," Mizuno attacked the warmongers for too lightly fomenting war. He asked what they thought they could do if things really came to war and pointed out to the Japanese that no amount of spiritual ideology could surmount military inferiority.

> An immoderate number of Japanese have irresponsibly been advocating a Japan-U.S. war. Do they really think that, armed with nothing but the Yamato spirit and rifles with fixed bayonets they can swim the Pacific and scale the Rockies? I believe that no one who is at all informed about Japan's situation can seriously consider a Japan-U.S. war or anything of the sort. If one is to wage war at all, one must be confident of victory. If one undertakes war on a speculative basis, people asked to serve essentially as targets for artillery practice will not put up with it. It is said (though I can't vouch for the truth of this) that during the Russo-Japanese War, the plan was that if by any chance Japan lost, it would cede Taiwan and maybe other territories to Russia. If we lost a war now, the entire country would be pushed into an abyss so deep we would never be able to crawl out.

Hector C. Bywater's *The Great Pacific War* was published four months after the manuscript was completed. It was not put out in Boston by Houghton Mifflin, but in London by Constable & Co. Greenslet, who had lauded Bywater's manuscript so highly, had ultimately concluded that it should not be published in America. The author agreed. Their thinking was that if a book like this were published in America, it might provoke the Japanese, inciting sensationalism, whereas an English publication would be accepted by Japanese readers with equanimity. It turned out that their caution was wasted.

No sooner had the book been published in England than the *Kokumin* newspaper began to serialize a translation on August 26, barely a month after the book had been released. On September 16, the translation was published in book form. The famous author Tokutomi Soho (1863–1957) went to the trouble of inserting a preface explicitly stating that "the total defeat of the Japanese navy depicted in the dénouement is off the mark." And the translation itself contradicted Bywater's intentions. For example,

252 | PART II

in the description of how the Philippines and Guam fell at the beginning of the war, the atmosphere is very different from the original. Consider one line from Bywater and its version as serialized in the *Kokumin* newspaper.

Bywater:

> It was clear that the military power of Japan was enormous. Her navy and army were obviously in a high state of efficiency, and her sailors and soldiers appeared to be fighting with all their traditional prowess.[18]

Kokumin newspaper translation of Bywater, translated back into English from the Japanese:

> Our mighty army and navy are brimming with combat prowess. The martial spirit that they have inherited from many generations back has reached the boiling point.

This spirited tone was received well in Japan, and after three weeks produced the following announcement in the same paper: "The blockbuster that continues to astonish the Japanese people—now in its eighth printing!"

Ishimaru Tōda's translation, *The Pacific War, with Critique* also appeared now (January 1926). As the title indicated, the translation incorporated the translator's opinions.

> Those who swallow Bywater's line so easily, and view our Empire's path ahead with pessimism, are showing contempt for our diligent officials at Kasumigaseki [Tokyo district where Japanese governmental offices are located] and for our courageous soldiers and sailors.

In the copy of this work at Japan's National Diet Library, an indignant reader wrote the following graffito at this very place in the text: "Nay, it were better to say they show contempt for the entire nation!"

It would seem that what Japanese found so objectionable about Bywater was not his views overall, but rather his book's ending with a defeat of Japan. Minuzo Hironori thought the same way as Bywater, and he was becoming isolated.

CHAPTER TEN

Seeking a Strong Japan

T HERE IS A TYPE of conversational pest who, when the cause is liquor,
the Japanese refer to as a "clinging drunk." Kept at a healthy distance,
such social predators pose no problem, but when they work for the same
company as you, take the same class, or belong to the same group, then
however much you may dislike them, you are nonetheless thrown together
with them.

Author Akutagawa Ryūnosuke (1892–1927) had just such a clinging friend
and was at a loss as to what to do about him. Ikezaki Tadayoshi (1891–1914)
initially wrote under the pen name Akagi Kōhei but later was adopted into
the Ikezaki family and wrote under that name. I shall refer to him as Ikezaki.
Like Akutagawa, he was a member of the Sōseki Sanbō (literally, "Sōseki
Mountain Range"), the group of literary disciples studying with Natsume
Sōseki. He considered himself Akutagawa's sworn rival.

Ikezaki (then still known as Akagi) makes an appearance in Akutagawa's
diary entry for August 29, 1914. Akutagawa relates that he himself was
casually perusing some classical text when Akagi "came by in his summer-
weight hemp kimono, with a striped crepe *haori* [traditional coat] over it,
and I was trapped."

Akagi had long been partial to the poetry of Li Bo, and was the kind of
fellow who would say, for example, that Li Bo's poem "Shō Shinshū" [C.
Jiang Jinjiu] exhibited "weltschmerz" [Akagi is using the German word for
a sentimental world-weary pessimism]. If the book I was reading had no
Li Bo in it, he was greatly contemptuous. But if I made no reply, I knew
he would consider that I had been defeated, so even though it was a hot
day, I argued the point with him a bit. This sort of argument is really just
for killing time, so it hardly mattered to me if I won or lost.[1]

In those days, Akutagawa was still a student in the Tokyo Imperial University English department. Ikezaki was at the same university, but in the German law department. They were both second-year students. Akagi was a year older.

A photograph in Akutagawa's *Collected Works* gives us a good look at his features. On a neck so scrawny it looks emaciated by illness sits a graceful, slender face with sharp eyes that stare straight out of the picture at us. The forehead is broad, and across it falls disheveled hair of the sort one expects of an artist.

Ikezaki, on the other hand, was round of face with arched eyebrows. Good-natured, amiable eyes squint out from behind his spectacles. But once he started speaking, those eyes would light up strangely. He had a grating, high-pitched voice that rang in one's ears and a confrontational attitude. He also had a winning smile and would take advantage of any indulgence to talk you to death.

With his grounding in classical Chinese, his quickness of mind, and his fondness for composing *haiku*, Ikezaki was not completely incompatible with Akutagawa. But the words that gushed from his lips were never directed inward, contemplatively. They were all externally oriented, aggressively forward-marching.

Ikezaki (still known as Akagi) makes another appearance in Akutagawa's diary some five years later, on June 8, 1919.

Afternoon. Akagi Kōhei, Kojima Masajirō, Tomita Saika, and Muroga Fumitake came by. Professor Kōhei was as grandiloquent as usual. He always uses me as the sounding board for his rants. Why do I lay myself open to this?

It was around this time, 1916 to 1918, that Akutagawa was publishing such stories as "Rashōmon"; "Hana" (tr. "The Nose," 1961); "Imogayu" (tr. "Yam Gruel,"1952); "Kumo no ito" (tr. "The Spider's Thread," 1930); and "Jigokuhen" (tr. "Hell Screen," 1948). His reputation was growing. Here, the gently mocking tone with which he treats his erstwhile rival, "Professor Kōhei," suggests that he could now afford psychologically to be a little indulgent. He was trying to let Ikezaki talk without actually becoming a conversational partner.

My object here, however, is not to write about Akutagawa Ryūnosuke. Rather, it is to write about Ikezaki. Later, he became a popular author in the genre of Japan-U.S. future-war chronicles. Literary histories slight this sort of popular literature; at best they merely number Akagi among the many who studied with the Sōseki Sanbō and ignore his later activities. Or rather, it would be more accurate to say that they know little about them.

Ikezaki's *Japan Need Not Fear the U.S.* was published in August of 1929. Two years had passed since the suicide, on July 24, 1927, of his rival, Akutagawa, at the age of thirty-five. Authorship of this new book was attributed to Ikezaki Tadayoshi. Ikezaki's pen name as a young literatus had been Akagi Kōhei. Now, at thirty-eight, he was in the prime of life, and this new name was his way of making a clean break with—as he would have put it—the "soft" literature of his youth.

This new work instantly won Ikezaki new renown. The sculptor Asakura Fumio, who was awarded the Order of Cultural Merit in 1948, had dealings with Ikezaki at this time and recounted after the war that "he must have sold out a printing of over a hundred thousand copies," and that "it was translated in America in the Hearst syndicate's *New York American*."[2]

This was a time when the mainstream *Asahi* newspaper ran an advertisement in which the message, splashed across the page in huge characters, read NO MORE U.S.-PHOBIA! JAPAN WILL NEVER BOW! (*Asahi shimbun*, September 6, 1929). To the side were carried the comments of a number of celebrities.

Nakazato Kaizan, for example, well known for his book *Great Bodhisattva Pass*, praised Ikezaki's work: "His lucid and sharp opinions are often more valuable than an expert's." On the other hand, Rear Admiral Nakajima Gonkichi's blurb accorded him something of the status of an expert as well: "Knowing that someone such as yourself, who is not a military man, has conducted so much research on this subject, I find not only worthy of the most sincere respect, but also enormously encouraging."

Sales did not drop off, even into the autumn. By November 9, the cheerfully bombastic advertisement in the *Asahi* was headlined IKEZAKI TADAYOSHI'S *JAPAN NEED NOT FEAR THE U.S.*—70TH PRINTING, and went on to emphasize the international nature of the book's reception in the following terms: "Look at the worldwide reaction! Why did the *Japan Times* carry this article? Ah, Nippon, never will you bow and scrape!"

They even put the title into English: *Japan Need Not Fear U.S.* (sic), and described it using the English loan words "sensational" and "best seller." It was indeed a bombshell.

What was Ikezaki's motivation in writing *Japan Need Not Fear the U.S.?* I should like to unravel this riddle gradually. This is necessary because in the process, we must determine why Hector C. Bywater and Mizuno Hironori disappeared so completely from the new landscape created by Ikezaki.

Japan Need Not Fear the U.S. made the Japanese feel courageous. Or rather, it gave them that illusion. We all want to be courageous, to take a clear stand. The fear of big bad America, the insecurity that had been ingrained in the Japanese psyche ever since Perry's Black Ships, was hereby decisively, absolutely negated. The advertising copy put on the book's cover by its publisher, Senshin Sha, was, if nothing else, full of verve. "Entertaining beyond compare! Myriad points of interest! Ah, Japan will not lose; absolutely Japan will not lose! Even if the Anglo-Saxon race attacks en masse, there is, in the end, no need for fear!"

The "Japan will not lose; absolutely Japan will not lose!" part is gratifying. However dubious the claim of greater strength, the feeling this claim generates is not a bad one. The reason Bywater's *The Great Pacific War* had incurred the displeasure of the Japanese public was that its conclusion was that Japan would lose. To become a best seller, there has to be a broad base of interest. If readers judge too superficially, then not much can be done about it. Ikezaki was well aware of how this worked. There had to be some concrete expression of proof that America was not to be feared.

> We must rid ourselves decisively of this illogical, unnecessary Americanophobia. If we do not, then the future that awaits Japan and the Japanese will be a gloomy one indeed.

Ikezaki went on to say that in the event of war between Japan and the United States, Japan would win easily. The war would begin with surprise attacks on the Philippines and Guam. Here, at the outset, Ikezaki was not following in the footsteps of Homer Lea and Bywater so much as patterning his predictions after the genre of U.S.-Japan future-war chronicles.

> The issue for Japan is just how easily the Philippines and Guam can come into Japan's possession. We feel so sorry for America: Japan will take possession with no trouble at all.

Japan Need Not Fear the U.S. was not a novel. It was a tract based on the stenographic record of a lecture by Ikezaki, so from cover to cover it has the flow of spoken language. The book's argument was extremely accessible, even the military analyses that tend to be abstruse to the layman. In this, *Japan Need Not Fear the U.S.* was diametrically opposed to the oppressive mood that characterized Mizuno Hironori's *The Next Battle*.

Ikezaki had the chutzpah to borrow the rationale for Japan's early victories directly from Bywater.

> Anglo-American military experts familiar with the ins and outs of this issue agree, to a man, that the Japanese Army will accomplish the occupation of Manila in just a few days. . . . The author of *The Great Pacific War* states that "if the Japanese fleet reaches Guam by daybreak, then that very day the sun will set on a Rising Sun waving over the island." This is by no means an exaggeration.

However, in Bywater's *The Great Pacific War*, as in his *Sea Power in the Pacific*, Japanese victories occur only in the first half of the hypothetical war. How does Ikezaki overcome the gradual worsening of the Japanese position?

> As I envision it, a bilateral Japan-U.S. war would be concluded in an extremely short time period. But even if it took an extremely long time period, it is virtually certain that the victory would be Japan's. . . . Any suffering Japan would incur as a result of prolonging the war would be trivial. Japan should confidently follow the natural course of a war with the U.S.

Such an assertion is all very well, but if the author does not describe the grounds for it, the reader is in trouble. The argument will seem like, "Japan is strong because it is strong."

> No matter how powerful the American fleet is, it must include some specially tasked ships with weaker fighting power, or transport ships with no combat capability at all. Like a parent and a child walking down the street, to the extent the parent protects the child, it is constrained in its ability to protect itself. It too will be as prey, merely stimulating the appetite of our falcon-swift surprise attack fleet.

Squadrons of special task ships and transports cannot move in an uncoordinated fashion. The assertion is stated up-front, and the conclusion then brought in smartly. Such decisiveness sounds good. At first glance it looks logical, and that adds rhetorical appeal.

Even if Japan and America are joined in battle, the Japanese fleet will employ its superior speed and range so as to strike from beyond the reach of the enemy fleet, and for the Americans the result will be the most miserable catastrophe.

Ikezaki's next metaphor is a simple and common one, but that only lends it more appeal and power.

No matter how grand the American armada may appear, in reality it must, undeniably, have certain shortcomings. It may have an absurdly large number of destroyers, but then it may have an absurdly small number of cruisers. If it emphasizes battleships, it may have not a single battle cruiser. To compare the fleets to individual persons, the Japanese fleet is like someone whose limbs and organs in all respects exceed the average, rendering him a man of massive and powerful physique, whereas the American fleet is the man of conspicuous height and weight, whose limbs and organs in all respects far exceed the average, but who is also, merely, obese. He may seem strong enough, but it's a dangerous state for a body to be in: one never knows when he may be struck by cardiac arrest or cerebral hemorrhage.

The Japanese had seen a great American fleet up close during the commotion over the White Ships. Their newspapers had apprised them of the more recent world cruise and exercise. But this was all negated by an appeal to the cliché that a large man can't be wise all over.

So the Great American Fleet was nothing but a big oaf. However, readers' doubts now shifted to whether the difference in the two countries' economies did not entail a difference in national strength.

In the April 1923 issue of *Chūō Kōron*, Mizuno Hironori had already addressed this issue of U.S.-Japan comparative economic strength in an essay titled "Anatomy of a New National Defense Policy," concluding that Japan could not compete.

The idea that war does not require money is limited to countries whose financial strength is greatly trusted by other nations, or which are self-sufficient both in war strategy and in the resources needed for daily life. That a country like Japan, which must import all the resources its citizens need for daily life (iron and oil and so on), requires sufficient financial

power is so obvious as to go without saying. . . . A Japan-U.S. war will
not be a military contest but a financial one.

Ikezaki's refutation took the following form:

> For all its wealth, [America] cannot compel Japan's submission. An
> abundance of gold merely poisons the body politic from within its very
> marrow. Even without the application of a powerful external force,
> America will nevertheless, and soon enough, begin to collapse internally.
> Wealth may be one way to obtain strength, but in and of itself does not
> confer strength.

So the almighty dollar is merely a matter of show: economic strength
and military strength are different.

Ikezaki closes by ingratiating himself further with the Japanese reader,
while shifting responsibility for the upcoming war onto America.

> Doubtless there are those who would point the finger at Japan; they are
> merely hastening their own demise. America, which has been assuming
> the unacknowledged role of a twentieth-century Roman Empire, must
> abandon its absurd fantasies regarding the Far East, leave Asia to the
> Asians, and allow Japan the freedom to pursue its own path. If it does
> not, then it will fall into the ridiculous plight of sacrificing its own na-
> tional prosperity in the pursuit of excess benefits not needed for its own
> survival. . . . Whether the waves of the Pacific Ocean remain eternally
> peaceful or not depends in large part on the degree to which America
> and the Americans repent and relent.

In any event, *Japan Need Not Fear the U.S.* sold well. Nowadays Ikezaki
is completely forgotten, but in his time his reputation surpassed even
Akutagawa's—perhaps not in the literary world, but among the general
public. Once he was invited to be the guest of Ogura Masatsune, managing
director of the Sumitomo Corporation's head office, who offered encouragement. Saying, "This is for your research expenses," Ogura handed him
a thick envelope containing fifty thousand yen, equal to about five times
the yearly salary of the prime minister.

Ikezaki had beaten Akutagawa, he thought. After years of rivalry, he had
finally won. Or so he tried to believe.

Japan Need Not Fear the U.S. became a best seller two years after the death of Ikezaki's perceived rival, Akutagawa Ryūnosuke. Ordinarily one tries to refrain from flogging a dead opponent who cannot respond, but Ikezaki's tenacity was extraordinary. Normally it is difficult to say things such as, "The skepticism that tormented you in this world: I now say, 'Feed it to the dogs!'" But Ikezaki spelled it out even further: "In my eyes you have always been a fanatic believer in knowledge." This string of invective appeared in "A Farewell to My Departed Friend, Akutagawa Ryūnosuke," which was published the year following the favorable reception of *Japan Need Not Fear the U.S.*

With this one book, *Japan Need Not Fear the U.S.*, Ikezaki vaulted into the ranks of celebrity. Overnight his name recognition was on a par with Akutagawa's. The many years of accumulated, pent-up bitterness were now blown clean away. But I think there is more to it than that.

Namely, the fact that Akutagawa committed suicide, attributing it to merely "a vague uneasiness." I am certain it was Ikezaki's view that this phrase had been internalized by the Japanese as a sort of loss of confidence. For Ikezaki to bury Akutagawa with his own hands, as it were, meant to bury at the same time the defeatism that held that if Japan and America fought, Japan would lose. It is a performance that could be given only by someone like Ikezaki, who knew Akutagawa personally.

Many commentators have offered interpretations of Akutagawa's suicide. His companions in the Sōseki Sanbō, other contemporary writers, those close to him, everyone pondered the reason for the suicide. Ikezaki seemed to base his strange confidence in his own interpretation on secrets that passed between only himself and Akutagawa.

I should like to give a concrete example showing what sort of relationship Akutagawa's death had to the zeitgeist of Japan in the late 1920s.[3] The day he died, July 24, 1927, it had been raining since dawn. A soothing balm sprinkled down as if expressly to relieve several consecutive days of fierce heat. On the second floor of the Akutagawas' house in Tabata, across the hallway from the Akutagawas' own bedrooms, was a six-tatami-mat room occupied by a nephew, Kuzumaki Yoshitoshi. He knew that for the past two years Akutagawa had been writing and rewriting his will.

Two days prior to his suicide, Akutagawa was visited by a friend, the artist Oana Ryūichi, who designed the covers for his books. Afterwards, Akutagawa called out to Kuzumaki, "Chat with me a bit?" He showed him the unfinished draft manuscript of *Western Man, Continued* and told him that since it was still unfinished he (Akutagawa) would not die that night.

The next day, Akutagawa worked on the manuscript all day. He had a pleasant lunch with his wife, Fumi, and his three children, Hiroshi, Takashi, and Yasushi, everyone chatting cheerfully together. Takashi kicked the dining table, and Akutagawa reprimanded him. Akutagawa had dinner on the first floor, with a guest. At sunset, he said to Kuzumaki, "Please give me a soft pencil." He had finished the draft of *Western Man, Continued* and now apparently wanted to paginate it. Then a square envelope concealed in his kimono dropped out. He picked it up. At that point Kuzumaki did not realize that this was Akutagawa's suicide note, addressed, "Memorandum to an Old Friend."

Akutagawa's seventy-one-year-old Aunt Fuki now came upstairs. Akutagawa's mother, Fuku, had died when he was ten years old. Fuki was her elder sister. Blinking away the tears, Fuki said to him, "You have been the only person I could depend on, but these days you keep saying you're having a nervous breakdown...." Aunt Fuki disappeared back down to the first floor, and Kuzumaki also returned to his room. At about 1:00 AM, Akutagawa handed his aunt a large, fancy card on which he had sketched a self-portrait and written a haiku titled "Self-Mockery":

> Dripping from the tip
> of the nose, glistening
> in the setting sun.

Then Akutagawa swallowed a lethal dose of sleeping pills. At about six in the morning, Fumi, who had been sleeping beside him, spoke to him but received no response. Kuzumaki and Aunt Fuki were alerted, and they rushed in. There was no pulse. The body was still warm.

Akutagawa's suicide note, "Memorandum to an Old Friend," ran to eighteen pages. The very next day, July 25, it was carried in its entirety in the *Tōkyō Nichinichi* (Tokyo Daily) newspaper.

No one has yet written an unvarnished account of suicide from the psychological standpoint of the suicide himself. This is due perhaps to the suicide's personal pride, or alternatively to his lack of interest in his own psychology. In this, my final letter to you, I would like to communicate clearly to you what that psychology is.... Doubtless you've come across many of the motives for suicide given in the newspapers in "Page Three" stories and so on: problems in one's living situation, the torments of illness, psychological suffering. But to judge from my experience, none of these is *the entire motive*. . . . At least, in my case, there is simply a vague uneasiness. Somehow, regarding my future, simply a vague uneasiness.

I should like the reader to bear in mind that repeated phrase, "simply a vague uneasiness."

All the newspapers competed to explain Akutagawa's unexpected suicide by soliciting the opinions of assorted writers, poets, university professors, lawyers, and others. The first thing that was apparent was what a shock this event was. Novelist Izumi Kyōka (1873–1939) was dejected: "Search as we may, we will not find another writer with so supple a style as Mr. Akutagawa. I wish it were a dream, or at least not true. We have no others like him" (*Ōsaka Yomiuri* newspaper, July 25, 1927). But Mushanokōji Saneatsu wrote, "To confront death directly and yet maintain such equanimity—this is marvelous" (*Yomiuri* newspaper, July 26, 1927). Mushanokōji applauded the prose of the suicide note, calling it "splendid."

Kume Masao, a member of the Sōseki Sanbō, was stumped by what he saw as the riddle of Akutagawa's death: "This suicide note speaks of some obscure uneasiness, but does that refer to the sort of struggles through which one must persevere in one's life, or to some more philosophically obscure uneasiness? This is so surpassingly difficult an issue that one cannot help referring to it with the phrase, 'obscure uneasiness.'" Kume seems to be sympathizing, but what he means by this comment I haven't the slightest idea.

Clearly the phrase, "simply a vague uneasiness," in the suicide note exacerbated the confusion. Suicide is, essentially, an extremely personal event. But it is tempting to think of the suicide of a writer as different from the death of an ordinary person and as something that serves to mirror his or her era. If the writer is taken to be a particularly sensitive indicator, and if this needle swings so wildly it breaks, that must be evidence of some particularly dangerous condition in the outside world. Many were the articles that tried to find some sort of explanation from that standpoint. The following appeared in the *Ōsaka Mainichi* newspaper for July 26:

If one takes the broad view, any event reflects its era. Just as the mountain peaks are the first to receive the dawn's rays, so too the attenuated nerves of our writers are the first to sense the sufferings of the age. The deaths of Kitamura [Kitamura Tōkoku] and Arishima [Arishima Takeo]; Akutagawa's death: we do see, greatly figured forth in the shadows cast by their deaths, the eras in which they lived.

The "shadows" of their eras: now that's a handy phrase. Anybody's mind is overshadowed by his or her era. Or consider the following, from the July 28 issue of the *Tōkyō Nichinichi* (Tokyo Daily) newspaper:

Arishima Takeo's death may be summed up as that of a spoiled young purist. The sensation caused by [Akutagawa's] death follows from the premise that his thought and art strike the keynotes of social anguish.

The phrase "the keynotes of social anguish" also seems understandable but resists easy explanation. This was not merely a suicide. Here is reflected the idea propagated by the phrase "simply a vague uneasiness": that this suicide is related to our own selves; that one cannot really ignore that. Later, the writer Matsumoto Seichō would suggest a new factor: "Essentially, the hellish predicament he faced in his liaison with Ms. 'H' was something about which he could unbosom himself to no one. He had to deal with it till the very end."

And then there is the matter of his concern over the possibility he had inherited his birth-mother's insanity. According to this explanation, the uneasiness that so tortured him was the fear that mental illness could emerge at any time.

What I should like to turn to now, however, is the question of the larger impact of this phrase "simply a vague uneasiness." And I want to show it as demonstrated in social phenomena. One cause of uneasiness is economic recession. This is true in any era.

The Taishō Emperor died on December 25, 1926. The first "year" of the Shōwa era thus lasted only one week, to the end of the year. On New Year's Day it was already Shōwa 2. Just two and a half months into the new era there was a financial crisis. In an unguarded moment during his March 14 appearance before the Budget Committee of the Lower House, Kataoka Naoharu, the minister of finance, misspoke himself: "Today," he let slip, "around noon today, the Watanabe Bank finally entered into bankruptcy." Watanabe Bank was not a first-tier bank. After the Great War it had made numerous bad loans, adversely impacting bank operations, but somehow it had muddled through.

Immediately a line of depositors wanting to withdraw their money began to form outside Watanabe Bank branches. This crisis of confidence spread to other banks. Eventually, thirty-seven banks were caught up in the panic and suspended their operations. At the time there were 3.5 million unemployed in Japan. In his autobiography, *My Shōwa: A History*, the novelist Yasuoka Shōtarō recounts an episode illustrative of the situation:

> This Kataoka who misspoke himself was my mother's grandfather's cousin. Seeing my mother and father spreading out the newspaper and discussing it, even I understood enough somehow to realize that this was a huge blunder and had made a mess of things. Akutagawa Ryūnosuke committed suicide that same year, in the summer. Around the same time, my uncle, the husband of my mother's elder sister, killed himself with a pistol over his stock-market losses. I had often been taken to his house to play and had stayed over a number of times, and I felt something terrible had happened there.

This is all highly reminiscent of Japan's current post-bubble economy. One heard stories everywhere of instant millionaires instantly going bankrupt and fleeing in the night. But recessions are sometimes long tunnels, with no end in sight. Soon, even hirings of graduates of Tokyo Imperial University dipped below the 30 percent level, and in 1929 Ozu Yasujirō's film *I Graduated, But...* came out.

Ever since Japan became a member of the winning side in the Great War, it had been spoken of as a first-world country. But as the economies of the war-torn European countries rebounded during the postwar era, Japan found its export markets being snatched back. Even domestically, Japanese products faced fierce competition from imported goods. And then there was the follow-up blow of the Great Kanto Earthquake. On the Ginza, "moga" and "mobo" (short for the English phrases "modern girl(s)" and "modern boy(s)") walked the walk and talked the talk of the new era, but in the background, Japan's economy was running out of steam.

In America, on the other hand, the postwar recovery was real, and its effects were felt all over the world. Movies, jazz, fashion, sports, automobiles—American culture and affluence flooded into Japan. At the same time, there was still no end to news of discrimination against Japanese immigrants. In the Japanese mind, these two distinct trends flowed together and began to merge.

Half a year before Ikezaki's *Japan Need Not Fear the U.S.* appeared, the same publisher put out Murobuse Kōshin's *America—Its Economy, Its Civilization*. His opening salvo was, "Know America!" Then he delivered a payload of heavy statistics. America had 22,137,324 automobiles. By comparison, Japan had only 42,727. Next was the diffusion of telephones. America had 16,935,918 telephones in service; Japan had 636,736. America's national wealth (equivalent to GNP) was $320,803,862,000. Japan's was $22,500,000,000 or about one-fifteenth that of America's. The theme penetrating the entire discussion: America is great.

But having sufficiently established the greatness of America, the canny publishers now had Ikezaki write *Japan Need Not Fear the U.S.*

Ikezaki could not stand the bandying about of such phrases as "simply a vague uneasiness"; he detested Akutagawa for it. In "A Farewell to My Departed Friend, Akutagawa Ryūnosuke," he ridiculed the popular mood that so accommodated the notion of uneasiness. It was as if to say, "Come on, everyone, don't be taken in!" Rhetorically addressing Akutagawa himself he wrote, "Your cunning strategy turned the criticism your death deserved into melancholy, and turned scorn into sympathy." In other words, the "simply a vague uneasiness" was merely an outlandish pose typical of Akutagawa. This was obvious to anyone who had known Akutagawa since they were both schoolboys. Why did others not see through it? The intensity of Ikezaki's disapproval knew no bounds: "You stirred up the world with your own death, eliciting its astonishment, its misgivings, its sorrow, in some cases even its admiration. Yet I must confess that I, for one, who once enjoyed your favor, received the news of your death coolly."

There was another critic of Akutagawa's suicide: Miyamoto Kenji, formerly the honorary chairman of the Central Committee of the Japanese Communist Party. While Miyamoto was still a student at Tokyo Imperial University, he submitted an essay to a competition held by the journal *Kaizō* (Reform) and won first prize, out of a submission pool of three hundred-plus essays. The title of his essay was "The Literature of 'Defeat.'" In it, he labeled Akutagawa a "petit bourgeois writer" whose suicide was due to his awakening to his own defeatism in the face of the rise of proletarian literature. He was of course propagating a Marxist-Leninist theme. Second prize went to Kobayashi Hideo for "Variety of Design." If we read them now, Kobayashi's essay is still interesting, but Miyamoto's is tedious. The background to awarding first prize to "The Literature of 'Defeat'" is not only the fashionable status of Marxism among the intelligentsia of the day, but also the exasperation of ordinary folk with "simply a vague uneasiness," which was hardly enough to help them cope with the unbearable insecurity of employment during the recession.

Though they stood at opposite ends of the ideological spectrum, both Ikezaki and Miyamoto picked Akutagawa as the handiest target. Pent-up feelings have to be released somehow.

The territory I am covering here is still the Japan-U.S. future-war chronicles of the early Shōwa period. But to do that I must first go a little deeper into Ikezaki's character. If he had not had Akutagawa as a rival, for example, would he ever have written such a novel? I can't get that nagging question out of my head. One frequently sees cases in which someone who purports to elucidate national affairs and to advocate justice is in fact transposing some personal complex onto august matters of duty and loyalty. Such people can be annoying in the extreme, but sometimes they can dominate the world.

Ikezaki was a disciple of Natsume Sōseki; he associated with the Sōseki Sanbō. How he managed to confuse public and private is the matter I should like to turn to next.

As I mentioned above, Ikezaki's real surname name was Akagi; his given name was Tadayoshi. He was born on February 9, 1891 in a remote village in the western part of Okayama Prefecture. Nearby was the Yoshioka Copper Mine, operated by Mitsubishi Mining. His father, Akagi Tatsusaburō, worked at the mine as an assistant engineer. As a boy, Tadayoshi was psychologically wounded as a result of his father's falling out with a superior at Mitsubishi Mining. Tatsusaburō's position in the company was rendered tenuous and he quit, buying a small mining lot and starting up his own small-scale copper mine. The community was a small one, and setting up in opposition to Mitsubishi Mining was a fatal move. He and his family were ostracized. Young Tadayoshi was rather openly ganged up on and ill-treated by bullies among the other children. It was one against many. There was no way for him to fight back successfully. It was the precocious discovery that his tongue provided the best defense that gave him a way out of his isolation.

Akagi Tatsusaburō's family owned a mountain, so everything went well for a while. Ultimately, however, a boundary dispute with Mitsubishi Mining led to a court case which Tatsusaburō lost. Tadayoshi's parents moved to Shikoku to seek employment at Sumitomo Metals' Besshi copper mine.

For his schooling, Tadayoshi commuted from his remote mountain village down to a middle school near to the plains, in a former castle town called Bitchū Matsuyama. His grades were good, and he proceeded to the No. 6 High School (the region's sixth-tier high school under the old system) in Okayama by recommendation, without having to take the exam. Though he now lived in a dormitory, he still had to face up to his father's defeat.

Tadayoshi participated in the debating club and the literature club; he even helped edit the alumni magazine. He was a passionate writer of haiku and other verse, and was partial to the work of Suzuki Miekichi, who was later to gain renown with his song "Red Bird." Miekichi had contributed material to Takahama Kiyoshi's journal *Hototogisu* (The Cuckoo) since he was a student of the English department at Tokyo Imperial University. He had graduated about three years previously, and was now selling well as a promising new author.

When Tadayoshi contributed an article titled "On Suzuki Miekichi" to the alumni magazine, he sent Miekichi a copy and a correspondence ensued. The article was then reproduced in the August 1912 issue of the journal *Shinchō* (New Tide). Ecstatic, this third-year student at a sixth-tier provincial high school made up his mind to move to Tokyo. But his father's business plans were not panning out. So it was decided that, through the good offices of a local notable, he would become the foster son and heir of one Ikezaki Kosaburō, who dealt in knitted goods in Osaka, and who would finance his education in Tokyo. In the spring of 1913, he graduated from No. 6 High School and matriculated at the German law department of Tokyo Imperial University. His dream of living in Tokyo was now becoming a reality.

For a Miekichi admirer, it might have made more sense to have entered a literature department than a law department, but Ikezaki was constrained by his arranged destiny as successor to a knitted goods business. Still, the law department left Ikezaki unsatisfied, and he began to associate with Miekichi. Thus it was that he came to know Sōseki Sanbō.

Sōseki's residence was in Minami-machi, Waseda. In addition to Miekichi, his disciples included Terada Torahiko, Morita Sōhei, Nogami Toyoichirō, Abe Yoshishige, Abe Jirō, and Komiya Toyotaka. Ikezaki visited there during the middle of October 1913, barely a month after entering university. This sort of alacrity is also one kind of talent.

Natsume Sōseki is so well known as to require only the briefest of introductions here. As a novelist, he left us a succession of masterpieces from 1905 to 1910: *Wagahai wa neko de aru* (tr. *I Am a Cat*, 1916), *Botchan* (tr. *Botchan*, 1972), *Kusamakura* (tr. *Three-Cornered World*, 1965), *Gubijinsō* (tr. *Red Poppy*, 1918), Sanshirō (tr. *Sanshirō*, 1977), *Sorekara* (tr. *And Then*, 1978), *Mon* (tr. *Mon*, 1972). But Sōseki came to suffer terribly from gastric ulcers. He went to Shūzenji for treatment, where he vomited blood. This was in 1913, when he was forty-six years old.

Ikezaki relates his first impression of the great writer in the following reminiscence:

> When I first saw Sensei himself with my own eyes, he did not conform to the ideal image I had constructed from the available materials (photographs, etc.). To my eyes, at least, he looked old before his time.[4]

When Ikezaki was visiting him, Sōseki was resuming work on *Kōjin* (tr. *The Wayfarer*, 1967), which he had suspended for half a year for treatments; in November he completed it. Then he continued to write: *Kokoro* (tr. *Kokoro*, 1957), *Garasudo no naka* (Inside the Glass Window), *Michikusa* (tr. *Grass on the Wayside*, 1969), and the unfinished *Meian* (tr. *Light and Darkness*, 1971). He died on December 9, 1916.

Ikezaki loved to debate; his classmates felt overwhelmed by his polemical skills. He seemed so self-assured. But during his first interview with Sōseki, he was tongue-tied.[5]

> I sat next to Mr. Suzuki [Miekichi], listening raptly to his conversation with Sensei. Sensei's attitude was extremely "easy"; from time to time he smiled as if there was nothing he was ever fussy about. And his speech was indeed as free as the breeze. He even addressed me, but although I was accustomed to speaking without reserve, my tongue did not smoothly voice my thoughts.

> This was not simply nervousness. The atmosphere in the room was like that of an audience with a religious leader.

> To somebody like this, one could reveal all, and all would be forgiven. It seemed as if he would understand everything.

This worshipful intensity lasted. Through Miekichi's introduction, Ikezaki was able to publish a sixty-page essay "On Natsume Sōseki" in the haiku journal *Hototogisu* (The Cuckoo) under the pen name "Akagi Kōhei," created for him by Miekichi. Forthwith, Ikezaki sent a copy of his article to the author he esteemed so highly. On January 5, 1914, even before the New Year's pine decorations had been taken down, Ikezaki received a reply from the great master.[6]

> Greetings.
> On New Year's Eve, after receiving your letter, I read the essay you were so kind as to write about me. Until then, I was so busy I had no time to read it. Your essay is a long one. And you have taken great pains over it. In addition to your wishing me (even more than others) to read it, I note that the essay is informed by goodwill: the motive was to write something for my sake. I am moved and grateful that for my sake you went to the expense of so much effort and time.

So far, so good. But then things turn circumlocutory. The gist of it is that there is nothing so bothersome as misplaced adulation. Being lauded to the skies as a man of character, a critic of civilization, or "an imperishable light" is, on the contrary, distinctly annoying.

> You have praised me highly. No doubt flattery was not your intention. I do not think that I am so exceptional a person as you say, but if I appear so in your eyes, so be it. To evaluate only your argumentation (looking at it separately from any praise or blame of me), I must say it is regrettably deficient. In a nutshell, I feel that the substance of what you write is comparatively weaker than the way you write about it. . . . Sometimes what you say so grandly is simply not sound.

He is clearly calling this exaggerated praise devoid of substance. And his final cut is, "You write so earnestly, however, that whatever I say here may not register."

The difficulty in understanding Ikezaki is that even though he was both quick and bright, he was also, in a way, impervious to insult. As if he minded not a whit, he attended the Sōseki Sanbō discussions. Supplementing his Sōseki article with others, he collected them all into his maiden publication, *Idealism in Art* (1916). The letter from Sōseki was included most deliberately—in fact, it was printed at the front of the book, in lieu of a preface.

Ikezaki was a hard case. And thus we see that Abe Yoshishige's assessment in his memoirs was generally correct. Ikezaki's prose, he wrote there, was

heavily larded with classical Chinese, and for a member of the "younger generation" (to borrow the English phrase) he was skilled in the use of *kanji*. He read voraciously; his literary criticism may be regarded as the product of the leisure hours of a law student. As with his view of Sōseki, he moves hastily from limited observation to conclusion without embarrassment: his are the arguments of a literary novice.

What sparked Ikezaki's sense of rivalry with Akutagawa was related to this matter of Sōseki-worship. Akutagawa's affiliation with the Sōseki Sanbō began two years after Ikezaki's, Ikezaki attending from his first year in the German law department, Akutagawa from his third year in the English department.

Together with friends from his high school days (Kume Masao, Kikuchi Hiroshi, Matsuoka Yuzuru, Yamamoto Yūzō, Tsuchiya Bunmei, Toyoshima Yoshio) Akutagawa formed and published a journal, *Shinchō* (New Trends). And he contributed short pieces to *Literature of the Empire*, such as "The Jester" and "Rashōmon." None was well received. However, his "The Nose," first published in *Shinchō*, garnered high praise from Natsume Sōseki. Sōseki's letter to Akutagawa is extant: "See if you can line up another twenty or thirty pieces like this one. You will become a writer like none other in our literary world." At Suzuki Miekichi's recommendation, "The Nose" was carried in the May 1916 issue of *New Fiction*. Akutagawa had made a spectacular debut on the literary scene and would now become a central figure in the Sōseki Sanbō.

Ikezaki's *Idealism in Art* was published several months later. His inclusion of Sōseki's letter to him can be seen as a competitive move, as if to say, "Look, Sōseki praised me too!" And it also proved that Ikezaki had known the great man of letters far longer.

Actually, at this point in time, with respect to sheer name recognition, Ikezaki (as Akagi Kōhei) topped Akutagawa. One of the essays collected in *Idealism in Art*, titled "The Literature of Dissipation and Its Imminent Extinction," had appeared in the *Yomiuri* newspaper recently, on August 6 and August 8, 1916, and had created a sensation. Ikezaki named as culprits such authors as Nagata Mikihiko, Yoshii Isamu, Kubota Mantarō, Gotō Sueo, and Chikamatsu Shūkō. He condemned their works as "coarsely vulgar," and he characterized their protagonists as nothing but variations of "Mr. Pleasure Fool" and "Miss Abominable Scandal," meaning respectively the men who overindulge themselves with women and wine, and the harlots who service them. Whereas art, he said, should aspire to the ideal of "an earnest contemplation of life; an attitude of sincerity."

It would be pointless to cite them all here, but numerous journals and magazines, such as *Chūō Kōron* (The Central Review) and *Shinchō* (New Trends), then carried articles condemning the works of authors identified as targets for extinction. On top of that, the reason for the warm reception accorded "The Literature of Dissipation and Its Imminent Extinction" was that there were many writers who took a dim view of the trend that under the banner of literature, anything goes. Even Akutagawa, though he was repelled by Ikezaki's stridency, wrote to a friend that "it is useful enough as a wake-up call" to their colleagues.

Both Ikezaki and Akutagawa compared themselves to their venerated sensei. In that one regard, they were comrades. But Akutagawa felt that with Ikezaki "his logic is a bit off." Once Sōseki had passed, their face-to-face encounters diminished. However, they continued to exchange letters. It was chiefly a haiku competition. For example, this letter from Akutagawa to Ikezaki (July 19, 1917):

> Here's a modern classic I composed:
>
> > In such a rain
> > the Snake Woman conceives.
> > Silk-tree blossoms.

Other messages suggest a cordial relationship, such as this one, dated November 3, 1917.

> This evening, gazing at the clear sky, I composed a verse:
>
> > Looking long at Heaven's River,
> > I work at night, piling up
> > seed eggplants.

> If you're free, won't you drop by? I'll be in on Sunday.

In reality, however, they were rivals. Referring to "The Literature of Dissipation and Its Imminent Extinction," Ikezaki had asked Sōseki, "Sensei, you have read my article, have you not?" This got him a curt "I saw it," in reply. Feeling deflated, Ikezaki pressed further: "How did you like it?" At which Sōseki smiled wryly, saying, "That article, it's as if you're flourishing a long-sword directly in front of you. You're going to injure your readers." Ikezaki hung his head. This was three months before Sōseki's death.[7]

"The Literature of Dissipation and Its Imminent Extinction" marked the high point but also the end of Ikezaki's early fame. Upon graduating university, he went to work as a correspondent for the *Yorozu Chōhō* newspaper. He must have felt it to be quite a turning point. He wrote of it as follows: "Now I am separating myself from over twenty years of academic life, urging on my mentally fatigued and physically exhausted self as I attempt to sail into the maelstrom of the real world."[8]

Akutagawa, on the other had, found his fame rising ever since his talent was publicly recognized by Sōseki. It was time to decide which man was the victor. They severed relations. Akutagawa referred to this in a letter to Ikezaki dated January 31, 1919: "Greetings. Are you still angry with me? If not, I want to present you with a copy of a book I've put out. How about it? If you're inclined to receive a copy, send a reply."

The specific origin of their quarrel is not clear, but Ikezaki's "A Farewell to My Departed Friend, Akutagawa Ryūnosuke," written after Akutagawa's suicide, gives us a general idea of what happened.[9] He writes there that "the greatly talented Akutagawa" was "a great plagiarist," whose works were clearly dressed up in "Ōgai's overcoat, Anatole France's shoes, Sōseki's hat." What bothered Ikezaki the most was the Sōseki part. Or rather, parts: "A Sōsekiesque manner of speech, Sōsekiesque feelings, Sōsekiesque interests: in every way, shape, and form, and at all times, he exuded Sōseki." Ikezaki confessed that he said things like this to Akutagawa's face before he died. "Ill-mannered yokel that I was, my pronouncements provoked your rage, and ultimately I lost the pleasure of associating with you." Until his second literary debut, as author of *Japan Need Not Fear the U.S.*, he was tormented deep down by a sense of playing second fiddle.

From the age of twenty-two to the age of twenty-nine, Ikezaki was active as a literary critic, using the pen name of "Akagi Kōhei." At the end of this seven-year period, he returned to Osaka. His feud with Akutagawa Ryūnosuke occurred during this seven-year period.

It was in order to return to Osaka that he jettisoned the pen name Akagi

Kōhei. He had become the adopted heir to Ikezaki Kosaburō, who had a large knitted-goods business in Osaka and who (in exchange for acquiring Tadayoshi as successor) had taken care of his university expenses upon his entering the law department at Tokyo Imperial University. However, after he had arrived in Tokyo, instead of studying law, the young man had become captivated by the "soft" subject of literature.

Ikezaki paterfamilias was a merchant from Ōmi; he had made a fortune in Osaka and become a figure of local importance. He had a daughter. Her name was Nobuko. He had her tutored in various accomplishments, including playing the piano. In those days, naturally, few houses had pianos. It was the mark of a "high-collar," meaning a Westernized Japanese. Nobuko went to a local girl's school and then to Tokyo for college, enrolling in the Tokyo Conservatory of Music (now the Tokyo National University of Fine Arts and Music) in Ueno.

It was Ikezaki Kōsaburō's intention that Tadayoshi become Nobuko's husband, continuing the family's name, preserving the family's business, and increasing the family's wealth. But Tadayoshi had no intention of returning to Osaka to become his heir and successor. Kosaburō gave up. He wished he had found a groom who would more loyally inherit the business.

However, as soon as Nobuko graduated the Tokyo Conservatory of Music, Tadayoshi went ahead and cohabited with her anyway. Kosaburō was livid. It was one thing for Tadayoshi to get the girl if he were going to continue the business, but forcing himself upon her with no such intent was unforgivable.

As Akagi Kōhei, Ikezaki Tadayoshi was still a darling of the literary world. A gap was beginning to open up between himself and Akutagawa, but still he had a certain level of renown. Given the source (Ikezaki himself), it is probably best to discount this, but apparently the day he graduated from Tokyo Imperial University in 1917, there was a student-professor mixer at the law department, and one of the professors made the following comment: "Amongst the graduates here, there may be present the distinguished literary critic, Mr. Akagi Kōhei. If he is here, would he please stand up and show us his face."[10]

Upon graduation, Tadayoshi became a correspondent for *Yorozu Chōhō*, and he and Nobuko began their lives together as newlyweds in a rented apartment in Ueno. Prior to that, he had resided at the Kikufuji Hotel in Hongo, near the university. This Kikufuji Hotel had a long and honorable history of providing first-rank student accommodations. Tanizaki Junichirō, Takehisa Yumeji, Ōsugi Sakae, Itō Noe, Uno Chiyo, and other intellectuals had periods of residency there, and the place was enveloped in a distinctive and lustrous aura of modernism. However high-collar Kosaburō thought himself, for a knitted goods manufacturer and wholesaler in the environs of Osaka, this was a world apart.

Kondō Tomie has written about the Hongo Kikufuji Hotel in a book of that title. One of the reminiscences she records takes the form of the following vignette.

I mean, imagine yourself standing in the dark vestibule of the hotel. From Room 3 (that's Uno Kōji's room) come the strains of "Gonjō," a Kiyomoto song. It's the shamisen-strumming of the Fujimichō geisha, Murakami Yae, who will later become the model for the heroine of [Uno Kōji's] *Omoigawa* [Love Stream]. She was Mr. Uno's lover, you know. In the communal bath, the head clerk is humming some revolutionary anthem. The philosopher Miki Kiyoshi is in the room directly above Uno's, writing "A Marxist Form of Humanist Studies" for the Iwanami journal, *Shisō* [Thought], while down in the dining salon Hirotsu Kazuo is playing ping-pong with Takao, the second-eldest son of the proprietor. Then some young fellow in a *happi* coat drops by, on the run, ringing the bell as he leaves off some newspaper extras about the general resignation of the Wakatsuki Cabinet. This would have been April of 1927, I think.[11]

Ikezaki, associating with the Sōseki Sanbō as Akagi Kōhei, longed to immerse himself in this world. Once he got his feet wet, he did not want to return to Osaka. And perhaps it was because he was so thoroughly steeped in this heady environment that he became enmeshed in scandal. It all started when he had the actress Shirai Sumiyo accompany him on a one-day, one-night trip to the Bōsō Peninsula.

In the September 1915 issue of *New Fiction*, one of Ikezaki's *sempai* (seniors) at the Sōseki Sanbō, Komuro Toyotaka, wrote a mercilessly critical review of a production of Chekhov's *The Cherry Orchard* directed by Osanai Kaoru.

Generally speaking, the actors think it sufficient to perform only as they

utter their own lines; after that, they just loll about. Strangely, they pay
no heed to what the others are saying. When their turn comes around
again, suddenly they begin to recite again.

Shirai Sumiyo played a supporting role in this production, that of the
governess, Charlotta.
Shirai had trained at the school for actresses established by Kawakami
Otojirō and his wife Sadayatsuko. She became an actress in the Imperial
Theatre, but it was not so glamorous an existence. Word did get around that
her hobby was raising snakes, but she never acquired much of a reputation
as an actress. One heard of her rather as an old trouper.
A love scandal is not a matter of one party's fault rather than the other's.
But in this case it seemed that the actress would not be appeased unless
Ikezaki were made out to be the villain. After their one-night stand, she
pressed the young writer to marry her. On top of that, she dropped by
Ikezaki's apartment, uninvited, and confronted Nobuko. Eventually she
went to cadge money from Tadayoshi's adoptive family in Osaka, who had
not been communicating with him. And she tried to sell her story to the
newspapers. This was one "bad actor."
The *Tōkyō Nichinichi* (Tokyo Daily) newspaper broke the scandal in its
March 9, 1919 issue. That was because Shirai Sumiyo had lodged a petition
for reprimand with the Ueno police chief. The petition for reprimand was
essentially a plea to have some alleged offender officially cautioned by the
police. No doubt she would have liked to ask them to indict him on charges
of both rape and breach-of-promise.

The aforementioned Ikezaki Tadayoshi, using the pen name Akagi Kōhei,
has, in the public press, been preaching humanitarianism and denouncing "the literature of dissipation," but his personal life belies his writings. He habitually tricks women into sacrificing their chastity.... [On
the way back from the Bōsō trip], seeking to seduce me, he led me to a
tavern in Kyobashi Ward, where he plied me with sake and violated me
notwithstanding all my efforts to resist.

Something like this coming out in a daily newspaper was devastating. It
struck a nerve. For the man who had made his reputation with the article
"The Literature of Dissipation and Its Imminent Extinction" to be accused
of raping a woman at a tavern certainly destroyed that reputation.

And the *Tōkyō Nichinichi* made no effort to substantiate the story. They got only the "she said" and did not even bother with the "he said." Their only concern was immediate titillation.

As Sumiyo tells it, she and Akagi had promised each other verbally that under no circumstances would they reveal to others what had happened at the tavern. But then the story began to be bruited about, originating presumably in Mr. Akagi's boasts that this had been a love tryst initiated by Sumiyo. This caused Sumiyo to suffer extreme emotional distress. To try to take him to task, Sumiyo called on his home two or three times seeking a meeting, but each time was rebuffed at the vestibule. Thus it was, she says, that she had recourse to the petition for reprimand printed on the right. It will be interesting to see how His Excellency the local Police Chief will decide this case.

In literary circles, a certain *senryū* (satirical haiku) made the rounds. It punned on Kōhei's name and other words in a way that will not survive translation into English, though some of the effects may be approximated by the following:

> Hey, hey, Kōhei!
> Don't you go away
> without your "suit"!

The famous literary critic Akagi Kōhei had nowhere to hide and no-where to go. His shocked foster parents came up to Tokyo. The incident itself Ikezaki Kosaburō settled with hush money, but this was only after Tadayoshi had resigned himself to moving to Osaka to inherit the knitted goods business—as Ikezaki Tadayoshi.

Ikezaki Kosaburō had constructed a 7,000 square-foot mansion on a 25,000 square-foot lot in the Osaka suburbs. The young couple, however, were ensconced in the Ikezaki Kosaburō trading store in downtown Osaka, a better way to learn the business, it was thought. Tadayoshi severed relations with his previous friends and acquaintances. He now sat in his shop, wearing an apron. He was responsible for directing affairs at the shop, managing its accounts, and making the rounds of regular customers. He was engrossed in work at which he was no good. For someone who normally thought only how to best others in argument, this was a tough job.

However, given his complete divorce from the literary world, this new life did not generate the same kind of stress as his former existence. As he threw himself into his work and began to forget Tokyo, he made new friends.

It so happened that back at Takahashi Middle School, there had been an upperclassman named Yamamoto Hatsujirō. Like Ikezaki, he had been adopted into the family of a knitted goods manufacturer and merchant in Osaka. And he was a graduate of the Tokyo Higher Commercial School (now Hitotsubashi University). In an industry dominated by self-made men who had worked their way up from apprentice, these two had similar educational backgrounds. They became friends.

As Ikezaki grew proficient at the family business, something began to gnaw at his heart. By the end of the Taishō period (1926), Akutagawa Ryūnosuke's fame seemed assured.

Through Yamamoto, Ikezaki widened his circle of acquaintances in Osaka cultural circles. From his Sōseki Sanbō days, he knew the Western-style painter Saitō Yori, who had studied in France with Tsuda Seifū, Yasui Sōtarō, and others. Now, Saitō was running an art school in Osaka. Ikezaki also came to know the poet Kawada Jun. Kawada was also general manager of the Sumitomo Corporation's home office. Associating with figures such as these, Ikezaki broadened his sphere of acquaintances in Kansai-area financial circles.

Early in the spring of 1928, at Yamamoto's invitation, Ikezaki undertook a trip to the Nanki area. The traveling party included a friend of Yamamoto from his Hitotsubashi days, Kabutoyama Hamago, then a company director of the forerunner of today's Nomura Securities, and also Katsuta Shin, an examiner at the Bank of Japan's Osaka branch. The Kisei Line did not extend as far as Kumano, so they went by boat both ways. During their long hours together on board, the conversation bloomed, covering myriad topics. The theme gravitated toward America's anti-Japanese immigration laws. Many villages in the Kishū region had sent immigrants to America.

At that point it became a one-man Ikezaki show. For over two hours he pontificated on the topic at hand, vehemently and volubly, as Kabutoyama's reminiscence attests.

For over two hours, he declaimed upon the subject that had just been introduced, giving a truly detailed account of America's foreign policy toward Japan since the Russo-Japanese War, subjecting its vicissitudes and plans to the most scrupulous analysis, mentioning all sorts of people by name and blasting our own government's lack of a foreign policy. At the same time, he warned that Japanese foreign affairs were on the verge of a crisis. In that, as in his comparison of the two countries' naval strength, and in matters of naval strategy and so on, he demonstrated profound knowledge.[12]

In fact, Ikezaki had been reading Hector C. Bywater's *The Great Pacific War*. But that is not the sort of content just anyone can master. Ikezaki had a gift for realigning material with his own polemics. In this case, he reworked the argument of "The Literature of Dissipation and Its Imminent Extinction," with America as the new target for extinction. Impressed, Kabutoyama made the following request: "Nomura Associates has a monthly lecture series. We invite distinguished speakers from all walks of life. I would very much like you to come and do one."

Ikezaki was a man who had competed with Akutagawa on an equal footing. But perhaps he was inclined all along not so much to literature as to speechifying. His lecture at Nomura lasted over three hours. Pleased with the positive reception it was accorded, Nomura had the stenographic record printed up and distributed to major clients. Copies were highly sought after. It was an expanded version of this lecture that became *Japan Need Not Fear the U.S.*

When *Japan Need Not Fear the U.S.* became a best seller, Mizuno Hironori could not remain silent. He wrote a refutation, which appeared in the *Asahi* newspaper on November 8, 1929:

From the opening sentence, the author's worldview is apparent. A virulent antipathy and burning hostility to the white man, above all the Anglo-Saxon race, spews out from between every line. That is the ideological context of this book, cover to cover.

Mizuno went on to explain calmly. Ikezaki placed extraordinary emphasis on America's weak points. It faced the internal threat of an insurrection by the black man and the external threat of a war with Mexico. But Mizuno pointed out that Japan had to deal with an independence movement on the Korean peninsula, and that a struggle was shaping up in China. To overlook all that, and to touch only on America's problems, was wrong, he said. And it was bizarre to hold that if a Japan-U.S. war were a long war,

America would be at a disadvantage. America wasted its military budget, its people were not unified, so it appeared beatable. But what sense did it make to boast extravagantly about Japan's naval strength while making light of America's economic might?

Mizuno thought that merely criticizing *Japan Need Not Fear the U.S.* was not enough. When a request came in from the Yokosuka Sea Scouts for a work marking the twenty-fifth anniversary of the Battle of Tsushima, he wrote *Air and Sea*. Later, in 1932, he wrote *The Japan-U.S. Battle for Dominance*, for which *Air and Sea* was something of a dry run. That earlier work ended with American air strikes turning Tokyo to rubble. But Mizuno was outnumbered, and his position among writers of future-war chronicles declined from this point.

In contrast, the happy-days-are-here-again line propounded by *Japan Need Not Fear the U.S.* sounded good to recession-weary Japanese who had lost their self-confidence. And when it became a hit, new writers of future-war chronicles emerged one after another. Hirata Shinsaku, whose writings later became a staple of youth magazines, made a brilliant debut in 1930 with a trio of books: *Will America Challenge Japan?*, *The Pacific War and the Insecurity of Arms Reduction*, and *War in the Far East and the American Navy*. In the same year were published such works as Murata Koimaro's *Our Navy and the Next War*; Satō Kiyokatsu's *Empire in Crisis: A Japan-U.S. War Draws Nigh*; Okada Meitarō's *Struggle for the Pacific: Realities of the Situation and the Empire's Self-Defense*; and Toyoshima Jirō's *Japan's Great Naval War*. Translations also proliferated, with works such as Elliot Fielding's *The Tide of Battle* lining the shelves of Japanese bookstores. Not to be outdone, Ikezaki continued to ride this wave successfully. Immediately after *Japan Need Not Fear the U.S.*, he wrote *Japan's Submarines*. Over the course of the next seven years, starting in 1930, he published one work after another: *The Global Menace of Americanism*; *Can a 60-Percent Fleet Fight?*; *A Pacific Strategy*; *Destiny: A Japan-U.S. War*. Every single one of these books adopted logic that defended Japan's positions and fixed blame on the United States.

Ikezaki was pleased, but not simply because his books were selling well. He had opened lines of communication with politicians and powerful military figures who agreed with him. Meanwhile, the lingering presence of his rival, Akutagawa, who had ended his own life, was now fading and receding into the distance. The way ahead was open. Ikezaki was confident. He now wanted to become a Diet member, the darling this time of the political world.

PART III

Blending Fiction
and Reality

If I were under orders, then for the first six months to a year I'd work like crazy carrying them out, and you'd see results, believe me. But if it were to take two or three years, I would have no such confidence. Now that we have the Tripartite Alliance, we have to deal with it, but since things have come to such a pass, I request that every effort be made to avoid a Japan-U.S. war.

—YAMAMOTO ISOROKU[1]

CHAPTER ELEVEN

Foretelling the Great
Tokyo Air Raid

I N MARCH, Tokyo weather is unstable. This writer has many memories of how, at that time of year, just when you're feeling nice and comfortable thanks to the sun's warm rays, along comes a fierce blast of wind, and you must go about with collar turned up.

March 9, 1945 was one of those gusty days. As dusk yielded to night, the wind grew even more violent. Remnants of the snow that had fallen some two or three days prior still remained where there was shade. The wind that raged through the streets was piercing cold. At 10:30 PM the first-alert siren sounded. This time, it was just one B-29, coming from the direction of the Bōsō Peninsula. Presently it circled around and went back. The citizens of Tokyo breathed a collective sigh of relief. As they were relaxing and going to sleep, a large formation of B-29s attacked. The first bombs were loosed upon the Fukagawa district at eight minutes past midnight (and thus technically on March 10). Soon incendiary bombs were raining down all over Tokyo.

The conflagration engulfed the middle-to-lower-class neighborhoods along the Sumida River, known as the *shitamachi* or "low-town" district. The first air raid siren sounded at 12:15 AM, seven minutes after the first bomb was dropped. As the flames were whipped up by the stiff winds, a sea of fire spread all around.

I have before me a five-volume Japanese compendium titled, *The Great Tokyo Air Raid: Reminiscences of Wartime Devastation.*[2] This resource exhaustively documents the ways in which the destructiveness of such air raids beggars the imagination. Many personal reminiscences are recorded here. One that strikes me in particular is the experience of a young female student.

Whirlwinds were swirling about incessantly. She abandoned her suitcase. She thought she saw Kōtō Bridge. It was hot; her body felt like it was catching fire. There were indeed people around her who rolled about bundled in flame, screaming as the flames enveloped them. People were jumping into the river. Try as they might, they could not outrun the flames. "Mother, we're going to die!" she cried. "We're catching fire! Let's jump into the river. All right? Hold my hand. Don't let go, okay?" Her mother said nothing, flinching from such a step. If she did not plunge into the river right here and now, she would be burned to death. "I can't die. I'm going to live. I'll go into the river." So the girl and her mother jumped down onto a raft together. Then immediately after them, people enveloped in flames came jumping down, one after another, inadvertently striking her and her mother on the head or elsewhere. And that became her eternal parting from her mother, who disappeared in the chaos and was never seen by her again. It all happened in a few moments. The girl was lucky enough to grab hold of the raft. But her mother, a quiet, timid sort of woman who was never seen to wear anything but a kimono, may have lacked the energy and will (thought the girl) to grab hold of that raft and live. Thinking only to help her child, she was probably praying to the Shinto and Buddhist gods for her daughter's salvation. But clutching onto the raft for dear life, the girl could not search for her mother. She could only drift with the raft, not even thinking about her own survival.

And there, at the border between life and death, a kind stranger put out the flames that had started to burn the girl's *zukin*—her air-raid hood. She could neither express her thanks nor shed a tear. Seized with terror, she clung to the raft like a wax doll. Red flames spread, covering the surface of the water, rising up at every point along the riverbank. She was brushing off sparks, dousing her head in the river, letting the raft take her where it would. Though she was wearing an overcoat, her body felt chilled. "Don't fall asleep," said someone in a loud voice, encouraging her. Bodies bobbed in the water: women, children, all dead. Now it seemed almost as though she were the only person alive in a river of corpses. A middle-aged woman floated on her back, dead. Here, there, everywhere: dead people. The horror of it began to fade for her, situated as she was on the fine line between life and death. Did she want to live or to die? What would happen to her? Even these questions did not occur to her.

The powerful winds and flames intensified, and the people clinging to the raft slipped away: first one, then two. And the girl felt the last of her own strength slipping out of her hands. When she grew sleepy, she heard again the voice of the man calling out, "Don't you fall asleep!" She heeded him and left the rest to Heaven. Just then the man grabbed her arm and saved her from slipping away. He used his own steel helmet to scoop up water to splash over her head.

There is much more in this girl's memoirs, but we will leave it at that for now and pick up the threads of our earlier historical narrative. Between the Russo-Japanese War and the Second World War, the destructiveness of war was not brought home to the Japanese in any serious way. Even in the Russo-Japanese War, there were no battles fought in the home islands. When Japanese armed forces charged up Hill 203 at Port Arthur they augmented the terrain with mountains of heaped-up corpses. But even that took place on foreign soil.

In Europe, however, in the Great War, even noncombatants were caught up in the conflict, and cities were scorched. Modern weapons reduced human beings to the most insignificant existence. This was the world that beggared the imagination of Mizuno Hironori, as he gazed firsthand upon the devastation wrought in Europe.

Ikezaki Tadayoshi's *Japan Need Not Fear the U.S.* was nothing more than an easy power game. Mizuno thought it terrible for writers who knew nothing of war to turn the boom in Japan-U.S. future-war chronicles into such lightweight entertainment. So thought Mizuno when he described an American bomber raid on Tokyo at the end of his *Sea and Air* (1930).[3]

In Mizuno's fictional climax, several of the enemy's planes finally enter the skies above Tokyo. Gas bombs and incendiary devices fall everywhere. The civilians have not been issued gas masks and are soon affected by the poison, victims collapsing to the ground in a heap. There is only one hour's warning of a raid by enemy planes. The fires start in the eastern and southern portions of the city. Before long, lines of flame extend to some thirty or forty locations in the north and west as well. The throngs of evacuees filling the streets prevent fire engines from responding. Unfortunately, the rain stops. Seeing red, the southeasterly wind grows all the more furious. The people of Tokyo find a raging inferno consuming their world, insatiable flames devouring everything, the sounds of things burning, of people screaming. Afterward, a horrific scene, one that cannot be described, one that cannot even be imagined. The fires continue for two days and nights. When everything that can burn has burned, the fires naturally die down. What remains is a city of ash, a city of scorched earth, a city of corpses. The skeletal remains of large buildings protrude like Roman ruins.

Mizuno's graphic description was like an eyewitness account of the future. Fifteen years later, reality matched what the writer had merely imagined. Reading it in conjunction with the girl's actual memoirs referred to above, one is cut to the quick by a feeling of helplessness. If people understood that such a calamity would ensue, why did they not avert it?

What Mizuno witnessed in World War I was not simply the horror of war in general. It was, specifically, the threat of aerial weaponry. He had personally experienced the German air attacks on London.

Even Hector C. Bywater's *The Great Pacific War*, noted for its detailed war scenarios, naturally tended to have fleets deciding the issue with naval battles. It was the same with Mizuno's *The Next Battle*. The reason Mizuno chose *Sea and Air* for the title of his latest book was due to his forecast that the war of the future would not be decided solely by naval combat but would instead center on air power, including carrier-based aircraft. And if aircraft were crucial in combat, then they would also be used for indiscriminate attacks on cities.

Charles Lindbergh's nonstop New York–Paris flight took place in 1927. It took 33.5 hours to cross the Atlantic, and it was hailed as one of the great feats of the century. From a military point of view, one could now expect flight ranges that would permit planes to invade an enemy's airspace and then return. Lindbergh was welcomed in Paris as a man of peace, but the aftermath of this great feat would include an endless parade of casualties in wars of the future.

Japan acquired this technology from more advanced nations, absorbing the know-how to manufacture aircraft. Ultimately it became capable of making warplanes on its own. It launched its first aircraft carrier at the end of 1922, but at that time its carrier planes were either imported or assembled in Japan under foreign direction. Domestic prototypes were prepared from blueprints drawn up by foreign advisers; engines were produced under license. The final products of domestic manufacture were in fact completely copied from existing foreign models, with barely a local touch or two.

The 1922 Washington Naval Limitation Treaty had restricted Japan's capital ship tonnage to 60 percent that of Britain's. The subsequent London Naval Conference in 1930 extended the same ratio to auxiliary ships.

On the oceans we are hemmed in. That leaves us the air. Such was the line of thinking upon which the Japanese navy now embarked. Thus it was also in 1930 that the Aircraft Research Laboratory (renamed Nakajima Aircraft the following year) developed the first truly domestically produced airplane. In the same year, *Sea and Air* was written. And this was also the year in which the navy established an air cadet system.

In *The Crucial Battle*, Mizuno had already conscientiously described the sheer power of the modern armaments he had witnessed during the Russo-Japanese War. With the First World War, he saw the next step. And he realized that he could envision no limit to the escalation of arms technology and scale.

For four years after he lost his wife Morie to tuberculosis, Mizuno lived as a widower. When she died, their son, Mitsunori, was a third-year student at the Musashi Elementary School. Mizuno's own needs were looked after by a live-in maid. Mizuno was entering his fifties, but he had to do something about this situation. As he confided to a young military man who admired him, being a widower was difficult.

Mizuno remarried in 1928. His new wife, Tsuya, was born in the outskirts of his old hometown of Matsuyama. She was forty years old; it was her third marriage. Tsuya's first marriage to a man in a nearby family had ended when she fled back home to her parents. She then married a lawyer named Ono in Matsuyama City, who suffered from mental illness and later died. For a second time she returned to her parents, where Mizuno's marriage proposal awaited her. Perhaps because of her two previous unhappy experiences, in her new marriage Tsuya was self-effacing and reticent in all things. The Mizuno household moved from Aoyama to Sasazuka and then to Komezawa. In 1930 Mizuno bought property in Sangenjaya and built a new house there. It was a humble two-story dwelling. The first floor had three rooms. One room was six tatami mats in size, one was eight mats, and the library was four-and-a-half mats. The second floor had Mitsunori's study room.

The focus of Mizuno's life was his writing. After *Sea and Air* he went to work on *Japan and America: The Battle for Dominance*. From time to time he would go out into his small garden where he was assiduously cultivating chrysanthemums, upon which he gazed with great satisfaction. Every evening without exception he had a drink with dinner. But Mizuno was conservative about the amount of liquor that he consumed. The author was happiest when the food came in many small dishes. Pecking at these various dishes, he sipped away at his drink over the course of a lengthy dinner.

Mizuno was working out a plot. In his head, the characters of *Sea and*

Air were holding a conversation. On the deck of a navy ship a number of officers stand about discussing the attack strengths of various aircraft.[4]

"Forget about the details. If you think back to the Battle of Tsushima, you realize that back then, warfare itself was still in its infancy."

"Yeah. Back in the Russo-Japanese War, no planes, no subs. We had wireless for only two or three hundred nautical miles out, and it was iffy at that. If there'd been planes and subs back then, we probably couldn't have blockaded Port Arthur. No Battle of Tsushima, either."

"And nowadays it isn't much of a contest when we can only aim for the enemy ship's smokestacks from twenty or thirty thousand meters away. We can hear them, we just can't see them. It's like watching a play with your eyes closed."

Scenes of war involving aircraft are followed by a conversation noting the coming ascendancy of the aircraft carrier over the battleship.[5]

"These high-profile, slow-maneuvering battleships make a great target for aircraft, don't they?"

"If you follow that logic, then next you'll say heavy cruisers are useless, and then after that light cruisers, and eventually it'll be all warships are useless. That means the death of the navy. No?"

"Yeah, I think that day is definitely coming sooner or later. Essentially, the warships' task is mastery of the seas, in the sense of controlling ocean-going traffic. When shipboard takeoffs and landings get a little easier, even commercial ships will be able to carry two or three aircraft to do their own reconnaissance, so they can travel sea lanes safely without the protection of warships. Then apart from the aircraft carriers you can scrap the others."

"I'd take an opposing view: I say abolish all aircraft carriers too. I mean, basically Japan is surrounded on all sides by ocean, so an enemy air assault could easily come from any direction. Aircraft carriers are the most dangerous warships of all. We'd never know when Tokyo or some other city would be set ablaze."

So Japan is a sea-girt archipelago, a fortress with a natural moat. Conventional war strategy called for Japanese forces to go out to meet any approaching enemy fleet. In historical reality, Japan had done just that in repulsing Russia's Baltic Fleet. But the advent of the aircraft carrier changed the situation completely. Wars of the future would make the broad Pacific look like a pond in a miniature garden. The day was coming when bombers launched from aircraft carriers packed with many such planes would swarm over the skies of Tokyo.

Sea and Air ends with the horrific scenes of the Tokyo air raids that we noted above. The protagonist then stands amid the charred ruins and mutters to himself:

> If you're going to go to war, you'd better be prepared for it. If you're not going to go to war, you have to stick to your principles. But this war began because we were aimlessly pulled into it by bravado and emotion, without being either prepared or principled.

And then comes the punch line:

> Everything rattled. It was an earthquake, and your author awoke from his dream.[6]

It was to be expected that such a clear-cut Japanese defeat would provoke a reader backlash. There was also reason to fear that publication would be banned. These concerns were natural. But there was no self-censoring blanking-out of material, nor were the official censors strict.

Mizuno's next book, however, *Japan and America: The Battle for Dominance*, was initially slapped with a stop-sale order. Issue No. 50 of the Police Report on Publications (November 1932), a secret document prepared by the Ministry of Home Affairs' Law and Order Bureau, justified this action as follows:

> This book takes as its subject a Japan-U.S. war. Although it is merely a fictitious novel, it does contain language that constitutes an attack on the Empire's conduct in the current China Incident. There is also libel of military affairs. Furthermore, some material is leftist propaganda. For these reasons, this book is banned.

The Police Report on Publications mentions "leftist propaganda," but Mizuno was no left-winger. However, saying Japan would lose a war was enough to get one classified as a left-winger. In those days the most obvious antiestablishment movement was the Japan Communist Party (JCP), so the Special Higher Police would infer their influence.

On June 29, 1932, the existing Special Higher Section of the Tokyo Metropolitan Police Department was raised to the status of a Special Higher Police Division. In line with the Comintern Thesis of 1932, the JCP took "abolition of the emperor system" as its slogan and goal, so the authorities were expanding and improving their organizations of control and choosing their moment to attack. For its part, the JCP attacked the Ōmori branch of the Kawasaki Daihyaku Bank on October 6, 1932 in order to obtain operating capital. This incident provided an excuse for a thorough crackdown. The JCP would receive a fatal blow.

It was immediately after this that Mizuno's *Japan and America: The Battle for Dominance* was published. It had absolutely zilch to do with the JCP, but the timing was certainly bad. The original title was *Dominance: The Next Crucial Battle*. The book's subtitle was was *Resolution or Destruction?*

Mizuno's second wife's nephew, Shigematsu Fukio, had moved from his hometown in Ehime Prefecture to Tokyo to attend the Tokyo College of Agriculture. He was often to be seen in the Mizuno home in Sangenjaya. On one occasion, he was given a copy of *Dominance: The Next Crucial Battle: Resolution or Destruction?* which had just been delivered by the publisher. On his next visit, sometime later, Mizuno told him with a cloudy expression on his face, "That book has been banned. Possession means trouble. Better give it back." On this point, however, Tōkai Shoin, Mizuno's publisher, soon educated their disappointed author. "Sensei," they said, "something that's been banned sells better!"[7]

The way the censorship system worked, prior to publication one had to submit a sample to the publications section of the Law and Order Bureau of the Home Ministry. But even if sale were initially prohibited, one could revise or blank out the offending portions and resubmit. If the portions flagged by the ministry had all been satisfactorily attended to, grounds for the ban were nullified and sales could proceed. Thus on publication, a book's advertising would sometimes proclaim, "Controversial! Originally banned!" And of course readers' interest would be piqued. They would want to know why the book had been banned, and they would want all the more to read something with such impact. And the publishers, counting on this psychology, played the system adroitly. Freedom of speech was indeed restricted, but market forces and marketing savvy proved quite resilient.

Mizuno's *Dominance: The Next Crucial Battle: Resolution or Destruction?* underwent a title change, to *Japan and America: The Battle for Dominance*.

He was following marketing advice that titles with Japan and America in them sold better. On November 15, merely a month after its initial ban, *Japan and America: The Battle for Dominance* appeared on bookshop shelves.

A section originally blanked out by the censors is reproduced below. One can see from this what sort of writing they thought was leftist propaganda.

> "So I thought, if you're going to be grabbed by the military anyway, better the navy, where you can read things a little more freely, and see the West at government expense. Of course, if war breaks out, you can't really run or hide. But I figure maybe there's more merit to becoming shark food than trench-filler. What, you wanted to know about my will? Well, no parents or siblings; no assets to bequeath, anyway. I'm a bachelor. No particular need for a will. But just to state my personal desire, it would be regrettable to die without seeing a more pleasant society, as I would be able to naturally if I were longer-lived."
>
> "And this 'pleasant society' you're talking about. What 'pleasant society' would that be?"
>
> "Well, for one thing, a society in which the rich man and the bureaucrat don't lord it over everyone else. Next, a society in which there are no more people who hang themselves because they can't make ends meet."[8]

The organizational upgrading of the Special Higher Police was done not only in response to the JCP, but also to assist surveillance of the right wing, which was burgeoning in strength and numbers. The Manchurian Incident of September 1931 and the Shanghai Incident of January 1932 were followed domestically by the "5/15" Incident of May 15, 1932. It was with the stench of these events still fresh in his nostrils that Mizuno began to write *Japan and America: The Battle for Dominance*.

There was an ex-army lieutenant named Matsushita Yoshio, two years younger than Mizuno and enamored of socialism. He also idolized Mizuno, so Mizuno's classification as having leftist tendencies may not have been without basis. In response to an overture from the young activist, Mizuno replied,

> Once again, the world has slipped back into an era of violence. . . . We have returned to the militarism of old, and until we collapse there will be an arms race, and there will have to be both a Japan-U.S. war and

a Japan-Britain war. Without this baptism into modern war, the Japanese people will not awaken to peace. As a result of this war, whatever physical hardships we suffer, we will long all the more for our spiritual freedom.[9]

In setting the stage for its narrative, *Japan and America: The Battle for Dominance* starts right off by positing an actual recent event, the Manchurian Incident, as the trigger for a U.S.-Japan war. In this future history, the U.S. protests that the establishment of Manchukuo is a foreign military violation of China's territorial integrity, and thus runs contrary to the Nine-Power Pact agreed upon at the Washington Conference. This leads Japan and the U.S. to break off mutual diplomatic relations, and then to declare war on each other.

In Japan, a general mobilization is announced. Patriot bonds are issued. Rings, watches, and other items made of precious metals are requisitioned for the war effort. To assist in air defense, regulations are issued restricting the burning of fuel and the use of electric lights. "Neon signs no longer sparkled on jazz clubs, the same with the cafes of Ginza and the bars of Shinjuku. This was now a city of shadowy streets, and of death."[10]

In America, on the other hand, martial law is declared on the West Coast, in Hawaii, and in the Panama Canal zone. Japanese are forbidden to enter or leave the country. All ethnic Japanese between the ages of fifteen and sixty living in Hawaii are sent to the mainland and interned. The U.S. Atlantic Fleet is moved through the Panama Canal to join up with the Pacific Fleet. As one joint fleet, they begin transferring to their forward base at Pearl Harbor.

What I should like to draw attention to here is that in both Japan and America, aspects of total-war ideology appear to have been present. In describing the general mobilization directive in Japan or the forcible incarceration of ethnic Japanese, Mizuno's forecasting was right on target.

One is also conscious of the relative importance laid on Pearl Harbor. Yamamoto Isoroku's surprise attack strategy was adopted only later and in extreme secrecy. Yet *Japan and America: The Battle for Dominance* is studded with prefigurations of Pearl Harbor.

A good example is the attack on San Francisco by carrier-based bombers. The first strategic phase involves, as it has in previous future-war chronicles, the conquest of the Philippines and Guam. However, in this scenario, an additional Eastern Expeditionary Fleet is formed.

The core of the Eastern Expeditionary Force that heads for San Francisco is comprised of the only four aircraft carriers in the Combined Fleet, protected by cruisers. Setting out from Yokosuka, it traverses the Pacific via the Mariana, Marshall, and Caroline islands. In *The Great Pacific War*, Hector C. Bywater had the U.S. fleet counterattack by hopping the same chain of island groups eastward. Mizuno simply has the Japanese fleet proceed in the reverse direction.

The aerial assault on San Francisco is a success. Dozens of bombers launched off the decks of the carriers before dawn penetrate San Francisco's air space. Complacent in the belief that Japan could not possibly attack, the city lies undefended. Here is how Mizuno describes the aerial bombardment.

> The whine of the airplanes, the antiaircraft fire, the pounding of the machine guns, the bursting of bombs, buildings collapsing: it was stupendous—one would think the entire universe was in upheaval. A severe storm had already exhausted people the previous day. Now, just before they awoke from their dreams at dawn, came a sudden aerial attack. The citizens of San Francisco, struck with fear and horror, fell into utter panic, screaming and shouting in scenes of truly hellish pandemonium. Large edifices were destroyed; fires raged everywhere. There was no one prepared to respond. The injured lay on the roadsides covered in blood, moaning.[11]

This urban air raid is meant to strike a psychological blow against the American people. But it also has another purpose: the utter destruction of the enemy fleet thought to be anchored in the naval harbor at San Francisco. But because the American Pacific Fleet is assembling in Hawaii, and what remains in San Francisco is only a single cruiser undergoing repairs and a few specially commissioned ships. For that reason, damage to the fleet itself is limited to these few ships. On the other hand, the shipyard—including the repair docks—is demolished.

Presently the Japanese bombers circle around to return to their carriers, but by now American planes are in pursuit. Half the Japanese bomber force is shot out of the sky. The American planes pursue the survivors and attack the carriers. Combat planes kept on reserve and on alert on the carriers now take to the air. A dogfight ensues. The Americans take heavy damage and losses, but the Japanese air force is annihilated. Finally, the

American planes devastate the flight decks of the carriers, which then lose their utility as carriers.

So Japan's Eastern Expeditionary Fleet successfully carries out its attack on San Francisco but suffers grievous damage and loss itself. Expecting further pursuit by the American Pacific Fleet assembling in Hawaii, the Japanese force has no choice but to beat a hasty retreat back to Japan.

* * *

TO EXPLAIN the "reality" of *Japan and America: The Battle for Dominance*, I should like to consider the meaning of the strange behavior of Vice Admiral Nagumo Chūichi during the surprise attack on Pearl Harbor on December 8 (Japan time), 1941, which has posed such a mystery for subsequent generations.

Gordon Prange's *Tora! Tora! Tora!*, the best seller made even more famous by being turned into a movie of the same name, is one work that raises doubts about Nagumo. The first wave of the surprise attack on Pearl Harbor was undertaken by 183 planes, of which only nine did not return. A separate force of 171 planes comprised the second wave. With these two strikes, the battleships anchored at Pearl Harbor were annihilated. However, twenty planes were lost from this second strike, over double the first wave's losses. At the same time, the damage done proportionately to the enemy dropped. In weighing the utility of a third wave, it was felt that relative damage to Japanese assets would increase further, and that one or two carriers might even be lost. Thus, even were a decisive victory secured, the price would be too high. Already, in addition to the twenty-nine planes that had been lost, seventy-four planes had been hit by enemy rounds. But should this have been viewed as too much? As negligible?

The last pilot to return from the first assault wave was Commander Fuchida Mitsuo. He could not imagine failing to mount another attack (a third wave) that afternoon. On his way back, he envisioned the targets of such an attack. Chief among them were the enemy's fuel depot and ship repair facilities. Commander Genda Minoru, who greeted Fuchida upon his return to the flagship *Akagi*, was of the same mind. But Vice Admiral Nagumo, commander in chief of the First Air Fleet (the Pearl Harbor Striking Force), had already declared "mission accomplished" and ordered that the striking force withdraw.

Whether Fuchida and Genda were right, or whether Nagumo's caution was correct, is something that will become apparent shortly. What was incontrovertible was that America had sustained serious damage from the surprise attack. However, with the fuel depot and ship repair facilities left unscathed, the overall damage to U.S. assets—apart from the 2,402 who lost their lives—was not as bad as it could have been. The battleships *Arizona*, *Oklahoma*, and *Utah* were sunk, but since all the other vessels were in the shallower parts of the harbor, salvage operations could restore them to active service. Furthermore, the lessons learned at Pearl Harbor stimulated the U.S. Navy to convert to a modern, carrier-based, rapid-deployment navy. Whereas six months later, out of the six Japanese carriers that had participated in the surprise attack at Pearl Harbor, four (*Akagi*, *Kaga*, *Sōryū*, *Hiryū*) were sent to the bottom of the sea at the Battle of Midway.

Japan and America: The Battle for Dominance was extremely rich in premonitions of the future. There are two key points here: Mizuno's scenarios placed great importance on attacking the ship repair facilities at San Francisco, and they showed an awareness that despite the success of the original mission, there was at the same time a high risk of counterattack. The correctness of Fuchida's and Genda's advocacy of a third assault wave at Pearl Harbor relates to the first issue. And Nagumo's determination to preserve his naval forces by withdrawing at the earliest possible moment suggests that his fear of the consequences of a counterattack engendered real timidity.

So how does Mizuno's tale unfold after that? Things go well for Japan in its occupation of the Philippines and Guam and in its attack on San Francisco, but eventually the war situation falls into a stalemate. A war of endurance plays into America's hand. The League of Nations approves a boycott of Japanese products. Japan gasps under the effects of an economic blockade.

> Look at people's living conditions. Their clothing and their food were a matter of daily distress, especially if you saw the plight of the farm villages, where there was neither food to eat nor money to spend. More than half the elementary school children were malnourished. Many people didn't show up for work because they lacked clothes. . . . Some even gave up on bartering. They just waited in empty rooms for death from starvation.[12]

There is no alternative but to go on the offensive, hoping to produce a turnaround in the war situation. The decision is made to attack the large American fleet based at Hawaii. Japan's Combined Fleet sets out from Tokyo Bay, intent on a general assault. But when the American fleet gets wind of this, they leave Pearl Harbor, bypass the Japanese fleet, and attack Tokyo. The story ends without a record of the result. Instead, "A Study of Our Pacific Strategy" was appended to the book. This appendix, however, made the author's point of view clear enough: "In a war with the United States, Japan [given its relatively inferior economic strength] can achieve victory only by avoiding a war of endurance and going for a quick military resolution." That Mizuno fudged the ending as much as he did was due no doubt to his concerns about both popular opinion and the authorities.

Japan and America: The Battle for Dominance led the Japan-U.S. future-war chronicle into new territory. To the scenes of a Europe devastated by World War I, it added the threat of a new weapon: the airplane, with descriptions of an air assault on Tokyo.

The future exists only in the imagination, but that does not mean that it is not based on past experience. Indeed, the only way to depict it is to keep one's eyes on the past and the present while adding elements of the unknown. People do not change much, but science and technology always march on. When you are foretelling the future, extrapolating the developments of science and technology creates something like a magnetic field that endows the narrative with a measure of credibility. In the case of the Japan-U.S. future-war chronicles, this meant imagining the progress of military technology.

If *Japan and America: The Battle for Dominance* is an example of adding unknown elements to a foundation of past experience, then Unno Jūzō's *The Capital Under Bombardment* is an example of sheer optimism regarding the progress of science and technology.

The Capital Under Bombardment was initially serialized under the title *Air Raid Dirge* in the May through September 1932 issues of the Hakubunkan journal *Asahi* (Morning Sun). It was a novel written during the same time period as *Japan and America: The Battle for Dominance*. And Unno's novel resembles Mizuno's, especially in describing a great air assault on Tokyo. However, the impressions they leave the reader with are diametrically opposed. Both are fine pieces, but *The Capital Under Bombardment* is inordinately sunny. It lacks the gloomy gravitas of *Japan and America: The Battle for Dominance*. And yet today Mizuno is entirely forgotten, while Unno has had a lingering impact upon people of a certain generation.

For example, Tezuka Osamu has stated, "I loved the science fiction novels of writer Unno Jūzō." Note that he calls Unno's works "science fiction novels," not "Japan-U.S. future-war chronicles." Indeed, Unno was what we would call today a sci-fi writer. His *Martian Army*, in which Martians invade Earth, borrowed ideas from H. G. Wells's *War of the Worlds* and met with tremendous success. Tezuka has declared that "every time an installment of *Martian Army* appeared in the *Mainichi Schoolchildren's Newspaper* I got so carried away I would forget even to eat, forget even to go to school. It was thanks to this same *Martian Army* that I got my start writing science fiction manga—got the idea of doing it."[13]

It was not only Tezuka who got "so carried away" that he would "forget even to eat." There were countless children like him. The writer Kita Morio also spent his childhood as an Unno fan.

> My middle school had a library where I worked to discharge the obligatory school chore. The most borrowed book in the library was Unno Jūzō's *Martian Army*, but not everyone who wanted to read it could do so. That was because I—taking advantage of my position—was reading it over and over again.[14]

There could be no greater compliment to a writer.

Martian Army may have been the product of Unno's peak period, but *The Capital Under Bombardment* was a product of his efforts to make a name for himself.

Unno Jūzō was born in 1897. In 1926 he graduated from Waseda University's Science and Engineering Division and found employment in the electrical examination laboratory of the Ministry of Communications. He was an engineer in wireless communications, who later became an author. It was an unusual background. Working at the laboratory, and at the same time contributing to youth-oriented science magazines, he was able to use his specialized knowledge to write novels. Unno began to make a name for himself when he was nearly thirty. He was no early bloomer.

The Capital Under Bombardment[15] was written when Unno Jūzō was thirty-four and his reputation was on the rise. It offers a fine display of his abilities. For one thing, his descriptions of various devices that were not yet well known stimulated the imaginations of his youthful readers. It was a veritable parade of truly colorful new military technology: gas masks, television, secret fortified underground bases, laser beams. These were imaginary prototypes, so to speak, of later developments. Television itself penetrated widely in Japan. Fittingly, in the late 1960s and early 1970s, the TV series *Ultraman* captivated children's imaginations by featuring other technologies Unno had described, proving their continuing appeal. It is not known just how far Unno, as a scientist, really believed this military technology could be achieved in reality. It would appear he was simply playing around with ideas in an imaginary world.

The gas masks appear at the very beginning of the novel. During the air raid on Tokyo, he envisions not only incendiary bombs being dropped but also poison gas being somehow disseminated.

The story begins with a scene of a father supping together with his family; they own a *geta* (wooden clog) shop in Asakusa in Tokyo. For his fiftieth birthday, his third son has given him an unusual present.

A gas mask! Ho, ho! Unusual product you've got here! So this is the latest toy, is it?

It is not clear whether the father is impressed or appalled. However, the son, who works at a rubber factory, wears a serious expression.

If Japan goes to war with foreign countries, these gas masks will definitely be needed. Tokyo? Bombers from enemy nations will fly over the city. Their five-ton bombs will leave the place as flattened and burnt out as it was after the Great Kanto Earthquake. And then enemy planes will surely come and spray poison gas as well.

But the father simply cannot fathom that enemy planes could attack Tokyo. The son tries hard to persuade him of the danger of such air strikes: "But there's no place easier to attack from the air than Tokyo! I read it in a magazine, and I heard some military officer give a speech about it." The father contradicts this, and they argue the point for a while.

"It's okay, son. The Japanese army has planes, the navy too. And plenty of them. On top of that, we [the citizenry] have contributed a hundred Patriot Planes. Besides, the Japanese military is powerful, my boy. This is Tokyo, where the Emperor himself resides. Do you think they would let enemy planes make even a move in this direction? You wouldn't know it yourself, but our defenses are very well drawn up."

"You can't secure the air! That officer said so!"

"Idiot! You say stuff like that in such a loud voice, you'll get scolded by the cops."

And so goes the conversation in this rather typical family. But the man's second son happens to work as seaman second class aboard a submarine stationed at Yokosuka. The submarine once crossed the Pacific all the way to the waters of California. The captain exhorted his men as follows:

The task of this craft is identical with that of our sister ships Nos. 102 and 103. Immediately before the American Atlantic and Pacific Fleets can move in concert to attack our land, we must intercept and inflict as much damage as possible. Our primary targets are sixteen battleships and eight aircraft carriers.

Meanwhile various political squabbles ensue and finally, on May 1, 193–, Japan and America break off diplomatic relations. Then, when declarations of war are issued, the content of newspapers and radio reports change completely. The following is typical of radio commentary at the time:

This just in: the main force of the joint U.S. fleet has finished assembling at Pearl Harbor, part of a larger effort now underway to merge the U.S. Pacific and Atlantic Fleets.

Ten days after war begins, a radio news program departs from its usual format. The Tokyo civil defense commander himself takes the microphone: "Attention: all Imperial subjects in the city and environs of Tokyo," he begins.

Our Empire has already issued a declaration of war against the United States of America. Our army and navy on the eastern front are waiting in the Pacific Ocean for the opportunity to attack, while in the west we are in the process of reducing Shanghai and the Philippines to our control. Hitherto, in the Sino-Japanese, Russo-Japanese, and German-Russian wars, and even after the Manchuria and Shanghai Incidents broke out in 1931 and 1932, the war zone has been located exclusively in foreign parts. Never have we permitted even a single enemy soldier to intrude upon the home islands. However, with the present Japan-U.S. conflict, circumstances have changed utterly. The battlefield cannot be restricted to foreign parts. We are forced to consider not only our colonies but even our own domestic areas, such as Tokyo and Osaka, as lying in the war zone. As you all know, this is because of the increase in the attack capabilities of military aircraft.

The commander concludes his address, "The fate of the Empire rests on your shoulders: give to this struggle your utmost efforts!" This is the best he can do—a plea for each listener to devise his own measures in response. In that respect, the *geta* manufacturer's third son showed clear foresight.

However, the preparations made by the Civil Defense Command against air raids are sufficient. Secret bases are constructed underneath Tokyo. The command post is one hundred meters underground and is provided with telephone service. There are also food and munitions, even a factory. All the necessary provisions have been made for living underground. But the details are somewhat dubious. For example, there is the method described for ensuring breathable air: the freshness of the air underground is maintained by fans in constant operation. In the event of a poison gas attack above, several layers of disinfectant doors will close automatically, sealing off and preserving the underground city. Additionally, microphones and "television swivel-scopes" (surveillance cameras) are mounted on the smokestacks of above-ground factories so that the underground city can always have some periscopic idea of what was happening up above.

At last an actual air raid warning is sounded in Tokyo. At the *geta* shop in Asakusa, everyone (thanks to the forethought of the third son) is provided with a gas mask. However, this third son has not yet delivered a gas mask to his eldest brother, who has set up a *geta* shop independently in Shinjuku, on the western side of Tokyo. So off he hurries to Shinjuku to deliver it.

While he is en route, the enemy planes arrive. This is described like a scene in a film:

The cluster of light shone in iridescent hues of apricot and white, indistinguishable as when molten iron flows. It fell rapidly, leaving behind it a string-like trail a foot wide as measured with one's outstretched arms.

Mizuno and Bywater came to fiction from backgrounds in military analysis and commentary. Many of their scenes smack of logic and ideation. They lack Unno's lively expressiveness. One understands how Tezuka Osamu could lose himself in Unno's writing.

Light and sound make a definite impression here. Although it is rather a case of beauty before fear.

Whoosh! A bolt of purple lightning! It came out of nowhere, flashing across the middle of the sky, crossing the beam of a searchlight.

"Oh," said someone, "that was an enemy plane."

How amazing. The plane's fuselage flashes like the iridescence of a dragonfly's abdomen. Taking aim, the antiaircraft guns let out a deafening barrage of concentrated fire and noise.

When I read this I was reminded of the following passage from Sakaguchi Ango's novel *One Woman's War*, written just after World War II:

As it floated into the shaft of the searchlight, even the pristine gray B-29 looked beautiful. The antiaircraft fire flashed, then in the midst of its "ack-ack-ack" came the scream of the B-29's bombs. Falling incendiary bombs, which spread and fell like fireworks. But only the vast, karmic conflagration down below could provide complete satisfaction.[16]

There are some definite points of resemblance.

The third son of the *geta* shop takes shrapnel in his left leg and is knocked to the pavement. He then crawls to a nearby farmhouse, seeking refuge. There, he hears on the radio the strains of Chopin's "Funeral March."

Meanwhile, the commander in chief of America's Pacific Fleet is monitoring the theater of operations via television. He orders all the air forces under his command to commence an assault. A giant air armada of two thousand planes heads for Tokyo.

But the curtain falls on this narrative all too soon. A new weapon developed by the Japanese military appears: a destructive "monster ray" that shoots down all two thousand American planes one after another.

* * *

UNNO'S FANS steadily increased. And from his novels the youth of the day learned no fear. What was transmitted instead was palm-sweating excitement and hope for the future that science would bring about.

Mizuno, on the other hand, having been stuck by the authorities with the leftist propaganda label, found his own sphere of activities shrinking under such constraints. His nephew, Shigematsu Fukio, who was extremely fond of him, reports the following incident.[17] Once, walking with his uncle in the vicinity of the house, they heard footsteps behind them. The steps kept to a fixed pace and followed them without pause. "Don't turn and look," said his uncle. "It's the *Tokkō* [Special Higher Police]." Mizuno himself faced forward and whispered to Shigematsu as he walked.

Nor was the harassment limited to the Special Higher Police. On August 25, 1933, inaugural ceremonies were held at the Toyōken restaurant at the Hibiya Civic Auditorium for the Association of the Far Eastern Friends of Peace, with Mizuno listed as one of the founding organizers. As Mizuno was delivering his welcoming comments, a group of right-wing men heckled him from outside, banging on the windows. Finally, they forced open a window and several of these men invaded the hall, treading on the tatami mats in their shoes. At that, a group of police, waiting in readiness, entered the hall through the doorway. Making a show of chasing away the rightists, they shouted, "Disperse! Disperse!" This forced both the rightists and Mizuno's group to quit the hall; the ceremony was halted. When the circumstances of this incident were reported incorrectly in the newspapers, Mizuno printed up a flyer of his own, "Concerning My Peace Movement," which he distributed as widely as possible. In it he wrote,

> As someone with military knowledge and experience, I know better than the average person the atrociousness and tragedy of modern warfare. My intention is to make sure that our nation and our people do not become mired in the horrors of this new war. . . . No matter how highly trained and skilled our armed forces, and no matter how arrogant the boastings of the military, it is not difficult to imagine the outcome of a war waged against the rest of the world. That is the true motive for my advocacy of peace.

The document continued, and its conclusion was, "The best defense is to take the offensive. But the surest victory lies in not fighting."

CHAPTER TWELVE

The Advent of Writers Who
Had Never Known War

A MERICA was and has been for Japan like some giant mirror ball reflecting myriad shards of light. Jazz, fashion, film, automobiles. Starting in the Taishō period (1912–26), this was the stuff that Japanese dreams were made of.

Even with regard to their own national status as a military power, the Japanese were content to flatter themselves on their brilliance when they were merely awash in the reflected illumination of the mirror ball. It was very sad, I feel. I wonder if this began with the sense of victimization Japanese have harbored deep down ever since the advent of Perry's Black Ships. The idea of an air raid on Tokyo was taken up thematically not only by the famous youth fiction writer Unno Jūzō, but by many Japan-U.S. future-war chronicles. My purpose in trying to pick them out now from the trash heap of history is to identify in them the original forms of specific mental constructs that must have shaped the consciousness of the present day. For military power could one substitute economic power? Well...I won't deny that such considerations inform my concerns.

Many of the Japan-U.S. future-war chronicles can be described as heroic. But is this true heroism, or is it rather the inverse of a sense of victimization? As we have already noted, awareness of the new threat posed by the military use of aircraft first appeared in Japan-U.S. future-war chronicles in 1932. Aerial weapons invade Tokyo Bay like new Black Ships. But while Mizuno Hironori's *Japan and America: The Battle for Dominance* gloomily indicted air raids as horrific tragedies, Unno Jūzō's *The Capital Under Bombardment* regarded air raids less as fearful calamities than as thrilling plot devices. I'd like now to introduce several archetypal authors of Japan-U.S. future-war chronicles who are similar to Jūzō, because collectively their awareness of "the enemy" was so remarkably different from Mizuno's.

The first one I want to take up is Fukunaga Kyōsuke, whose "Blazing Super-Ray," which appeared in the April 1932 issue of *Tatakai* (Battle), told of a new Japanese weapon that handily knocked enemy aircraft out of the sky as they attacked Tokyo. It thus bore a close resemblance to the conclusion of Unno's *The Capital Under Bombardment*. But its publication preceded that of Jūzō's book. His conception was not original. In any event, in Fukunaga's story the Japanese Combined Fleet is annihilated by America's Pacific Fleet. "The mystery as to why this happened was revealed in a newspaper interview with a crew member of a submarine that was the sole survivor of the battle." As the crew member puts it,

> The problem, bud, was the planes. Even with the planes the army brought in from Island X, we only had 400 planes. Against that, the enemy fleet's expeditionary air force sent up 1200 planes. This wasn't even close to being a match.

By the time that the Japanese could regard their Combined Fleet as world-class in terms of actual fighting strength, they had a new and difficult problem to face: a new weapon, the military airplane. In youth-oriented tales such as Fukunaga's, it was common to achieve an instant turnaround by entrusting the task of defense to a fictional weapon.

In Hirata Shinsaku's *Task Force Shōwa*, serialized in *Shōnen Kurabu* (Youth Club) in 1934, the Super-Ray becomes the Aoki Ray, after its inventor, a Dr. Aoki. Once again, there are strong similarities to Unno (and Fukunaga). Consider the following scene:

> The four surviving seaplanes made a beeline for us: now they were human-guided missiles. Enemy though they be, they were brave. But when they were struck by the Aoki Ray, every one of the poor pilots and their planes became bundles of flame and went down ablaze.[1]

In all such tales, Japan is at the mercy of the airplane, but the airplane is in turn done in by a superior new weapon. In reality, however, these new Japanese weapons did not exist. As a product of military training, Mizuno thought logically about war. His gloominess was a matter of course. He knew that new weapons could not be made to spring forth by sleight of hand.

The Japan-U.S. future-war chronicles, on the other hand, were all products of the authors' imaginations. But among these imaginative authors, the perspectives of those who had experienced war and of those who had not proved vastly different.

By 1932, already a quarter-century had elapsed since the Russo-Japanese War. That real war would soon begin to recede in memory. It was by no means strange that mainstream Japan-U.S. future-war chronicle writers would begin to be comprised of a generation for whom battle scenes did not correspond to personal experience.

Bungei shunju (The Literary Arts in All Seasons), a prestigious literary and general interest magazine, organized a roundtable discussion that threw together both military men and civilians, from both the Russo-Japanese War generation and the postwar generation. The transcript was carried in the magazine's April 1932 issue and was titled "The Shanghai Incident and the World War: A Roundtable Discussion." Two notable participants were Fukunaga Kyōsuke and Hirata Shinsaku. Comments were also contributed by Mikami Otokichi, author of *The Transformation of Yukinojō* and *Lady Yodo*. Hirata was twenty-eight years old; Fukunaga was forty-three; Mikami was thirty-eight.

Mizuno Hironori was not invited, but retired Lieutenant Commander Ishimaru Tōda did appear. Ishimaru attended the Naval Academy three classes behind Mizuno and three ahead of Yamamoto Isoroku. He was now fifty-three years old. He had served in the Russo-Japanese War. With regard not only to his career trajectory but also his expressed views, Ishimaru— who was also a military commentator and a writer of Japan-U.S. future-war chronicles—held the position closest to Mizuno's. He may not have been as radical as Mizuno, who was deemed worthy of surveillance by the Special Higher Police, but he also kept the lid on any pro-war rhetoric. One would have to classify him as a moderate.

The roundtable discussion led off with the Shanghai Incident, but gradually the topic shifted to the matter of a Japan-U.S. war. As the ripples of the Shanghai Incident spread outward, international opinion had mounted against Japan, leaving it isolated. Ishimaru clearly stated the pessimistic outlook: that the West would impose an economic blockade.

The only way to defeat Japan would be to make it a war of endurance. It's the same with an economic blockade. The Westerners know this, too. So if we do not construct a plan that will let us persevere for four years or even five years, we will be defeated. But if we are subject to an economic blockade, can we really persevere for four or five years? I think it is dangerous.

Hirata, who was born the year the Russo-Japanese War broke out (1904), argued a contrary position, saying, "All we need in this time of crisis is the sense of crisis." If they only had that, they could make do or do without, so that "even a complete rupture of economic relations is nothing to be afraid of." This nicely brings out the contrast between Ishimaru, who remembered that in the Russo-Japanese War Japan was not a powerful nation and scored a pyrrhic victory over Russia, and Hirata, who had had no actual experience of war.

At this point, a reporter for *Bungei shunju* asked Hirata, "If a Japan-U.S. war came about, do you think Japan would win?" Hirata stated his basic theory as follows:

> [America] will build aircraft carriers and 10,000-ton cruisers, and the skies over Tokyo and other cities will be filled with their attack planes. Or they'll attack our provincial cities. If they adopt such stratagems they'll catch us off guard and we'll be in trouble.

So, he added by way of explanation, "The only way to win will be to smash whatever the other side sends up against you." In his own novel for boys, that is achieved by the Aoki Ray, which knocks the enemy's planes out of the sky, but...

At this point, Fukunaga broke in. "It'd be an easy win, wouldn't it—if it happened now." One assumes that his phrase "if it happened now" implies that once the air war became central, Japan might not win.

> [In the event of an air attack] in rather short order, we'd be in trouble. They'll be able to hit Japan from Honolulu. Either that, or they'll come via the Aleutians. We don't know what direction they'll come from. So Tokyo has to be prepared for the worst. Even so, it's not as if we'll be wiped out. We shall endure. And those underground shelters should do the trick.

This phrase "underground shelters" recalls the facilities described in Unno's *The Capital Under Bombardment*.

Why Mikami, author of *The Transformation of Yukinojō*, was included in the roundtable is unclear—perhaps it was to represent the readers. But his comments were breathtakingly irresponsible:

> To hear you experts talk, America is about to start a war with us in short order. But why shouldn't we be more aggressive? Why wait?

This flummoxed even the wily Hirata. His arguments had been based on counterattacking the adversary as it struck. That was how his novel was written.

Mikami now spoke even more forcefully.

> Isn't it weak just to strive to pay our taxes and wait for a losing struggle? Better to forge ahead.

I think this exchange gives an idea of the general atmosphere prevailing among the participants.

Other active-duty military officers were present: from the navy, Captain Yasutomi Shōzō and from the army General Staff, Lieutenant Colonel Nemoto Hiroshi. Both were in their forties. From *Bungei Shunju*, not only were its columnists present, but President Kikuchi Kan and Sasaki Mosaku also attended in the capacity of emcees.

Let us return to Mikami's question: rather than wait, wouldn't it be better to go on the attack? Hirata countered with a last-ditch proposal: "We must become so powerful that our adversary would never dare to attack us."

Mikami consented with the proviso, "Well, then, we have to build up our military." But he was still racked with uneasiness. "Isn't the U.S. a step ahead of us?" Hirata replied,

> As things stand now, I think that is the case.

Kikuchi Kan had been listening to this exchange in silence. Now, unable to bear it any longer, he intervened:

> But even if we wage war against the U.S., we have no chance of conquering it, right?

It was a commonsensical point. Mikami replied dejectedly, "I guess in the end it wouldn't work, would it." But Hirata remained supremely confident:

"We can control them [America] by the use we make of our air force."

Starting perhaps last year, the navy has been building the best flying boat in the world. And our army is building the best airplanes in the world. So our aviation community gives us a hint as to how to achieve a breakthrough success."

This business about a "hint" entailed some problems. They were building "the best airplanes in the world," but no one knew when these would be completed. As in the conclusion to his novel, we get a substitution—wishful thinking.

If our technical experts apply themselves rigorously and make something great, then even if we can't compare in quantity, we can still put up a good fight, can't we?

Thus we see an unfolding of the most arbitrary, self-indulgent imaginings. In contrast to this, the military men reacted coolly. Yasutomi was clear: "The U.S. will not unilaterally undertake a Japan-U.S. war." And when Mikami asked, "Don't military commanders ever find their passions inflamed, so that they just leap into action?" Lieutenant Colonel Nemoto turned a cold shoulder: "Providing levelheaded judgment is the core responsibility of the Central Command."

When we consider the meaning of militarism, I think that we might find here something that could shatter conventional wisdom. There is no question that military men led the nation into war. But it is also true that popular opinion overrode the doubts of some military professionals, calling them to war regardless. One might also say that the Japan-U.S. future-war chronicles, situated on the tricky border between the military and popular opinion, served as both listening posts and loudspeakers.

In any event, it was commonly accepted among writers of Japan-U.S. future-war chronicles that if war broke out between the two countries, enemy aircraft would drop bombs on Tokyo. From Mizuno to Hirata, notwithstanding differences of opinion or of generational outlook, their forecasting in this regard proved to be right on target. So it would be fair to say that the Japanese public—the readers of these Japan-U.S. future-war chronicles—had some presentiments as well.

In fact, both military thinking and popular opinion were running along the same lines. In August of the following year, 1933, a large-scale Kanto air defense drill was held. The hypothetical basis was formulated by the Tokyo Civil Defense Command as follows: "At the height of the naval battle in the Pacific, enemy aircraft carriers, one by one, approach the coasts of the home islands. There is considerable reason to fear that in ten days time our Imperial Capital will come under aerial attack." In addition to Tokyo itself, four adjacent prefectures participated in the drill: Kanagawa, Chiba, Saitama, and Ibaragi.

The scenario called for American airplanes to invade Tokyo airspace, scattering poison gas and incendiary bombs. The military had their own drills to follow. They primed their antiaircraft guns to knock enemy planes out of the sky, and they scrambled combat aircraft to intercept the invaders. For the city's residents, their main efforts were directed at practicing evacuations and firefighting.

From far away, Kiryū Yūyū, the editor in chief of the *Shinano Mainichi* newspaper, mocked this overblown event in an August 11 editorial titled, THE GREAT KANTO AIR DEFENSE DRILL: WHAT A LAUGH! This incurred the wrath of the military, and Kiryū was obliged to resign from the paper. When we reconsider this famous event in the light of Japan-U.S. future-war chronicles, we have a much better understanding of what Kiryū was trying to suggest. Specifically, that the very idea of intercepting enemy planes in the Kanto skies, in the skies above the Empire's capital, signals the defeat of the Japanese military. If enemy planes were intruding to such an extent, Japan had already lost the war. (And indeed the Great Tokyo Air Raid proved that to be the case at the end of the Pacific War.) Besides, Kiryū added, if such an incursion were made, no matter how many enemy aircraft were intercepted, they could not all be stopped. Even if only two or three got through and dropped their bombs, Tokyo would be a sea of flames.

Kiryū no doubt had read the Japan-U.S. future-war chronicles of Mizuno, Hirata, and Fukunaga. He pointed out that if the enemy used infrared rays, then no matter how dark or recessed the hiding places, Japanese would be targeted and destroyed. And while the enemy already had infrared, no one on the Japanese side had any Super-Ray.

[It was] a bright, hot day. One's very shadow seemed sun-bleached. The B-29s, which usually appeared against the sky like scattered, silvery sand, were today nowhere to be seen. The sky was achingly blue. It was a fantastic scene. I was playing at my favorite spot, a shrine to Inari.[2] The trees provided shade, and I climbed a pine tree and sat on a branch with my legs dangling down. A fourth-grader who was a friend of mine came by.

"Hey, Japan lost!" he said.

"What do you mean, 'lost'? We've got *Submarine Fuji*, don't we?" I said.

"Yeah, but we lost," he said.

"So what happened to the *Fuji*?"

That was how, as a second-grader at a public school, the children's literature author Futagami Hirokazu experienced Japan's actual defeat.[3]

In Hirata Shinsaku's *Task Force Shōwa*, one finds not only the Aoki Ray but also a submarine that flies through the air. This is *Submarine Fuji*. The comment, "We've got *Submarine Fuji*, don't we?" makes it seem as though the child is missing a marble or two. However, there is also something here that tugs strangely at our heartstrings. The students at the public school believed that *Submarine Fuji* really existed as some sort of super-weapon. Youth-oriented Japan-U.S. future-war chronicles thus achieved a narrative space that comprised an imagined reality in which the imaginary was also felt to be real.

How could I, as someone born in the postwar period, make sense of this sort of mindset? I can't say I didn't rack my brain over it. I tried multiple readings of Hirata Shinsaku's works. As I closed and opened his books, I began to feel my way toward some sort of understanding.

And then one day, I had a chance revelation. As I was seated on a bench on the subway platform with a copy of *Girl's Club* magazine (which I had just obtained from the library) open to Hirata's "High Seas in the Pacific," an elderly man of an agreeable appearance spoke to me. "Hah, you've got yourself something unusual there!" The old man immediately arrived at the conclusion that I had been struggling toward myself.

Hirata Shinsaku, huh? To us, his stuff's like [Defoe's] *Robinson Crusoe* or [Verne's] *A Two-Year's Holiday*. Adventure stories.

He began to tell me about himself, how he had wanted to be a sailor and had finally joined the navy. But then the subway train pulled in with a deafening roar. The old man made a dash for it, and he disappeared through its doors. It was all over in an instant. I realize it may sound as though I'm taking liberties here, but this episode really happened!

The Akutagawa Prize–winning author Otsuji Katsuhiko, who also works as an artist under the name Akasegawa Genpei, has described in a newspaper article the excitement with which he read Hirata's work. It was a piece in the *Sankei* newspaper for May 15, 1988, and it carried the subtitle, "A Scientifically Realistic, Militaristic Sci-Fi Thriller That I Read Bursting with Excitement."

> The content was that of a militaristic sci-fi novel, so I read it bursting with excitement. It concerned an Oriental country called Yashima. This was perhaps Japan. Then there was some katakana [foreign] country whose name I have forgotten. This was perhaps America. The two countries go to war, and a variety of new weapons take the stage. It wasn't simply some fantastic tale constructed out of whole cloth: it was extremely realistic. I thought the airship that can stop in midair, which appears toward the end of the novel, was terrific. There were no helicopters at that time, or if they existed they were not in widespread use.

Otsuji is full of expressions such as "the metallic sounds were . . ." and "a naked human voice" and "it made me feel grown-up." But he does state that "I'm not sure if I read it during the war or after the war. At war's end I was in third grade, so perhaps I read it after the war. But I was so cocky as to read the books my elder brother read."

I should like to offer some further proofs of Hirata's influence. The poet and radio author Kawasaki Hiroshi was fifteen at the end of the war. His *My Youth in a Militarist Nation* includes reminiscences of Hirata's *The New Warship Takachiho*.

> What I recall straight off is Hirata Shinsaku's *The New Warship Takachiho*. It was serialized in 1935 in *Shōnen Kurabu* [Youth Club], but I think I read it when it came out later as a book. I've almost completely forgotten the contents, but this was a truly amazing warship. After it sees tremendous action, it is greeted in the Japan Sea by the *Nagato* and other ships the Japanese navy actually had at the time. The *Nagato* looked outclassed. Somehow I remember this strange stuff.[4]

Hirata's widow Yōko told this author in 1992 that every month *Youth Club* and Hirata's other publishers would receive several cardboard boxes' worth of fan mail, which they would deliver to his home. Japanese kids would write things like, "As long as Mr. Hirata is around, Japan will not lose." Even as an eighty-three-year-old she remembered such sentiments vividly. Which is why this lady, in her chaste purple kimono, could comment that "if anyone, because they read his books, died thinking they did so for the nation, to that extent I myself have no right to happiness."[5]

At the 1932 *Bungei shunju* roundtable, Hirata commented, "If Japanese engineers work hard and produce something good, then even if we're out-numbered we'll be able to put up a pretty good fight, don't you think?" Writers of the generation that had not experienced the Russo-Japanese War heard this message of scientific and technological optimism—and believed that putting up a good fight was the most important thing. One might say that Hirata's Japan-U.S. future-war chronicle was itself an expression of this wish. However, at this point we must ascertain precisely what significance he placed upon America as the hypothetical enemy in that novel.

The protagonist of *Task Force Shōwa* is Dr. Aoki's younger brother, Kiyo. He is still a middle school student (under the old school system), but is so brilliant that even at this age he compares favorably to students in the engineering department of Tokyo Imperial University. Also featured is Dr. Aoki's beautiful young niece, Akiyo.

The scenes in which these two youngsters appear are shot through with fantasy. For example, at the secret Blue Sea Island naval base south of Hachijōjima, the destroyer *Mogami* traverses a cliff-lined passage on its way into the harbor. The passage looks like a ravine, with banks of the black-est black extending indeterminably. In the channel at the bottom of the ravine proceeds our battleship, the *Mogami*, propelled ever farther along by tremendous ocean currents. Two small figures appear, moving on the deck near the bow. One of the figures is that of a young woman whose beauty could conquer even the black of night. A red wool hat is perched on her head; she is wrapped in a panther-skin overcoat.

"I'm a bit frightened. How far in do these locks go?"

With her round, jet-black eyes she peers deep into the distance. The towering cliffs soar high, and in the distance they appear to converge enough to obstruct the passage of the ship. They cannot discern how far the channel extends before it opens onto a harbor.

"Akiyo-chan, this is the entrance to Hell," murmurs the second tiny figure, a handsome, ruddy-faced youth wearing the uniform of a chief petty officer. The color in his cheeks, the sparkle in his eye. You're sure that you've has seen this somewhere before. Oh, it's Kiyoshi! There at the bow of the light cruiser *Mogami*, he draws himself up to his full height, crosses his arms, and stands, stock-still.

In fact it is a four-cruiser battle group spearheaded by the *Mogami*, and it is called Task Force Shōwa. One gets an impression of sci-fi elements added to Jules Verne's *A Two-Year Holiday*. And if it seems strange that two teenagers, one boy and one girl, should be chatting familiarly on the deck of a warship, well, perhaps it is best not to demand too many answers. The evening of their deployment, the young lad and lass are asked by the task-force commander, "I am about to lead you now into battle. How about it, Akiyo-san? Are you afraid?" Her reply: "Oh, my! No." And thus the adventure-loving lass acquiesces on the spot. The writer knows full well that in reality, war is no picnic, yet he finds the young boy and girl perfectly suited as stand-ins for his readers, reporting on the events of the story and sharing their experience of this adventure called war.

In one scene, Task Force Shōwa clashes with the American navy at Midway Island. The Task Force Shōwa flagship, the *Mogami*, is equipped with the Aoki Ray mentioned above. The vast, 324-ship American armada—comprised of 15 battleships, 7 aircraft carriers, 15 heavy cruisers, 15 light cruisers, 3 aircraft-equipped cruisers, 164 destroyers, 57 submarines, and 48 special-duty ships—is entirely obliterated by a single Japanese cruiser, the *Mogami*. On the deck of the *Mogami*, a boastful commander brags to the young boy and girl about the result: "What did you think of that? Just like hunting, wasn't it?" Akiyo replies, "Yes, a grand hunt over the entire Pacific!"

As the narrator explains to the reader, "Akiyo-san wants to die a martyr's death, but the enemy's bullets have not found their mark, and she has not yet become a Jeanne d'Arc."

The account continues. The *Mogami* forces the enemy to retreat, but the enemy then develops a new bomber aircraft, which drops poison gas on Task Force Shōwa. But never fear: the Japanese then invent *Submarine Fuji*.

Its gunwales concealed wings. These giant wings were now outstretched, emitting jets of pale bluish-white sparks: rocket plumes. Ah, hah: so this is how the *Fuji* manages to navigate the heavens: it is rocket-propelled! But it makes no sound. This is a silent airship.

With the advent of this matchless new weapon, *Submarine Fuji*, the Japanese finally succeed in forcing a complete enemy withdrawal, and the story's ending is a happy one.

Task Force Shōwa thus captured the hearts of the youth of Japan, who cried as one, "How could we lose? We've got *Submarine Fuji!*" And what could be more natural when war is presented as an adventure than for youngsters to want to participate in that adventure?

The enemy referred to in this novel is unquestionably America. However, America's role is itself merely symbolic and instrumental. It is essentially a device in an adventure story.

Hirata's view of war is clear and simple, as he demonstrates in a passage from *Our Army, Our Navy*, published in 1932:

> There are two kinds of war. One is the unjust war. The other is the just war. We must absolutely never engage in an unjust war. Japan's military forces would absolutely never engage in a dishonorable war. But a righteous war, a just war, they will fight no matter how far afield they must go. No matter how strong the enemy, no matter how great the enemy, if the war is just, our military will not be the least afraid but will rise to the occasion and face their foe.

One craves some explanation of the meaning of just and unjust, but Hirata merely concludes with simplistic moralizing:

> The Japanese military does not want to become an unjust military. They want to push through to victory, no matter where or when, as a just military force. And as long as they obey the Emperor's commands, there will be no stain of dishonor upon the Japanese military.

Hirata's Japan-U.S. future-war chronicles, starting with *Task Force Shōwa*, were published mainly in *Shōnen Kurabu* (Youth Club). This magazine was founded in November 1914 by a forerunner of the Kōdansha publishing company. By 1935, circulation reached 750,000; it had become a major periodical. In its issues were published many famous works, whose names still ring bells: Satō Kōroku's *A Cherry Petal in My Sake Cup*; Ōsaragi Jirō's *The Goblin Man of Mt. Kurama*; Yamanaka Minetarō's *Three Hundred Leagues Behind Enemy Lines* and *Dawn in Asia*; Takagaki Hitomi's *Our Hero, Black Hood*; Tagawa Suihō's *Blackie, the Stray Cat*; Shimada Keizō's *Adventures of Dankichi*; Edogawa Ranpō's *The Man with Twenty Disguises*... And that is just to list a few that come immediately to mind. Other regular contributors included Yokomitsu Riichi, Kataoka Teppei, Yoshiya Nobuko, Uno

Kōji, Naoki Sanjūgo, Kojima Masajirō, and Mikami Otokichi. *Shōnen Kurabu* sold well, and the books it spawned also sold well. Hirata was the preeminent author of Japan-U.S. future-war chronicles.

However, as I have already noted above, the reason these works sold so well was not because they fanned the flames of war. They sold as adventure tales and as science fiction. This is because readers were able to indulge in such things. In *My History of the Shōwa Period*, Yasuoka Shōtarō includes a reminiscence indicative of the prosperity of that era.

> It was from around that time [i.e., the Manchurian Incident of 1931] that—even if we were ultimately fooling ourselves—things definitely started looking up economically. Even my aunt, who used to use words like "fired" and "unemployed" a lot, stopped using them so much. And my mom stopped grumbling about "salary cuts."[6]

Between the Manchurian Incident of 1931 and the inception of an all-out Japan-China war in 1937, Japan's economy showed an upward trend. People felt that their lives were getting easier, and that encouraged boys to set their hearts and minds on the future. They felt that science promised a better future.

Both Hirata Shinsaku and the author we shall examine next, Fukunaga Kyōsuke, targeted these affluent youngsters and were able to amass fortunes writing Japan-U.S. future-war chronicles. Hirata began his writing career in earnest when he was twenty-five years old. Three years later he was living in a 1,155 square-meter mansion, with numerous disciples—live-in students or young writers who studied with him and also did chores about the house. And yet his widow Yōko says that contrary to the clear message of his novels, he told her he really felt that "if we fight America now, we'll lose. We don't have enough airplanes."

Rather than Mizuno Hironori's accurate reporting of Japan's gloomy prospects, it was Hirata's rosy visions of the future, laced with lies, that made readers feel good.

* * *

SINCE THE ELITE of the Japanese navy breathed a different atmosphere from that of the rest of tiny Japan, relatively more of them were high-collar types, meaning Japanese proud of their Western lifestyle. Fukunaga Kyōsuke, for example, resigned his commission as lieutenant commander at the age of thirty-four when he was diagnosed with tuberculosis, but later become an author of Japan-U.S. future-war chronicles. Fukunaga lived in Kamakura and had a villa at Lake Nojiri in Nagano Prefecture. He engaged in outdoor recreations such as yachting and skiing. He owned a German-made camera and developed the film himself. He would even go backstage at the SKD (Shōchiku Kageki Dan [Shōchiku Song and Dance Troupe]) and take pictures of his old acquaintance, the singer-actress Mizunoe Takiko, in the green room. His house in Kamakura was a Western-style building without a single tatami room. Naturally enough, he did not take off his shoes in the Japanese manner, but instead wore them around the house. Fukunaga had a bed to sleep on, not a futon, and the house was equipped with a Western-style toilet as well. Even on New Year's Day, that most central and traditional of Japanese holidays, he had bread and coffee. In his leisure time he would listen on the latest gramophone to French *chanson*.

Previous writers of Japan-U.S. future-war chronicles had had their own independent, even warped, sentiments, but as this lifestyle of Fukunaga's suggests, he presented a somewhat more clear-cut, distinctive profile. Mizuno Hironori, born into a lower-ranking samurai family, had grown up in extreme poverty, experienced the Russo-Japanese War, had personally witnessed a Europe devastated by World War I, and then took up writing because he had something he wanted to say. Homer Lea, for all his lucidity, bore up under serious handicaps, his twisted frame embodying a romantic desire to be respected as a general. Hector Bywater's experiences as a spy for England during World War I cast a shadow across his countenance. Even the Sōseki disciple Ikezaki Tadayoshi (originally known as Akagi Kōhei) was constantly tormented by his feelings of rivalry with Akutagawa Ryūnosuke. All these men wrote Japan-U.S. future-war chronicles from personal motives. But Fukunaga was free of all such feelings.

In the preface to one of his best-known works, *A Future Chronicle of the Japan-U.S. War*, Fukunaga asserts that all previous such works were "like chewing wax, they're so tedious, full of theorizing about strategy on too difficult a level." Not entertaining in the least, he states. Their authors prided themselves on their abilities as professional writers. But "to conjure up a castle in the air, to make the readers thirst for more, and then still more, requires skills of no ordinary caliber."

If we posit Mizuno and the others as authors of pure literature, then Fukunaga was a writer of entertainment literature. Having said that, we should recognize that he was at first a military man, who had had to cut short his hopes of a career in the military, his tuberculosis proving too much of an obstacle. He had attended the Naval Academy, a minority of whose graduates—those of great promise and with superior records—went on to the Naval War College. Fukunaga Kyōsuke was one of the chosen, and his career proceeded on track. In 1917, he served as staff officer on a special convoy escorting a destroyer, custom-made in Japan for France, to Malta in the Mediterranean. It was immediately upon his return to Japan that he entered the hospital.

His illness was not that grievous at first. For a time it looked like he was heading for recovery, and he even went off to France in hope of becoming a painter. This sort of maneuver would have been impossible had he not come from a wealthy family. While he was in France, a publisher asked him for a translation of a French novel, and he was gradually drawn into the writing business.

It was around this time that Fukunaga published in the mass-circulation journal *Chūō Kōron* (The Central Review) his arguments for the "roman-ization" of Japanese. Everything in our outmoded language—the *hiragana* and *katakana* syllabaries and the *kanji* or Sino-Japanese characters—should be converted, he said, into romanized (read Latin) script. This would seem to be a brutal approach to language, but his manner of stating it was mild, consistent with his elegantly narrow features, the pleasingly defined ridge of his nose, the gentle image he projected.

This romanizing modernist-cum-entertainer was hardly interested in dragging along the burden of the past. Rather, he frankly (or perhaps I should say, naively) obsessed about the future. As to why—that was because the future was where his readers were going to come from.

In *A Future Chronicle of the Japan-U.S. War*, Fukunaga Kyōsuke projected that air supremacy would become a key factor in war. This novel was pub-lished by Shinchō Sha as a special supplement to the 1934 New Year's issue of their monthly periodical *Hinode* (Sunrise). While a supplement, it took the form of a paperback book. *Hinode*, by the way, had been founded two years earlier to compete with *King*, a major periodical put out by the Dai Nippon Yūbenkai Kōdan Sha, a forerunner of the Kōdansha publishing company.

The Washington Naval Limitation Treaty, it will be recalled, required Great Britain, the United States, and Japan to maintain a 5:5:3 ratio in the tonnage of capital ships in their navies. The treaty was set to expire in 1936.

Fukunaga's narrative begins with a breakdown in a Second Washington Conference on Naval Arms Limitation held in 1935. At last there dawns an era of unrestricted competition in naval shipbuilding. Given the differences in economic strength between Japan and the U.S., a gap begins to grow between the two countries in terms of numbers of ships.

A young officer reflects sensitively on this state of military tension. One day, a hot-blooded young destroyer commander, Lieutenant Maki Eitarō, launches—on his own initiative—a torpedo strike against an American cruiser anchored off Shanghai, blowing it up. His scheme is to bring the two countries into a state of war before the gap in fleet size can grow any larger. More news is carried on the radio:

> To repeat this stunning special report: at 4:15 this afternoon, the *Houston*, a ship in America's Asiatic Fleet, was attacked and sunk today off Ulsan. More news is coming in: stay tuned.

America's Pacific Fleet is now heading for Japanese waters. Japan's Combined Fleet heads east across the Pacific to engage the approaching foe. The ensuing description is certainly more skillfully drawn than what one finds in Mizuno's writing. A table lamp throws into relief the profiled features of Admiral Nagano as he pores over his nautical charts. His salt-and-pepper hair, his broad, wise forehead. The light of a keen intelligence gleams in his eyes. His large mouth expresses the gravest determination.

"Humph," says the captain, raising his head, to the chief of staff beside him. "So how do the two forces compare with respect to air power?"

The chief of staff is a small man but a font of knowledge. He reels off statistics pertaining to combat aircraft. Thus the war's conclusion is presented as being all about air supremacy: 126 American military aircraft vs. 105 in the Japanese fleet's air wing. America is superior.

However, under the cloak of night, a Japanese destroyer sinks an American aircraft carrier. The Japanese Air Force's chief of staff reports that "the enemy's combat aircraft now number 72. With our 105 aircraft, we now definitely have superiority." But the developments around this part of the narrative come a little too conveniently. And finally, holding air supremacy, the Japanese Combined Fleet finds the American fleet to be nothing more than a paper tiger.

> If you're shooting at a completely silent enemy—in other words, even when you get a hit, you're also not getting any return fire, not so much

as a single shot—then it isn't really a battle. It's just target practice. And so it was in this case. For the Japanese fleet, it was about as tough as twisting a baby's arm. The distance was short, but not a single enemy shell came in. For our part, we could, at our own unhurried pace, use aerial spotting to sink ship after ship.

The battle now over—the victory awarded to Japan—the novel concludes with the following description of the protagonist's postwar activities:

Half a year later, he set sail from Yokohama on the *Chichibu Maru*, bound for the new colony at Honolulu. Loaded on board was a bronze statue of Admiral Maki, to be erected in a public park at Waikiki in commemoration of Japan's victory.

So Hawaii was now a colony of Japan.

That this ending would stir up controversy in America was something even a dove like Fukunaga Kyōsuke did not imagine. But the Hawaiian vernacular newspaper, the *Hawaii Hoichi*, reported the following on December 14, 1933:

The No. 1 Supplement of the magazine *Hinode*, brought into port on the 12th inst. by the *Chichibu Maru* and containing the novel *A Future Chronicle of the Japan-U.S. War* by navy lieutenant commander Fukunaga Kyōsuke, was abruptly seized by local customs authorities. . . . Customs Commissioner Doyle sent several copies to authorities in the U.S. Army and Navy, and incinerated almost the entire rest of the 2,000-copy shipment.

This news also reached Japan. It also transpired that newspapers affiliated with the Hearst syndicate had translated and printed the novel in their papers, raising quite a fuss. As the *Ōsaka Mainichi* newspaper reported on January 17, 1934:

The U.S.-Japan war hypothesis carried in the magazine *Hinode* (Sunrise), which was the object of the confiscation incident at Honolulu, has struck a nerve with the American public, and is increasingly serving as fuel for inflammatory newspaper articles. The *Washington Herald* began serializing the entire work in English translation on the 15th, and the Hearst syndicate's newspapers around the country have followed suit, giving it special prominence.

Undoubtedly it was not simply the Japanese victory but Japan's acquisition of Hawaii as a colony that made the novel's outcome so unpleasant for American readers. And yet, as the *Hawaii Bulletin* noted, "It has the same character as some record of the exploration of Mars, or a work of science fiction." This was, after all, entertainment. So why did it provoke such an extreme response?

The genre of the Japan-U.S. future-war chronicle was a product of fantasies shared and fostered by both Japan and the U.S., two nations that faced each other across the Pacific. Homer Lea's *The Valor of Ignorance* and Parabellum's *BANZAI!* fanned fears of the Japanese threat; Mizuno Hironori's *The Next Battle* urged that measures be taken against the threat posed by America.

Moreover, the merchants of crisis who hyped the threat of the "other" nation were not simply authors and critics. Hearst newspapers used these controversies to boost circulation, and military backers contributed their own information in efforts to curb trends in public opinion that favored arms limitation.

But things were not that simple either. The fatalistic schemata one sees in the Japan-U.S. future-war chronicles take on forms different from ordinary xenophobia. Just as the Black Ships deeply wounded the Japanese psyche in ways that were not easily healed, so too in America the Japanese immigrant problem was rooted in fears of an inscrutable alien culture.

Prior Japan-U.S. future-war chronicles on the American side all had plots that involved residents of Japanese ancestry in Hawaii or the West Coast rising up and taking action in concert with the Japanese military. From this it is easy enough to see which way the wind was blowing in the U.S. Then there is the actual incarceration of Americans of Japanese descent— but not those of German or Italian descent—during World War II. One has to think that, among Americans, some fear of Japan as an inscrutable alien culture was indeed in play.

That Fukunaga Kyōsuke's *A Future Chronicle of the Japan-U.S. War* was confiscated by U.S. Customs and incinerated confirms that a tale that was considered to be fantasy in Japan was taken more literally in America. Perhaps it was the serialization of *The Tide of Battle* in the monthly *Our Navy* for over six months in 1930 that served as the trigger for the book's confiscation.

The author of *The Tide of Battle*, Elliot Fielding, was an army major who had served in Japan as a military attaché. His future-war chronicle begins with a surprise attack on San Francisco and Pearl Harbor. A scene featuring a flustered communications operator at a coastal wireless radio station on Oahu is strikingly reminiscent of the corresponding scene in Parabellum's *BANZAI!* The enemy comes out of nowhere. The undersea cable is out of commission. San Francisco—no response. Same with Midway. The operator tries to call the wireless station at Pearl Harbor, but they are also unreachable. Finally he establishes communication with a submarine anchored in the harbor. The radioman there shouts back that it is an uprising, that they can hear gunfire on the island, that it looks like someone tossed a bomb into the wireless station at Pearl Harbor. The culprits, he stated, are Japanese.

So the Oahu operator tries urgently to call up San Francisco. Finally he gets a response, to the effect that Japanese are— Midsentence, the line is cut, for at that instant a bomb is hurled into the station there, too. In short order, the wireless station is engulfed in flames.

Next, less than twenty minutes later, a report is made to Pearl Harbor by telephone from the lighthouse on Kaena Point on Oahu to the effect that planes of unknown nationality are approaching fast. Aircraft with the Rising Sun insignia painted on their wings have dropped bombs on the airfield at Pearl Harbor, destroying facilities and aircraft.

The Japanese strike force is launched not from aircraft carriers but from Kauai Island, sixty miles west of Oahu. An insurrection has been raised there by residents of Japanese descent. Around the time of the insurrection, a Japanese task force centering on the aircraft carriers *Akagi*, *Kaga*, and *Hōshō* approaches. The Japanese military swiftly builds an airfield, executing plans for a surprise attack on Oahu. A description of the ensuing battle by a participating American pilot is reminiscent of the later, historical, sneak attack on Pearl Harbor. The military port is being destroyed. Transport ships and magazines packed with torpedoes and explosives are blown up; flames swirl about everywhere. Smoke billows from burning warehouses and oil tanks.

And thus it is that the Japanese military are able to occupy Hawaii and San Francisco and prosecute the war from a position of advantage.

Japanese military control of America's West Coast is a staple of the Japan-U.S. future-war chronicle. However, in this particular chronicle, Britain, Australia, and other allies now come to the aid of the U.S. The fortunes of war are reversed, and the curtain closes with an American victory. Japan avoids payment of an indemnity, but loses Okinawa, the Ogasawara Islands, Taiwan, and the Marshall, Caroline, and Mariana islands.

If we cross Fukunaga's *A Future Chronicle of the Japan-U.S. War* with Fielding's *The Tide of Battle*, the result is a good profile of the start of the historical Japan-U.S. war.

* * *

AROUND the time *A Future Chronicle of the Japan-U.S. War* was published, Japan's leading engineers were gathered at the Yokosuka Navy Yard, gazing in admiration at a shipment that had just been brought all the way across the Pacific. It was the beautiful, silvery figure of a long-distance light bomber, the latest in American technology, purchased expressly for purposes of examination. The engineers could tell at a glance that it was superior to the biplane that had just been adopted the previous year by the Japanese navy.

That biplane, manufactured by Mitsubishi and dubbed the Type 89 Carrier Attack Bomber, had already gone into mass production. A carrier attack bomber was armed with both bombs and torpedoes and launched from aircraft carriers to attack enemy ports and vessels. It was a mainstay of naval aviation. Mitsubishi's Type 89 was made of both metal and wood. But the American plane was Northrop's Gamma monoplane, all metal but of a design and structure so unconventional that it managed to remain lightweight. Furthermore, after take-off, its wheels retracted. Nowadays that seems like an obvious, standard feature, but the Type 89's wheels were fixed and exposed.

"This won't do," was the dry comment made by Rear Admiral Maehara Kenji, chief of military aircraft construction. He sighed a long sigh and stood there, looking overwhelmed. According to Yanagida Kunio's *The Zero Fighter Plane*, the shock these engineers felt on that day was greater than that produced years later by the advent of the B-29. In the real world, the gap was great.

The Japan-U.S. future-war chronicle always gave pride of place to Japanese science and technology. And to be sure, for the first half of the Pacific War, the Zero was a champion fighter, greatly feared by American pilots. As its name indicates, it made it to the war just in time: "Zero" pays homage to the double-zero ending for the year of its introduction, in the Imperial Japanese dating system by which 1940 was the year 2600.

The Northrop Gamma light bomber was a new Black Ship. The overwhelming technological superiority of this "other" was known to an extremely small number of navy personnel. However, even if the specifics stayed under wraps, what did manage to spread far and wide was the vague sense of a threat posed by imminent attacks from some new and powerful carrier-borne aircraft.

In *Air and Sea*, and in *Japan and America: The Battle for Dominance*, Mizuno Hironori—fully aware of the mindset of the navy brass—had warned of the danger of a great air raid on Tokyo. And in a letter to Matsushita Yoshio, dated September 22, 1934, he commented as follows on what amounted to a military-industrial complex of a psychological sort, concerning air power:

> The reason that the military and the imperialists cannot successfully prosecute a war against America and Russia today is that they fear an aerial attack. I do believe that that is the chief reason. If America did not have its aircraft carriers—if there were no fear that Tokyo would burn—then a Japan-U.S. war might well have begun already.

The era had arrived in which airplanes and aircraft carriers would play a central role in warfare. Mizuno held the inconvenient view that since Japan lagged so far behind in this regard, it could not wage war even if it wanted to.

I mentioned above that 1936 was the year the Washington Treaty expired. The era of naval limitation had ended, and a new era of competition in naval shipbuilding began. The same year, 1936, was also the year in which Hitler and his Nazis tightened their grips on the reins of power in Germany and displayed their strength to the whole world at the Berlin Olympics. And in Japan, 1936 was the year of the "2/26" incident, an event that rocked the military and political landscape of Japan with cataclysmic force.

It was basic to the development of the plot of Fukunaga's *A Future Chronicle of the Japan-U.S. War* (1934) that the abandonment of the Washington Treaty was followed by an era of world chaos, triggering a Japan-U.S. war. Also in 1934, Hirata Shinsaku wrote *For 1936*; the previous year, Ishimaru Tōda had written his own *1936*. War between Japan and the United States did not occur as predicted in that very year, but such works did raise, among the general public, a crisis consciousness that half-believed in the predictions' validity.

As the general sense of crisis mounted, two writers of Japan-U.S. future-war chronicles were to step to the front lines of politics.

On January 21, the Lower House of the Japanese Diet was dissolved. Hirata

Shinsaku then stood for election from Hyōgo Prefecture's Fourth District, and Ikezaki Tadayoshi became a candidate in Osaka's Third District. Hirata stood at the invitation of the Shōwakai, a splinter group of the Seiyūkai. The Shōwakai, for their part, seem to have planned on exploiting Hirata's name-recognition by running him as a celebrity candidate. Fate had other plans, as the following *Ōsaka Mainichi* newspaper obituary reveals:

> On the 25th of this month, Hirata Shinsaku, preparing to stand in the general election as a Shōwakai candidate for the Hyōgo 4th district seat, suffered a serious fracture of the base of his skull in an accident on the Kobe highway near the Hanshin Railway Line at Motoyamamura. He was being treated at Tōmei Hospital in a suburb of Mikagecho, but finally passed away at half past eight in the evening on the 28th.

Hirata Shinsaku was the second son born to a family that had for generations been pharmaceutical wholesalers in Akō, Hyōgo, the town famous as the locale of *Chūshingura*, the tale of the forty-seven samurai. Shinsaku, however, was poor at math and science, and withdrew from school in the fourth year of middle school. As one of his schoolmates relates, he had a loud voice, "and he'd grandstand, almost foaming at the mouth."[7] This sounds right, and in that, he resembled Ikezaki. Hirata Shinsaku was just thirty-one years old when he died.

Hirata's accident occurred when he was rushing back to Kobe from Akō and his taxi collided with a truck. The way in which he died mirrored his era. The novelist appeared like a comet, exciting the interest of young people, only to pass forthwith into the next world. He lived life super-fast. Underlining his contemporaneity, his unfortunate demise involved the automobile, which to the bulk of the population was still practically a device out of science fiction.

The editors of the magazine *Shōnen Kurabu* (Youth Club) felt a responsibility to let children know of the author's death.

> Mr. Hirata has passed away! Could any news be more untimely, more sorrowful? He has been so energetic in relating to all of you a variety of tales filled with the martial spirit we Japanese should all take pride in, tales informed by his expertise on the latest in military affairs. We believe that the best expression of thanks we could offer to his soul would be to nurture that knowledge and that spirit.[8]

THE ADVENT OF WRITERS WHO HAD NEVER KNOWN WAR | 325

The readers also contributed eulogies. From the following estimation of a fourth-grade Kobe elementary school student, one can gauge the commanding position Hirata occupied in the literary landscape of the Japan-U.S. future-war chronicle.

> Every school kid in the country went crazy over *Task Force Shōwa*. If Mr. Hirata hadn't been alive, we wouldn't have had such fun stories to read. And his *Our Army, Our Navy* made me a little more clever. Not a little—my father says it made me double, triple-clever. It's a pity we can't read the continuation of Mr. Hirata's latest story, *The New Warship Takachiho*. My father and mother say it's too bad to lose this man.

Ikezaki, however, was one of the election's biggest victors, making it something of a vindication of his honor after his loss the first time he stood, in 1932. Following his election, he joined the Unaffiliated Club in the Diet. According to the reminiscences of fellow Club member Koyama Ryō, Ikezaki felt somewhat at a loss in the Diet. Wanting to know how Koyama saw things, Ikezaki asked him if he'd read his book.

> "You've read my *Japan Need Not Fear the U.S.*, haven't you?"
> "No, never heard of it."

The instant Koyama had responded, Ikezaki let loose a second shaft:

> "Do you know of the literary critic Akagi Kōhei?"
> "Nope."

At that, Ikezaki stood up with a rather disappointed look on his face.

> "You don't read many books, do you?"

Ikezaki may have been both naive and sensitive, but he also recovered quickly. After he had learned his way around the Diet, he published *Memoir of the World War*. It was a grandiose title.

It was apparent that Ikezaki had no use at all for the military's air-raid phobia. For him, America must never be worth fearing. The view he stressed in *Memoir of the World War* was that the damage done by the German air raids on London during the war was surprisingly light.

In bombing from the air, aiming is extremely problematic, and hitting one's designated target is not easy.

* * * * *

If the firefighting infrastructure is there, then this fear of fires caused by bombs is unnecessary.

* * * * *

Even the primitive antiaircraft guns they had in those days were quite useful in preventing the enemy from approaching.

* * * * *

If civilians remain indoors as much as possible during enemy air raids, bombing casualties will be extremely light.[9]

Bombing fears intensified with the realization that whereas London's buildings were made of stone, Japan's were made of paper and wood. But to Ikezaki this was not a problem.

When Ikezaki was at the zenith of his career as a Diet member, Ishimaru Tōda was arrested for violating the Military Secrets Protection Law. Ishimaru never indulged in Ikezaki-style flights of fancy, nor was he an antiestablishment type like Mizuno Hironori. He maintained the stance of a coolheaded analyst of military affairs. But now the era was approaching in which his sort of Japan-U.S. future-war chronicle was meeting with the opprobrium of the authorities. Reading over the transcript of his trial, one gets the strong impression that the charges were trumped up (or nearly so), and that his arrest and prosecution were intended very much as a warning to others. He was supposed to have violated the Military Secrets Protection Law, but all he had done was to obtain, as background data for his novel, a copy of the Order of Battle. This did not rise to the level of what one might call a military secret. It was the sort of material anyone with a friend in the army could obtain.

One can get a sense of the atmosphere of the era from the dramatic report of Ishimaru's arrest in the legal press.

If someone violates the Military Secrets Protection Law simply to write a novel, there is no issue to think about here. It is worse than a monkey falling out of a tree. For starters, trading so portentously on the current situation in order to write and sell a sensational war novel is disgraceful. It leads the citizenry badly astray. One must respect works that elucidate the gravity of our situation, and informational literature, but frivolous, provocative works, it would be well to control without compunction.[10]

Ishimaru Tōda was sentenced to one year and six months confinement in prison. He appealed, and when his appeal was denied in Tokyo on May 26, 1939, he was obliged to begin serving his sentence.

It was around this time that Mizuno Hironori's *Knowledge of War* was also accused of violating the Publication Law. That was settled with a fine of thirty yen, which was possible only because Mizuno had been under surveillance by the Special Higher Police and had given up on information-gathering activities like Ishimaru Tōda's. Mizuno wrote satirical verses on the subject:

> When what I write is banned before it's sold,
> I think: I'll write no more, lest I grow old...
>
> ...with grief, lamenting this land's parlous state;
> I think: what comes will surely come; it's only fate.

CHAPTER THIRTEEN

A Murder Mystery
Heard in New York

I MUST BEGIN this chapter by describing an event that took place in London just as the authors of Japan-U.S. future-war chronicles were busy commercializing their "crisis."

The date was December 3, 1934. The place was the five-star luxury hotel Grosvenor House, an imposing structure with a brown exterior and a height of six stories. Even in the dark of night it was clearly bathed in an atmosphere of insular arrogance and pomposity. We shall peek into a three-room suite, Nos. 345–347.

In his suite in the hotel, a Japanese man somewhat past his prime, sporting a buzz-cut hairstyle and nicknamed by the press "The Man with the Smile of Steel,"[1] awaits an English visitor who has an appointment to call on him at seven o'clock. Two of the rooms in the suite are bedrooms; the third, the farthest back, is a sitting room. There waits the aforementioned Japanese man with hair cropped as close as a Buddhist priest's.

In December in London the sun sets earlier and earlier: four o'clock, even moving into the three o'clock range. From the sitting room one can look down on Park Lane, the broad boulevard connecting Marble Arch and Victoria Station. Beyond lies an expanse of green—Hyde Park. At this hour, the headlights of the vehicles traveling on Park Lane repeatedly sever the boulevard from the deep and dark expanse of park in a momentary but bold chiaroscuro. If you can also imagine the sensation of five degrees below zero, you'll get a feeling for the frigidity of that evening.

The sitting room is heated by steam radiators. There is a sofa with a floral pattern and a desk colored dark brown. Wall and floor are unified by pastel green wallpaper. Indirect lighting further harmonizes the room's decor.

The Japanese man has only just returned to his rooms himself. Without changing clothes, he has flung his tired body down on the sofa and is now sunk deep in meditation.

He is dressed in the white cloth and gold buttons of the uniform of the Imperial Japanese Navy. He is barely over five feet tall and slight of frame. When he entered the Naval Academy, he was just one kilogram over the forty-five-kilogram minimum weight. His friends teasingly called him "Skin-and-Bones." Now, slightly past his prime, he weighs some fifty-six or fifty-seven kilos. He had scored low at the Academy in physical education, receiving (on a scale of 1 to 5, with 5 at the top) a grade of 3 in kendo and a 2 in swimming. But in his middle school days he had mastered the giant swing on the high bar. He was skinny, but muscular nonetheless, and overall his physical ability was not bad. Although he was not the sort to project the dauntless image that is stereotypical of the military man, he conveyed an air of being master of an inner strength that he would not reveal.

What was this officer of the Imperial Japanese Navy doing in a luxury hotel suite in London? What were his duties? We shall uncover these matters presently. Our immediate interest is his frame of mind.

A military uniform has insignia on the collar from which one can tell the rank of the wearer. In this case, the collar badge had a yellow ground and black trim. On the yellow ground, a single white cherry blossom indicated that the wearer was a rear admiral. In the hierarchical society of the military, one's duties are in a general sense defined by one's rank. However, just two weeks earlier, on November 15, this man had received news from Japan that he had been promoted to vice admiral. In addition to the new collar badge that he would be sent at some point, there would now rest on his shoulders new expectations as to the role he must play in London. His promotion to vice admiral at around the age of fifty indicated a smooth rise through the ranks. However, he was not about to give himself over to unrestrained rejoicing. That is because he also knew that from now on, he would be burdened with even more difficult duties than his title might seem to warrant.

Later, this man was to serve as commander in chief of the Combined Japanese Fleet, spearheading the Imperial Navy's surprise attack on Pearl Harbor. His name was Yamamoto Isoroku. And back in London, on that December day of 1934, he had taken one giant step toward his new destiny.

＊ ＊ ＊

YAMAMOTO ISOROKU is well known for a comment he made at the time of the war with America, that "for the first six months to a year I'd work like crazy carrying out" orders, and "you'd see results." There was no way to defeat the overwhelmingly superior Black Ships with a smaller and weaker military force. However, if he was ordered "Do it!," then as the commander in charge on the scene, he had no choice. We can say that Yamamoto's comment suggests a certain resignation. The only way out was a narrow path that would be open only at the beginning and would not last long. From his manner of speaking, his stance, it is possible to isolate certain character traits by considering such factors as historical context, social or professional position, and age.

There was something unconventional about Yamamoto Isoroku. During breaks in discharging his fleet-related duties, he would become so engrossed in betting on cards that in London he sometimes kept his subordinates up past three in the morning playing with him.

Yamamoto's given name, Isoroku, is unusual in Japanese especially in the more common pronunciation of the three characters (*i*, *so*, and *roku*) making up that name: *gojūroku*, meaning "fifty-six." At least *Isoroku* sounds a little more like a name. But were it not for his fame as a war hero, enduring into and through the postwar period, his name would surely seem odd. It is only when we know its origin that we understand. Isoroku was born to his father's third wife, when his father, Sadakichi, was fifty-six years old.

Meanwhile, the eldest son by another of Sadakichi's wives, Yuzuru, was named with an alternative reading of the character *jō* in Sonnō-Jōi, the nationalist slogan of the 1860s that meant "Respect the Emperor, Expel the Barbarian." This half-brother was thirty-two years Isoroku's senior. Yuzuru's own eldest son, Tsutomu—Isoroku's nephew—was over ten years older than Isoroku. Tsutomu was top of his class at Niigata Prefecture's Nagaoka Middle School.

Tsutomu returned to Niigata from Tokyo, where he had been studying, to convalesce from an illness, but died a month after his return. This happened when Isoroku was in the second year of middle school. Distraught at the death of his beloved grandson, Sadakichi said to his youngest son, Isoroku, "It would have been better if you had died instead." No words could have wounded the heart of the fourteen-year-old Isoroku more greatly than these. It was around this time that he began to devote himself to exercising on the high bar on the athletic field. This must have stemmed from the reflection that if he continued to be physically weak, he could do nothing to improve his humiliated state. But such enthusiasm in perfecting the giant swing, which makes one see the world go round and round, requires a greater impetus than mere self-reflection. In which case, we are left with his father's comment.

However, we cannot delve too deeply into such matters. Everyone internalizes some sort of adversity in his youth.

Yamamoto Isoroku arrived in London aboard the British liner *Berengaria* on October 16, 1934. He had left Yokohama on board the Japanese ship *Hie Maru* on September 20, crossing the Pacific and arriving at Seattle on October 2. From there he proceeded by transcontinental railway to New York via Chicago. Then he crossed the Atlantic, which took him almost another month. Nowadays a direct flight only takes twelve hours, but his was a very long journey. Prior to his departure, a newspaper carried this announcement: "Ambassador Yamamoto will be negotiating substantive matters concerning the navy, particularly strength levels, with Great Britain and the United States."[2]

In London, Yamamoto was awaited by the resident ambassador, Matsudaira Tsuneo. The two of them would be teaming up at the foreign policy negotiations. However, the topic of the negotiations was principally "substantive matters concerning the navy," the negotiations were "expected to be fraught with difficulties," and "these proceedings were considered to be of the utmost importance." So even though Yamamoto was lodged in a luxurious suite, he could hardly relax.

I should like now to reflect on the historical significance of these military limitation talks and in particular on the meaning of the date December 3, 1934. The starting point is the Washington Conference. There, the tonnage of capital ships for the navies of the United States, Great Britain, and Japan was fixed at a ratio of 5:5:3. A faction of the Japanese navy found this unsatisfactory. Young officers preferred a pro-growth position; at first Yamamoto too was inclined to favor expansion. The Washington Treaty was due to expire after fifteen years. If, two years prior to expiry, one of the parties to the treaty announced its intention to withdraw, the treaty would automatically expire in 1936. In that case, preliminary negotiations would be necessary with a view to concluding a new treaty.

On October 23, one week after his arrival in London, Yamamoto attended the first such meeting at the British prime minister's residence at No. 10, Downing Street. The following day, the twenty-fourth, he headed for Claridge's, the hotel where the American delegate was staying. In principle, negotiations proceeded in the form of this round-robin of bilateral discussions between the U.S. and Great Britain, Great Britain and Japan, Japan and the U.S.

The British representatives were, in addition to Prime Minister James Ramsey MacDonald, most notably foreign secretary Sir John Simon, navy secretary Bolton Eyres-Monsell (Viscount Monsell), and chief of naval staff Lord Chatfield. The American participants were Ambassador Norman H. Davis and sometime acting secretary of the navy William H. Standley. As the *Asahi* newspaper's special correspondent reported,

> At these naval negotiations, the British pronouncements use polite language but remain guarded; the Americans, after their fashion, are openly aggressive. The Japanese representatives have learned how to deal with such attitudes and are landing some telling blows of their own.

For example, one of the Americans observed that "America is not at all pleased with the 5:5:3 ratio either. Currently, it puts Alaska, Panama, the Philippines and so on under threat." Yamamoto responded, "All the more reason for you to subscribe to our no-threat plan." This "no-threat" plan was an offer to structure fleets for defense rather than offense. For example, it proposed the complete abolition of aircraft carriers. Japan put forward these proposals seriously, but the United States did not believe so. This exchange gives us a glimpse into the world of diplomatic thrusts, parries, and feints. Or as Yamamoto told the *Asahi* correspondent, "If we compare this match-up to a baseball game, the score is zero–zero."[3]

Yamamoto's position was extremely precarious, with adversaries to both front and rear. The tiger in front of him was the Anglo-American axis; the wolf behind him was the hard-line faction in the Japanese government. One can readily appreciate that the confrontation with the U.S. and Britain was fraught with tension. Unfortunately, Yamamoto was also threatened by enemies within. The government's cunning, irresponsible strategy was to shift to the arena of international negotiations matters that should have been settled in domestic politics. Reading primary materials as carefully as I can, I can come to no other conclusion.

The day Yamamoto arrived in London, "Foreign Ministry sources" in

Japan spoke about "the fundamental policies of the Empire," and were so quoted in a Japanese newspaper article appearing the following day.[4] The mission of the ministers plenipotentiary was (according to sources) "to assert the right of self-defense," "to achieve substantive arms reduction," and "to reduce offensive weapons." The article incorporates the military expansionists' opinion that arbitrarily fixing a 5:5:3 ratio amounted to (for Japan) an abandonment of the principle of self-defense; on the other hand the same article provides wiggle room by suggesting that the result was the achievement of arms limitation and a refocusing of military efforts on defense. These different lines of argument were clearly contradictory, and for Yamamoto to be ordered to go and resolve such contradictions at the level of diplomatic negotiations was a hard duty indeed. Since 5:5:5 was not in the cards, his only option—if mandated to abandon 5:5:3—was to propose 3:3:3. This last ratio never actually made it onto the table during these negotiations. But one can easily surmise that if Yamamoto had had to declare his position, that would have been it.

On October 23, Yamamoto's official position at the first round of negotiations in London was outlined and announced as follows, in language that was, deliberately, both abstract and abstruse:

The Powers are to agree on the principle that military preparedness is based on the necessity of national self-defense.

The current ratio is abolished; in its place the Powers will fix common maximum limits, within which each nation is free to build and possess as many of whatever kind of warship it pleases. [No specific figures were offered.—Inose.]

Extreme reductions are to be made in offensive warships, offensive war is to be eradicated, and fleets are to be restructured on defensive principles.

I would like to focus on the third item above, which reveals the Imperial Japanese Navy's true position.

"Offensive warships" had hitherto been defined as capital ships: namely, battleships or cruisers. But this was no longer the era of the Russo-Japanese War. In just a few years, radical changes had occurred. Specifically, capital ships were now defined as including not only battleships but aircraft carriers as well. The thinking was therefore that if "extreme reductions" encompassed this new weapon of the aircraft carrier, then offensive war could be "eradicated." Whatever England might do about it, one could hardly imagine that America would swallow such a proposal.

In his magnificent *Yamamoto Isoroku*, Agawa Hiroyuki offers the following elucidation of Yamamoto's aircraft carrier abolition strategy, based on an interpretation of his psychology:

> The Japanese government had Yamamoto propose the abolition of the aircraft carrier. They even permitted Yamamoto to bring up, as a part of conference maneuverings, the abolition of all capital ships. . . . For his part, Yamamoto believed the era was coming in which the currently subordinate Japanese air forces would take precedence over the navy. So he must have found somewhat odd the government's tactical proposal to abolish capital ships in general, when the real intent was to abolish aircraft carriers in particular.

We must remember that Japanese discourse at the time was dominated by fear of air raids. Without aircraft carriers, American planes, no matter how outstandingly superior in quality, did not have the range to conduct air raids on the Japanese home islands. If the war were a matter of dueling warships, then the calculation was that even if the Japanese fleet was no more than 60 percent the size of the American fleet, its submarines could bring the larger American fleet down to parity as it traversed the Pacific, softening it up for the final battle.

The Japanese were that fearful of American air power. But the government's attitude was contradictory. On December 3, the Japanese cabinet issued an "Announcement of Abrogation of the Washington Treaty." This was tantamount to removing all discretionary latitude from Yamamoto as minister plenipotentiary.

That day, a luncheon party was held at Claridge's by the American delegate. As someone commented ironically, it was "just like a farewell party, wasn't it?" This was followed by cocktails, hosted by the English representatives. There, someone made his way through the crowd toward Yamamoto. The man was tall, with a broad forehead and bluish-gray eyes. The color of his skin was somewhat dark for an Englishman. The man began to introduce himself. As soon as Yamamoto heard the man's name, he arranged to meet him at Grosvenor House.

* * *

IT IS SEVEN O'CLOCK in the evening on December 3. In his suite at the Grosvenor House Hotel overlooking Hyde Park, Vice Admiral Yamamoto Isoroku, tasked with representing Japan at the preliminary negotiations for a new arms limitation treaty, prepares to greet a single British visitor in absolute privacy. Since the diplomatic negotiations are not going well, one may imagine Yamamoto as sunk in the sofa in the sitting room, awaiting his guest in a gloomy mood. Until, that is, he hears a knock on the gray-painted wooden door.

In the three-room suite, the room farthest back is the sitting room. Next to it is Yamamoto's bedroom. Just beyond another door is a second bedroom where Lieutenant Commander Mitsunobu Tōyō, a subaltern who accompanied Yamamoto from Japan, serves as gatekeeper.

Now the lieutenant commander comes down the corridor of the suite to inform the vice admiral of the arrival of his English visitor. Yamamoto tells Mitsunobu to show the visitor in. And, he adds, Mitsunobu's own presence will not be necessary during the interview.

The tall English visitor introduces himself again: Hector C. Bywater. Bywater was a common enough surname in England, perhaps on the order of Kawabata in Japan, but Hector is unusual. It is the same name as the hero who won fame during the wars between Greece and Troy. But in fact, Yamamoto Isoroku has heard this distinctive name before. And that was why, even though he routinely responded to reporters' questions with "No comment," he had instantly agreed to a private interview with this man. It was an encounter between the man who would soon be entrusted with the execution of the surprise attack on Pearl Harbor and the author of a Japan-U.S. future-war chronicle who had, early on, predicted a war between the United States and Japan. Bywater had declared to Yamamoto that he wanted information for an article he was writing as correspondent for the *Daily Telegraph*. Yamamoto, for his part, wanted to learn what Bywater was thinking. He did not know that Bywater's complex career included a period during which his main work was as a spy. Bywater held interest for Yamamoto as a writer, as an analyst of military affairs, and above all as the author of *Sea Power in the Pacific* and *The Great Pacific War*.

Hector C. Bywater was born in London on October 21, 1884. Yamamoto Isoroku was born on April 4 of the same year—Meiji 17—in the city of Nagaoka in the Japanese prefecture of Niigata. They were both fifty.

Yamamoto's hair, flecked with white, was cropped in a buzz-cut. Bywater's hairline had receded considerably. Although the two men had been born on opposite ends of the globe and led very different lives, they were now arriving at common views regarding war strategy. This is something I should like to explicate further.

When was it that Yamamoto first learned of Bywater? I do not know the precise moment, but there is no difficulty fixing the general period. It was the beginning of the summer of 1921, back when his close-cropped bristles were fuller and stiffer, and Bywater's hair had not thinned so much. They were both in their late thirties and at the height of their vitality.

Yamamoto Isoroku had been selected to attend Harvard University, mainly to improve his English. He studied there from May 1919 until his return to Japan in July of 1921. He could not possibly be indifferent to the just-published *Sea Power in the Pacific*. By that time, the Japanese navy had already designated America its hypothetical enemy. America had returned the favor. Speculations concerning the real possibility that this opposition between the two Pacific nations would devolve into a war of horrific duration are recorded in detail in *Fifty Years in Foreign Affairs*, by Shidehara Kijūrō, the special minister plenipotentiary and—for a time—resident ambassador in the United States. As Shidehara muses,

> I have forgotten which book it was, but I remember finding it extremely interesting. So I said to Yamamoto, "Here, you give this a read; if you think it's good, send a report on it to the navy minister." It was such a thick tome, I thought it would take him two or three weeks to read it and write a report. For an ordinary person that would be par for the course. But he brought me a fair copy of his report the third day after I'd handed the book to him.[5]

Shidehara was flabbergasted. Yamamoto's response was, "I thought it so important to report on this promptly to the navy minister that I have not slept these two nights writing it up."

Yamamoto's next period of residence in the United States was from 1926 to 1928. His previous stay had been in Boston; now he was sent to the capital, Washington, as naval attaché to the Japanese embassy. In Washington, Hector Bywater's *The Great Pacific War*, published in 1925, was a hot topic of conversation. In it, Bywater clearly predicted that the coming war would begin with a surprise attack by the Japanese navy.

This English author, who so accurately foretold the destinies of Japan and America sixteen years in advance, did not fabricate his novel out of whole cloth. Given the 5:5:3 ratio in capital ships between America, Great Britain, and Japan (as set by the Washington Conference), if some touchy situation were to arise, the only way for Japan—at 3—to prevail in an armed conflict would be by initiating hostilities with a surprise attack. Bywater had applied deductive reasoning to identify the sole option open to Japan.

Returning to Japan in 1928, Yamamoto was made captain of the cruiser *Isuzu*. He revealed his own thinking on the subject of a future war in a lecture he gave at the Torpedo School at Yokosuka:

> In the future, airplanes will supplant fleets. And in the event a Japan-U.S. war occurs, I believe that there is no way to win other than by attacking Hawaii, rather than adopting a defensive strategy.

That is according to the recollection of Ōshima Ichitarō, at the time an upper-level student at the Torpedo School and later a navy captain. We also have the following testimony left us by Vice Admiral Hori Teikichi, a close friend of Yamamoto:

> In total war, it goes without saying that a country's resources, its economic power, its industrial power, are decisive factors. Between Japan and the United States, in this regard, there are differences that are beyond comparison. Particularly with respect to the quality and production capacity for the air force, the gap is absolute, and fatal. From that point of view, it is entirely understandable why Yamamoto opposed a war with the U.S. and Great Britain, and therefore why he recognized that fighting a war against the United States would be truly difficult. He was convinced that if Japan were to wage war with the U.S., the only possible way to prosecute it would be to obliterate the enemy's main force at the very start, upsetting the unfavorable balance and securing a sufficient handicap. It was precisely in this logic that he found grounds for considering an attack on Hawaii to be essential.

Initially, the military command was opposed to the Pearl Harbor strategy. To that extent, this strategy was a product of Yamamoto's own belief; it could not have been the doing of any other military officer. That is, Yamamoto's perspicacity stood out alone on the extremely dangerous horizon of Japan's domestic affairs, even within the navy. At the preliminary arms limitation talks in London in 1934, it looked as if things were proceeding willy-nilly in a negative direction for Japan. Given that situation, the strategy he was later to put into effect must have presented itself to him like a smiling devil, sidling up to him gradually, growing more and more real.

Yamamoto wanted a comrade. He wanted someone to stand with him on the same frontlines. If not a comrade, then someone who would understand him; someone who could alleviate his loneliness; someone who would be sympathetic toward him. In his situation this was hardly strange.

Bywater's article was carried under his byline in the *Daily Telegraph* on the following day, December 4, and it was given quite a bit of space. The article was favorable to Yamamoto. Bywater reported that during their interview the previous night, Admiral Yamamoto, Japan's chief delegate, had stated that the primary goal on the Japanese side was to reduce the possibility of war by achieving large-scale reductions of offensive weapons. Yamamoto had pointed out how regrettable it was that public opinion in England seemed to have missed that crucial point. He added that Japan was clearly opposed to a shipbuilding race, and that Japan was prepared to use any rational means to avoid such an unfortunate international situation. The admiral also "expressed himself frankly" regarding the issue of naval bases in the Pacific:

"I and many other Japanese naval officers do not regard Singapore as a menace," he said. "It is too far away from our country to cause us worry. We should, however, be seriously perturbed if the United States were to create a powerful base in the Philippines."[6]

Furthermore, Bywater wrote that Japan in general fully understood that if it unilaterally announced it was abrogating the Washington Treaties, yielding a situation in which there were no governing treaty, the great powers would recover the freedom to build military bases within the sphere of Japan's military security competence—which for the Japanese was not a situation to be desired.

Bywater also appreciated the rather epoch-making nature of the arms limitation proposals Yamamoto had brought to the negotiating table. Admiral Yamamoto, he wrote, had made it clear that Japan's current offer to scrap certain warships included not only those whose construction was projected but also those already completed and those presently under construction. He also made it clear that Japan's intention was to eliminate all large ships, and to reduce all the signatories' navies practically to the status of coast guards. The admiral acknowledged that this proposal had not been welcomed by the British government. If capital ships could not be scrapped in this way, Japan was hoping to continue the shipbuilding holiday by extending the service life of ships currently in service. Such were the main points of Bywater's article.

There are indications that the Americans wanted to assign Japan the blame for a collapse in the preliminary negotiations and were scheming to get Japan to be the first to mention scrapping the Washington Treaties. If the arms limitation treaties were scrapped, a new era of unrestricted naval shipbuilding would ensue. England itself no longer possessed the glory it once had. In an era of free competition, it would lose to America; it could not maintain its 5:5 ratio. America saw that and was throwing its weight around. The American representatives could not say so directly to the British, but if Japan were dissatisfied with 5:5:3 and proposed 5:5:5, America would reject it. The only move left for Japan would be treaty abrogation. This was a ploy to make Japan the villain while keeping the American position superior vis-à-vis England.

Ultimately the Japanese hard-line position played into the American hand. Yamamoto understood this. So did Bywater. That is why Bywater took care to convey Yamamoto's disclosure that

> Japan's plan . . . was not only to reduce current building programmes, but to scrap many ships already built or on the stocks. [Yamamoto] made it clear that Japan wishes to get rid of all large men-of-war and reduce navies virtually to the status of coast defense forces.[7]

Yamamoto and Bywater both thought that if it came to war, the only military strategy left to Japan would be a surprise attack. Even so, if the war lasted as long as four years, it would end in Japan's defeat. Bywater's *The Great Pacific War* had forecast this. Indeed, it was Bywater's express purpose in writing this book to issue a warning to Japan not to engage America in a war.

In Yamamoto's estimation, Bywater had correctly predicted the processes likely to be at work, and it was the vice admiral's desire that such a situation not come about. It would be sufficient to obtain a 3:3:3 ratio, rather than to be so greedy as to insist on 5:5:5. A "coast guard" navy would be just fine.

Unfortunately, the preliminary negotiations in London did not yield good results. All the participants were predicting that the full arms limitation conference, to be held two years later, would end in failure. On January 28 of the following year, after a stay of three months, Yamamoto Isoroku left London and returned to his native country via Siberia. The meeting at Grosvenor House between Yamamoto and Bywater, when the two opened their hearts to each other and talked openly, was both the first and last such occasion for the two men.

* * *

THE RESULTS of the preliminary arms limitation negotiations in London, in which Vice Admiral Yamamoto Isoroku had participated with full negotiating powers, were unfavorable to Japan. Neither America nor Great Britain favored a continuation of the Washington Conference regime. But even the government that dispatched Yamamoto to these negotiations did not have any settled policy. Nevertheless they placed on him the burden of achieving some result. It is said that after his return to Japan he confided to a friend, "I may want to quit the navy."

It was not only Yamamoto who was dogged by such pessimism. Bywater began to feel disappointed about his own country's military strategy. The naval might of the great seafaring nation of Great Britain was gradually fading before the raw power of such countries as America and Germany. Bywater still believed that a Japan-U.S. war would be decided by battleships. That is how navies at war operated, he continued to think. In *The Great Pacific War*, airplanes were given only the supporting role of providing reconnaissance. Even after he had completed *The Great Pacific War*, Bywater continued to assert that the chief role would be played by battleships rather than airplanes.

When the torpedo has acquired the range and precision of a 16-inch gun; when submarines have become as swift, as seaworthy, and as habitable as big surface vessels; when the radius and carrying power of aircraft have increased tenfold, and bomb dropping is as accurate as gun practice: then, but not till then, will the primacy of the battleship be endangered.[8]

Those words are from a short piece that won Bywater first prize in the annual essay competition administered by the United States Naval Institute. As an organization affiliated with the United States Navy, the association was located on the campus of the U.S. Naval Academy at Annapolis. It had authority. The naval affairs journalists in London began to admire Bywater even more than before.

Bywater's thinking here coincided with his country's global strategic interests, since Britain laid great importance on battleships as the means of securing the sea lanes that linked British colonies scattered across the world. However, in the 1930s, England's throne as queen of the seas began to be shaken. Her navy's budget began to shrink. As Bywater wrote to Nobel Prize–winning author Rudyard Kipling, revealing his gloomy state of mind on this subject, "To be a naval correspondent today is a rather thankless task, for the fleet has become a mere skeleton. Some of the effects of consistent malnutrition are obvious enough, but the worst are hidden from public view. It is tragic to one who, like myself, knew the navy at the zenith of its power."[9]

Bywater's discussion with Yamamoto occurred the year after he wrote to Kipling. With aircraft carriers and bombers now appearing on the world military stage, it looked as though the curtain would be drawn on a history of brilliant performances by the British navy. A sharp journalist like Bywater simply could not shut his eyes to the truth. A few weeks after his encounter with Yamamoto, he sent an article to the academic journal *Pacific Affairs* stating that a few emendations of *The Great Pacific War* were in order.

Previously, he had indicated in *The Great Pacific War* that the Japan-U.S. war would begin with the Japanese military launching a surprise attack on the Philippines and Guam. He had not changed his opinion, except with regard to the means of attack. He wrote that Japan was likely to adopt a strategy using not battleships and cruisers as he had anticipated before, but aircraft carriers.

It was the trend of the times to shift from battleships to aircraft carriers and bomber aircraft.

For ten months after returning to Japan, Yamamoto Isoroku allowed himself to be tasked ambiguously both to the Navy Ministry and Naval Command. Agawa Hiroyuki puts it thus in his *Yamamoto Isoroku*:

Although excellent people are always chosen as plenipotentiary representatives to international conferences, upon their return they all, without exception, are made to suffer in some way. Some trivial infraction of orders or protocol is detected and magnified, and they are made to fail. Yamamoto found himself in just such a position. Many military insiders were sympathetic and even angry that he should be treated like that when he had been reluctant to go in the first place, but there was nothing they could do about it.[10]

As 1935 drew to a close, Yamamoto was given the post of chief of naval aviation. In July of the next year, the decision was made to construct the battleships *Yamato* and *Musashi*. The new aviation commander was strongly opposed, asserting that, "in the future, aircraft attack power will greatly increase, to the point that before the battleships engage they will be destroyed by aerial attacks. These big battleships will be useless." But in the navy, the big ships, big guns philosophy was still the mainstream.

In December, Yamamoto became vice minister of the navy in the Hirota Cabinet. He served in that capacity until August 1939, when he was made commander in chief of the Combined Fleet. The navy minister was Yonai Mitsumasa. Yamamoto, Yonai, and chief of staff Inoue Shigeyoshi were referred to as the "pro-Anglo-American trio." By maintaining their opposition to Japan's participation in the Tripartite Pact with Germany and Italy, they became targets of attack by right-wingers and army hard-liners. It was thought that when Yonai resigned as navy minister, he would be succeeded by Yamamoto. However, Yamamoto did not become a minister. Instead, he was named commander in chief of the Combined Fleet.

"If we force through Yamamoto's appointment [as navy minister], one worries that he might be killed."[11] So thought Yonai, who thought it just might save Yamamoto's life if he were not in Tokyo for a while. Yamamoto had a very open, even careless personality. His relationships with geisha in the Shimbashi district in Tokyo were well known. He loved to gamble. There were plenty of chinks in his armor. But that very breeziness was one of the reasons for his popularity.

On September 1, Yamamoto entered the captain's cabin of the *Nagato*, the flagship of the Combined Fleet, anchored at Wakanoura in Wakayama. That very evening he heard the news that the German army had invaded Poland. A second world war had begun—two years, as it would turn out, before the start of the Japan-U.S. war.

Mizuno Hironori wrote with a sigh, in his diary entry for September 2, "The German army has finally invaded Poland, with air raids on Warsaw and elsewhere. Extremes of violence and cruelty have been reached." But

England and France did not immediately issue declarations of war on Germany. Mizuno felt frustrated.

> From France and England: just talk. Their parliaments are mired in use-less debates. A delay of one day at the start of a war can mean a month of calamity later. These "gentlemen" have no idea how to conduct military affairs. I despise the pusillanimity, indecisiveness, and sheer slackness of the democracies.[12]

It was September 3 when France and England finally got into gear. Mizuno, who had been waiting impatiently, wrote excitedly, "8 PM. England finally takes a stand." And he predicted, "Can Hitler have any hope of success? The day of his decline must be drawing nigh." Mizuno was sixty-four years old and had no arena in which to publicize his opinions—all he could do was to jot down this brief line in his diary.

For Hector C. Bywater, who had had the experience of immersing himself in German society as a spy, the despotism of Nazi Germany was unbearable. Before Germany invaded Poland, the British government had not worked out any settled policy toward it. The articles that Bywater had written for the *Daily Telegraph* had incurred the displeasure of the paper's managers. In them, Bywater had repeatedly asked Prime Minister Chamberlain, who had been adopting a policy of appeasement toward Nazi Germany, why he had not strengthened the navy. The gulf only deepened between Bywater and the paper's staff, who were sensitive to the government line.

As a highly specialized journalist, Bywater considered himself a walking encyclopedia of information on navy strategy and equipment, and on war in general. Because he was self-confident and would not yield to others, he appeared to be stubborn. When it came to the point that Europe was about to be plunged into another nightmare, Bywater could stand it no longer. He quizzed editor in chief Arthur Watson until the latter was red in the face. When Bywater finished arguing, he was also finished at the newspaper. It was announced that he was fired.

It was after he had left the *Daily Telegraph*, for which he had worked for eleven years, that Bywater began to drink heavily. He had already divorced his first wife, Emma, in 1930. The next year he had married Francesca Dorothy Gross, a divorcée eleven years his junior. After being driven out of the *Daily Telegraph* he freelanced for a while. He was then picked up by the *News Chronicle*, but never regained his former panache. His private life also fell apart; his second marriage failed.

Around March 1940, when Bywater was making his second start as a journalist at the *News Chronicle*, a simulation war exercise was conducted on the deck of the *Nagato*, the flagship of Japan's Combined Fleet. The result was that in a fight between battleships and an air squadron, the battleships would lose. Yamamoto muttered to chief of staff Rear Admiral Fukutome Shigeru, "Couldn't you do Hawaii with airplanes?"

In a Japan-U.S. war, Japan could not win by following a straightforward strategy. So it would develop just as Bywater described it in *The Great Pacific War*. Was there no other way out, not even a crack through which to escape an otherwise probable dead end? Not without the advent of some new weapon that did not appear in *The Great Pacific War*.

Bywater's life ended at age fifty-five, not half a year after Yamamoto's comment about an attack on Pearl Harbor.[13] It was August 17. The previous day, London had suffered a massive raid by the German air force. Bywater was living on the first floor of a five-story brick apartment building in the London suburb of Richmond. So weakened was he by his alcoholism that he was essentially bedridden, unable to move about. Some of his fellow tenants started to carry him out of the building on a stretcher, but when the building across the street collapsed during the air raid, with all the horrific crashing and tearing of exploding aerial bombs, they took fright and flight but left Bywater and his stretcher on the landing of the stairway while they scattered like baby spiders.

For Bywater, Germany had been the archenemy since the Great War. Now German bombers had insolently invaded London's airspace and were dropping bombs. Pale and immobile, Bywater could do nothing other than lie there listening to the blasts and the screams. The next morning, Mrs. Margaret Perrin, the housekeeper, knocked on his door, but there was no answer. She entered to find Bywater sleeping, with perspiration on his face. After lunch, when she visited him again, he looked as though he were sleeping, with a placid expression on his countenance. Feeling her heart race, the housekeeper rushed over to him and took his pulse, but in vain. She rang up his personal physician. The doctor came over, and after a simple check, he placed a white cloth over Bywater's face. On the medical report he wrote, "Consider death due to alcoholic poisoning."

The following day, once again, a fierce air raid was visited upon London. The intervals between the raids gradually grew shorter, and starting September 7, there were raids every night, for sixty-five nights in a row. It was during this period, on September 27, that Japan, Germany, and Italy signed the Tripartite Alliance in Berlin.

Yamamoto issued specific instructions concerning the Hawaii strategy just after New Year's Day, 1941. He reported to navy minister Oikawa Koshiō that in waging war against America, Pearl Harbor must be attacked at the very outset. Then, to make the plan more concrete, he wrote a letter to Rear Admiral Ōnishi Takijirō, the chief of staff of the 11th Air Fleet (the base fleet) at the Kanoya base in Kagoshima, ordering him to "make a thorough examination of all problems relating to [the Hawaii strategy]." The rear admiral summoned Commander Genda Minoru, air chief of the First Air Battle Squadron on the aircraft carrier *Kaga*, anchored at Sasebo. Genda's response: "The plan is a difficult one, but not impossible."

Gordon Prange's *Tora! Tora! Tora!* begins with a scene of the task force just before the surprise attack on Pearl Harbor, and it fully depicts Commander Genda's contribution to the strategy. Since his days at the Naval Academy, it had been Genda's dream to become a pilot. When he entered the Kasumigaura Naval Air Fleet at the end of his first term of instruction in 1928, he was at the top of his class. His piloting skills were impeccable, and his facility at aerial stunts was such that he was teased as the star of "the Genda Circus." During his time at the Naval War College, Genda submitted an essay proposing that since the mainstay of the navies of the future would be not the battleship but the aircraft carrier, the Japanese navy could do without battleships entirely and gain in offensive power if instead it had aircraft carriers, destroyers, and submarines. It was the sober opinion of his instructors and classmates at the Naval War College that "Genda is nuts."

As air power in fact grew in importance, Genda's reputation within military circles grew proportionately. At the end of 1938 he was dispatched to London as a naval attaché. His primary objective was to observe British air power. However, as he remarked in his postwar memoirs, *Naval Aviation*, "Since we never showed anything to attachés from Great Britain or the U.S. on the ground that they were unfriendly nations, it was only to be expected that even though I was in England, I was not able to see anything." Although Genda was stationed in London for almost two years, he obtained hardly any results. Instead, since the Second World War broke out during his tour of duty there, he got to experience air raids by Nazi Germany. He left London just after Hector C. Bywater drew his last breath.

. Genda did what he could in London. In New York, there is even someone who seriously believes that Genda murdered Bywater, who knew too much, on the orders of Yamamoto Isoroku.

The *New York Times* building is on 43rd Street in Manhattan. It is near Times Square, which at night is ablaze with the neon signs of Japanese electronics manufacturers. When I announced myself to the receptionist, a huge white-haired man appeared from the direction of the elevator, smiling broadly. William Honan, at that time the culture editor of the *Times*, was born in 1930, so when I met him he was over sixty, but his step was light. In Japanese newspaper companies, a journalist who had reached this age would have retired and be either gardening or decked out on a sofa in some VIP lounge. But in America, it is not unusual to see a white-haired journalist still on duty.

We struck up an immediate friendship. Honan had begun to pay attention to Bywater early on and devoted considerable time to tracing his life story. I myself became interested in Bywater while unearthing the genre of the Japan-U.S. future-war chronicles. The feeling was, as Confucius puts it in the *Analects*, "Is it not a pleasure when friends come from afar?"

William Honan first encountered the forgotten Hector C. Bywater in the 1960s. He casually picked out a copy of *The Great Pacific War* from a random pile in a secondhand bookstore. It cost twenty-five cents. Flipping through the pages once he had returned home, he was surprised by how closely the development of the story mirrored the actual course of the war. When Pearl Harbor was attacked, Honan was eleven years old, content in his community of family and school. He received what he terms a shock as great as if the whole world had exploded.[14] The reason he majored in history in college was that this shock still remained in the core of his being, and it was the same obsession that led him to respond to the words *Pacific War* on a book cover in a secondhand bookstore. After he had accidentally obtained *The Great Pacific War*, whenever his work permitted he delved deeply into the history of the Pacific War. What sort of person was this author Bywater?

At first Honan had no idea. In between his regular work assignments, he would travel frequently to England, hunting up materials and searching out Bywater's acquaintances. He carefully perused contemporary newspaper accounts. After he had a general picture, he traveled to Japan in 1982. There was one question he could not get out of his head. So he decided to meet Genda Minoru and ask him about it in person.

Genda died in 1989 at the age of eighty-four. When William Honan came to see him, he was seventy-eight and a Japanese National Diet representative. He was a captain at the end of the war. After the war, he entered the Air Self-Defense Force and rose to the level of chief of staff and air force general before turning to politics and becoming a Diet member at the age of fifty-eight.

Honan's biography of Bywater, titled *Visions of Infamy*, was evaluated by University of Pennsylvania professor Stanley Weintraub in a book review appearing in the November 1, 1991 edition of the *New York Times*. Weintraub describes the book as "part ingenious speculation, part detective story, part biography." In the course of shedding light on the generally obscure career of Hector C. Bywater, William Honan became possessed by an overwhelming suspicion. And that had to do with the part that was not "biography" but "detective story," and it was related to Genda Minoru.

Honan himself told me, quite seriously, that Yamamoto Isoroku was responsible for, and in fact personally ordered, the assassination of Hector Bywater.

Visions of Infamy does not go so far. What it does do is develop with great care the hypothesis that Bywater may have been murdered. The British journalist's personal physician had written, "Consider death due to alcoholic poisoning." When I visited Bywater Jr. at Derby, he was eighty-one years old, but he responded decisively that his father's heart was weakened and grew progressively debilitated until he died. But in *Visions of Infamy*, Bywater's biographer is greatly concerned with the postmortem.

Honan obtained a copy of the postmortem report. At 5:40 PM on the day after Bywater's doctor had written the death certificate, an autopsy was performed at the temporary public morgue. Had there been no suspicion as to the cause of death, surely they would not have conducted an autopsy. In the report, written by Dr. R. Donald Gere, who conducted the autopsy, several of the symptoms of alcoholism are noted. However, what is noted is merely that he had gastritis and that his liver was somewhat enlarged; the conclusion: "Sudden death. No suspicion of foul play." Since, on that day,

London was being bombed, Dr. Gere's report was terribly incomplete; it omitted the usual tests for poisons.

Honan reasons that there is a possibility that Dr. Gere overlooked evidence that Bywater was murdered. But his suspicions were initially piqued by someone else's suggestion.

E. A. Harwood, a friend of Bywater's when he worked at the *Daily Telegraph*, declared to the *New York Times* editor that (in Honan's words) "he believed Bywater was killed by a Japanese agent possibly acting on instructions from Isoroku Yamamoto." And Harwood was one of the few surviving witnesses close to Bywater. Harwood remembered distinctly what happened immediately after Arthur Watson, Bywater's editor in chief at the *Daily Telegraph*, had fired him. An ashen-faced Bywater opened the door to the newspaper's research library, where Harwood was chief librarian. Bywater had occasionally looked in on him and taken afternoon tea with him. That day he just stood there, stock-still, saying nothing.

Harwood had always been worried about Bywater. When World War II broke out, Bywater took to carrying a handgun on his person. He seemed to think that some danger was pressing in upon him and ordered a tailor to sew special leather webbing into his suit jackets so that he could carry the pistol about undetected. He joked to Harwood that this way his suit wouldn't get wrinkled—also that with an ordinary holster one couldn't draw and shoot fast enough.

Harwood appealed to Honan, asking if there were not some connection between Bywater's death and the death of James (Jimmy) Melville Cox, the Reuters correspondent in Tokyo. On July 29 of that year, Cox, age fifty-five, died after falling out of a third-floor window of the headquarters of the Kempeitai, or military police, in Tokyo. Bywater died just nineteen days later. Harwood stated that it wasn't that Cox had suddenly jumped of his own suicidal volition, as the Kempeitai announced, but rather that he was either pushed or forced to jump. It is certainly true that two days later the British foreign secretary, Edward Halifax, remarked in the House of Lords that the government was "entirely unable to accept" the official Japanese version of events. This statement was greeted with cheers by his listeners and was also made much of in the Japanese press, where the Cox incident was reported in a rather sensational manner. Simply the capture of a British spy was news enough, but that fall from the window was like a scene in a movie. Alternatively, the reportage assumed the characteristics of a detective novel; that, too, stirred up public sentiment:

The suicide, Cox, had been living with his wife and their maid at Higashi Kaigan in the town of Chigasaki, Kanagawa, since around 1936. It was a lonely life, without much interaction with the townspeople. The house stood alone in the middle of pine woods right at the shore, near the Shōnan Yuhō Dōro hiking trail. They kept six fierce dogs. Fearing the dogs, no one went near the house. Even the merchants who had business with them were quite limited in number. None of them knew anything about the family; they even commented, "Foreigners are usually friendly, but that family is different." Once the Kanagawa prefectural police searched the place, and after that people avoided it even more. On the evening of the twenty-ninth, this reporter tried to pay a call on the Cox home, but was greeted only by the ominous snarling of the fierce dogs. There was no other response.[15]

Harwood's hypothesis is as follows. When Yamamoto decided on the attack on Pearl Harbor, he feared that the plan would leak. Any prior detection of a surprise attack means its failure. He thought to himself, who would be likely to notice such a plan in the offing? Bywater was the very person who had come up with a similar strategy fifteen years earlier. And Bywater's own current source of information must be Cox, at the Reuters Tokyo bureau. Add Cox's information to Bywater's analytical powers, and Yamamoto's strategy would be seen through. Accordingly, first Cox was liquidated. Then the devil extended his hand to London. If an assassin snuck into Bywater's bedroom one summer's night and injected him with poison . . .

William Honan himself wrote in *Visions of Infamy* that all this rested on circumstantial evidence.

Tantalizing as is such speculation, it remains only guesswork and seems more the stuff of thrillers than history. Hard evidence of foul play, as Harwood was the first to admit, is simply lacking. Bywater's sense of personal jeopardy toward the end of his life may well have been a case of alcohol-induced paranoia. Furthermore, not only Bywater's physician but also his brother and son were of the opinion that he had become alcoholic by the end of his life.[16]

I did not believe that Bywater's death was a murder. However, in the process of exchanging information about Bywater with Honan, we had hit it off, and things began to look different to me. We parted at his newspaper's offices and arranged to meet later at one of New York's many Japanese restaurants.

That evening, we ate sukiyaki and drank beer. When the conversation turned to the topic of Bywater's death, suddenly Honan grew excited, and his voice louder.[17] I think it was when I said, "Harwood's theory is nonsense. I mean, Yamamoto himself was a Kempeitai target." Honan's rebuttal: "We just can't prove it." He went on, speaking rapidly,

Whether or not Cox was murdered can be proved if there's a Kempeitai record. But when I tried to research this in Tokyo, I was told that the Kempeitai records had all been incinerated. And there was a limit to what I could do during my brief stay in Tokyo. But there may be some proof extant somewhere in Japan. That possibility can't be denied.

Honan said that he had then changed his focus and gone to see Genda himself.

Honan points out that anyone who looks into the subject of Yamamoto Isoroku and the surprise attack on Pearl Harbor naturally cannot ignore then-Commander Genda, who appears so prominently in *Tora! Tora! Tora!* As one delves further into Genda's history as Yamamoto's right-hand man, one grows concerned about his period of residence in London. One can say that his objectives constituted a type of espionage. Honan said that although he had initially laughed off Harwood's theory as preposterous, it had grown on him, with a strange sense of reality about it.

"Bywater died on August 17, and Genda returned to Japan in September as if fleeing the country," said Honan—as if that clinched his argument.

"So when you interviewed Genda, you asked him about this point, right?"

Honan nodded vigorously in the affirmative and leaned forward.

I wondered, "How did you broach the subject?"

"I asked him, once he had completed his mission by killing Bywater, did he return to Japan immediately?"

"You asked him *that*?!"

"Straight out."

Americans certainly are straightforward. But entertaining.

"So what kind of face did Genda make?"

"The interpreter was a former navy officer, and he said, 'Mr. Honan, I did not want to pass along that question just now. I was afraid. I thought he might bite someone's head off.' But in the end, Genda flatly denied it."

"So that's the end of your theory, right?"

"No, I still have my suspicions about Genda. All the former Japanese navy brass I met knew Bywater's name. But Genda said he'd never heard of him, had absolutely no recollection of him. It doesn't seem natural, does it? Isn't he hiding something?"

Japanese are not as good as Americans at handling direct questions. They don't have the custom of fearlessly insisting on the legitimacy of something even when it is disadvantageous to oneself. Genda must have thought Honan to be a rude character, intent on besmirching his good name. So it is possible that even if he knew of Bywater, he became cross and responded negatively. Such subtleties of Japanese behavior are more apparent to a Japanese.

I am impressed by Honan's courage. Such behavior serves as a reference point for a way of thinking that does not occur to Japanese. On the other hand, it's rather like a wild pitch that's hard to get your catcher's mitt around.

"If you're so obsessed with this, why didn't you touch on the Genda question in your book? And you've stated rather negatively that this theory was 'the stuff of thrillers, rather than histories,' haven't you?"

"If I wrote up things like that, it would be misunderstood as sensationalism, pandering to the masses. I'd never get reviewed in a reputable paper like the *New York Times*!" William Honan gave a hearty chuckle.

To a Japanese like myself, Honan's thesis that Yamamoto Isoroku had Bywater killed is wildly unexpected. I think it's an untenable hypothesis, but when one sets up such a bold hypothesis one nevertheless takes a detour into a surprising world that can yield an unexpected harvest.

Let's distill the circumstantial evidence adduced by Honan. First, there is the apparent murder of Melville Cox, the Tokyo bureau correspondent for Reuters (and Bywater's presumed source of information), in Kempeitai custody, just nineteen days before Bywater's own death. Second, there is the return to Tokyo, from London, of Lieutenant Commander Genda Minoru, Yamamoto's confidant, immediately following Bywater's death.

After I returned to Tokyo myself, from New York, I scavenged around for material on the Melville Cox incident. Fortunately, the Kempeitai official in charge of the matter, Ōtani Keijirō (section chief, First Section, Special

Higher Branch, Tokyo), has left us detailed handwritten notes. The Special Higher Branch of the Tokyo Kempeitai was divided into two sections. First Section was in charge of external matters, Second Section handled police matters. Counterespionage was the purview of First Section. Ōtani became Chief of First Section in 1938 at the age of forty. By war's end he had been promoted to colonel and was commander in chief of the Eastern Division of the Kempeitai. This sort of résumé is a source of misfortune when one's country loses the war. Ōtani was prosecuted as a war criminal at the International Military Tribunal, Far East (the Tokyo War Crimes trials), and was sentenced to ten years' hard labor. He was released on parole in September 1956. It was the same year that the Economic White Paper declared that "the postwar is now over," that Ishihara Shintarō's novel *Season of the Sun* was turned into a movie by Nikkatsu, and that the Sun Tribe in their bold aloha shirts strutted about the Shōnan seacoast.

Ōtani's notes were published in book form in 1966, under the title *A History of the Military Police in the Shōwa Period*. The Kempeitai (as they are usually called in English writings on the subject) were a police department within the military; their duties (Ōtani wrote) typically included such things as admonishing the cadet who stole five hundred yen from his colleague's pocket, or arresting the private second class who had made off with the family jewels from some count's residence in Azabu. However, after the 5/15 Incident and the 2/26 Incident, the military became more deeply involved in politics, and the Kempeitai became more involved in intelligence matters.

Ōtani and the Tokyo Kempeitai had for some months been clandestinely observing Melville Cox's movements. Cox was known to the other foreign correspondents stationed in Tokyo as a capable person. And he was particularly active during a period in which he was in close communication with Sir Robert Craigie, the British ambassador to Japan. He also had dealings with Richard Sorge, the German journalist known from the Sorge Incident. The suspicion was that Cox knew too much about the Japanese military's formations and equipment, its strategic circumstances, the movements of its fleets, and so on, but whether this was the activity of a professional spy or merely the overzealous action of a reporter collecting information for a story was hard to judge.

The Kempeitai obtained proof that Cox was delivering this information to Craigie. However, since it would only be natural for an Englishman to furnish his government information he came across that he thought beneficial to his own country, this was not conclusive. They were determined to get to the bottom of it.

On July 27, the Kempeitai arrested Cox at his home in Chigasaki and transferred him to Tokyo. The headquarters of the Tokyo Kempeitai were at the Ōtemon, one of the gates to the Imperial Palace. Day after day, Cox was questioned in a third-floor interrogation room. He simply would not confess. On the third day, the twenty-ninth, shortly after noon, he suddenly jumped out of the window, or so it was reported. A military doctor attempted emergency treatment, but Cox's skull was fractured, and he was barely breathing.

What instantly flitted across Ōtani's mind was not the failure of the interrogation, but the concern that this would become a diplomatic issue. When he received a report on Cox's "jump" from the chief of external affairs, he issued the following instructions.[18]

This incident is a regrettable one, and it is not possible to prevent an interruption of our interrogations. What is of primary importance is that the disposition of the case be above reproach. For that reason, internal assessment of responsibility will be postponed. However, it will not do for anyone to try to cover up the failure of supervision that has led to this bombshell of an incident. Nothing is more important than to expose the actual reality of the event. If foreigners want to know every last detail, we can open up our headquarters to them. We can leave the spot he landed and the interrogation room as they are and show them. You must make this crystal clear to your subordinates. Inspection and verification should not be conducted by Kempeitai personnel. Contact Prosecutor General Hirano at the public prosecutor's office, and have him handle it directly. And we must exhaust all possible treatments in caring for the Englishman who has received such critical injuries. And if by chance he dies, unfailingly observe all due propriety.

The motive for this suicide, Ōtani stated, was unclear, but there was no question of any violent interrogation.

We found something that looks like the deceased's last will. As Cox lay groaning on a bed, a Kempeitai member found in his trouser pocket a crumpled up bit of paper. It was the torn-off corner of a larger sheet. A closer look revealed it to be a news bulletin from the Dōmei [United] wire service. I flipped it over and found something scribbled in pencil, together with Cox's signature.

That scribbled hand read, "I was treated well at the Kempeitai. I just can't take it anymore."[19] The content was in the nature of a will, addressed to his wife. But whether what Ōtani was writing in this record was true or false, I cannot tell.

Cox's wife brought him a homemade boxed lunch every day. The "will" had been roughed out on the paper that had wrapped one of those lunch boxes. Ōtani writes that "it was from this will that I realized that his suicide was something he had made up his mind to do." He states this in terms of a conclusion from evidence, but considering the attitudes of the Kempeitai in that era, it is only natural to be skeptical. One wonders whether Cox was not in fact killed after being forced to write out this will.

As if attempting to dismiss these very suspicions, Ōtani chronicles the events immediately preceding Cox's "suicide" in some detail. Let us consider a précis of his account.

As it was a hot summer's day, the windows of the room were wide open. The way they opened the windows was to push up the lower half of the windows. Thus, the bottom halves were all open. This was the source of the custodial lapse. In the middle of the room was a square table. Near a window was a Kempeitai guard, leaning back in his chair with his back toward the window. On that day, after the morning interrogation by Second Lieutenant Nemoto, Cox was given lunch in the interrogation room. Since he was a foreigner, whose eating habits were different, his wife's lovingly prepared boxed lunches were passed along to him every day after his arrest.

This time too he finished with evident satisfaction the boxed lunch assembled with such tender care by his wife. And again as usual, he was permitted a postprandial promenade about the table. Because it was normal, the Kempeitai guard paid no particular attention. Cox suddenly stopped and picked up from the table a glass that still had some water left in it, and took a drink. Next, he took out a cigarette from a pack of Cherry brand cigarettes, also lying on the table, and lit it. He smoked slowly, exhaling slowly, as if relishing it. With the cigarette still in his mouth, he started to walk again. Before he reached the Kempeitai guard, he swiftly placed a foot on the windowsill, and sprang up to it. By the time the shocked guard realized what was happening, the center of gravity of Cox's 190-pound body was already past the falling point. It was all over in a flash.

When Ōtani looked out that same window, he could see clearly the disturbance in the sand and gravel where Cox had fallen. The site had been left unaltered after the removal of the gravely injured Cox, and that was clear to Ōtani. He remembered in particular seeing, lying on the ground, the cigarette butt that Cox had had in his mouth. The cup on the table in the room was still one-third full of water; the pack of Cherry brand cigarettes was still there too.

I mentioned above that Ōtani Keijirō was concerned lest the Cox affair develop into a diplomatic issue. Immediately after the incident, when Ōtani contacted the British consulate general in Yokohama, the reply was that the consul would come that evening. Around six o'clock the consul came, accompanied by a British physician who would conduct an autopsy. Cox's body was laid out on a bed in the infirmary on the third floor. At the foot of the bed, flowers and incense had been hurriedly arranged and placed. According to military protocol, a Kempeitai soldier stood ceremonial guard. The two or three Kempeitai officers in charge of Cox's interrogation were also by the bedside. The consul announced that the English doctor wished to conduct an autopsy. First, the doctor listened to a rough account by the attending Japanese military doctor. Then he began his own careful examination. He investigated the key points relating to suspicion of torture or murder by the Kempeitai, inspecting every square inch of the body. It took thirty minutes. It seemed longer. He whispered something into the consul's ear. The consul nodded.

When the autopsy was concluded, Ōtani showed the two Englishmen into the interrogation room. He explained in detail the circumstances of Cox's suicide. The consul asked no questions, merely nodding as he listened. When this explanation was over, one of Ōtani's subordinates, a lieutenant in the Kempeitai, handed the consul a one-page statement and said, "Please sign this." It was a receipt for Cox's body.

This was the climax. With bated breath, Ōtani Keijirō and his subordinates looked at the two Englishmen. If they did not accept delivery of the body, it would mean they had not accepted the cause of death. The receipt, written in formal Japanese, read roughly as follows:

TO: Commandant, Tokyo Kempeitai
RECEIVED: The body of James M. Cox

At or around 12:30 PM on July 29, 1940, the above-mentioned deceased leaped from the third floor of Kempeitai Headquarters into the courtyard, sustaining critical injuries. At 3:12 PM on the same day, at the headquarters infirmary, he was pronounced dead.

RECEIVED BY: The Consul General of Great Britain
DATE: July 29

It was clear that the consul had reading ability in Japanese. When he had finished reading, he acquiesced, took out his fountain pen, and signed swiftly. It was as simple as that.[20]

Ōtani was greatly relieved. Now there would be no trouble between Japan and Britain on this account. Even if Britain were to revisit the matter later, this one receipt ensured it would not become a serious problem, as the receipt itself clearly specified suicide as the cause of death. Since a public official of the status of the consul acknowledged this with his signature, there would be no grounds for picking a fight with the Kempeitai.

The army thought the Cox spy incident worked out perfectly. As Ōtani put it in general terms, "The populace has now been enlightened and educated in an Anglophobic and counterespionage direction," so that the objectives of the military in arresting Cox had been fully satisfied. Certainly journalism was made to dance to the tune called by the authorities.

Thanks to the political, economic, legal, intellectual, and cultural intercourse with foreign countries ever since the Meiji Restoration, the network of foreign spies in our own country has been expanding in every place and direction, like masses of barnacles on a ship's bottom. It has extended its tentacles steadily and deeply throughout ordinary times and by legal means, and its penetration has developed so greatly as to be astonishing.[21]

The same article gave concrete examples of these "tentacles": missionaries, missionary schools, amateur theatrical groups, yacht clubs, golf clubs, patent offices, foreign trading companies, the Salvation Army. The entire tone was retrogressive, redolent of the era of National Seclusion.

And in fact, after this Cox Incident, the Salvation Army was chosen as a specific target for suppression. The reason was that its headquarters were in England. The objective was not suppression in and of itself, but the counterespionage campaign. The Defense Section of the Personnel Bureau of the Army Ministry submitted a request to the Tokyo Kempeitai: "We have already reached an agreement with the Home Ministry, but now that it has come to the final stage, they are dragging their feet. Can you not take this business in hand now?" Ōtani summarily rejected their request, saying arrests were impossible on the basis of the evidentiary materials supplied. They repeated the request, saying, "They don't have to be found guilty of a crime. Administrative suppression is fine." And finally they had their way.[22]

Two weeks after the Cox incident, the Kempeitai searched the head-quarters of the Salvation Army in Jimbocho and arrested the entire top echelon. The basis for suspicion was that "since the principal management were in England, and since they received operational funding from there, this enabled conditions in Japan to be reported easily." But no proof could be found that they had committed any infractions of the Military Secrets Protection Act. So the Kempeitai tried to urge upon them a compromise solution. Finally, the Salvation Army's Japan branch cut off all connection with their English headquarters and became reborn as the headquarters of the Japan Salvation Army.

Ōtani regrets this Salvation Army incident as a blotch on the history of the Kempeitai.

> No question, this left the bad aftertaste of religious oppression. It would be convenient to say that these arrests were not originally the unsolicited idea of the Kempeitai, and that it would have been difficult not to respond to the army's request, but in fact this was a conscious, if minimalist, response to pressure by army brass. Moreover, when one bears in mind that the organization in question was a group of devout Christians, I feel that we cannot simply let this go as merely an excess of zeal on our own parts.

We probably should not consider Ōtani's memoirs to be entirely false. My reason is that one can trace in his memoirs a particular current of thought.

On September 27, 1940 the Tripartite Pact was signed by Japan, Germany, and Italy. One faction of the powers-that-be in the army pushed hard for this. The midsummer Cox and Salvation Army incidents were used in the

Eliminate English Ideas and Prevent Espionage campaign. And thus this was not a scene in which Yamamoto Isoroku, who was opposed to the Tripartite Pact, had any part.

One column of Honan's theory thus crumbles. But thanks to him, the meaning of Genda's stay in London, which I had not appreciated sufficiently before, has become clearer.

CHAPTER FOURTEEN

Why Pearl Harbor?

I T TRANSPIRED from our examination of the memorandum of Ōtani Keijirō (former Chief of First Section, Special Higher Branch, Tokyo Kempeitai) that the death of Melville Cox was instrumental in the campaign to expel British influence and prevent espionage.

After Japan's war with China had begun in earnest, the military's tension level, especially the army's, had risen. In April 1938, a national mobilization system was put into effect, as advocated by Satō Kōjirō in his *Dream Tales of a Japan-U.S. War.* The Counterintelligence Institute, a forerunner of the army's famous Nakano School, was born in July of the same year.

Future-war chronicles also began to take on a rather moralistic cast, reflecting both the general national mobilization and the heightened counterespionage consciousness. Fukunaga Kyōsuke's *Defending Our Land*, published in 1939, sensitively incorporated this atmosphere. In the copy of this work that I obtained from a secondhand bookshop, the following inscription was written in the hand of a young woman: "Received as a prize for good health, 1942." To this was added the girl's signature: "Katō Hideko, Japan Commercial High School for Girls, Freshman Year." This work was one of the twenty-four-volume paperback series put out by the publisher Shinchō Sha, titled "Literature of the Youth of New Japan." Other works in the series include Kikuchi Hiroshi's *People Who Won Success Overseas*, Satō Haruo's *Paths Artists Trod*, Osaragi Jirō's *Selections from Japanese Literature*, and Shimazaki Tōson's *Selections from Western Literature.*

The photographic inserts to Fukunaga's book are exclusively of warships, airplanes, and infantry charge practice. The protagonist is a young man who aspires to be a navy pilot. Though this may have been difficult for a young woman like Katō Hideko to relate to, she must have received it gratefully since it was wartime. No doubt she would soon be mobilized to work at a military supply factory and no longer be able to attend school. Assuming she did not fall victim to the Great Tokyo Air Raid, she may even be alive today.

Defending Our Land identified readers' needs in a literary style different from that of science fiction. It offered a sense of contemporary reality; indeed it induced young men and women to understand that the war was coming home to them, entering their daily life and space. The enemy lay hidden all about, even near to hand.

The initial setting of Fukunaga's *Defending Our Land* is as follows.[1] The young male protagonist's maternal uncle, whom he calls Uncle Unno, is a navy lieutenant. The father of one of his classmates, whom he calls Uncle Hoshino, is an ex-navy doctor. The two of them sometimes visit the hero's home and tell stories about war and navy life.

One day, Uncle Unno, who has served in the Canton Campaign and is now home on furlough, drops by the hero's house for a visit. As luck would have it, so does Uncle Hoshino. And as always, they begin a lively exchange about matters of war. Uncle Unno, fresh from battle, begins to address Uncle Hoshino in a somewhat formal tone.

"I heard today from someone that before the ***** [Canton] Campaign, some of the plans had already leaked to the general public."

"As for that, it was sketchy, but we knew about it too."

"How did you know about it?"

"From the mobilization of military doctors and the arrangements made for equipping *****. Even if we didn't know the exact place, we got the impression that at any rate they were being sent somewhere south. And then some magazines and other publications had editorials saying, 'We Need an ***** Campaign,' so I thought, 'Ah, hah!'"

"You think the military doctors who were drafted would blab about something like this?"

"No, but even if the doctors don't, their wives and family members would spill something eventually. That news would spread like the wind, and there's your rumor."

"Troublemakers, those wives are, aren't they! When the military is taking such precautions to keep secrets, still there are leaks. Those wives chatter thoughtlessly, and we don't know where or when enemy spies may be listening."

Uncle Unno, who participated in the Canton Campaign, seems truly embittered by this. Uncle Hoshino interjects sympathetically.

"Japanese are a little careless in that regard, aren't we."

Then the two men begin talking about spies active during the Russo-Japanese War. As the young narrator listens (and this narrative is actually in the first person), he has the hair-raising realization that he "is ignorant and unaware, but there may be spies all over the place!"

"Uncle, what does a spy look like?" he asks, bursting with curiosity.

"Oh, there's no specific appearance, you know. 'Cause if there were, they'd be spotted right off."

The boy, who has been imagining a strange man with dark sunglasses and a hat pulled down low over his forehead, is a bit disappointed.

"The ones we have to be most careful of are the 'pro-Japanese' foreigners who are quoted in the press."

"Huh? The pro-Japanese foreigners?"

"Spies know that if a foreigner claims to be pro-Japanese, the Japanese will lower their guard. Counting on that, they imitate the pro-Japanese foreigners. Giving money for national defense, visiting the tombs of the White Tiger Regiment, and so on."

"So the ones who say things like 'I love Japan' are all suspicious, right?"

"Not all of them, no. There are some who truly favor Japan. It's just that there are also phonies mixed in among them."

And Uncle Unno lists a few foreign examples. A high-ranking French officer, who loved horseracing, bet and lost heavily on a certain horse, unaware that the horse's jockey was in league with a foreign spy. When the officer was so overcome by debts he had nowhere to turn, the spy pressed him to leak military secrets. Then there are the golf-course spies disguised as caddies who eavesdrop on the confidential conversations of military men and diplomats on the golf course. Spies, he explains, can glean secrets from the slenderest of clues.

The boy, now alarmed, remembers that one of his classmates is the son of the president of a news agency. This classmate is proud to be informed—and to talk—about matters that have not made it into the newspapers.

"That's bad," says Uncle Unno, frowning. "There certainly won't be any spies among the students, but as such stories get bandied about, there's no denying a spy might catch wind of it somewhere. When you go to school next, you should warn that student that such things can happen." Uncle Unno concludes his comments as follows:

> Those in charge, be it in the government or in the military, are doing their utmost to take care that state secrets and military secrets do not leak out. But this cannot be accomplished by our civil servants alone. The general populace, cognizant of the havoc spies can wreak, simply must join with our civil servants in conducting counterintelligence.

After a London sojourn of a year and a half, Genda Minoru returned to Japan in September 1940, immediately after the death of Hector Bywater. He had engaged in just the kind of activity that *Defending Our Land* had warned against—but in England, on behalf of Japan.

According to Genda's memoirs, *The Naval Air Corps: Battles*, in the midst of an extremely ordinary day's business, he would manage to gather a great deal of information from the smallest of clues.

> When I went for a drive in the suburbs, or when I went golfing, I would see combat aircraft that had taken off from a nearby airfield. They would be engaged in aerial training exercises, and by observing their maneuverings I could get some idea of the skill of the pilots. It would have been dangerous in the extreme to infer from one training exercise the condition of the entire British air force, but if one observes it often enough, one can get a general idea.

Genda Minoru's memoirs do not reveal precisely what his espionage activities were as an adjunct military attaché, but he does seem to have posted sufficient results just from the sort of observation he describes.

The Second World War broke out half a year after Genda's arrival in London, providing him with the perfect opportunity to observe wartime conditions. British and German combat aircraft engaged in aerial dogfights in the skies above London. Observing these battles from the ground, Genda could observe the capabilities of the aircraft and the skill of the pilots. "The fighting strength of the British fighter squadrons is far lower than that of the Japanese navy's. And the German fighter squads are even less effective than the British." The conclusions Genda reached on the basis of his observations are self-confident to a strangely supreme degree.

The famous Zero fighter was finally introduced, formally, in the summer of 1940. As we saw in chapter 12, Japan was naturally behind in aircraft design and production. We recall the comment gasped by the Japanese military aviation expert when he first saw the Northrop Gamma: "This will not do." Since then, Japanese engineers had strived mightily to catch up to the West and surpass it. According to Yanagida Kunio's *The Zero*, by 1937 the new Japanese "96" was decisively beating the Chinese air force.

> The air battle over Nanjing lasted a mere fifteen minutes. By the end, the only planes flying about were the "96s"; there was not even one Chinese plane. Twelve "96s" had shot down twenty-one Chinese air force fighters, leaving not a single one remaining.

All of the Chinese planes were Western-made, so rather than a feeling of having beaten China, this was understood as Japanese technology outstripping that of the advanced nations. In terms of operational skills as well, Japanese were gaining confidence. As the American scholar Martin Caidin acknowledges in his *The Ragged, Rugged Warriors* (1985), the Japanese pilots handled their deadly machines with an unbelievable agility. To outstanding group performance they added outstanding individual technique.[2]

Genda had been at the forefront of the upgrading of Japanese fighter plane performance and operational technology, so as he watched the air war over London, his confidence deepened. The destiny of the Hawaii strategy depended on this confidence.

When Genda returned to Japan, he was asked by Rear Admiral Ōnishi Takijirō (to whom Yamamoto had conveyed his intentions in this regard), "How about a surprise air strategy for Hawaii?" From the moment that Genda declared, "It's not impossible," the bows of the Combined Fleet began to point in the direction of Hawaii. This means that while he was stationed in London, Genda had obtained a result more important than any killing of Bywater.

In the movie version of *Tora! Tora! Tora!* (1970), the following scene occurs:

Soon after Genda Minoru is selected for the air command wing of the task force, he makes a jaunty landing on the deck of the *Akagi*, as it lies anchored at a military port. Commander Fuchida Mitsuo and other colleagues run over to Genda's plane, staring at it, dazzled.

"Is this the new Zero?"

"Type 21; foldable wings. Boosts the carriers' loading capacity. She's got long legs and turns a mean corner. Best fighter in the world."

"Wouldn't lose out to a Messerschmitt or a Spitfire?" asked Fuchida delightedly.

"Never. When I was naval attaché I got a good look at them over London."

"So this is the real deal, huh?"

This scene does not appear in the original book by Gordon Prange. It must be something reconstituted by the scriptwriters after reading Genda's memoirs.

The reason William Honan brings up the theory of Bywater's assassination by Genda Minoru on Yamamoto Isoroku's orders is actually to suggest an even more comprehensive formulation.

Until now, historians have believed that Yamamoto's war plan was conceived independently, or at least that its origins "remain obscure," as the American military writer Ronald H. Spector recently observed in his authoritative *Eagle Against the Sun*. But today, half a century after Yamamoto unleashed Japanese forces in the Pacific, it can be shown that while serving as naval attaché in Washington in the late 1920s he reported to Tokyo about Bywater's war plan and then lectured on the subject, adopting Bywater's ideas as his own. Years later—long after it had become encoded in his mind—Yamamoto followed Bywater's plan so assiduously in both overall strategy and specific tactics at Pearl Harbor, Guam, the Philippines, and even the battle of Midway, that it is no exaggeration to call Hector Bywater the man who "invented" the Pacific War.[3]

It is certainly true, as I have remarked more than once, that the surprise attacks on the Philippines and Guam at the beginning of *The Great Pacific War* strongly resemble the actual inception of the war between Japan and the U.S. Did Yamamoto get a hint from Bywater's strategy?

Unfortunately, however, Honan's theory embraces an enormous contradiction. Bywater's *The Great Pacific War* ends in Japan's defeat. Yamamoto was obliged to assume a Japanese victory. And to achieve that, he had to bet he could pass his fleet through the eye of a very small needle.

Hector C. Bywater was someone who placed his faith in the brilliant history of the British Royal Navy. And the decline of that navy coincided with Bywater's own affliction with alcoholism. Yamamoto Isoroku's point of view was, in contrast, future-oriented. In his view, the strategy of employing aircraft carriers and carrier-borne bombers was the only way to break free of the spell of Bywater's scenario.

In *The Great Pacific War*, there was no surprise attack on Pearl Harbor. So who thought of Pearl Harbor and when, and how was the plan actually put into effect? When Yamamoto muttered, "Couldn't you do Hawaii with airplanes?" it was during Combined Fleet battle maneuvers in March of 1940. This is the established opinion of all the biographies, from Agawa Hiroyuki's *Yamamoto Isoroku* on down. Battle maneuvers meant, for example, loading planes with real torpedoes and estimating how well they could do attacking real battleships. The torpedoes carried no explosive charges, and their traveling depth was adjusted so that at best they would pass under their target battleships. There was no actual damage, but an assessment could be made as to accuracy and so on.

In the postwar period, former navy personnel have left many a testimonial of their experiences. Taking a cross section of a few of these accounts will allow us to build up a picture of how the surprise attack on Pearl Harbor emerged as an option.

Commander Miyo Kazunari of Section One (Operations) of Naval Command observed the Combined Fleet's battle maneuvers from the bridge of the flagship *Nagato*. Aircraft packed with torpedoes, called torpedo at-tack planes, encircled a battleship, bringing it to a standstill and "sinking" it. Commander in chief Yamamoto's inspiration had been borne out by verifiable, actual results.

Commander Miyo remarks that the command officers "were not in agreement with the Hawaii strategy." The standard move was to mount a forward defense in the event of an American attack. This basic navy policy was quite old, having been sanctioned on June 29, 1918. Here, "sanctioned" means receiving the emperor's imprimatur. The right of supreme command belonged to the emperor; approval by the National Diet was not necessary. In effect, the army and navy general staffs directed military policy themselves. The policy in question was the First Revised Strategy Outline.

Broadly speaking, the Combined Fleet was comprised of First Fleet, Second Fleet, and Third Fleet. In phase one of a war with America, a force built around Second Fleet was to attack and destroy the U.S. Asiatic

Fleet stationed in the Philippines. A force built around Third Fleet was to make Manila Bay its objective as it backed up the army in their landing on, and conquest of, Luzon. But the plan was not to force a direct entry to Manila Bay. Rather, it was to move in from the rear, via Lingayen Bay and Ramon Bay.

In phase two, the main force, First Fleet, which had been held in reserve, was to play the major role. A showdown between the U.S. fleet (intent on recapturing the Philippines) and the Combined Fleet would probably come either in the seas near Japan or in the seas near the Philippines. While First Fleet would see the main action, Second Fleet would assist with reconnaissance and apply guerilla methods during preliminary skirmishes.

The basis for the First Revised Strategy Outline was the eradication of the American presence in the Philippines and a victorious forward defense to the predictable rescue mission by the U.S. Pacific Fleet. It was extremely simple and clear. In the Russo-Japanese War, the Japanese had attacked the harbor at Port Arthur from the rear. Then, when Russia's Baltic Fleet came from afar to right the situation, the Japanese fleet had gone out to meet it and prevailed. This was the same pattern.

At the outset of the war, the Philippines would be conquered. That scenario is the same as what Homer Lea gives us in *The Valor of Ignorance.* You can find it also in Parabellum's *BANZAI!* And it is also described in Hector C. Bywater's *The Great Pacific War.* Japanese Japan-U.S. future-war chronicles were exploring the same territory. You could say it was that era's international common sense.

Where Japan-U.S. future-war chronicles exhibited variation was in their latter halves. In Mizuno Hironori's *The Next Battle,* the showdown between the two fleets ends in Japan's defeat. Mizuno was suggesting defeat because at the time he was in favor of expanding the armed forces, and wanted to warn Japanese of the result of not doing so. In Homer Lea's *The Valor of Ignorance,* simultaneous with the conquest of the Philippines the Japanese army attacks the United States. Both Homer Lea and Parabellum saw their homelands as losing such a struggle, and in that respect they were quite similar. Their common goal was to awaken Americans to what they saw as the new threat from the Orient.

Japan-U.S. future-war chronicles were generally composed in the above manner from the end of the Meiji era to the middle of the Taishō era. That is, from Japan's victory in the Russo-Japanese War to the end of World War I. Roughly speaking, they correspond to the First Revised Strategy Outline.

WHY PEARL HARBOR? | 369

Next, a Second Revised Strategy Outline was sanctioned on February 28, 1923, immediately after the signing of the Washington Treaties. In response to the Washington Treaties, which fixed Japan's fleet at 60 percent the size of America's, a partial revision was sought in the country's basic strategy. Phase one was the same; phase two differed somewhat. Before the American fleet could reach the seas near Japan, Japanese submarines, destroyers, and torpedo boats would subject it to harassing attacks, successively reducing the size of the American fleet until the numbers were about even. Then Japan would bring on the final battle. There was no change to the strategy of invading the Philippines or of the forward defense; it really amounted to no more than a technical adjustment. The basic philosophy was the same: the forward defense of engaging the enemy. In the late 1930s and into the early 1940s the Second Revised Strategy Outline saw a number of minor revisions, but every year it was renewed along the same basic lines.

If one thinks about it, there is nothing more odd than this strategic stance. The only way to interpret it is that deep down, the navy was not overly determined to fight its hypothetical enemy, America.

Two months after Yamamoto Isoroku muttered his line about "doing" Hawaii with airplanes, a circumstance arose which demanded a revision of the Second Revised Strategy Outline. It was announced that the U.S. Pacific Fleet would be stationed at Hawaii. This was no mere temporary positioning for the purpose of maneuvers. It seemed more like the fleet now had a permanent offensive base and was waiting for an opportunity to attack.

Section One of Naval Command felt obliged to set forth a new strategy. The section chief at that time was Captain Nakazawa Tasuku, who as a lieutenant commander had studied at Stanford University, where he jotted down the following reflections:

I had thought that because the American population was comprised of diverse ethnic and racial groups, it would be weak in forming a collective will. But contrary to my expectations, the entire populace is vigorous in the defense of America. The country is replete with a domineering ethos whose motto is, "In All Things, Number One in the World." Its resources are abundant beyond comparison with Japan. In a crisis, Japan will have its back against the wall. That is especially so in regard to military aviation.

Now, as section chief, Nakazawa conducted large-scale, week-long, simulation Japan-U.S. war games at the Naval War College, from May 15 to May 21, 1940. To use the naval lingo of the day, it was a "map exercise."

Battle maneuvers were rich in technical elements such as real ships and planes. A map exercise was conducted on a giant map spread out on a table. One says "on a table" but in reality, this was a large-scale event, taking up the entire fourth floor of the Naval War College and involving over thirty personnel. In the center conference room on the fourth floor were situated the judges, drawn from the college's administrative staff. Flanking both sides of the large conference room were over a dozen smaller rooms, equipped with telephones connecting them to the large conference room. The competitors were divided into the Red Force and the Blue Force. Each had a command center, to which staffers in the small rooms reported the progress of the exercise. The staff judges would confirm the moves made by each side on the map spread out on the huge table and decide who had won or lost. This exercise had the following results:

First, Blue Force (Japan) progressed extremely smoothly in its operations, until as a result of events its fighting strength gradually decreased, and its hands were full dealing with repairs to its damaged vessels. With respect to those repairs, and to fleet augmentation with new vessels, a gap opened up between Blue Force and Red Force (America).

Second, strategically, Blue Force was relying completely on a war of endurance. But, given its evident force degradation, no matter how favorably one juggled the numbers, they did not add up to victory.

Third, from the above vantage point, it was clear that if a Japan-U.S. war could not be brought to a conclusion within two years, Japan could not win. It was inevitable that such a Japan-U.S. war would become a war of endurance.

Fourth, the gap with respect to war materiel and raw materials was larger than expected. Items which Japan had in sufficient supply still came to one-tenth of what America had. Items in which Japan was deficient totaled less than a hundredth of what America had. Moreover, Japan had the disadvantage of having to import raw materials vast distances by ship from areas to the south and then process them in Japan, before transforming them into constituents of military strength. In the southern territories themselves, there was essentially zero manufacturing capability of which Japan could avail itself. In respect to these conditions, Japan and America were polar opposites.

As chief of naval operations, Nakazawa reported these results to navy minister Yoshida Zengo.

It was four months after the map exercise, at the end of September 1940, that Yamamoto Isoroku had his famous interview with Konoe Fumimaro, in which he said,

> If I were under orders, then for the first six months to a year I'd work like crazy carrying them out, and you'd see results, believe me. But if it were to take two or three years, I would have no such confidence. Now that we have the Tripartite Alliance, we have to deal with it, but since things have come to such a pass, I request that every effort be made to avoid a Japan-U.S. war.[4]

There was a relationship between the results of the map exercise and the language in which Yamamoto expressed himself to Konoe. Yamamoto found it hard to take the plunge. When Combined Fleet chief of staff Fukutome Shigeru was considering the following year's training policies for the Combined Fleet, he asked Yamamoto if it was all right to introduce the Hawaii surprise attack. Yamamoto replied, "Wait a bit."

In the second half of November there was a map exercise modeling the conquest of the Dutch colonies in Indonesia. The way it developed made it clear that there was no other way than to preemptively attack the U.S. fleet at Hawaii. As a practical matter, Japan was economically blockaded. Indonesian raw materials were thus seen as the only way to break the noose of the encircling "ABCD" powers (America, Britain, China, the Dutch). But if Japan invaded Indonesia, its hypothetical enemy would no longer be just the U.S.—England and Holland would be added. And most of the Japanese navy would have to be tasked to the resource-rich southern territories. The Combined Fleet would exhaust itself effecting this Southern Strategy, and the American fleet would not wait for it to recover, but attack from Hawaii. Not only would they destroy the Combined Fleet, but bombers operating from American aircraft carriers could then strike the home islands.

When this map exercise had been concluded, Yamamoto Isoroku verbally informed Oikawa Koshirō, who had taken over from Yoshida as navy minister, "There is no means of commencing a war with the United States other than by a surprise attack on Pearl Harbor."[5]

A letter is extant, addressed to Navy Minister Oikawa Koshirō and dated January 7 of the following year. To paraphrase: We ended the map exercise after the general trend had become apparent, so it's just a determination based on that situation. At that point, we were not running a simulation on how to win the war.

As to how to win the war (the letter basically argued) there was only one way. And that one method was, "when most of the enemy fleet's main force is at anchor in Pearl Harbor, to destroy it utterly by attacking it with a fleet of aircraft, at the same time blockading the harbor."[6]

This is the first mention of the Pearl Harbor surprise attack strategy in the public record. Yamamoto also conveyed his intentions to Naval Command. If Command staff were to consider it and propose it, it would formally become policy.

Nakazawa Tasuku was transferred from his post as chief of naval operations to that of captain of the cruiser *Ashigara*. The position he left was filled by an instructor at the Naval War College, Captain Tomioka Sadatoshi. One of Tomioka's subordinates was someone who had been in Genda Minoru's cohort at the Naval Academy: Commander Uchida Shigeshi.

Uchida finished drafting a strategy proposal toward the end of January. After it had passed under Tomioka's pen, it was sent along to Nagano Osami, chief of Naval Command (chief of staff), in June.

The Pearl Harbor surprise attack plan hardly sailed through this policy vetting process with no crosswinds. The draft strategy required the approval of the chief of staff. In July, the draft was returned to Commander Uchida: it had on it the stamped approval of the section head and division head, but not that of the chief of staff. Uchida asked Tomioka, "Why did it not get the chief's stamp of approval?" Tomioka gave no direct reply and instead answered evasively, "Maybe you should bring it to him for approval yourself."

So Uchida pressed Nagano: "May I have your approval, sir?" Nagano was famous for napping during meetings and conferences. In the end, he even napped in the defendant's chair at the Tokyo War Crimes trials. Despite his impressive eyebrows and strong facial features he gave the impression, in navy circles, of undependability. This time, he played dumb, asking, "Don't you have any explanation?"

Uchida Shigeshi had worked hard on this draft strategy and seethed with anger. Heedless of the difference in rank, he answered boldly, "If you read it, sir, everything should be clear." Faster than one could say, "Pearl," there was the chief's stamp. Nagano's backing and filling on the question had simply reflected the atmosphere within the Command staff.

WHY PEARL HARBOR? | 373

In October, Captain Kuroshima Kameto, chief of staff of the Combined Fleet, visited Naval Command. He requested that six aircraft carriers be tasked to the Pearl Harbor surprise-attack force. Operations chief Tomioka Sadatoshi replied, "Look at the total picture. Naval Command lays great stress on securing the vital areas to the south. We can split off no more than three aircraft carriers for the Hawaii strategy."

Frustrated, Commander Kuroshima played his trump card: "Commander in Chief Yamamoto has said that if this proposal is not adopted, he cannot be responsible for the security of the Empire; he will have no choice other than to resign as commander in chief."

Nagano's eventual reaction was, "If Yamamoto is so committed to this, why don't we try and give him a shot." This was not complete approval. Nagano was rather perceptive about the prevailing atmosphere within the navy. Yamamoto was sensitive to atmospherics as well. But in Yamamoto's case, what he sensed was not the mood within the navy, but the reactions of the general populace. As Yamamoto put it,

> If there's any chance that enemy planes could suddenly attack Tokyo and Osaka, so that in one morning both cities would be burned to the ground, or even if the damage were not so great, what then would national opinion—the ignorant masses—have to say about the navy? When I think back on the Russo-Japanese War, it's not difficult to imagine.[7]

This was in a letter addressed to the incoming navy minister, Shimada Shigetarō, immediately after the Pearl Harbor surprise-attack strategy had been formally approved by Naval Command.

That Yamamoto could so blithely refer to the public as "the ignorant masses" is a measure of how easily he was made to dance to the tune of pied-piper agitators like Ikezaki Tadayoshi. In 1941 Ikezaki published a speech titled, "If Japan and America Fight: Theory and Practice of the Pacific War." It exhibited his characteristic dash:

> The notion that planes packed with bombs could be dispatched from the American mainland to attack our cities is of course nothing we need to consider. . . . But there must be people who would ask, what if they come here by aircraft carrier? Come they may, come they might. The possibility is undeniable. On the other hand, if they come, they come with full awareness that they will be attacked and sunk by the Japanese

navy. And even if they are lucky enough to slip past the watchful gaze of the Japanese Fleet, our army and navy planes will be waiting to greet them. So even if one or two aircraft carriers made it over, what kind of business could they hope to accomplish?[8]

CHAPTER FIFTEEN

War Plan Orange

IN THE DAYS preceding Japan's surprise attack on Pearl Harbor, Ikezaki
Tadayoshi, who had debuted with *Japan Need Not Fear the U.S.*, came
out repeatedly with characteristic pronouncements of the "Japan is strong"
variety. Writers of best sellers for youth magazines also found in war the
perfect setting for their romantic tales of adventure.

The prospect of betraying such public acclaim is a frightening thing.
What Yamamoto Isoroku feared most, if the myth of the invincible navy
were to crumble, was "what then would . . . the ignorant masses . . . have to
say about the navy?"

What set Yamamoto Isoroku's mind on the Pearl Harbor strategy was
the likelihood of otherwise falling into a war of endurance with the United
States. His plan therefore differed from the Japanese navy's traditional
strategy of a forward defense, the type of engage-the-enemy scenario by
which they crushed Russia's Baltic Fleet.

It is worth asking at this point what sort of strategy America had delin-
eated in order to cope with Japan.

America's Japan strategy was code-named War Plan Orange. As we observed in passing in chapter 3, the plan, as worked out immediately after
the Russo-Japanese War, envisioned a Japan-U.S. war adhering to the following outline.

At the outset of the war, the Japanese army would invade the Philippines
and Guam. The U.S. Navy would immediately dispatch reinforcements to
the Philippines. But the broad Pacific constituted a great wall obstructing
any such relief effort. Or rather, as the U.S. fleet traversed the Pacific, it
would be subjected to devastating attacks by Japanese submarines. How
to break free of such potential damage was the question. It was a puzzle in
need of solution.

The framework for War Plan Orange had, in the main, been roughed out just prior to the First World War. Since then, it had gone through a number of iterations. The history of the strategy's recombinant genetic makeup is now a matter of events in the distant past, on their way to being forgotten even by the principal itself, America. But a commendable scholar emerged to address these issues. Edward S. Miller is his name, and the results of twenty-five years of his research finally came to fruition at the end of 1991, just in time for the fiftieth anniversary of the Pearl Harbor attack: *War Plan Orange: The U.S. Strategy to Defeat Japan*, a massive tome nearly two inches thick.[1] A jacket blurb attributed to Tom Clancy, author of *The Hunt for Red October*, praised it as "a superb piece of scholarly research into previously virgin territory." And William J. Crowe Jr., Admiral, USN, and former chairman of the Joint Chiefs of Staff, was quoted as calling it "a must read for historians, strategists, military planners, and students … a highly enjoyable account for even the casual reader of American history."

To start with the results, War Plan Orange was a successful strategy. This is clear at the very beginning of the book from Miller's description of a comment by Admiral Chester Nimitz that "the war unfolded just as predicted in naval war games applied to the plans as well."[2] Today, Nimitz's name recognition among Japanese is at a lower point than General Douglas MacArthur's, but in World War II he was commander in chief of the Pacific Fleet. Japanese children were made to learn a song called "The Battle for the Philippines" (Japanese lyrics by Saijō Yaso; music by Koseki Yūji) that went, approximately,

> If Nimitz and MacArthur come,
> And try to ring our bell,
> We'll give 'em marching orders
> Back to where they came from: Hell!

If MacArthur was America's land hero in the Pacific War, the sea hero was Nimitz.

Let us continue with Miller's analysis of War Plan Orange. Phase one of the war scenario played out much the same way the Japanese saw it. The Philippines and Guam both fell early on. In phase two, the Japanese plan called for the advancing U.S. fleet to be attacked and destroyed. The American side, however, had no intention of falling into that trap. They considered two strategic paths. Each proposal had its proponents:

the relatively radical group referred to as the Thrusters and the relatively conservative group known as Defensivists.

The Thrusters proposed heading straight for the Philippines without putting in to port at Hawaii. If the garrison at the Philippines could hold out, the relief might arrive in time. But this plan was the same as the Japanese phase one scenario. In other words, it would play right into the Japanese hand.

The Defensivists recommended a counterattack that would hop from island to island across the Pacific, roughly east to west—the Marshall, Caroline, and Mariana islands, and so on—occupying each in turn. However, this would take time. In the interim, the Philippine garrison would find itself in an extremely perilous situation. They would be like sacrificed pawns.

At first, the Thrusters had the momentum. What turned the tide in favor of the Defensivists was the altered situation following the end of the First World War. Under the Treaty of Versailles and the League of Nations Covenant, the Marshall, Caroline, and Mariana island groups were made Japanese mandates. If they had remained as German protectorates, then (as they were not independent participants in the war) they could not be occupied. But if they fell under Japanese control, then Japan could be made to give them up. The island-hopping strategy began to feel doable.

However, when word of War Plan Orange was leaked to Philippine Governor General Leonard Wood, it breathed new life into the Thrusters. The plan essentially called for Wood to be sacrificed. Since Wood lodged objections on that score with the secretary of war, President Warren G. Harding ordered the navy to make changes to War Plan Orange. This episode gives a sense of what a heavy burden it was for the United States to maintain the Philippines.

It was Japan's fault that the Philippines exacted such a high price for serving as America's forward base in acquiring rights in Asia. That an Asian nation with an outstanding military would come onto the scene was contrary to all American expectations, and as ill luck would have it, that nation was located uncomfortably close to the Philippines. Later, even General MacArthur had to submit to being sacrificed to this strategic burden.

The Thrusters and the Defensivists, in other words, represented the horns of a dilemma. To the garrison in the Philippines, the Thrusters offered some consolation. Nevertheless, it was also recognized that for America to secure a final victory, the Defensivists' proposal was the correct one. So in 1924 (the year Bywater was writing *The Great Pacific War*), a compromise plan was laid down. The decision as to which of the two courses to adopt would be left to the discretion of the commander in chief of the United States fleet.

As I was navigating Miller's *War Plan Orange*, I could see the context for the powerful realism of Hector C. Bywater's *The Great Pacific War*. A savvy journalist with experience as an intelligence agent, Bywater became aware of the give-and-take between Thrusters and Defensivists and positioned himself to benefit from their war of leaks, skillfully assimilating information. Ultimately it was the Defensivists' plan that Bywater developed most completely. By adding his imaginative powers to his knowledge as a journalist of naval affairs, he was able to describe convincingly an American victory.

* * *

BEFORE HE WROTE his novel *The Great Pacific War* in 1924, Hector C. Bywater published an analysis of naval affairs titled *Sea Power in the Pacific* (1921). The book garnered praise from Rear Admiral William Sims (promoted to full admiral only in 1930 on the retired list), former commander in chief of U.S. naval forces in Europe during World War I and one of the string-pullers for the Defensivists.

The Thrusters went on the offensive. At their leading edge: Admiral Robert Coontz, former chief of naval operations and incoming commander in chief of the U.S. Navy. Coontz was thinking in terms of assembling the main fleet in Hawaii as soon as war broke out, then taking the attack straight to the Philippines with a force of three hundred ships without putting in to harbor. The operations element of this plan, a version of what was called the Through Ticket option for Plan Orange, was formalized as Fleet Plan O-3, and it constituted the core of Plan Orange for the next decade.

To corroborate his conceptions with empirical proof, Admiral Coontz assumed command of an American fleet and took it on a grand exercise from Hawaii to Australia nonstop, a distance equivalent to the planned dash to the Philippines. However, since mid-ocean refueling proved more difficult than anticipated, the exercise actually wound up giving aid and comfort to the Defensivists.

Indeed, the more one was forced to consider experimental data, the worse things looked for the Thrusters. The long, nonstop routes increased the risk of ambushes by Japanese submarines. A number of simulations were run to explore this issue. In 1923, it was forecast that some fifteen ships of the main force would make it to the Philippines. In 1928, that calculation was revised downward to ten ships. And by 1933, the estimate had fallen to seven ships. This nearly sealed the fate of the Through Ticket strategy advocated by Admiral Coontz and the Thrusters. That is, the concept of a nonstop dash to recover the Philippines.

But this revival of fortunes for the Defensivists did not mean the end of the dilemma for Plan Orange. The Philippines remained America's Achilles' heel. In 1922, Philippines Governor General Wood had objected to Plan Orange when it appeared to sacrifice the Philippines. But in 1933, Brigadier General Stanley Embick, commander of the fortress at Corregidor, called the Through Ticket version of the Plan "madness."[3]

When the Defensivists came to constitute the mainstream, there remained only one way for the otherwise sacrificed Philippine garrison to resist a Japanese assault. It was Brigadier General Embick who made the following proposal. If the goal were really to retain the Philippines, a large fleet would have to be provided for at Manila itself. To that end, the U.S. would have to be prepared to expend vast sums in a shipbuilding program. There is no question that it was a sound argument. However, Embick knew such an increase in funding was impossible. Logically, then, the U.S. would have no choice but to withdraw immediately from Asia.

The U.S. Navy found no logical counterargument to Embick's proposal. At the same time, however, the navy was hardly about to withdraw to the eastern Pacific, just like that. So the rebuttal to Embick took the form of a scheme to retake the Philippines if and when they were lost. Once the Philippine garrison had been evacuated, they would not retreat any farther than a line running from Hawaii to Alaska. There they would hold out for three years, subjecting the Japanese fleet to harassing submarine attacks while the U.S. built up a fleet four times the size of Japan's. Then, gradually, they would tighten the noose around Japan.

The Defensivists were also emboldened by advances in aviation. The Marshalls, Carolines, and other Japanese trust territories covered a distance of some one thousand miles. This distance made extended flight range a necessity. In October 1933, the Catalina flying boat was developed, with a range of one thousand miles. With this, it was possible to encompass Japanese bases scattered all across the Pacific, with a plan that would turn them from safe havens into targets of U.S. reconnaissance and bombing.

Finally, the ascendancy of the Defensivists was confirmed. Embick was transferred from his post as commander of the fortress at Corregidor back to the U.S., where he became involved with the army General Staff's work on Plan Orange. His proposal was adopted by the navy, and he joined the Defensivists.

The U.S. Army's chief of staff was Douglas MacArthur. Embick concealed from MacArthur his conversion to the Defensivist position and reported to him that Plan Orange had "not been changed materially." According to its current drafters, the new version of the Plan should consider moving promptly from Toraq (then called "Truk") to "Manila Bay or some other location." Embick told Macarthur that (in the words of Edward S. Miller) "the fleet merely wished to perfect its line of communication before setting sail for the western Pacific, that the army should support it, and that the amendments altered only the *initial* goal of the offensive."[4] MacArthur then effectively put his own signature to a strategy that was to put him in a predicament in the future. It was one of history's ironies.

When MacArthur signed off on the revised Plan Orange in May 1935, it also meant that now there was no question that the twenty-thousand-man garrison in the Philippines would be sacrificed. The Defensivists had triumphed completely. The strategy was designed to lead inexorably to an American victory in a future Pacific War. It was permeated with the coolheaded (if not cold-blooded) calculation that great victories require small sacrifices. One of the chief merits of the Defensivists' island-hopping counterattack was that it drew Japan into a war of endurance, putting the screws to it economically.

So Plan Orange meandered in its development but eventually returned to a point that Hector Bywater had predicted in his *The Great Pacific War*. In *Japan and America: The Battle for Dominance*, Mizuno Hironori had written that Japan would be drawn into a war of endurance, which it would lose. And Ishimaru Tōda, of the same naval generation as Mizuno, had also expressed anxiety regarding a war of endurance. He became aware of *War in the Pacific* (1936), a joint work by two members of the new generation of Japan-America future-war chroniclers, which spoke of the efficacy of a war of endurance from the American point of view. In 1938, Tōda translated an excerpt from this work in the magazine *Kaizō* (Reform). And when he published a full translation in 1940, he praised the stance taken by the authors, Sutherland Denlinger and Charles Gary:

> With thoroughgoing logic and also with realism, the authors have written an excellent work that permits not only specialists, but also the general reader, to comprehend the true character of a Pacific War.[5]

War in the Pacific drew attention not so much to military might as to industrial might. In overall national power, Japan could not compare to the United States. Therefore any war with the U.S. would be one of endurance. Statistics showed just how dependent Japan was on international trade. So Japan would have to devise ways and means to secure the importing of oil, cotton, rubber, nickel, and iron even in the event of war. America, however, would establish its main Pacific fleet at Pearl Harbor in Hawaii, from which it could patrol the Aleutians, Midway, and the Panama Canal. For the space of at least one year, the American fleet would watch and wait at Pearl Harbor in Hawaii, sending out submarines to interdict traffic on the sea lanes by which Japan imported raw materials from the south. Inevitably, this would lead to the economic exhaustion of Japan. America should tighten the noose slowly but surely. In this approach there was no emotional evocation of the inscrutable Japanese sneaking up on America from behind. Rather, it was a coolheaded view that simply and matter-of-factly favored driving the Japanese into a corner.

Whereas the Japanese aimed for a limited war settled by a climactic naval battle, the Americans planned for total war, including economic war. That is what determined the direction taken by Plan Orange.

Plan Orange, for its part, did have its conflicting partisans of the Thrusters and Defensivist approaches. The eclipse of the Thrusters and the ascendancy of the Defensivists confirmed that a war of endurance was in fact a shortcut to victory in war. What buttressed the arguments of the Defensivists (the faction supporting the island-hopping counterattack strategy) was aircraft development. Ironically, it was air power that also led Yamamoto Isoroku in the direction of Pearl Harbor.

After becoming commander in chief of Japan's Combined Fleet, Yamamoto reportedly told a journalist the following:

> The future of our naval strategy lies in the navy seizing a given island, then within one week constructing on that island an airfield from which our air force will advance, gaining air mastery over the next designated sea area. But I wonder whether Japan can do this at our current level of industrial capacity.[6]

Commander Yamamoto was displaying an intuitive appreciation of the island-hopping counterattack strategy given structure in Plan Orange. While Japan couldn't do it, it seemed that America could. So if the alternative was a slow strangulation, the only solution was an all-out preemptive strike.

This is not to say that on the American side the island-hopping strategy was free of its doubts and doubters. Under the Treaty of Versailles that concluded World War I, Japan had assumed control of the former German protectorates in the South Sea islands north of the equator. But construction of military facilities on these islands was expressly forbidden. However, if an impregnable fortress were to be built secretly...

In *War Plan Orange*, Miller comments, "For two decades Japan had shrouded the Mandated Islands in mystery."[7] But rumors were rampant in U.S. naval circles about a fortress on Toraq, about ten-inch guns on the highlands of Palau, about artillery batteries on Saipan as well. The army's G2 section (army intelligence) submitted a report estimating that in at least thirteen locations, the Japanese mandates had submarine or air bases.

The United States repeatedly lodged requests stating its desire for an investigation into the question of whether or not Japan were abiding by its treaty commitments. Japan rejected these requests every time they were made. It was announced that the American cruiser *Milwaukee*, newly constructed, would go on a shakedown cruise, stopping at a number of ports around the world in a test of its seaworthiness and handling. This was an internationally accepted maritime practice. To no one's surprise, some of the ports they stopped at were in the Japanese mandated territories. That was, after all, the main objective. But all they could confirm was the existence of a small fuel storage facility on Toraq. Surely that was not all there was.

Just at that time, there occurred the death, from causes unknown, of Lieutenant Colonel Earl Hancock "Pete" Ellis of the U.S. Marines. To confirm his own theories, he had boarded a Japanese passenger ship and visited the Marshall and Caroline island groups before dying at Palau. Rumors of Japanese machinations were impossible to quell. But there was no proof and no memo by Ellis to offer any other explanation.

After Japan withdrew from the League of Nations, the Americans grew even more frantic. The first crossing of the Pacific on a flying boat, the adventure of a round-the-world voyage by a light plane: these and other such stunts camouflaged a continuing effort to canvass the same area.

I am reminded of Hirata Shinsaku's *Task Force Shōwa*. Its secret naval base is located south of Hachijo Island, in a place unknown to the enemy and surrounded by cliffs. It can be reached by ship only via a long, long passageway through that steep canyon, which continues so far that the outlet is shrouded in darkness. However, the Americans' genuine worries were an overreaction. What the Japanese military was trying so hard to conceal was no giant fortress. In fact, before 1939 there was nothing of a size that could be called a fortress on any of these various islands. Yamamoto's subordinate, Rear Admiral Fukudome Shigeru, who served as chief of staff of the Combined Fleet, has left us the following account:

> Before the war, in all of Saipan, Toraq, and Palau, the only facilities built by the Japanese navy that could be called military facilities were communications facilities and small fuel storage facilities. Apart from those, the only thing that stands out is the airfield the army set up at Aslito in Saipan in 1935. . . . The Americans claimed we were unquestionably maintaining military facilities that may have violated certain prohibitions, and the American military attaché in Tokyo petitioned persistently, every year, to inspect the areas in question. Each time the request was denied.[8]

Japan was neglecting to prepare for such a threat as an island-hopping counterattack. Or rather, in terms of their overall thinking, they were not honestly confronting the reality of a war of endurance.

And that was because Hirata was not the only one who was content with a hazy conception of the region, as indicated by the notion of a Shōwa Task Force somewhere "south of Hachijo Island."

In a war plan, as one might guess, there are certain specialized military or diplomatic matters pertaining to realms that can be called technical. But in War Plan Orange, and in Japanese strategic planning, these technical realms occupied comparatively little space.

One might well say that war planning in general is rather a matter of imaginative power. Many are the cases in which it is not the military professionals but the journalists and the novelists who see most clearly into the future. Mizuno Hironori and Hector C. Bywater are two examples, representing the genre of what I have called Japan-U.S. future-war chronicles.

War changes the fates of individuals. I have just used the phrase "war planning," but it would be more accurate to call it a program for mass murder in the near future. And if that's what it is, then military and nonmilitary alike had better devote some planning for their own imminent deaths. Reality is a great leveler.

The reason so many authors of Japan-U.S. future-war chronicles appeared in rapid succession was because of the leveling conditions that obtained in the twentieth century. The motives of such authors were many and varied. There was the patriot who wanted to sound the alarm to his fellow citizens. Another professed to be writing in a spirit of humanism. Still another might be angling for military funds. One author would be using war's risks to life and limb as plot mechanisms in a tale of adventure. Then there was the ideologue who thought the genre a bully pulpit for proselytizing his beliefs. And the hobbyist intoxicated with a fetishism for the machinery of war. And the writer trying to project onto affairs of state his own psychological struggles. For one reason or another, these authors all attempted to predict the onset and course of war.

In terms of sensitivity, writers are not inferior to professional military personnel. Indeed, the military may reflect politics, but writers reflect the people. Still, just as a capable officer may produce an outstanding strategy, and an inferior one may produce an inferior plan, so it is with the authors of Japan-U.S. future-war chronicles. One author may see with great clarity into the future; another may be essentially the spokesman of the "ignorant masses." And while the military may lead the people, it is also true that the people lead the military.

Yamamoto Isoroku was terribly concerned that if Japan were the target of air raids, "what then would . . . the ignorant masses have to say about the navy?" At the beginning of the war, the navy—in contrast to the army—was somewhat reticent. That was because they knew better than the army just how hopeless it was for Japan to try to match America in terms of national strength. But if that were so, why did they not state definitely that they had little confidence of success?

After the war was over, Fukutome reminisced about this very question.

As to why the navy did not state this definitely, it was hardly as simple as a deficiency of bravery. Was it really the kind of cut-and-dried affair in which a simple declaration would prevent war? The decision to go to war was not based on anything so practical as whether the war's outcome would be profitable to us. The situation was such that we were driven into desperate straits. If you object that "driven" is deficient, I will add that in our predicament, with no way out in sight, we willingly rushed into the jaws of death.[9]

As to who did the "driving," I want to suggest that this was the result of both external pressure (the U.S.) and domestic public opinion (in Japan). I have commented on this in my *The Defeat of the Summer of '41.*[10] Tōjō Hideki, who had assumed the post of prime minister just before the war with America began, hesitated just at the point when a decision had to be made as to whether or not to start the war. In contrast to the fiercely pro-war stance he had adopted in his days as army minister, now his posture was clearly irresolute. It was at this point that a Resolution on Accomplishing National Policy formally passed the Diet (on November 18).

> Turmoil continues to spread throughout the world. Hostile countries have distorted the true intentions of the Empire; their rhetoric has grown increasingly radical. . . . Accordingly, be it resolved that we must dauntlessly establish the existence and authority of the Empire, constructing the Greater East Asia Co-Prosperity Sphere and thereby securing world peace.

When Diet Representative Shimada Toshio rose to introduce the resolution, he faced Tōjō and other cabinet members present on the dais and in a greatly agitated manner asserted, "This is the collective will of the people!" Another Diet member present was Ikezaki Tadayoshi. At that time, Tōjō kept an ambiguous poker face, avoiding any clear statement. The people had already passed him by.

* * *

IT WAS DECEMBER 8, 1941, before sunrise. Diet member Ikezaki is dozing in a second-class sleeper car on a train going from Aomori in the north to Osaka in the west of the main island of Honshū.[11]

The previous day Ikezaki had been invited to talk at Ōsawano-machi in the suburbs of Toyama. For three hours he had held forth in his high-pitched grating voice on the theme of a Japan-U.S. war: the showdown is inevitable; its day is nigh; Japan will win. The auditorium in the public school was packed. He had boarded the Ōsaka train home in high spirits.

At 8:26 AM the train arrived at Ōsaka Station. The Diet member had reason to remember the exact time. It was at that moment that a station employee holding an extra edition of a newspaper in his left hand ran up to the ticket gate and handed it to his colleagues. Ikezaki cast a casual glance. The words that danced before his eyes proclaimed that America and England had just declared war on Japan.

"We've finally done it."

He rode a subway to Honchō, then transferred to a city tram. All the way back to his office in Tokiwachō, he muttered the same words over and over to himself. He was excited. He immediately flipped the switch on the radio. His wife, Nobuko, also poked her head in at the office. His assistants as well—everyone gathered around the radio. The title, *Winning a Protracted War*, came to him in a flash of inspiration, and he began to rough out an outline.

"For some thirteen years I have incessantly warned my countrymen about the coming of the day that has now, truly, dawned."

That evening, at the Asahi Hall, the *Asahi Shimbun* held a lecture meeting. Naturally Ikezaki Tadayoshi was the lead-off batter, preceding the military speakers. The *Ōsaka Asahi* newspaper reported that, "As if by prior agreement, the listeners were all carrying copies of the newspaper and spent the few minutes before the meeting began, not wasting precious time in private conversation, but silently consuming—as they were consumed by—the news." The paper also carried a précis of Ikezaki's speech.

I have a certain way of looking at the present conflict. That is, "the worst of times" will not last three years. But we must be resolved to prepare ourselves mentally for five years, even ten years. I say three years because after three years there will be another presidential election campaign year. And I should like to predict that the struggle will be not between Democrats and Republicans, but between the "war" party and the "stop" party—and that the "stop" party will win overwhelmingly.

One of the excited listeners called out, "Motion!" The motion was to send a telegram of support to Tōjō Hideki. Straightaway, Ikezaki composed the following telegram:

We hereby make obeisance to the Imperial Rescript declaring war on England and America; our awe and excitement cannot be suppressed. We trust in the valor and exertion of our army and navy, and with the country united in this effort we expect the utter chastisement of our benighted enemies.

To the very end, Ikezaki Tadayoshi did not believe that it would be a war of endurance.

On the same day, Mizuno Hironori received a visit at his home in Sangenjaya from one Matsushita Yoshio. "Look what they've done!" was Mizuno's sole comment, delivered with a glum expression. His conversation with Matsushita was disconnected, awkward.

Between "We've finally done it!" and "Look what they've done!" the difference is 180 degrees.

As a Diet representative much in demand as a speaker, Ikezaki was more than ever the darling of the age. Mizuno, arguing that a protracted war was inevitable, was the opposite case. Already in February, the Cabinet Information Bureau had given editors of general-interest magazines a list of those whose opinions were not to be printed. Mizuno's name was among them.

Having successfully directed the surprise attack on Pearl Harbor, Yamamoto Isoroku became a hero of the people.

Ikezaki Tadayoshi's *Winning a Protracted War* was published in book form in March of the next year (1942). But on April 18, sixteen bombers under the command of Lieutenant Colonel James Doolittle suddenly attacked the home islands of Japan. They dropped bombs on Tokyo, Kawasaki, Yokosuka, Nagoya, Yokkaichi, and Kobe before departing for the Chinese mainland. It was an isolated incident, not to be compared to the Great Tokyo Air Raid at the end of the war, but it gave Yamamoto a shock. It was the situation of which he had been most fearful.

At the time of the surprise attack on Pearl Harbor, it so happened that the American aircraft carriers were all out of port. Now that carrier-based bombers had actually attacked Tokyo, Commander Yamamoto (being of the opinion that Japan would lose a war of endurance) resolved to attack Pearl Harbor once again. This time, Midway Island was to be made the forward base, and the raid on Pearl mounted from there. However, the movements of Japan's Combined Fleet had been detected by the enemy's reconnaissance planes, and Yamamoto suffered a miserable, crushing defeat.

The defeat in the naval battle at Midway occurred on June 5, 1942. Six months after starting the war, Japan was put into something of a predicament with the loss of four aircraft carriers. Under War Plan Orange, Japan was now methodically being driven into a corner and strangled.

Two months later, on August 7, the Americans landed on the island of Guadalcanal. The island-hopping counterattack had begun.

Then, on April 18, 1943, Yamamoto took off from Rabaul for an inspection tour, only to be attacked in the skies over Bougainville Island by sixteen enemy fighters that had been waiting in ambush. The U.S. military had intercepted and decoded wireless transmissions that revealed his destination. Thus Yamamoto met his death. With the loss at Midway, his scheme to choke off War Plan Orange at its inception had already met its own untimely end.

Epilogue

IN THE SUMMER OF 1943, a little over two months after Yamamoto Isoroku was killed in action, Mizuno Hironori felt a sharp pain in his lower abdomen. He sought admittance to a naval hospital but was refused. Eventually, he was carried to a small clinic that did not even have inpatient facilities. The diagnosis was acute appendicitis.

Convalescing at home, he wrote a letter to Kiyosawa Kiyoshi, a friend. Kiyosawa was fifty-three, some fifteen years younger than Mizuno. Kiyosawa had studied in the United States, returning a liberal and becoming a prolific writer. Like Mizuno, he had been blacklisted by the cabinet's Information Bureau and banned from publishing in general-interest magazines. Mizuno informed him,

> Already this old man has but a few years left. Withering on the vine will be my last contribution to my country. You and others in whom the sap of life still flows in abundance must devote your strength to the struggle for Japan's rebirth.

With no public forum available to him, Kiyosawa recorded his thoughts in his diary. Reading Mizuno's letter, the younger author wrote,

> Kobayashi Seizō [an admiral], Nomura Kichisaburo [an admiral; Japanese ambassador in Washington at the start of the war], and others of our classmates [at the Naval Academy] have reached positions of fame and influence. Here's a man with even more talent. What a pity!

Kiyosawa's diary was published after the war under the title *Diary of the Dark*.[1]

In the autumn of that year, Mizuno's nephew, Shigematsu Fukio, came to visit.[2] Shigematsu had enrolled in the Matsuyama regiment and spent five years in military campaigns on the Chinese mainland and had just been honorably discharged. Knowing that Mizuno was fond of sake, he brought a large bottle he had somehow managed to acquire: "Good thing you survived and got to come home."

Mizuno had not had sake in a while. It put him in a good mood. But in his condition he was probably not ready for it. Once again, he was struck down by illness. This was diagnosed as a pancreatic cystoma. When he was released from the hospital, he went to recuperate at the Shigematsu family home. This was on Ōshima, near which the Seto Inland Sea Bridge now connects Onomichi on the island of Honshu with Imabari on the island of Shikoku. Back then it took a full day and night to get there from Tokyo. Mizuno rested on Ōshima for two months, then returned to Tokyo. Soon it was New Year's Day, 1944.

The American island-hopping counterattack was posting steady results. In February, 6,800 members of the Marshall Islands garrison died with honor. In June, in a sea battle off the Mariana Islands, the Combined Fleet lost three aircraft carriers. In July came the loss of Saipan, in which 30,000 members of the garrison and 10,000 noncombatants died. The Tōjō Cabinet fell, and the Koiso-Kuniaki Cabinet was established. This hardly meant that the war situation improved. In August, 8,000 men died in action on the island of Tinian. On Guam, the figure was 18,000. In October, at the Battle of Leyte Gulf in the Philippines, the Combined Fleet was practically wiped out.

Then, on November 24, from the Mariana Islands, the B-29 "Flying Fortresses" took off on their first bombing runs over Tokyo. Their target was the Nakajima aircraft factory in North Tama County. No one yet suspected that this was a prelude to ordinary civilians becoming embroiled in the war the next year (1945), with the Great Tokyo Air Raid of March 9 and the subsequent raids on April 13 and May 25. Mizuno composed the following *kyōka* (satirical verse):

> Fight on, fight on, fight on, fight on, fight on:
> The race of fighters fights till fighting's done.

He decided he had no choice himself but to evacuate to Ōshima. At Onomichi his abdominal pain became unendurable. At the inn the pain was such that he was unable to sleep.

Two days after Mizuno arrived on the island, the Koiso-Kuniaki Cabinet resigned en masse. When word of this reached Mizuno, he predicted to Shigematsu, "I'd say the next prime minister will be Suzuki Kantarō, and the next foreign minister will be Tōgō Shigenori," and "The war will be over by September."

Mizuno's life on Ōshima was a life of routine. When he learned that his home in Sangenjaya had been burned, he was silently tending the field he had leased from Shigematsu. Finally, even his birthplace, Matsuyama, was bombed—not far away.

On July 26, incendiary bombs were dropped in a ring about the hill on which stood Matsuyama Castle: downtown was almost completely razed to the ground.

Over cities all across Japan, the American military scattered leaflets in Japanese, advising surrender. On one side of the flyers was the comment, "The militarists have underestimated America." On the other side, the message included a quotation from Mizuno's own writings.

> To all Japanese:
> In the April 1925 issue of *Chūō Kōron* [The Central Review], Mr. Mizuno Hironori said the following:
> "Along with the idiocy of giving too much credit to the spirit of the American people, we must also not make the huge mistake of underestimating America. Since, in studying their military capability, we do not respect their human factors as equal to ours, I fear we risk repeating the mistake by which the people of Germany erred in their assessment of the English."
> Your military leaders have indeed repeated the very mistake that Mr. Mizuno warned against.

On August 15, Mizuno heard over the radio an announcement that "at noon there will be an important broadcast." He muttered, "So we've lost." And indeed, as it turned out, the announcement referred to the emperor's famous broadcast declaration that Japan had lost the war—the first time most Japanese had heard the emperor's voice.

Now all he could do was await the demobilization of his son, Mitsunori. Unlike his father, Mitsunori was a slender lad with a narrow face, who had graduated from Tokyo Imperial University's German law department and

gone to work in the mining industry. He married a graduate of Sacred
Heart Women's Academy. Within half a year, however, they were divorced.
Mitsunori, despondent, now volunteered to be stationed in Manila. Called
into military service at Manila at the end of the war, he was wounded. While
he was recuperating in a field hospital, an American bomb ended his life
on August 12. Mizuno knew none of this.

One autumn festival day on Ōshima, Mizuno cried, "I have a toothache!"
and spat out dark blood. For a week he gasped with abdominal pain. It
looked like some sort of intestinal blockage. And if that were the case, there
was no point in trying to treat it on Ōshima; he had to be moved to facilities
at Imabari on Shikoku. That evening, they got hold of a small motorboat,
and both Shigematsu and his wife accompanied him as escorts. But midway
the engine failed. A fishing boat came to the rescue and returned them to
Ōshima, where they made arrangements to transfer to another boat. It
wasn't until the following morning that they finally reached Imabari. The
hospital there had been bombed half to bits. The abdominal operation took
two hours. They didn't have enough space to keep him there. Mizuno was
transported on a door to a nearby civilian home. It was right after this that
the author drew his last breath. He was seventy years old.

* * *

ON DECEMBER 7, 1991, I covered the fiftieth anniversary ceremonies at Pearl
Harbor. American veterans who had survived the Japanese surprise attack
were by then in their seventies. Around the event site one noticed many old
couples. The proceedings began early, at 7:00 AM. At 7:55, the time of the
first wave of Japanese bombers, the schedule called for President George
Bush to dedicate with a silent prayer the memorial built above the battleship
Arizona, which had been sunk with one thousand sailors aboard.

The next day, I received word that before the battleship *Missouri* was to be
scuttled it would be opened to the public. The *Missouri*—on whose decks,
on September 2, 1945, Japanese leaders formally surrendered to the Allied
forces. On that occasion, Douglas MacArthur, supreme commander for the
Allied powers in Japan, had the *Missouri* fly the very Stars and Stripes that
had flown on Commodore Perry's flagship, the *Powhattan*. This was the
flag that was fluttering on the mast when Matsuzaki Mitsutarō, the government's advisor on Confucian protocol, his breath redolent with the French
wine he had so freely imbibed, grasped Commodore Perry in a drunken
embrace and cried, "Japan and America, all the same heart."

Putting the fiftieth anniversary ceremonies behind me, I walked farther and farther back into the American military base at Pearl Harbor. As I passed the giant nuclear submarines, their cylindrical fuselages exposed, I saw, on the other side of some barbed wire, that a long queue had formed. Not a Japanese in sight. I felt strange and embarrassed, thinking that all these people lining up knew about the role of this battleship in avenging the abominable "Day of Infamy."

In the unforgiving blaze of the sun on this tropical isle, that pile of ugly metal seemed to be sweltering all the more. Its 16-inch deck guns protruded so far one would think them off balance. On the fateful day of surrender, Shigemitsu Mamoru, the Japanese plenipotentiary representative, suffering from the tension and the heat, asked for a glass of water but was coldly refused. I could not help but think of that episode now.

Indeed, we were more than once obliged to the Black Ships.

In 1854, Perry had insisted on negotiating at the capital, but the Tokugawa Bakufu (the Shogunate) had held him in check at the village of Yokohama.

On August 30, 1945, General MacArthur alighted at the Atsugi airfield. The airfield was pockmarked with bomb craters. Not six months earlier, Kamikaze Special Attack Forces had used this airfield for training.

But MacArthur did not make straight for the capital. The Japanese government had stipulated that Yokohama be made the site of his general headquarters. Official instructions sent to the Kanagawa prefectural administration at Yokohama, the prefectural capital, made it clear that the enemy must be held in check at Yokohama, and not a single soldier permitted into the imperial capital. The meaning was that U.S. General Headquarters must not be set up on the Tokyo side of the Tamagawa River.

This was certainly a familiar line of thinking.

GHQ accordingly set up shop at the Yokohama Tax Offices. It looked as though the Japanese maneuver was working. From Atsugi, MacArthur headed for Yokohama's Hotel New Grand.

The Hotel New Grand was—and is—situated in front of Yamashita Park. MacArthur had stayed there once before with his wife Jean, so he was familiar with the location. That part of town now lay in ruins, but the four-story hotel itself remained standing, unchanged in appearance. To take him there, the Japanese supplied a dilapidated Lincoln of uncertain vintage. During the twenty-five kilometer trip from Atsugi on that broiling hot day, MacArthur must have wished he could arrive quickly at this familiar hotel and get some rest.

MacArthur was met at the entrance by "an elderly Japanese dressed in a wing collar, swallow-tail coat, and pin-striped trousers," who "bowed deeply."[3]

"How long have you been the manager of this hotel?" asked MacArthur.

The seventy-five-year-old Nomura Yōzō replied, "I am not the manager. I am the owner," and bowed several more times. Saying, "I hope you'll like the room I'm going to show you," he padded quickly down a corridor, leading the way. The suite he showed the general was of the highest class, but it had a lower ceiling than MacArthur had imagined.

MacArthur entered and lay down on the bed. In the corridor outside, a hundred staff officers bustled about, seeking their billeted quarters with loud voices. He could get no sleep. Gazing out the window at Yokohama harbor, which was visible over the branches of the gingko trees lining the street outside, he rang the bell for service. Three maids rushed in all aflutter, like so many butterflies, followed by the swallow-tailed Nomura. MacArthur announced he would like to dine with his staff.

The menu featured walleye pollack with carrots, onions, potato, and also frozen whale meat cooked up as a steak. Nomura intended this cuisine as the hallmark of a cordial reception, but the general took one bite and then lay down his fork.

The entire area was declared off-limits, and the first day of the new coming of the Black Ships was over.

John Gunther, later famous for travel books such as *Inside Europe* and *Inside Asia*, stated in *The Riddle of MacArthur* (1951) that when MacArthur made arrangements for the surrender aboard the Missouri before sufficient troops had arrived to provide security, "professors who studied Japan all their lives, military experts who knew every nook and cranny of the Japanese character, thought that MacArthur was taking a frightful risk."[4] As Gunther explained it,

> There were some—in those days—who in fact believed that the concept of any kind of occupation in Japan would turn out to be impossible. There would be guerrilla warfare for years within ten miles of Tokyo. No American administrator would be safe without permanent heavy guard. The Japanese would devote themselves to passive resistance mingled with the most savage type of organized brigandage. The country would blaze with a permanent flame of hatred for the conquering Americans. And so on.[5]

This anxiety was seriously felt at the time. And thus, said Gunther,

> MacArthur's decision to accept the capitulation on the *Missouri* in Tokyo Bay before more than a handful of American airborne troops arrived has been called the greatest gamble in modern history.[6]

For all that, MacArthur spent three leisurely days at the New Grand in Yokohama before attending the surrender ceremony.

Then, on September 5, MacArthur directed the Japanese government to requisition the Daiichi Seimei (First Insurance) building opposite the imperial palace to use as his general headquarters.

While MacArthur was setting up his headquarters in the Daiichi Seimei building, Unno Jūzō, who had gained fame for importing science fiction elements into the genre of Japan-U.S. future-war chronicles, was busy penning an article titled "The Atomic Bomb and World Security," carried in the October issue of *Hikari* (Light). For Unno, America was already yesterday's enemy.

> I must confess: when I first learned that America had succeeded in creating an atomic bomb, it transcended considerations of enmity in war, it transcended the holocaust of Hiroshima. I felt I owed America awe and respect for this epoch-making event in the history of science and technology. And I must also confess that I felt extremely envious.

Is it possible to say that this imprudent generosity was confined to Unno? By this time, how could anyone "feel envious" toward an enemy who had brought so much death and destruction to their country?

For Unno, "transcending considerations of enmity in war" was not that difficult.

> The Black Ships will eventually enter the harbor. And when they do, raising a hue and cry about it will serve no purpose. We earthlings will have no choice but to unite and cooperate without delay, welcoming these apparently threatening alien life forms that are about to invade, at last, from outer space.

Such a leap of imagination might seem unusual, but one can also see an example of the brutish fiend transformed into its opposite in the "What Should We Learn from America?" roundtable discussion published in the same October 1945 issue of *Hikari* (Light) that carried Unno's essay. The participants included the vice president of the Dōmei wire service, the former New York correspondent for the *Asahi* newspaper, and the former London correspondent of the *Mainichi* newspaper, among others—all prominent intellectuals. The consensus was that from now on, "we Japanese" must radically change our "Japanese" ways of thinking—our Japanese spirit, our feelings as Japanese.

The loss in war, followed immediately by remorse. But remorse in an individual applies to an effort to rid oneself of defects. Here, it was more a matter of seeking to acquire one's opponent's strengths. It was the same when Perry came. The "expel the barbarian" movement was always paired with this sort of "opening the country" argument.

Unno died of tuberculosis early in the summer of 1949. He was fifty-two years old.

* * *

ON DECEMBER 1, 1945, the Allied powers' General Headquarters published a list naming Tōjō Hideki and fifty-nine others Class A War Criminals. Among the names was Ikezaki Tadayoshi. On the eleventh he was transferred from Ōsaka to Sugamo Prison in Tokyo. When asked by the American prosecutor why he began to study military affairs, Ikezaki replied that the impetus was America's anti-Japanese exclusion laws. When asked about sources, he said that he had mostly relied on Hector C. Bywater.

Ikezaki was arrested as a wartime ideologue, but he was not so big a catch. Occupation authorities hesitated over an indictment. They asked him what sort of influence his books had had on the government or military. Asking the author himself such a question was a hopeless proposition, and indeed Ikezaki replied that they had best ask the government or the military.

Unindicted, finally, and released, Ikezaki returned home and made a bonfire of dried up old leaves in a corner of his garden. He gazed at the smoke for a long time.

At the end of the summer of 1949, Ikezaki Tadayoshi too passed away. He was fifty-eight years old. The cause of death was the same as for Unno: tuberculosis.

Thus the authors of the Japan-U.S. future-war chronicles passed from the scene right after the war was lost. Between those who favored war and those who were opposed, there were great disparities. But uniformly they directed their readers' attention to the vast Pacific. Somewhere in that expanse of ocean was a mystic space that fathered forth the unsettling vapors of external pressure. And from that place, even after the war, the Black Ships would surely come again.

When accused by the American prosecutors of crimes against peace, Ishihara Kanji, formerly a lieutenant general in the Japanese army (also author of *The Final World War* and one of the plotters behind the Manchurian Incident), made the following reply:

If Perry hadn't come, Japan would have been peaceful enough under its National Seclusion policy of *sakoku*. If you're going to try someone, try Perry![7]

Afterword

T HIS NARRATIVE has unfolded from the arrival of Commodore Matthew C. Perry's Black Ships to the end of the Second World War, a period of about a century. Another half-century takes us to the present.

I have lived in a Japan that has had no connection with war, and I have chosen here to focus on the genre of Japan-U.S. future-war chronicles because I have been struggling to find a way to delineate the modern spiritual history of the Japanese people. For now, I believe I can say the following: It is simply not the case that the Japanese have been living according to two diametrically opposed value systems, namely prewar militarism and postwar pacifism. What, then—and how?

It all began with the Black Ships. It was the Black Ships that provoked the Revere the Emperor, Expel the Barbarian movement; it was they who perpetrated, upon a newborn nation state, the centripetal fiction of the Mikado. Before then, the Japanese archipelago was a world unto itself; such a boundary as a national border merely dissolved into the vast ocean, disappearing beyond the sea.

From across that sea came the Black Ships, messengers of ill omen. They brought, ambivalently, both militarism and pacifism—both as the result of external pressure. So who was it that dispatched the Black Ships?

It would be too narrow a definition to think of external pressure as a matter merely of military compulsion. External pressure is, rather, a somewhat broader concept. Perhaps it reflects certain monstrous mutations in modern European civilization.

Modern European civilization brought quantum leaps in the spread of industrial production. At the same time, it engendered, worldwide, the madness of survival of the fittest. And the mechanism for suppressing this madness was also held in its sole grasp. It was called *democracy*. The best exemplar of this conjoint madness and democracy was the United States. Perry brought us modern European civilization; MacArthur brought us democracy. Together they forced upon us the global standard of European modernity.

In the mid-nineteenth century, an island nation in the Far East was incorporated, willy-nilly, into international society. Japanese were hard-pressed to cast off their old shells and change into new ones so fast.

The century of the Black Ships had begun.

External pressure breathed new life into the sleeping Mikado. The two combined as a two-faced god enshrined in the heart-of-hearts of the Japanese. Subsequently, Japanese emotions were expressed in relative terms, as a function of external pressure.

Modern Japan was devoted to war. War was something you had to wage, or you would find others waging it upon you. Japanese lived and died by that obsession. The simulation narratives I have been calling Japan-U.S. future-war chronicles were sensitive seismometers of external pressures. Any shifts in the indicators, or in the scales of measurement, were a matter of concern.

Mizuno Hironori's *The Next Battle* (1914) is a tale of how a Japan at peace after its victory in the Russo-Japanese War became embroiled in a war with the U.S. It ends with the following lament:

"Ah, what a sight, this sea of destruction, this graveyard of the Japanese Fleet! Even if the Black Current of the Japan Sea were now to flow to the West, our enmity will last forever!"

These were his very last moments; and thus did a drowning man suffer his final agonies, gasping out, "Ah, we won on strength but lost on numbers!"[1]

This island nation's destiny of destruction by external pressure was foreseeable—exactly the way the Heike, before their own destruction at the hands of the militarily superior Genji, could sense their own unhappy fate.

"Here, a hundred leagues from hearth and home..." goes the military song "Battle Buddies." It should be expressive of the spirit of the valiant soldiers as they advance in war, trampling some foreign country, but it is shot through and through with the same pathos as the fall of the Heike. Behind all that valor lies sorrow.

On my bookshelves sit a large number of Japan-U.S. future-war chronicles, obtained from secondhand bookstores. There must have been more than five hundred of them published, many of them once best sellers, not a few now scattered and lost. A number of them were read avidly at the time they were published but then neglected. Their covers' fading colors give one a sense of how much time has passed, yet there are also those in which the reader's notes, written in pen or pencil in the margins, are still fresh: comments such as *Stupid! Stupid!* and *Of course!* and *No! No! No!* and *If we really fought a war, Japan would win.*

War was the only means of ensuring survival in a Darwinian world. In those days, one had no choice but to believe that. But one wonders, for how long were we supposed to continue this struggle for survival? The undercurrent of sorrow in the Japan-U.S. future-war chronicles was based on this consciousness of Japan's fate.

How long must Japanese continue the competitive economic struggle, when they are disdained for fomenting trade friction? The agonies of today's businessmen must be no less than those suffered before. Rather than perfecting and fulfilling their lives, they must beat the competition and expand market share, and strive not to be gobbled up by the monster of external pressure. These are today's priorities.

It has been little more than half a century since we severed our connection with war—at the cost of many lives. In exchange for making war with weapons taboo, we have, undaunted, transposed our valorous efforts to economic war. Instead of sending expeditionary troops out to the continent or the Pacific islands, we have dispatched our business samurai all over the world. We part now, not at trains and wharves, but at airports. We have shifted the object of our loyalty from our country to our company. Once again, it is felt, Japan is challenging modern European civilization.

As this book has shown, the wellsprings of Japan-bashing are deep and can be traced back to books published in America after the Russo-Japanese War, such as Homer Lea's *The Valor of Ignorance* and Parabellum's *BAN-ZAI!* Each such work was followed by an overreaction on Japan's part. The situation remains unchanged today. With the collapse of the Soviet Union and the conclusion of the Cold War, such works as *The Coming War with Japan* (by George Freidman with Meredith LeBard) and *Rising Sun* (by Michael Crichton) became best sellers. Especially notable is *Rising Sun*, which immediately rose to number one and sold nearly three million copies, including the paperback edition. The film version, released by 20th Century

Fox, directed by Philip Kaufman and starring Sean Connery, provoked the Media Action Network for Asian Americans, with the particular support of the Japanese American community, to launch a protest movement. The protestors argued that the film ought to include disclaimers to the effect that this film is purely fictional, and that not all Japanese are trying to take over America.

With respect to Japan-U.S. relations, we have changed from an era in which Americans imported people (Japanese) to one in which they import automobiles and electronics. Nevertheless, misunderstandings remain on both sides. Even when Japanese-made cars and radio-cassette players are viciously smashed with metal bats, the Japanese reaction is not as violent as in the past, but our pain is deep nonetheless. So when we are asked to contribute internationally, it is only natural that we may wait to see what others are up to first.

The Japan-U.S. future-war chronicles form part of Japanese spiritual history. And it is fair to say that another reason they deserve a fresh look is that they provide an inside story—a back story—to the history of Japan-U.S. relations.

—NAOKI INOSE
May 1993

A Note from
the Translator

THIS CROSS-CULTURAL STUDY of "future war" scenarios, mainly those devised in Japan and the United States during the first half of the last century, seemed timely enough when its original publication coincided roughly with the fiftieth anniversary of the Pearl Harbor attack. Today, tragically, it is pertinent to the analysis of a new surprise attack on America, and (once again) to a "never again" discussion of how to prevent a future attack. In seeking to discover why the 9/11 attacks were not prevented, the U.S. government's own 9/11 Commission has identified four kinds of failures, chief among them being "failures of imagination."[1] As the Commission itself notes in the very first sentence of its subsection on "Imagination,"[2] the Pearl Harbor attack provides a useful historical perspective. And the exercise of imagination in the run-up to Pearl Harbor is precisely the subject of Mr. Inose's book, originally published in Japanese in 1993.

"War," declares Mr. Inose in chapter 2, "is summoned by acts of the imagination." Later in the book, considering technical military matters as they impinge on future-war scenarios, he observes that "war planning in general is rather a matter of imaginative power" (chapter 15). Referring in this regard to two authors he has discussed at length, he comments,

> Many are the cases in which it is not the military professionals but the journalists and the novelists who see most clearly into the future. Mizuno Hironori and Hector C. Bywater are two examples, representing the genre of what I have called "Japan-America future-war chronicles."

In the course of arriving at such judgments, Mr. Inose places this literary genre in a wide-ranging historical and national-security perspective. He declines to segment the undifferentiated aesthetic continuum of his larger subject in the usual way, instead identifying the genre of "future-war chronicles" as part of a milieu that encompasses not only fiction (and science fiction, as with Hirata Shinsaku's awesome Aoki Ray and his flying *Submarine Fuji* with its radio-guided airborne torpedoes in chapter 12), but also professional military forecasting, war simulations and games and exercises, and such exemplars of hegemonic ideology as the cinematic products of Hollywood. In short, Mr. Inose's work transcends conventional analytical boundaries.

The topics in this book therefore range from such "hard" matter as the conduct and outcome of the Russo-Japanese War (1904–1905), or the parameters of naval balance-of-power issues before and after the Washington Conference of 1921 (in chapter 13), to the formulation and extended evolution of the American military's War Plan Orange (chapter 15), the future-war scenarios of Japanese and Anglo-American popular fiction, and even (as discussed in chapter 7) something as "soft" as the romantic spirit of adventure—shading into a conviction of invincibility and a triumphalist spirit of conquest—inculcated by boys' magazines in prewar Japan. One convenient example of the overlap, as introduced in chapter 8, is the work and person of the English journalist, spy, and naval expert Hector C. Bywater, whom American journalist William Honan has called "the man who invented the Pacific War." In the course of writing his hypothetical *The Great Pacific War* (1925), Bywater made notable use of game playing and simulations (see chapter 9). Another example would be the equally cautionary imaginary wars of Mizuno Hironori, a chronically insubordinate Japanese naval officer and author whose views on modern war were radically altered by visiting Europe during and after the First World War. Tracing lines of literary influence, Mr. Inose notes (in chapter 10) the impact of Bywater's work on the bellicose Japanese writer Ikezaki Tadayoshi, whose *Japan Need Not Fear the U.S.* became a best seller in 1929—provoking a counterblast by none other than Mizuno. Mizuno's *Sea and Air* (1930) then took on the critical question of sea power vs. air power, essentially predicting America's March 1945 firebombing of Tokyo (see chapter 11).

In chapters 6 and 14, Mr. Inose speculates fruitfully as to the relationship between softcore "future-war chronicles" and hardcore military planning. Perhaps we are starting to see something like that interplay in America today in novels and computer gaming—not only as a top-down fulfillment of the 9/11 Commission's earnest call for an "institutionalization" of imagination,[3] but in response to other imperatives, including military training and market forces. Yet there remains the question of whose imagination should be employed, and to what ends, and at what costs. Our novelists and journalists may well be able to see something of the future, as Tom Clancy did in a novel a decade ago (*Debt of Honor*, 1994) when he envisioned the deliberate crashing of a commercial airliner by a foreign pilot in such a way as to inflict tremendous harm on the United States. But the politicians and policy makers and functionaries who did not forestall 9/11 yet did lead America into Iraq also have their visions of the future. And if, at crucial strategic and operational junctures, clear-sighted soldier-statesmen are ultimately disregarded by their military or civilian bosses (I am thinking of the fates of former commander in chief of U.S. Central Command Anthony Zinni, former U.S. Army chief of staff Eric Shinseki, even former chairman of the Joint Chiefs of Staff—and now former secretary of state—Colin Powell) then the Commission's suggestions will also come to naught. Powell, Shinseki, and Zinni all understand better than the current civilian leadership (and followership) that there is more to the exercise of national power than the decisive application of lethal or destructive force. (Zinni's professional life story has been told by Tom Clancy, with the help of Tony Koltz and Zinni himself, in *Battle Ready*, published in hardcover in 2004.)

For his own part, Mr. Inose is conspicuously alert to the distinction between "hard" and "soft" power, a formula first adumbrated by Joseph Nye in the 1980s and recently experiencing a revival in public discourse. Hence the observation, in chapter 4 of the present work, that while the Japanese annexation of Korea in 1910 (for example) is unavoidable as a "hard" historical fact, the full significance of "soft" events that also contributed to the formation of Japanese national consciousness (or subconscious) easily drops out of the conventional historical record. As an example of the latter type of event, Mr. Inose cites the port calls by the American "Great White Fleet" in 1908, and its not-so-subtle reinforcement of the somewhat "harder" port-opening visits by Commodore Perry's "Black Ships" in 1853–54. (Perry's Black Ships in fact become the book's original sin, so to speak, and its leading metaphor for the motif of recurring "external pressure.") Overall, Mr. Inose makes a clear case for the importance of "soft" power to our understanding and manipulation of the world around us.

The world seen through the translator's narrow spectacles presents unending vistas of translation issues. Without being entirely reductive, one can at least think of "future war" scenarios as being, in and of themselves, a kind of translation. In ways large and small, our common, bootstrapping human psychology constantly has us reasoning, by transposition and transformation, from what we know to what we need or want to know. Forecasting and projections, gaming and role-playing, hypotheticals and counterfactuals: all involve such processes in one way or another; sometimes it is the philosophy of "as if" that provides the enabling fictions upon which (for reasons good or bad) we stake our lives, our fortunes, and our sacred honor. Mr. Inose undertook his cross-cultural study to familiarize Japanese with the ways in which such efforts both reflected and shaped the attitudes and actions of an era. This translation of his work into English is presented in the belief that Americans also have much to learn about assessing future risks and options. And learn we must, lest we either become "lost in translation" or allow ourselves to be misled as to the meaning of it all.

In dialectical, futurological fashion then, we look forward by first looking back—and across. In this case, back to the first half of the twentieth century, and across the Pacific.

—JAMIE WEST (DIPLOMATT, INC.)

Notes

Prologue

1   James Joyce, "A Painful Case," in *Dubliners* (Penguin Books, 1992), p. 112.
2   Bushū Ishikawa Gō Meishu [A Notable Inhabitant of Ishikawa Village in the Province of Bu], *Afurika-sen torai nikki* (Diary of an African Ship Coming to Japan), 1854, as quoted in Miyanaga Takashi, *Perii teitoku—Nippon Ensei to sono shōgai* [Commodore Perry: His Career, Featuring the Japan Expedition] (Yūrindō, 1981), p. 119.
3   Francis L. Hawks, comp. (abridged and edited by Sidney Wallach), *Narrative of the Expedition of an American Squadron to the China Seas and Japan under the Command of Commodore M. C. Perry, United States Navy* (New York: Coward-McCann, 1952), p. 156.
4   Hawks, *Narrative of the Expedition*, p. 156.
5   Hawks, *Narrative of the Expedition*, pp. 198–199.
6   Hawks, *Narrative of the Expedition*, p. 201.
7   Samuel Langhorne Clemens (Mark Twain; ed. Charles Neider), *The Autobiography of Mark Twain* (New York: Harper & Brothers, Publishers, 1959), p. 94.

Chapter 1

1   Natsume Sōseki (trans. Alan Turney), *Botchan*, (Kōdansha International, Ltd., 1972), p. 9.
2   Sōseki (trans. Turney), *Botchan*, p. 21.
3   Sōseki (trans. Turney), *Botchan*, p. 23.
4   Natsume Sōseki, *Botchan*, in *Sōseki zenshū* [Works of Sōseki] (Iwanami Shoten, 1979; 1956), p. 215.
5   Sōseki (trans. Turney), *Botchan*, p. 30. The original specifies a value of 250,000 *koku*: see Natsume Sōseki, *Botchan*, in *Sōseki Zenshū* [Works of Sōseki], p. 220.
6   For this scene, see Sōseki (trans. Turney), *Botchan*, p. 36.
7   Sōseki (trans. Turney), *Botchan*, p. 31. The ellipses indicate material omitted from this excerpt.

8   Sōseki (trans. Turney), *Botchan*, p. 29. The Heian period extended from 794 to 1185.

9   For this scene, see Sōseki (trans. Turney), *Botchan*, pp. 50–54.

10   Sōseki (trans. Turney), *Botchan*, p. 84.

11   A traditional Chinese medicinal therapy that involves applying the heat of burnt *moxa*, or mugwort, to specific pressure points on the body.

12   Sōseki (trans. Turney), *Botchan*, p. 23.

13   Quoted in Japanese in Yasuo Wakatsuki, *Hai Nichi no rekishi—Amerika ni okeru Nihonjin imin* [A History of Japanese Immigrants and the Anti-Japanese Movement in America], Chūō Shinsho 274 (Chūō Kōronsha, 1972), p. 29.

Chapter 2

1   C. Lushun; J. Ryojun—the Chinese and Japanese names for Port Arthur.

2   See Mizuno Hironori's "Ken wo toku made" [Until We Take Off the Sword], in Mizuno Hironori, *Hankotsu no gunjin, Mizuno Hironori* [The Defiant Officer: Mizuno Hironori] (Keizai Ōrai Sha, 1978), p. 299.

3   A major Tokyo daily, well known for its anti-war politics and its translations of Western literature.

4   Tayama Katai, *Yorozu chōhō* (January 1, 1912).

5   Mizuno Hironori, *Kono issen* [The Crucial Battle] (Hakubunkan, 1911), p. 212.

6   Mizuno, *Kono issen* [The Crucial Battle], p. 213.

7   Mizuno, *Kono issen* [The Crucial Battle], p. 216.

8   Shiba, Ryōtarō, *Saka no ue* [The Cloud Above the Hill] (Bungei Shunju, 1969), p. 257.

9   Mizuno, *Kono issen* [The Crucial Battle], p. 165.

10   Mizuno, *Kono issen* [The Crucial Battle], p. 190.

11   Powerful feudal lords who owned land and were vassals of the shogun from the tenth century to the early nineteenth century in Japan.

12   Mizuno Hironori, *Tsugi no issen* [The Next Battle] (Kaneo Bun'endō, 1914), pp. 124–125.

13   The following exchange is paraphrased from Mizuno, *Tsugi no issen*, pp. 128–131.

14   Quoted from Mizuno, *Tsugi no issen* [The Next Battle], pp. 224–225.

15   Mizuno, *Tsugi no issen* [The Next Battle], pp. 252–253.

16   Mizuno, *Kono issen* [The Crucial Battle], p. 164.

17   Mizuno, *Tsugi no issen* [The Next Battle], p. 255.

18   The following two passages are from Mizuno, *Tsugi no issen* [The Next Battle], p. 257.

19   Mizuno, *Tsugi no issen* [The Next Battle], p. 260.

20   The following description and quotations are from Mizuno, *Tsugi no issen* [The Next Battle], p. 305.

21   The original reads, "Japan is now supreme, in a military and naval sense, on

the Asian coast north of Hong-Kong. . . . There now remains but one power for Japan to put aside in order to make her supreme in the Pacific. . . . That nation is the United States." See Homer Lea, *The Valor of Ignorance* (New York: Harper & Brothers Publishers, 1909), p. 192.

Chapter 3

1 Eugene Anschel, *Homer Lea, Sun Yat-Sen, and the Chinese Revolution* (New York: Praeger Publishers, 1984), p. 2.

2 Key Ray Chong, *Americans and Chinese Reform and Revolution, 1898–1922* (Lanham, New York, London: University Press of America, 1984), p. 41.

3 Anschel, *Homer Lea, Sun Yat-Sen*, p. 3.

4 Marshall Stimson, "A Los Angeles Jeremiah. Homer Lea: Military Genius and Prophet," *Quarterly of the Historical Society of Southern California* (March 1942): 6; quoted in Anschel, *Homer Lea, Sun Yat-Sen*, p. 3.

5 Comment attributed to "a Chinese who had been with him in battle," cited in Boothe, "The Valor of Homer Lea," in Homer Lea, *The Valor of Ignorance*, (1942 ed.), p. xvii.

6 Anschel, *Homer Lea, Sun Yat-Sen*, p. 5.

7 Dr. David Starr Jordan, *The Days of a Man* (Yonkers, N.Y., 1922), vol. 2, p. 32; quoted in Anschel, *Homer Lea, Sun Yat-Sen*, p. 5.

8 Anschel, *Homer Lea, Sun Yat-Sen*, p. 5.

9 Anschel, *Homer Lea, Sun Yat-Sen*, p. 9.

10 *San Francisco Call,* June 1, 1900, p. 1; quoted in Anschel, *Homer Lea, Sun Yat-Sen*, p. 12.

11 The following encounter between Kang and Lea is paraphrased and quoted from the account reported in Anschel, *Homer Lea, Sun Yat-Sen*, pp. 20–21.

12 O'Reilly, as quoted in Thomas, *Born to Raise Hell*, p. 176, as cited by Anschel, *Homer Lea, Sun Yat-Sen*, p. 29.

13 From the "Articles of Incorporation" as cited by Anschel, *Homer Lea, Sun Yat-Sen*, p. 40.

14 See Anschel, *Homer Lea, Sun Yat-Sen*, pp. 42–44.

15 *Los Angeles Times*, December 31, 1904, p. 6; as cited in Anschel, *Homer Lea, Sun Yat-Sen*, p. 44.

16 Letter from Kang Yuwei to Homer Lea, October 10, 1910, Powers Papers; as cited in Anschel, *Homer Lea, Sun Yat-Sen*, p. 47.

17 *Los Angeles Times*, March 29, 1905, p. 10; as cited in Anschel, *Homer Lea, Sun Yat-Sen*, pp. 50–51.

18 *Los Angeles Times*, April 8, 1905, pt. 2, p. 6; as cited in Anschel, *Homer Lea, Sun Yat-Sen*, p. 57.

19 English translation of Japanese version given in Eileen Sunada Sarasohn (trans. Nanjō Shunji), *Za "Issei"—paionia no shōzō* [The *Issei:* Portrait of a Pioneer] (Yomiuri Shimbun Sha, 1991), p. 68.

20 English translation of Japanese translation of Pauline Kael (trans. Koike Misako),

Skyandaru no shukusatsu [Scandal on Holiday] (Shinshokan, 1987), p. 167; orig. titled "Raising Kane" (*The New Yorker*) and reprinted in Kael, Mankiewicz, and Welles, *The Citizen Kane Book* (c. 1971).

21 English translation of Japanese version given in Eileen Sunada Sarasohn (trans. Nanjō Shunji), *Za "Issei,"* pp. 68–69.

22 Sunada Sarasohn (trans. Nanjō Shunji), *Za "Issei,"* p. 69.

23 See Hata Ikuhiko, *Taiheyō kokusai kankeishi* [A History of International Relations in the Pacific] (Fukumura Shuppan, 1972), p. 72.

24 Nagai Kafū (trans. Mitsuko Iriye), "Bad Company," in *American Stories* (New York: Columbia University Press, 2000), p. 81.

Chapter 4

1 Parabellum (pen name of Ferdinand Heinrich Grautoff), *BANZAI!* (Leipzig: Theodor Weicher; New York: The Baker & Taylor Co., 1909), p. vii.

2 Parabellum, *BANZAI!*, p. 1.

3 The following synopsis of chapter 4 is paraphrased and quoted from Parabellum, *BANZAI!*, pp. 61 ff.

4 Parabellum, *BANZAI!*, p. 193.

5 Parabellum, *BANZAI!*, p. 193–194.

6 Paraphrased and quoted from Parabellum, *BANZAI!*, pp. 295–296.

7 Homer Lea, *The Valor of Ignorance* (New York and London: Harper & Brothers Publishers, 1909), pp. 19–20.

8 Lea, *The Valor of Ignorance*, pp. 276; 295–297.

9 Lea, *The Valor of Ignorance*, p. 344.

10 H. G. Wells, *The War in the Air* (London and Glasgow: Collins Clear-Type Press, 1921 [1908]), p. 178.

11 Wells, *The War in the Air*, pp. 173–4. The ellipses are Wells's, marking the speaker's pauses, not words deleted from the quotation.

12 Gaimushō [Ministry of Foreign Affairs] (ed.), *Nippon gaikō monjo* [Japanese Diplomatic Documents] 41:1 (Nippon Kokusai Rengō Kyōkai, 1960), p. 151.

13 Gaimushō (ed.), *Nippon gaikō monjo* [Japanese Diplomatic Documents] 41:2 (Nippon Kokusai Rengō Kyōkai, 1961), p. 563.

14 See Etō Jun, "Ningen, hyōgen, seiji" [People, Expressions, Politics] in his *Etō Jun chosaku shūzoku 3* [Works of Etō Jun, Supplement, v. 3] (Kōdansha, 1973); Hata Ikuhiko, *Taiheyō kokusai kankeishi* [A History of International Relations in the Pacific] (Fukumura Shuppan, 1972); and Ōe Shinobu, *Taiheiyō kokusai kankei shi* [History of Diplomatic Relations in the Pacific] (Fukumura shuppan, 1972).

15 Mizuno Hironori, *Tsugi no issen* [The Next Battle] (Kaneo Bun'endō, 1914), p. 258.

Chapter 5

1 Mochizuki Kotarō, *Nichibei hissen ron* [On the Inevitability of a Japan-U.S.

War; a Japanese Translation of Homer Lea's *The Valor of Ignorance*] (Rikugun Shō [Ministry of the Army], 1911), p. 2.

2 At the time, the highest court in Japan.

3 Treaty of Commerce and Navigation, Feb. 21, 1911, U.S.-Japan, art. I, 37 Stat. 1504.

4 *Nihon oyobi Nihonjin* (Japan and the Japanese), 1911: 4.

5 Kokumin Gunji Kyōkai [People's Committee for Military Affairs], *Nichibei kaisen—yume monogatari* [The Outbreak of the Japan-U.S. War: A Dream Tale] (Chūō Shoin, 1913), pp. 64–65.

6 Eugene Anschel, *Homer Lea, Sun Yat-Sen, and The Chinese Revolution* (New York: Praeger Publishers, 1984), pp. 4–5.

7 Homer Lea, *The Valor of Ignorance* (New York and London: Harper & Brothers Publishers, 1909), pp. 9–10.

8 Lea, *The Valor of Ignorance*, pp. 19–21.

9 Lea, p. 26.

10 Mishima Yukio, *Mishima Yukio hyōron zenshū* [Critical Works of Mishima Yukio], Vol. 2 (Shinchō Sha, 1989), pp. 531–532.

11 Claire Boothe, "The Valor of Homer Lea," Introduction to *If America Fights with Japan* (New York: The Hokuseido Press, 1942), pp. 1–2.

12 Letter #7 (September 5, 1910) and #8 (September 29, 1910), both from Homer Lea to Sun Yatsen, as printed in Eugene Anschel, *Homer Lea, Sun Yat-Sen*, pp. 205–207.

13 Letter #11 (August 10, 1911), in Anschel, *Homer Lea, Sun Yat-Sen*, p. 210.

14 Letter from Ethel Lea to her sister Agnes, November 16, 1911 (Powers Papers), as cited in Anschel, *Homer Lea, Sun Yat-Sen*, p. 162.

15 Undated copy of letter from Homer Lea to Senator Elihu Root, probably of November 2, 1911 (Powers Papers), as cited in Anschel, *Homer Lea, Sun Yat-Sen*, p. 159.

16 Miyazaki Tōten, "Untitled Manuscript," in *Miyazaki Tōten zenshū* [Complete Works of Miyazaki Tōten], vol. 5 (Heibon Sha, 1976).

17 David Starr Jordan, *The Days of a Man* (Yonkers, 1922), vol. 2, p. 30; as cited in Anschel, *Homer Lea, Sun Yat-Sen*, p. 197.

18 Henry Donald, as cited by Earl Albert Selle, *Donald of China* (New York, 1948), cited in Anschel, *Homer Lea, Sun Yat-Sen*, p. 175.

Chapter 6

1 Erich Maria Remarque (trans. A. W. Wheen), *All Quiet on the Western Front* (Boston: Little, Brown and Company, 1958 [1929]; orig. *Im Westen Nichts Neues*, 1928), p. 115.

2 Mizuno Hironori, *Tsugi no issen* [The Next Battle] (Kaneo Bun'endō, 1914), pp. 37–38. Mizuno's quotation of Lea is in Japanese translation, presumably Mochizuki's translation for the military; here it is translated back into English. However, the Japanese is not a close translation but a considerably simplified

précis of Lea's rather elaborate prose in *The Valor of Ignorance* (pp. 25–27).

3   Mizuno Hironori, *Hankotsu no gunjin, Mizuno Hironori* [The Defiant Officer: Mizuno Hironori] (Keizai Ōrai Sha, 1978), p. 306.

4   Mizuno Hironori, *Hankotsu no gunjin* [The Defiant Officer...], p. 307.

5   Mizuno Hironori, *Hankotsu no gunjin* [The Defiant Officer...], p. 320.

6   Mizuno Hironori, *Hankotsu no gunjin* [The Defiant Officer...], p. 333.

7   As quoted in Japanese in Mizuno, *Hankotsu no gunjin* [The Defiant Officer...], p. 348.

8   This excerpt is not the version carried in the *New York Sun* but a fresh translation of Mizuno, *Tsugi no issen* [The Next Battle], pp. 20–21.

9   Mizuno, *Hankotsu no gunjin* [The Defiant Officer...], pp. 349–350.

10 The following description of Mizuno in Germany is based on Mizuno, *Hankotsu no gunjin* [The Defiant Officer...], pp. 385 ff. Description and dialogue alike are translated from Mizuno's Japanese-language account.

11 For the following two comments about the situation of women, see Mizuno, *Hankotsu no gunjin* [The Defiant Officer...], p. 408.

12 Mizuno, *Hankotsu no gunjin* [The Defiant Officer...], p. 424.

13 Mizuno, *Hankotsu no gunjin* [The Defiant Officer...], p. 425.

14 For the following comments on the German Jews, see Mizuno, *Hankotsu no gunjin* [The Defiant Officer...], p. 399.

15 For Mizuno's speech at the Kaiserkeller, see Mizuno, *Hankotsu no gunjin* [The Defiant Officer...], pp. 418–419.

Chapter 8

1   Hector C. Bywater, *Sea Power in the Pacific: A Study of the American-Japanese Naval Problem* (Boston & New York: Houghton Mifflin Company, 1921), pp. 260–261. Originally published in London by Constable & Co., in 1921.

2   Quoted in Wiliam H. Honan, *Bywater: The Man Who Invented the Pacific War* (London: Macdonald & Co., 1990), p. 74.

3   Bywater, *Sea Power in the Pacific*, p. vi.

4   Bywater, *Sea Power in the Pacific*, p. viii.

5   The following account is from Hector C. Bywater and H. C. Ferraby, *Strange Intelligence: Memoirs of Naval Secret Service* (London: Constable & Co., 1931), pp. 141–145.

6   Bywater and Ferraby, *Strange Intelligence*, p. 145.

7   The following account of Bywater's initiation into the Secret Service is taken from Honan, *Bywater*, pp. 31–34.

8   Honan, *Bywater*, p. 30.

9   William H. Honan, *Visions of Infamy: The Untold Story of How Journalist Hector C. Bywater Devised the Plans that Led to Pearl Harbor* (New York: St. Martin's Press, 1991; orig. pub. in 1991 in Great Britain as *Bywater: The Man Who Invented the Pacific War*), p. 23.

10 Bywater and Ferraby, *Strange Intelligence*, p. 182.

11 Mary Doyle, quoted in John Dickson Carr, *The Life of Arthur Conan Doyle* (New York, Evanston, and London: Harper & Row, 1949), p. 123.

12 Conan Doyle, quoted in Carr, *The Life of Arthur Conan Doyle*, p. 124.

13 Mempes, quoted in Carr, *The Life of Arthur Conan Doyle*, p. 131.

14 Conan Doyle, quoted in Carr, *The Life of Arthur Conan Doyle*, pp. 134–135.

15 Carr, *The Life of Arthur Conan Doyle*, p. 134.

16 Witness quoted by Conan Doyle in *The War in South Africa: Its Cause and Conduct*, as cited in Carr, *The Life of Arthur Conan Doyle*, pp. 156–157.

17 Arthur Conan Doyle, "His Last Bow," in the collection also titled *His Last Bow*, in A. Conan Doyle, *The Crowborough Edition of the Works of Sir Arthur Conan Doyle* (Garden City & New York: Doubleday, Doran & Co. 1930), vol. XX, p. 198.

18 Conan Doyle, "His Last Bow," p. 190.

19 Conan Doyle, "His Last Bow," p. 193.

20 Conan Doyle, "His Last Bow," p. 195.

21 Conan Doyle, "His Last Bow," p. 208.

22 Conan Doyle, "Great Britain and the Next War" (*Fortnightly Review*, February 1913), cited in Carr, *The Life of Arthur Conan Doyle*, p. 227.

23 Arthur Conan Doyle, *Great Britain and the Next War* (Boston: Small, Maynard & Company, 1914), p. 48.

24 Arthur Conan Doyle, *The New Revelation* (New York: George H. Doran Company, 1918), pp. 38–39.

Chapter 9

1 This and other quotations below are translated from the author's Japanese language account of his personal interview with Hector C. Bywater Jr. on September 21, 1991.

2 Hector C. Bywater, *Sea Power in the Pacific: A Study of the American-Japanese Naval Problem*, rev. ed. (London: Constable and Co. Ltd., 1934 [1921]), p. 1.

3 Bywater, *Sea Power in the Pacific*, pp. 260–261.

4 Bywater, *Sea Power in the Pacific*, p. 264.

5 Hector C. Bywater, *The Great Pacific War* (Boston, New York: Houghton Mifflin Co., 1932) [orig. London: Constable & Co., Ltd., 1925], p. 30.

6 Bywater, *The Great Pacific War*, p. 38–39.

7 Bywater, *The Great Pacific War*, p. 40.

8 Bywater, *The Great Pacific War*, p. 31.

9 For this account of the hypothetical invasion, see Bywater, *The Great Pacific War*, pp. 41–44.

10 Bywater, *The Great Pacific War*, p. 153.

11 The following fictional battle-log entries are from Bywater, *The Great Pacific War*, pp. 272–277.

12 Bywater, *The Great Pacific War*, p. 304.

13 Bywater, *The Great Pacific War*, p. 107.

14 Letter from Hector Bywater to Ferris Greenslet, dated June 12, 1924. Copied in longhand by Naoki Inose with permission from the owner, Hector C. Bywater Jr.

15 The following passages are taken from a letter from Ferris Greenslet to Hector Bywater, dated August 19, 1924. Copied in longhand by Naoki Inose with permission from the owner, Hector C. Bywater Jr.

16 Mizuno Hironori, "Umi" [The Sea], in *Chūō Kōron* [The Central Review] (July 1922).

17 *Kokumin shimbun* (October 22, 1924).

18 Bywater, *The Great Pacific War*, p. 97.

Chapter 10

1 These and subsequent quotations from Akutagawa's diary (hereinafter identified by date only) are taken from the following edition: Akutagawa Ryūnosuke, *Akutagawa zenshū* [Complete Works of Akutagawa] (Iwanami Shoten, 1955), p. 187.

2 Nagai Tamotsu (ed.), *Ikezaki Tadayoshi* (Chūō Kōron Jigyō, 1962), p. 45.

3 These details regarding Akutagawa's last days are based on the "Commentary" by Usui Yoshimi in *Akutagawa Ryūnosuke shū*, in *Nippon bungaku zenshū* [Collection of Japanese Literature] (Chikuma Shobō, 1970), vol. 25, pp. 492–494.

4 Ikezaki Tadayoshi, *Natsume Sōseki* (Shinchō Sha, 1917), *Appendix*, p. 3.

5 For this episode, see Ikezaki, *Natsume Sōseki, Appendix*, pp. 3–4.

6 For this letter, see Ikezaki, *Natsume Sōseki*, pp. 1–4.

7 Nagai (ed.), *Ikezaki Tadayoshi*, p. 113.

8 Nagai (ed.), *Ikezaki Tadayoshi*, p. 197.

9 Ikezaki Tadayoshi, *Bōyū Akutagawa Ryūnosuke he no kokubetsu* [A Farewell to My Departed Friend, Akutagawa Ryūnosuke] (Tenjin Sha, 1930), p. 33.

10 Nagai (ed.), *Ikezaki Tadayoshi*, p. 113.

11 Kondo Tomie, *Hongo Kikufuji Hoteru* (Kōdan Sha, 1974), p. 14.

12 See Nagai (ed.), *Ikezaki Tadayoshi*, p. 237.

Chapter 11

1 Quoted in Agawa Hiroyuki, *Yamamoto Isoroku* (Shinchō Sha, 1969), vol. 1, p. 378

2 *Tōkyō daikūgeki • sensai shi* [The Great Tokyo Air Raid: Reminiscences of Wartime Devastation] (Tōkyō Kūgeki wo kiroku suru kai [Tokyo Air Raids Memorial Committee], 1973), 5 vols.

3 Mizuno Hironori, *Umi to sora* [Sea and Air] (Kaiyō Sha, 1930), pp. 142–143.

4 Ibid., pp. 27–28.

5 Ibid., p. 74.

6 Ibid., pp. 149–150.

7 In *Kokusai panfuretto tsūshin* [International Pamphlet Communications] pub. by Taimuzu Tsūshin Sha (December 1, 1932).

8   Mizuno Hironori, *Nichibei kōbō no issen: dakai ka, hametsu ka* [Japan and America: The Battle for Dominance] (Tōkai Shoin, 1932), p. 205.

9   Matsushita Yoshio, *Mizuno Hironori* (Shishū Sha, 1950), p. 214.

10 Mizuno, *Nichibei kōbō no issen* [Japan and America: The Battle for Dominance], p. 92.

11 Ibid., pp. 217–218.

12 Ibid., pp. 293–294.

13 Tezuka Osamu, as quoted in Kita Jun-ichirō's comments in *Unno Jūzō zenshū* [Complete Works of Unno Jūzō] (San-ichi Shobō, 1990), vol. 9, p. 431.

14 Kita Morio, in ibid.

15 The following account of Unno's story, *Bakugeki-ka no teitō* [The Capital Under Bombardment], is based on the edition in *Unno Jūzō zenshū* [Complete Works of Unno Jūzō] (San-ichi Shobō, 1990), vol. 1.

16 Sakaguchi Ango, *Sensō to hitori no onna* [One Woman's War], in *Sakaguchi Ango senshū* [Selected Works of Sakaguchi Ango] (Kōdansha, 1982), p. 240.

17 Author's interview with Shigematsu Fukio at Mr. Shigematsu's residence in Aichi Prefecture, August 1991.

Chapter 12

1   Hirata Shinsaku, *Shōwa Yūgekitai* [Task Force Shōwa], in Aizu Shingo (ed.), *Hirata Shunsaku / Ran-iku Jirō shū* [Works by Hirata Shunsaku and Ran-iku Jirō], in *Shōnen shosetsu taikei* [Youth Novels: A Survey] (San-ichi Shobō, 1994), p. 70.

2   Inari was originally a god of harvests, later the tutelary deity of any locality.

3   Futagami Hirozoku, *Shōnen shōsetsu no keifu* [Youth Novels: A Genealogy] (Gen-ei Jō, 1978), pp. 139–140.

4   Kawasaki Hiroshi, *Watashi wa gunkoku shōnen datta* [My Youth in a Militarist Nation] (Shinchō Sha, 1992), p. 159.

5   Mrs. Yoko Hirata, personal interview with author, October 14, 1992.

6   Yasuoka Shōtarō, *Boku no Shōwa-shi* [My History of the Shōwa Period] (Kōdansha Bunko, 1991), p. 41.

7   Kureki Ken (ed.), *Hirata Shunsaku shi wo shinobu* [Remembering Hirata Shunsaku] (Manuscript, 1936), p. 33.

8   The editors' message and subsequent readers' eulogies are taken from *Shōnen Kurabu* [Youth Club] (March 1936).

9   Ikezaki Tadayoshi, *Sekai Taisen Kaikoroku* [A Memoir of the World War] (Daiichi Shuppan, 1938), p. 146.

10 *Hōritsu Shimbun* [Legal News], June 30, 1939.

Chapter 13

1   From the Japanese translation by Togawa Yukio in *Ningen teitoku Yamamoto Isoroku* [Admiral Yamamoto Isoroku, The Man] (Kōjin Sha, 1987 [1976]), p. 59.

2   *Asahi shimbun* (newspaper), September 19, 1934.

3   As reported in the *Asahi shimbun*, November 2, 1934.

4   The following account is taken from the *Asahi shimbun*, October 24, 1934.

5   Shidehara Kijūrō, *Fifty Years in Foreign Affairs* (Chūkō bunkō; Chūō Kōron Sha, 1986), p. 282.

6   Hector C. Bywater, "U.S. Policy in Naval Talks," in *Daily Telegraph*, Tuesday, December 4, 1934.

7   Ibid.

8   Hector C. Bywater, as quoted in William H. Honan, *Visions of Infamy: The Untold Story of How Journalist Hector C. Bywater Devised the Plans that Led to Pearl Harbor* (New York: St. Martin's Press, 1991), p. 204.

9   Hector C. Bywater to Rudyard Kipling, as quoted in Honan, *Visions of Infamy*, p. 214.

10 Agawa Hiroyuki, *Yamamoto Isoroku* (Shinchō Sha, 1969), p. 56.

11 Agawa, *Yamamoto Isoroku*, p. 186.

12 Mizuno Hironori, *Diary*, entry for September 2, 1939.

13 The following account of Bywater's death (together with the determinations of his personal physician, the results of the County inquest, and the suspicions of E. A. Harwood) are based on Honan, *Visions of Infamy*, pp. 244-250.

14 William Honan, in an interview with the author.

15 *Yomiuri* newspaper (July 30, 1940).

16 Honan, *Visions of Infamy*, p. 250.

17 Author's interview and conversation with William Honan; quotations are approximate.

18 The following account of Ōtani's instructions, etc., is paraphrased and condensed from Ōtani Keijirō, *Shōwa Kempei-shi* [A History of the Military Police in the Shōwa Period] (Misuzu Shobō, 1966), pp. 392-394.

19 Ōtani, *Shōwa Kempei-shi*, p. 394; the version of Cox's note given here is translated from the Japanese given by Ōtani.

20 Ōtani, *Shōwa Kempei-shi*, p. 396.

21 *Yomiuri* newspaper (July 30, 1940).

22 Based on Ōtani, *Shōwa Kempei-shi*, p. 397.

Chapter 14

1   The following synopsis and dialogue are loosely quoted and paraphrased from Fukunaga Kyōsuke, *Kuni no mamori* [Defending Our Land] (Shinchō Sha, 1939).

2   Martin Caidin, *The Ragged, Rugged Warriors* (Bantam Books, 1985).

3   William H. Honan, *Visions of Infamy* (New York: St. Martin's Press, 1991), p. xiv.

4   Agawa Hiroyuki, *Yamamoto Isoroku*, vol. I (Shinchō Sha, 1969), p. 378.

5   Sanematsu Yuzuru *Shinjuwan made no 365 nichi* [365 Days to Pearl Harbor] (Kōjin Sha, 1975), p. 22.

6 Sanematsu, *Shinjuwan made no 365 nichi*, p. 22.

7 Yamamoto, quoted in Takagi Sōkichi, *Yamamoto Isoroku to Yonai Mitsumasa* [Yamamoto Isoroku and Yonai Mitsumasa] (Bungei Shunjū, 1968), pp. 81–82.

8 Ikezaki Tadayoshi, *Nichi-Bei tatakawaba: Taiheiyō sensō no riron to jissai* ["If Japan and America Fight: Theory and Practice of a Pacific War"] (Shinchō Sha, 1941), p. 259.

Chapter 15

1 Edward S. Miller, *War Plan Orange: The U.S. Strategy to Defeat Japan, 1897–1945* (Annapolis, Maryland: Naval Institute Press, 1991).

2 Miller, *War Plan Orange*, p. 2.

3 Miller, *War Plan Orange*, p. 183.

4 Miller, *War Plan Orange*, p. 183.

5 Tōda Ishimaru (trans.), *Taiheiyō Sensō* [The Pacific War; a translation of *War in the Pacific* (1936) by Sutherland Denlinger and Charles Gary] (Jitsugyō no Nippon Sha, 1940).

6 Hiroyuki Agawa, *Yamamoto Isoroku* (Shinchō Sha, 1966), p. 133.

7 Miller, *War Plan Orange*, p. 173.

8 Naoki Inose (comp.), *Mokugekisha ga kataru Shōwa-shi, Dai 6-kan, Taiheiyō sensō I* [A History of Shōwa as Told by Eyewitnesses, vol. 6, Pacific War I] (Shinjin-butsu Ōrai Sha, 1989), pp. 71–72.

9 Fukutome, as quoted in ibid., pp. 72–73.

10 Inose Naoki, *Nippon jin wa naze sensō wo shita ka? Shōwa 16 nen natsu no haisen* [Why did Japanese Make War? The Defeat of the Summer of '41], vol. 8 of *Nihon no kindai: Inose Naoki chosakushū* [Modern Japan: The Works of Inose Naoki] (Shōgakukan, 2002).

11 This account is drawn from Tadayoshi Ikezaki, *Chōki sen hisshō* (Shinchō Sha, 1941), p. 684 and *passim*.

Epilogue

1 For Mizuno's letter and Kiyosawa's thoughts on it as recorded in his diary, see Kiyoshi Kiyosawa, *Anmoku nikki* [Diary of the Dark] (Hyōron Sha, 1979), p. 105.

2 Author's interview with Shigematsu Fukio, August 1991.

3 This account of MacArthur at the Hotel New Grand is based on William Manchester, *American Caesar: Douglas MacArthur, 1880–1964* (Boston and Toronto: Little, Brown and Company, 1978), p. 447, and on Hideshi Shirato, *Hoteru Nyū Gurando 50 nen shi* [Hotel New Grand: Fifty Years of History] (Chūō Kōron Jigyō Sha, 1977), pp. 232–233.

4 John Gunther, *The Riddle of MacArthur: Japan, Korea, and the Far East* (New York: Harper & Brothers, 1951), p. 2.

5 Gunther, *The Riddle of MacArthur*, p. 2.

6 Gunther, *The Riddle of MacArthur*, p. 1.

7 Ishihara, quoted in Yokoyama Shinpei, *Hiroku: Ishihara Kanji* [Secret Annals: Ishihara Kanji] (Fuyō Shobō, 1971), p. 33.

Afterword

1 Hironori Mizuno, *Tsugi no issen* [The Next Battle] (Kaneo Bun'endō, 1914), pp. 259–260.

A Note from the Translator

1 National Commission on Terrorist Attacks Upon the United States, *The 9/11 Commission Report: Final Report on the National Commission on Terrorist Attacks Upon the United States* (New York: W. W. Norton, 2004), p. 339.
2 Ibid.
3 Ibid., p. 344.